Alter

Fairer taxes. Reinvesting in health care,

Federal Budget

education and the environment.

Papers 1998

Sustaining the recovery and job creation.

Canadian Centre for Policy Alternatives
CHO!CES: A Coalition for Social Justice

Canadian Cataloguing in Publication Data

Main entry under title:

The alternative federal budget papers 1998

Includes bibliographical references.
ISBN 0-88627-942-9

1. Canada -- Economic policy -- 1991- I. Canadian Centre for Policy Alternatives. II. Choices (Association)

HJ793.A77 1998 338.971 C98-950056-X

Printed and bound in Canada

Published by the Canadian Centre for Policy Alternatives
804-251 Laurier Avenue West
Ottawa, Ontario
K1P 5J6

Distributed by Formac Distributing
5502 Atlantic Street
Halifax, Nova Scotia
B3H 1G4

Table of Contents

Preface

This is the fourth year that the Canadian Centre for Policy Alternatives and CHO!CES have co-hosted the Alternative Federal Budget project (AFB). Each year involvement has broadened and each year the AFB's central message of hope—that there are sensible and credible progressive alternatives to the current government's policy direction—is reaching a larger and larger audience.

The project provides a meeting place for activists, academics and policy researchers; a place where citizens from a broad range of progressive national and community organizations can come together and create under the discipline of a fiscal plan, a common set of budgetary alternatives embodying values and priorities that differ markedly from those of the current political/corporate elite.

Our latest Alternative Budget was released in 30 centres across the country on February 10, 1998, two weeks before Paul Martin unveiled his budget. It was the result of six months of intense discussion around budget tables in Winnipeg and Ottawa, the result of budget schools and consultations in communities across the country, the result of economic and social policy round tables. Coordinators of some 25 policy working groups drafted and reworked, after much debate, the various pieces that make up our budget. Economic and social targets were established. Parameters were set and then reset. A credible and workable fiscal plan was drawn up.

In the end, after much give and take, we were able to agree on a document that everyone around the two tables felt they could live with even though it might not fully meet everyone's expectations. This is the essence of budget making in our project.

The *Alternative Budget Papers 1998* contains the two core documents: the Budget and the Framework Document. In addition, it contains an edited transcript of presentations at our Round Table by leading Canadian economists. This is followed by five background papers prepared specifically for this year's AFB: an analysis of the provincialization of social policy making; a path-breaking paper on incorporating gender considerations into budgets; an analysis of how we got to balanced budgets and how to maintain them; a background paper on taxation issues; and an examination of environmental issues and how to deepen the environmental dimension of the AFB.

This year's Alternative Budget focuses on reinvesting in our badly damaged public infrastructure while maintaining budget balance. The hallmark of our monetary and fiscal policy is sustained economic recovery, creating over 450,000 jobs per year and reducing poverty and inequality. On tax issues, our emphasis is on redistribution giving relief to low-and middle-income people while financing these cuts through new taxes on wealthy individuals, superprofitable financial institutions, etc. Thus, under our alternative, virtually all of the so-called fiscal dividend would go to health care, education and other public investments. Finally, our fiscal plan would create the momentum for a rapid reduction in the debt burden (debt/GDP ratio) and in debt interest payments.

Paul Martin brought down a budget that reflects very different priorities. Remarkably, it continues, even as it moves into budget surplus, to cut overall program spending, a few highly touted initiatives notwithstanding. It continues to apply tight monetary and fiscal brakes that breed chronic stagnation, insecurity and mass unemployment.

This may be good for paper wealth-holders, financial speculators and businesses for whom high unemployment and weak social supports are a key way to keep wages low and the workforce compliant. It may also be good for wealthy Canadians who want to avoid any increase in their taxes and want to ensure that Canadians' expectations remain low. But it is not in the best interest of most Canadians. As you will see, the Alternative Budget's priorities are very different, but its plan is equally workable if only the political will existed.

As with previous alternative budgets, this year's effort would not have been possible with out the generous contribution of time, energy and expertise of many people from unions and universities, from a broad range of social and environmental organizations across the country.

Nor would the project have been possible without cash outlay from some of the participating organizations. The bulk of financial contributions again this year was provided by the Canadian Labour Congress and its major affiliated unions. Contributions were also received from the Canadian Conference of Catholic Bishops, the International Fund for Animal Welfare, the Canadian Association of University Teachers and the Confé-dération des syndicats nationaux.

The Budget

Overview

This year marks the 50th anniversary of the Universal Declaration of Human Rights, which outlines the fundamental social and economic rights that should be guaranteed for all people. Unfortunately, for several years public policy in Canada has undermined the realization of these rights for a growing number of Canadians.

The federal budget shapes the social and economic realities of our lives. It represents the government's basic values and priorities, and reflects political choices. For a single mother earning low wages with two children to support, or for an executive or professional with money to invest in the stock market, the budget's choices mean very different things.

For several years, each federal budget has brought more bad news for most Canadians. The government has protected the wealthy by pursuing low-inflation at any economic cost—throwing hundreds of thousands of Canadians out of work in the process. It has increased the misery and desperation of the unemployed by cutting UI benefits and income support programs.

In its lopsided battle on the deficit, the government has slashed funding for health, education, and other services that Canadians value and are prepared to support. It refuses to impose a fair share of the burden of deficit-reduction on those most able to pay—wealthy individuals and the increasingly profitable business community.

These choices dramatically reveal that the values and priorities of this federal government are fundamentally one-sided.

Since the first Alternative Federal Budget was released in 1995—the same year that Finance Minister Paul Martin began his "hell-or-high-water" war on the deficit—the federal government has cut annual program spending by $15 billion. Together with rising revenues and additional savings on government interest payments, this has allowed the federal government to eliminate the deficit faster than even the most optimistic observer could have predicted in 1995. So where do we go from here, now that the magical "fiscal dividend" is about to arrive?

Sadly, this year's federal budget promises little different from the ruling Liberals. Incredibly, program spending is scheduled to *be cut* by another $2.5 billion—with still more money taken away from social programs and other basic services. "New" federal initiatives are typically funded by cutting another needed program somewhere else. The result will be more pressure on the provinces to cut their own budgets, more public sector jobs lost, deepening poverty, and rising income inequality.

The Time is Now

Our lopsided, shaky, private-dominated economy is leaving millions of Canadians out in the cold. The time is now for government to correct the imbalance. The deficit was a phony but powerful excuse for government inaction. Now that the deficit is history, there are no excuses left. Governments must act, and act quickly. The time is now for the federal government to lead the way. The Alternative Federal Budget shows how this can be done in a fiscally responsible manner.

The time is now to:

- sustain economic growth at its recent pace (4% per year after inflation) for at least another four years, through low interest rates and injections of federal program spending;
- rebuild federal program spending in the first year of our budget to its pre-cutback level, and increase spending by another $8 billion in the second year;
- maintain a balanced budget in fiscal 1998, and target a small nominal surplus (of $1 billion) in subsequent years;
- freeze aggregate federal taxes at their 1996-97 level in fiscal 1999 and beyond, while taking significant measures to improve the fairness of the tax system;
- reduce the federal debt burden (measured as a share of GDP) below 60% (the European Community's Maastricht criteria) by the turn of the century, and below 50% by fiscal 2002;
- reduce the official unemployment rate to 5% or lower by the end of fiscal year 2001; and
- reduce the poverty rate by at least six points over the next four years.

Highlights of our fiscal and economic projections are provided in Table 1. A detailed breakdown of program spending initiatives is provided in Table 4.

The 1998 Alternative Federal Budget is a blueprint for how the federal government can create the kind of country Canadians want. The time is now for a federal budget with a renewed vision and sense of purpose. The time is now for a federal budget that provides Canadians with the opportunity and well-being that we deserve—and can clearly afford.

OUR GOALS, AND HOW WE GET THERE

The 1998 Alternative Federal Budget is designed as an integrated program for economic and social change. By keeping interest rates low, we stimulate the economy and reduce debt-servicing costs, both of which free up resources for federal programs. Higher federal spending puts hundreds of thousands of Canadians back to work. Newly-employed Canadians will pay taxes instead of needing income support. Lower unemployment further reduces poverty. And fair taxation measures reduce income inequality.

PROGRAM SPENDING:
PAUL MARTIN VS. ALTERNATIVE FEDERAL BUDGET

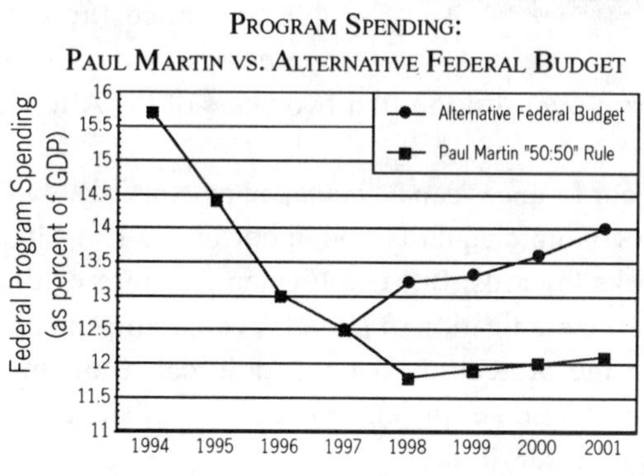

We aim to direct and channel economic growth so that it is based less on the exploitation of our human and natural resources. Job-creation emphasizes "green" growth— environmentally sustainable work such as housing retrofits, park construction, and toxic clean-ups—and work that fulfills social needs (such as health care, child care, education and culture).

Special effort is made to direct government spending toward improving equity for the disabled, Aboriginal peoples, visible minorities, and youth. Our budget is meant to benefit women on an equal basis with men, and values both the paid and unpaid work that women contribute to Canadian society.

The Alternative Federal Budget describes an ambitious plan for rebuilding financial support for important social and public programs. Under our strategy, federal program spending (measured as a share of our GDP) would gradually recover about one-half of the ground that has been lost since 1994 (see figure). In contrast, the Liberal government's "50:50" strategy for spending the fiscal dividend would lock in place the current atrophied state of federal programs.

Yet the Alternative Federal Budget is financially responsible. We are committed to maintaining a balanced budget or small surplus throughout our forecast period (barring a recession, in which case it is prudent for the federal government to tolerate temporary cyclical deficits).

And, by the most crucial indicator of fiscal stability—reduction of the government's debt burden—our emphasis on job-creation and social reinvestment pays off handsomely. Indeed, the Alternative Federal Budget attains a *faster* pace of debt reduction than is expected under a "status-quo" Liberal strategy, even one that allows for significant annual debt repayment (see figure). Thanks to stronger economic growth, we are able to reduce the debt burden by 1.5 percentage points more than Paul Martin over just the first two years of the Alternative Federal Budget.

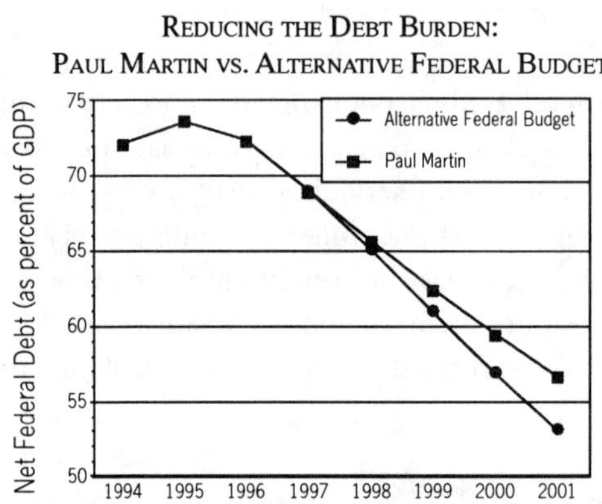

In short, we show that our finances can be managed responsibly, without sacrificing social and economic equality and opportunity. The Alternative Federal Budget works towards: full employment; a more equitable distribution of income; the eradication of poverty; economic equality between men and women; the protection of civil, political, economic, social and cultural rights; protection of the environment; and strengthening social programs and public services.

These are the choices reflected in our budget—very different choices, indeed, from those of the Liberals.

This document encompasses the views of hundreds of participants in dozens of workshops, conferences, and priority-setting meetings across the country. It is supported by over 50 national social, community, and labour organizations—and by thousands more Canadians working at the grass-roots level to preserve, improve and reweave our social safety net. It is a budget that provides a blueprint for a more humane, more liveable Canada. The time is now to enact it.

TABLE 1: ALTERNATIVE FEDERAL BUDGET, FINANCIAL PROJECTIONS
($ BILLIONS)

FISCAL YEARS	1997(FCST.)	1998	1999	2000	2001	2002
BUDGET COMPONENTS:						
Revenue	148.2	160.2	167.3	179.0	191.6	205.0
Program Spending	105.8	118.7	127.1	139.7	153.1	167.4
Debt Service Charges	43.8	41.5	39.2	38.4	37.5	36.6
Total Spending	149.6	160.2	166.3	178.0	190.6	204.0
Surplus (Deficit)	(1.4)	0.0	1.0	1.0	1.0	1.0
Net Debt	585	585	584	583	582	581
GDP	849	900	958	1025	1097	1174
AS PERCENT OF GDP:						
Revenue	17.5%	17.8%	17.5%	17.5%	17.5%	17.5%
Program Spending	12.5%	13.2%	13.3%	13.6%	14.0%	14.3%
Debt Service Charges	5.2%	4.6%	4.1%	3.7%	3.4%	3.1%
Surplus (Deficit)	(0.1%)	0.0%	0.1%	0.1%	0.1%	0.1%
Net Debt	68.9%	65.0%	60.9%	56.8%	53.0%	49.5%
ANNUAL PERCENT CHANGE:						
Revenue	+5.2%	+8.0%	+4.4%	+7.0%	+7.0%	+7.0%
Program Spending	+1.0%	+12.2%	+7.1%	+9.9%	+9.6%	+9.3%

OTTAWA, QUEBEC AND THE PROVINCES

The Alternative Federal Budget continues to subscribe to the historic view of progressive English Canada that the federal government should play a leading role in economic, social and cultural policy, in developing national cultural institutions, enforcing national standards for social programs, and building a strong national economy. However, such a strong federal role should not infringe on the expression of Quebecers' national identity and social rights. The key issue for English Canadians should not be the accommodation of Quebec's uniqueness, but the way that uniqueness is accommodated.

Until there is a resolution of the Quebec-Canada relationship, the AFB's approach to federal-provincial fiscal relations recognizes the need for special arrangements with Quebec which may not be open to the other provinces. We recognize that Quebec has primacy in its jurisdiction over social policy and the right to opt out of joint federal-provincial programs in this area; and, for the rest of Canada, we recognize joint federal-provincial responsibility, with a federal leadership role in funding social programs, as well as in setting and enforcing national standards. Common standards throughout the whole country, including Quebec, could be achieved through the negotiation of a social charter.

Macroeconomic and Fiscal Context

Current Economic Environment

The state of Canada's overall economy has a crucial impact on the state of federal finances. Relatively strong economic growth over the past year has greatly improved the government's fiscal position. Thanks especially to lower interest rates, Canada's economy grew by close to 4% (after inflation) in 1997, creating almost 400,000 new jobs, and pushing the unemployment rate below 9% by the end of the year for the first time in over seven years.

This recent economic growth and job creation is obviously a welcome relief from the Depression-like circumstances of earlier in the 1990s. However, the economy still has a long way to go just to make up for ground lost during the years of recession and stagnation. Real living standards are lower for most Canadians than they were a decade ago, and millions of citizens remain unemployed, underemployed, and underpaid. A shocking 1.5 million *more* Canadians have fallen into poverty since 1989.

Worse yet, by accident or by design, the continued strength of this badly-needed economic recovery is now very much in doubt. And if the recovery evaporates, so too will the much-anticipated federal "fiscal dividend." Instead of debating how this dividend should be "spent," Canadians may be left scratching their heads about how the promise of better economic times managed once again to slip through their fingers.

Two factors in particular now threaten future economic growth and continued improvement in government finances:

First, the financial powers-that-be in Canada continue to express a near-hysterical fear of inflation—and continue to demand restrictive policies that will keep inflation as close to zero as possible, regardless of the consequences for the rest of the economy. These powerful vested interests (the banks, bond-holders, and other financial investors) successfully pressured the Bank of Canada to increase interest rates in 1997, despite ultra-low inflation and stubbornly high unemployment.

What was long-delayed good news for most Canadians—stronger growth and job-creation—set the alarm bells ringing in the corridors of Bay Street. The financiers demanded that the economy be deliberately slowed down, to ensure that unemployment didn't fall too low or Canadians' expectations rise too high.

Second, to make matters worse, Canada was caught in the crossfire of the Asian financial meltdown. This crisis is just the latest in a whole string of needless human catastrophes wrought by the power of unregulated global finance. Asian workers are bearing the brunt of this crisis: massive spending cutbacks by businesses and governments, layoffs, poverty, and deflation. But Canadians are at risk, too: our currency is falling as financiers rush to convert their assets into safe U.S. dollars, the Bank of Canada is increasing interest rates even higher, Canadian exporters warn of collapsing sales to Asia, and the confidence of average consumers is being rattled yet again.

In the wake of rising interest rates and the Asian crisis, mainstream economists have scaled back their forecasts of economic growth in Canada next year—from 4% initially to 3% or lower. If the Asian turbulence gets any worse, Canada's economy could be hit even harder. Each point of slower growth removes at least $1.5 billion from the federal government's expected surplus; each point of higher interest rates does the same. If the slowdown tips over into a recession, then the much-vaunted surplus is likely to disappear altogether.

We draw one obvious conclusion from the financial instability of recent months: contrary to the claims of financiers and budget-cutters, simply eliminating the deficit and reducing the debt burden are not going to solve Canada's financial problems. The high interest rates and financial instability we suffered before 1995 were not the result of deficits: they were the result of a deregulated, self-interested financial system run amok. Even though the deficit is now history and Canada is a "Nirvana" for bond-traders, we will continue to be subject to the same financial pressures so long as we allow private financial markets to exercise such unrestrained and unaccountable economic power.

Incredibly, most Canadian interest rates are actually significantly higher now (after inflation) than they were in 1993—which was, supposedly, when financial markets were so "spooked" by our debts and deficits that they "dictated" the huge cutbacks we have endured since then (see figure). For example, the prime rate paid by the best private customers of chartered banks is almost two points higher, relative to inflation, than in 1993. The "tough medicine" of fiscal restraint has not brought us

INTEREST RATES: WITH AND WITHOUT DEFICITS

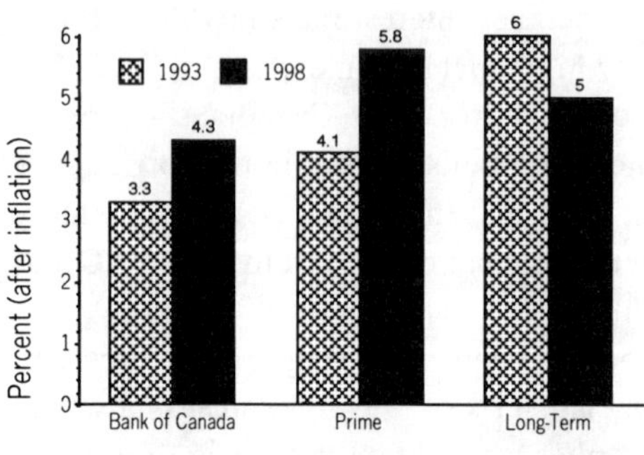

relief from the financial markets.

If we truly want low interest rates and financial stability, we will have to do much more than simply downsize government and then hope for the goodwill of the financiers. Rather, we must reimpose some rational oversight on the financial sector: maintain interest rates that make sense to Canada's real economy (rather than just the bond-holders), begin to regulate global financial flows, and make job-creation and real production the top priorities of our economic policies.

OUR MACROECONOMIC STRATEGY

The response of the Alternative Federal Budget to the deceleration and instability that erupted at the beginning of 1998 is clear and decisive. We will not allow this long-delayed recovery to be derailed, by accident or design, by the selfish actions of financial investors and speculators. We reject the incredible argument that recent growth in Canada has been "too fast" or threatens our monetary stability. We commit ourselves to keeping interest rates at low, stimulative levels until the economy approaches genuine fully-employed capacity limits. And we will supplement that monetary stimulus with major inputs of new public spending power—creating jobs, restoring the economic confidence of average households, and reducing our vulnerability to the whims of private investors.

We will instruct the Bank of Canada to restore monetary conditions to roughly the same levels that prevailed in mid-1997. Depending on the value of Canada's dollar, this implies short-term interest rates of about 3.5%. (If the dollar remains low, thus stimulating Canada's exports, then interest rates do not need to fall as far.) Thanks to sustained low interest rates and a recovery in federal program spending, we thus expect to be able to maintain real economic growth at its 1997 pace—about 4%—for at least another four years.

This would be sufficient to reduce the official unemployment rate to 5% or lower by the end of fiscal 2001, coincident with the expected return to the labour force of just some of the hundreds of thousands of discouraged workers who abandoned the work world since the last recession.

We need this kind of vibrant, sustained economic growth to fi-

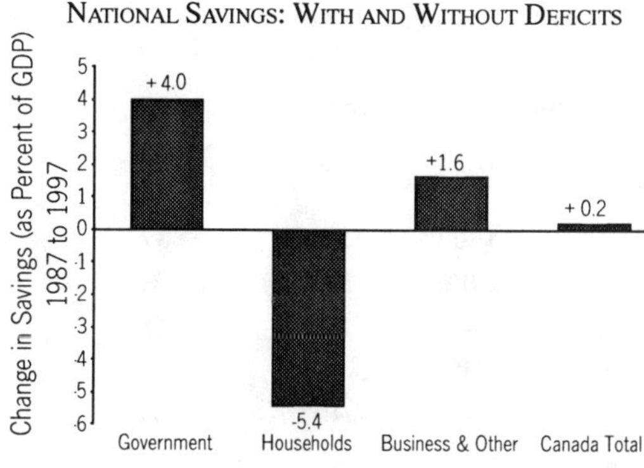

nance an improvement in government finances and public programs. It is also the type of growth needed to repair the simultaneous damage that has been done to *household* finances by years of unemployment and stagnation. After all, personal savings in Canada have fallen to all-time record lows through the 1990s, while personal debts for credit cards and other loans continue to soar. In fact, the decline in personal savings more than offsets the improvement in public finances over the past decade (see figure), with the result that national savings as a whole have not improved at all. By encouraging rising household incomes (through strong employment growth, higher wages, and better income security), we can help to ensure that future economic growth is balanced, stable, and beneficial for average Canadians.

As a consequence of strong growth and lower interest rates, we expect the rate of inflation to gradually increase over the next three years to about 3%. Moderate inflation in this range would be no higher than typical inflation rates in the U.S., and poses no danger to the well-being of average Canadians (especially in light of the expansion and indexation of social benefits that we also propose). Interest rates would rise gradually with the inflation rate. The Alternative Federal Budget would target after-inflation rates of over 1% on short-term bonds and 3-to-4% on long-term loans, both of which are in line with historical standards and represent a more-than-adequate return for investors in low-risk government bonds.

Financial investors, of course, will complain about higher inflation:

MEASURES TO SUPPORT A MADE-IN-CANADA INTEREST RATE:

- require commercial banks to reinvest a share of their assets in the communities where they operate;
- phase out the 20% allowable foreign investment of tax-subsidized pension and RRSP funds;
- develop alternative financial institutions (such as a National Capital Investment Fund) which keep their money in Canada;
- use the Bank of Canada to refinance 2% of the outstanding federal debt per year over the next five years (so that the government pays interest to its own bank, instead of a commercial bank); and
- work internationally towards a Tobin Tax and the establishment of global regulations on international financial flows.

TABLE 2: MACROECONOMIC & FISCAL PROJECTIONS

FISCAL YEARS	1996 (ACT.)	1997 (FCST.)	1998	1999
PAUL MARTIN'S OUTLOOK				
GDP (nominal, $billion)	$807	$849	$887	$927
Real GDP Growth Rate (%)	2.0%	3.7%	3.0%	2.5%
Inflation (% rise GDP deflator)	1.4%	1.5%	1.5%	2.0%
90-day Interest Rate (%)	3.73%	3.90%	5.25%	5.50%
Real Interest Rate (%)	2.34%	2.40%	3.75%	3.50%
Average Interest Rate on Federal Debt (%)	7.78%	7.50%	7.75%	7.75%
Employment (million)	13.71	14.08	14.36	14.58
Labour Force Participation (%)	64.8%	65.0%	65.0%	65.0%
Unemployment Rate (%)	9.7%	8.9%	8.5%	8.5%
ALTERNATIVE FEDERAL BUDGET OUTLOOK				
GDP (nominal, $billion)	$807	$849	$900	$958
Real GDP Growth Rate (%)	2.0%	3.7%	4.0%	4.0%
Inflation (% rise GDP deflator)	1.4%	1.5%	2.0%	2.5%
90-day Interest Rate (%)	3.73%	3.90%	3.50%	3.75%
Real Interest Rate (%)	2.34%	2.40%	1.50%	1.25%
Average Interest Rate on Federal Debt (%)	7.78%	7.50%	7.25%	7.00%
Employment (million)	13.71	14.08	14.50	14.94
Labour Force Participation (%)	64.8%	65.0%	65.25%	65.5%
Unemployment Rate (%)	9.7%	8.9%	7.9%	6.9%
Poverty Rate (%)	17.9%	18.0%	16.0%	14.0%

after all, each point of inflation eats away 1% of their paper wealth, and they will fiercely resist any macroeconomic strategy which elevates job-creation above inflation-control on the list of our economic priorities. We will require the active cooperation of the Bank of Canada in this shift in monetary policy; we expect that the Bank's "target range" for inflation would be increased by one point (to between 2% and 4% per year). And we will simultaneously need to develop and introduce a range of institutional and regulatory reforms aimed at insulating our financial markets from global pressures and protecting a made-in-Canada low-interest regime (see box on previous page).

Table 2 summarizes the macroeconomic assumptions and targets that are adopted by the 1998 Alternative Federal Budget.

STARTING TO UNDO THE DAMAGE

We expect (like most other observers) that the federal budget will be balanced during the current (1997-98) fiscal year. (Final figures will not be released until October.) Indeed, by November 1997 the government had already recorded a rolling 12-month surplus—its first in almost 30 years—and the numbers are only getting better as the fiscal year progresses. Finance Minister Paul Martin will thus have balanced the budget a full two years ahead of his own original timetable (according to which the deficit would have been eliminated in fiscal 1999-2000).

Surprisingly, the most important factor behind the faster-than-expected elimination of the federal deficit was *not* the historic cutbacks in program spending imposed by the Liberals over the past three years (see box). More important was the combination of low interest rates and accelerating economic growth—which together account for almost 60% of the federal deficit reduction achieved between 1995 (when Paul Martin released his "hell or high water" budget) and 1997. This experience provides a dramatic verification of the Alternative Federal Budget's consistent claim that deficits could be eliminated in a humane fashion by lowering interest rates and stimulating growth.

Indeed, Paul Martin's *initial* deficit-reduction timetable could have been surpassed without any program spending cuts whatsoever—purely on the strength of the lower interest rates and stronger growth that have prevailed since 1995.

We continue to disagree strongly with the means that were followed to eliminate the federal deficit, and we stress the dramatic increase in Canada's social deficit which has accompanied the decline in the fiscal deficit. Nevertheless, we do not disagree that the budget had to be balanced, and we recognize that the federal fiscal outlook now looks con-

HOW THE WAR ON THE DEFICIT WAS WON:

Sources of Deficit Reduction, 1995 to 1997

Pro-Growth Macroeconomic Policy (low interest rates, faster growth):		59%
Spending Cutbacks:		45%
Tax Increases:		10%
Cost of Increased Debt Burden:		-13%
Total Deficit Reduction ($30 billion):	100%	

Source: 1998 Alternative Federal Budget Technical Paper #1, "Over the Rainbow".

siderably brighter in the wake of attaining that balance. With an end to chronic deficits, the federal debt burden (measured as a share of GDP) will decline rapidly, and hence the government's own interest payments will diminish in importance, since tax revenues rise in step with economic growth. And all of this opens up significant room for new federal program spending initiatives, while still maintaining the balanced budget and even freezing tax levels.

This is the so-called "fiscal dividend" that has been much-discussed in Canada over the past year. Three options are usually presented on how to "spend" this dividend: 1) cut taxes, 2) pay off some of the accumulated debt, or 3) reinvest in repairing the public programs and social infrastructure that were so badly damaged by the retrenchment of the 1990s.

We think that most Canadians reject the false promise of widespread tax cuts: they recognize that lower taxes must ultimately translate into continued deterioration of our health care, education, and other services. Furthermore, most tax-cut proposals would offer the biggest benefits to high-income earners and businesses—hardly a good way to address the already significant and still-growing inequality in Canadian society.

The debt-repayment option is also doomed to political failure, we believe: Canadians are learning that the debt burden will fall quickly as a share of GDP simply thanks to ongoing economic growth, even without any budgetary surpluses. It would be politically impossible and socially destructive for a federal government to sock away billions for *extra* "debt repayment" each year, at the same time as Canadians are crying out for the repair of our social infrastructure.

The Alternative Federal Budget loudly and proudly comes down in favour of allocating the fiscal dividend in its entirety to starting to rebuild the important and valuable public programs that have been so badly damaged by the budget-cutting of the 1990s. We have designed a macroeconomic strategy aimed at maximizing the size of that "dividend"—by keeping interest rates low and sustaining growth. And we plan to spend every penny of it on necessary reinvestment in our social fabric.

Regarding tax levels, participants in the AFB exercise this year faced a genuine quandary. On the one hand, the potential clearly exists in coming years for massive increases in program spending, even within the constraint imposed by existing tax levels (which equalled about 17.5% of GDP in fiscal 1996-97). As the debt burden declines, the share of tax revenues wasted on government interest payments will steadily fall. These funds can then be reallocated to useful social programs, without increasing tax levels.

Together with policies aimed at lowering interest rates and accelerating economic growth, we estimate that program spending could grow by more than $10 billion per year over the next several years, without any increases in the overall burden of taxation.

On the other hand, however, we are also highly sensitive to the growing emergency in Canadian social conditions that is the legacy of the cutbacks of the 1990s. The frightening deterioration in our key social indicators—income levels, health, education, economic and political participation—cries out for immediate attention. We cannot wait long for the arithmetic of the fiscal "dividend" to work its magic, before beginning to reinvest as strongly as possible in the repair of our tattered social fabric.

The Alternative Federal Budget therefore adopts the following approach to fiscal policy. In the medium-run (for fiscal 1999 and beyond), we will maintain the overall federal tax rate at its actual 1996-97 level: 17.5% of GDP. New funds generated by ongoing economic growth and the falling debt burden will permit very substantial annual increases in program spending while still maintaining a balanced budget and unchanged tax levels.

In the first year of the Alternative Federal Budget, however, we must work faster to address the growing social crisis in our communities. We thus commit ourselves to an aggregate level of program spending in fiscal 1998 of $118.7 billion—exactly the sum spent by the federal government in 1994, immediately prior to the historic spending cuts implemented by Paul Martin. We thus aim to undo, in a single year, the cumulative and unprecedented nominal spending cuts engineered by the federal Liberals since the infamous "hell or high water" budget of 1995. This represents an increase of almost $13 billion over the actual federal program spending budgeted in 1997. Program spending will grow by another $8 billion in the second year, to some $127 billion.

Of course, in the wake of inflation and ongoing population growth, $118.7 billion will not replace the real value of the services that have been cut over the past several years. The budget bombardments of the 1990s have shattered Canadian public programs to such a degree that it will take years of rebuilding to undo the damage. But our aggressive stance in the first year of the Alternative Federal Budget marks a dramatic first step—a big down-payment on the rebuilding that needs to occur. This major injection of federal spending power into our economy will also go a long way toward ensuring that the current economic recovery maintains its momentum in the face of rising interest rates and global financial instability.

To restore program spending to its pre-cutback levels in a single year will require some additional tax measures, above and beyond the considerable sums freed up by lower interest rates, the falling debt burden, and ongoing economic growth. The Alternative Federal Budget will thus increase aggregate federal taxes, *for one year alone*, by $3 billion above

1998 ALTERNATIVE FEDERAL BUDGET FISCAL AND SOCIAL TARGETS:

- Balanced budget in all years.
- Program spending rebuilt to 1994 levels in the first year.
- Aggregate tax levels frozen at 1996 levels, in 1999 and beyond.
- Official unemployment rate reduced by at least 1 point per year.
- Poverty rate reduced by at least 1.5 points per year.

the level that would be provided by the average tax rates that prevailed in 1996-97. Extra taxes will be targeted at super-profitable banks and other vested interests—those that have done so well during the 1990s, while other Canadians tightened their belts. In the second year of our program (fiscal 1999), we will *cut* aggregate taxes by the same amount, bringing the aggregate federal tax rate back to its 1996-97 level (17.5% of GDP).

Over the first two years, therefore, the tax package of the AFB is "revenue-neutral": all new taxes imposed on particular interest groups or industries are offset by targeted relief offered elsewhere in the tax system. And thanks to a sweeping reform of our income tax and tax expenditure systems, virtually every Canadian earning less than $60,000 will pay lower federal taxes. Three-quarters of the new revenue received by the federal government in the first year of the AFB is provided simply by economic growth, not by the one-time tax increase.

Unlike the Liberals, we believe that deficits and debt are not the only economic and social indicators worthy of being targeted by federal budgetary action. Our budget also sets targets for reducing the unemployment rate and the poverty rate (see box on page 12). We hold these targets to be just as important as our fiscal targets, and we will adjust our fiscal and economic strategies mid-stream if it becomes necessary in order to meet these targets.

We expect to be able to reduce the unemployment rate by at least one full percentage point per year, to 5% or lower by fiscal 2001, while still allowing for some recovery in labour force participation (as formerly discouraged workers re-enter the workforce) toward its pre-1990 level. Partly thanks to falling unemployment, and partly thanks to the pro-active social policy measures outlined in this budget, we also expect to be able to reduce the poverty rate by at least one-third (to 12% or lower) over the same time frame.

ECONOMIC GROWTH AND THE ENVIRONMENT

The Alternative Federal Budget relies centrally on renewed economic growth to generate the revenues needed to rebuild social programs in Canada. We also think that stimulating and sustaining economic growth, together with appropriate interventions aimed at regulating the nature of that growth, is the best way to create jobs and generate badly-needed income for average households.

At the same time, however, we are acutely sensitive to the growing ecological constraints limiting traditional, resource-intensive, expansionary models of economic growth. We do not believe that strong growth and environmental sustainability are incompatible. In fact, the major investments that we collectively need to make in preserving our environment would be a major contribution to future economic growth. But we recognize that this growth will be a very different *type* of growth—and that we need to monitor and regulate it closely to cushion its ecological impacts.

By focusing on rebuilding public services as a major source of future economic growth and job-creation, we are immediately avoiding many of the environmental problems associated with private-sector, profit-led growth. Other of our job-creation strategies will carry environmental benefits (see box).

These measures alone will not be sufficient, obviously, to fully address the ecological issues raised by ongoing economic development. In particular, we view these measures only as a down-payment on our obligation to constrain greenhouse gas emissions in line with Canada's commitments in Kyoto. But by attempting to generate "greener" forms of growth and job-creation, while simultaneously providing substantial funding for environmentally-friendly projects, we think that we can move our economy toward a better balance with our natural environment.

"GREENING" THE ALTERNATIVE FEDERAL BUDGET:
ENVIRONMENTALLY-SENSITIVE JOB-CREATION INITIATIVES

- Subsidies for energy-conservation retrofits of existing housing.
- Significant investment in improving Canada's environmental infrastructure: park construction, toxic waste clean-up, and support for environmental research and development initiatives.
- Two "green" tax reforms: a tax on fuels contributing to atmospheric warming, and the elimination of favourable tax treatment for oil and gas exploration and development.
- Green tax revenues are fully devoted to greenhouse-gas reduction projects across Canada and the conversion of fossil-fuel industries toward sustainable purposes.
- A Forest Investment Fund to finance intensive, sustainable forestry practices.

Putting Canada Back to Work

A New Vision

Stronger economic growth brought some welcome relief to Canada's job market over the past year, generating close to 400,000 new jobs, and cutting the official unemployment rate to under 9% for the first time in seven years.

But this improved employment performance is too little, too late. The official numbers hide important signs of continuing job weakness: too many jobs are part-time, insecure, and low-paid. So-called "self-employment" constitutes a shocking proportion of all new jobs in Canada, typically offering poor income and lack of security. And the official numbers don't even count those Canadians who would work if jobs were available, but who have given up hope of finding work in the depressed 1990s.

Until recently, economic policy in Canada was rooted in the idea that unemployment had to be *deliberately* maintained at 8.5% or higher, in the interests of keeping workers economically disempowered, restraining wage increases, and maintaining ultra-low inflation. Most Canadians never accepted this policy of official unemployment (often called the "non-accelerating inflation rate of unemployment," or the NAIRU). But recent events have demolished its rationale once and for all.

By the end of 1997, the unemployment rate had fallen to 8.6%—just a hair above the former "natural" level. Yet inflation over the previous year had totalled just 0.7%: significantly slower than in recent years, and well below even the Bank of Canada's own stringent targets. As 1997 drew to a close, consumer prices in Canada were actually *falling*, raising the spectre of deflation.

Clearly, the official model is discredited. The Alternative Federal Budget rejects the notion that Canadians must be kept deliberately insecure in order to keep inflation close to zero, protecting the paper wealth of the financiers. We aim to put as many Canadians as possible to work in productive, well-paying jobs. There is no "natural" rate of unemployment in Canada. There is plenty of room in our labour force for the economy to expand vibrantly for years to come, and in our view job-creation belongs at the very top of our list of priorities.

OUR PLAN FOR JOBS

Job creation is a crucial plank in our overall strategy to build a society based on security, cooperation, and solidarity. We *can* afford a first-class social security system, even within our existing level of taxes—but only if we find well-paying jobs for more Canadians. That way, fewer members of our society will need to fall back on the safety net, while simultaneously more of us are helping to pay for it.

As described in Section 2, we pledge to reduce the unemployment rate by at least a full percentage point per year over the next four years, reducing the official rate to 5% or lower by the end of fiscal 2001. We achieve this target even though we expect labour force participation to recover somewhat from its low 1990 levels, rising by a quarter-point per year in response to our rapid pace of job-creation.

JOB CREATION:
STATUS-QUO VS. ALTERNATIVE FEDERAL BUDGET

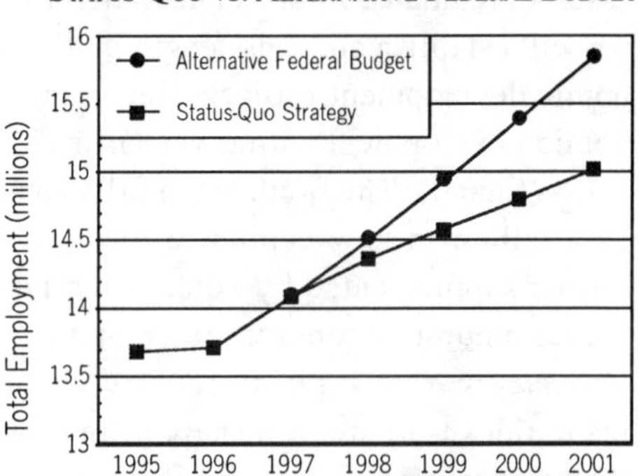

The best job-creation program of all, of course, is a healthy, growing economy. But growth cannot be sustained without a commitment to an interventionist full-employment policy by our government and financial regulators. That's why our macroeconomic and fiscal strategy—combining sustained low interest rates and major injections of federal spending power—is the centrepiece of our job-creation program. Thanks to lower interest rates and rebuilt federal program spending, we expect to create 1.8 million new jobs over the next four years: 800,000 *more* than are likely under current macroeconomic policy (see figure).

At the same time, however, the federal government can play a more direct and interventionist role, both in directly creating jobs (rebuilding a stable and well-paying public sector component within the overall job market), and in regulating and tailoring the type of jobs that are being created, so that they are better-paying, more secure, and more accessible to those who have been hardest hit by the stagnation of the 1990s (young people, women, visible minorities, and persons with disabilities).

Here are several of the specific programs, described in more detail elsewhere in this budget, that will underwrite our job-creation targets, and help to ensure that work in Canada becomes more accessible, productive, and rewarding for Canadians. In all of these initiatives, special emphasis will be placed on opening up positions for people currently receiving social assistance or other forms of income support, and on ensuring that complementary training and personal supports are in place, so that our job creation strategies generate real opportunities for those groups traditionally excluded from the benefits of economic expansion.

Rebuilding Public Services: The AFB will double federal transfer payments to the provinces for health, education, and other social programs in just two years. Moreover, our "social investment fund" approach ensures that these funds will be spent in the targeted areas. Over $10 billion in new funding for provincial, municipal, and community services over the next two years will translate into some 100,000 new public-sector jobs in each year.

National Capital Investment Fund: By requiring the deposit of a very small portion (starting at 0.1%, rising to 0.3% over three years) of the assets of regulated financial institutions and tax-subsidized pension funds, we will establish an arms-length public investment bank to finance economic development projects (including non-profit and community economic development initiatives) in hard-pressed regions and industries across Canada. The fund, when fully established, will direct an estimated $4.5 billion in new capital to local communities. These funds will be further supplemented by voluntary private contributions to RRSP-eligible Community Economic Development Corporations.

Community Reinvestment Act: We will further require private financial institutions to reinvest a share of their assets in the communities where they do business.

Social, Environmental and Physical Infrastructure: The federal government will provide up to one-half of the funding for a three-year joint program with the provinces, municipalities, and public-sector and community organizations for investments in public housing, municipal services, parks, environmental clean-up, and construction. Projects will be proposed by lower levels of government or by community sponsors. Funding for these infrastructure initiatives will total $1 billion per year over the next two years.

National Youth Job Strategy: Some $350 million per year will be devoted in the first two years of the AFB for pilot projects aimed at employing young people, aged 16 to 29, in long-term community development initiatives. Projects would be designed and proposed by youth, both single-job initiatives and group projects. After a two-year phase-in, the fully-implemented project would generate an estimated 50,000 youth jobs in the third and subsequent years.

Canadian Atmospheric Fund: All the proceeds from two "green" tax reforms (a new tax on greenhouse-gas fuels and the elimination of tax preferences for oil and gas development, generating total revenues of $1 billion per year) would be allocated to this fund, with significant job-creation benefits. The Canadian Atmospheric Fund will support community-based climate change initiatives across Canada, which typically have a high labour content; additional measures will support efforts to re-employ workers displaced from traditional fossil fuel industries.

Working Time Reduction: The reduction of average hours of work can play a significant role in reducing unemployment. AFB initiatives in this area include changes to the Canada Labour Code to facilitate shorter worker hours in areas of federal jurisdiction, facilitating voluntary leaves and early retirement through changes to UI and pension legislation, and working towards a restructuring of the UI and CPP premium structures to eliminate their present distortionary impact on hours of work.

Research and Development/Industrial Policies: The AFB contains numerous initiatives intended to strengthen Canada's traditionally poor R&D record, especially in public or non-commercial areas. Budgets for both internal research and external granting councils are substantially increased in several federal departments, including Natural Resources, Industry, and Agriculture. We significantly increase federal support for research and technology diffusion through the successful IRAP program of the National Research Council. And we establish sector-based training and procurement councils to facilitate labour force and market development in key Canadian industries.

Program Spending Initiatives

Once again this year, the Alternative Federal Budget's priority is to restore federal government support for vital social programs and public services. Total program spending of $118.7 billion in the first year will restore in a single year the nominal cuts Paul Martin has made since 1995. But after adjusting for inflation and population growth, real per capita program spending in the first year of our program is still significantly lower than was the case four years ago. Our initiatives are thus only a first step towards social and economic equality.

While our focus is on reinvestment, we do more than simply restore spending levels. We propose some new ways of thinking about how to meet our fundamental goals. We set new priorities which focus government attention on addressing poverty, creating jobs, sustaining our environment and natural resources, and building a common sense of community and shared citizenship within Canada and globally. Details of our program spending budget are provided in Table 3 on Page 28.

ZERO TOLERANCE FOR POVERTY

The contrast between the winners and losers in the federal government's war on the deficit is stark. While a fortunate few—bankers, bondholders and shareholders—have become immensely richer, many more Canadians are suffering poverty and deprivation. Over the last eight years, 482,000 more children and one million more adults have been plunged into poverty (see figure). The incomes of the wealthiest 20% of Canadians increased on average by $2,000 in 1996, while the incomes of the poorest 20% of Canadians, on average, fell by $500. On average, the incomes of our 1.1 million poor families with children are close to $9,000 below the poverty line. The average income of single-mother-led fami-

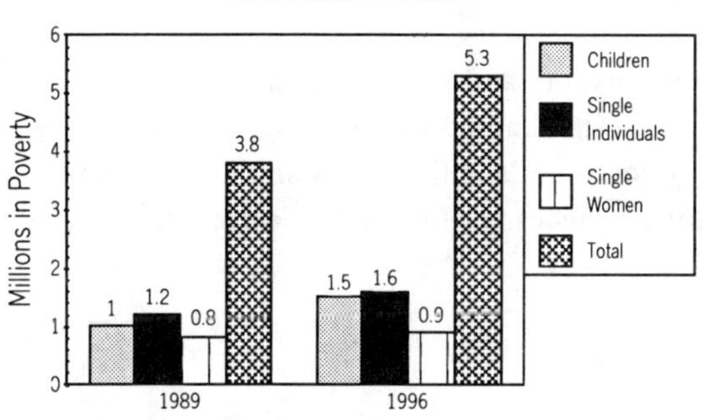

lies is just $14,998. At last count, over 2.5 million Canadians depended on food banks to survive.

The AFB recognizes the multiple causes and faces of Canadian poverty. Our solutions, therefore, are also multiple. Our economic strategy stimulates the Canadian economy and helps create balanced growth through low interest rates, job creation initiatives, and a combination of fair taxation measures and government spending. It is our goal to reduce the number of poor Canadians from 18% of the population to 12% over the next four years.

Reducing unemployment is clearly essential to reducing poverty. For every percentage point drop in the unemployment rate, poverty also falls by one percentage point. Our employment targets will begin to reduce poverty by creating quality jobs for young people, the disabled, Aboriginal peoples, and other marginalized communities.

Job creation is supplemented with programs to alleviate poverty immediately, by providing income assistance and a range of supportive services, providing the poor with the opportunity for full economic and social participation. The programs necessary to lift the burden of poverty, especially from the shoulders of women and children, are listed in the adjoining box.

Measures to Reduce Poverty

Reinstating funds cut from income support: $1.9 billion
National Drug Plan: $0.65 billion
Enhanced Child Benefit: $4.4 billion
Child Care Investment Fund: $0.5 billion
National Advance Child Maintenance System: no cost
Increased tax benefits for people with disabilities: $290 million
Increased retirement benefits: $0.6 billion
National Housing Fund: $0.4 billion
Higher Unemployment Insurance benefits: $1.0 billion
National Youth Employment Strategy: $350 million
Additional funding for Aboriginal health: $0.4 billion
Reduction in taxes on low incomes: $2 billion
Increase in low-income GST credits: $720 million

Our approach to social spending and job creation will reduce poverty by one-third over the next four years. These measures are a combination of compassion, social justice, and common sense. An Anti-Poverty Commissioner will be appointed and directed to make an annual report to Parliament on the government's anti-poverty initiatives, on their impact on women, and on their success or failure in meeting the poverty reduction targets.

NATIONAL SOCIAL INVESTMENT FUNDS

The Chrétien government will be remembered as the government which destroyed a set of social programs which took more than a half century to construct. The Canada Assistance Plan is gone, unemployment insurance has been cut savagely, and Old Age Security and the Guaranteed Income Supplement are to be replaced. Medicare is struggling under the impact of massive federal spending cuts and rapid privatization. Post-secondary education is becoming less accessible as tuition fees skyrocket.

The AFB's National Social Investment Funds offer a real alternative to the cuts to federal spending implemented by the Canada Health and Social Transfer (CHST), reversing federal offloading and the erosion of national standards. We propose to replace the CHST with a set of seven National Social Investment Funds, separately funded and with national standards attached to each. The need for national standards in Canada is clear. Students in New Brunswick, for example, pay tuition fees twice the level of students in Quebec. Social assistance rates vary widely across the country. Canadians are not guaranteed the same level of quality in home care across the country.

Our Investment Funds begin a process of reinvestment in Canada's greatest asset, its people. Our strategy will create thousands of badly-needed jobs in the public sector, while returning a measure of economic stability to millions of Canadians.

I. The Health Care Fund

The National Health Care Fund will immediately restore federal health care transfers to the 1995 levels of $6.7 billion. Funding in future years will increase in line with growth in the economy, and will be equalized so that poorer provinces can maintain health care systems on par with wealthier regions. Increased federal funding is essential in order to prevent the creep of for-profit health care, as is the enforcement of strong national standards.

The AFB will introduce legislation which will restrict privatization occurring through public-private partnerships, and will create an organization (arms-length from government), to collect and publicly disclose information on for-profit health care in Canada.

We will initiate a public review of health care funding models—comparing alternative methods such as the public health insurance model (which describes our current system) and a public health delivery model (under which government directly delivers health care programs).

We will also introduce a National Drug Strategy, to make pharmaceutical drugs fully available to all Canadians. First, the AFB will phase-in a National Drug Plan, allocating $650 million to the initiative this year, and $1.3 billion in 1999. Second, a series of measures will make drugs cheaper and ensure the safety of our food and drug supply. Bill C-91, the Act which excessively protects the patent rights of pharmaceutical manufacturers, will be repealed. The purchasing of drug supplies for federal and provincial governments will be coordinated through one agency. The budget of the Health Protection Branch will be restored to its 1993/94 level of $237 million.

Equal access to quality health care is a priority for the AFB, and we introduce several measures to improve equity. Provinces will be required to provide home care as a public service within their health care plans, thereby greatly improving the lives of the disabled, the chronically ill, and the elderly, who are heavily reliant on quality home care services. We will increase funding to the National AIDS strategy by $8 million this year, and by another $25 million in each of the following five years. The AFB also implements the recommendations dealing with health in the report of the Royal Commission on Aboriginal Peoples, with an increase in funding of $50 million this year, and another $20 million in 1999.

II. The Post-Secondary Education Fund

The AFB will increase access to post-secondary education (PSE) for students from all socioeconomic backgrounds. Tuition fees in Canada are the third highest of all OECD countries, having increased by 45% since 1993. At a time when average full-time earnings for young people are falling, students are experiencing ever-higher debt loads upon graduation.

A National Advisory Council on Post-Secondary Education and Research will ensure that community needs are met by the PSE system. The Council will be headed by a federal Minister, and will bring together representatives from the education and research communities, students, constituency group representatives, faculty, support staff, administration and government, democratically elected or selected by their peers.

The AFB also provides for the passage of a National Post-Secondary Education Act, and the creation of a corresponding Post-Secondary Education Fund, to guarantee all Canadians the right to a quality post-secondary education. All provinces (with the right for Quebec to opt out) will adhere to standards of public administration, full accessibility, comprehensiveness, transferability of credits, and mobility with regards to student grants and awards.

The federal government has cut $2.3 billion from PSE funding since 1993. The PSE Fund will be set at the 1995 level of federal government transfers to the provinces ($2.1 billion) and will grow with the national economy, providing an additional $80 million in 1999. This funding increase will total $760 million over the next five years, and should significantly reduce tuition levels across the country and improve the quality of PSE.

The second strategy for improving access and reducing student debt is the National Student Grants Program. It replaces the current system of loans, loan interest relief, and loan remission with direct grants to institutions and students—a more effective and equitable way of delivering federal funding. The National Student Grants Program will provide grants based solely on need, and specifically acknowledge students with special needs, such as disability, or regional differences in cost of living. Actual spending on grants in 1998 will total $400 million, rising to $575 million in 1999. Funding for First Nations' education will be increased to $21 million this year, and to $23 million in 1999.

The AFB's job-creation initiatives will include a Student Employment Program to help provide students with quality jobs during the summer months. It will form part of the National Youth Job Strategy.

III. The Income Support Fund

In 1996, 5.3 million people in Canada were living below the National Council of Welfare's poverty line. One out of every five children lives in poverty, and one-quarter of these children have at least one parent who works full-time but earns inadequate wages. The National Council on Welfare has calculated that the total amount needed to raise all Canadians to an acceptable level of income is $16.3 billion per year. In reality, the measures proposed in the AFB for income support for poor Canadians are modest and only a step in the right direction. Even if our plan were implemented, the elimination of poverty in Canada would still be far off.

When the Chrétien government ended the Canada Assistance Plan, the right of Canadians to income support on the basis of need alone was eradicated. A climate of scapegoating the poor for joblessness has led to social assistance benefits being cut by 21% in Ontario and by 17% in Alberta, among other provinces. Poor people are treated as criminals: they are fingerprinted and forced to work for welfare in several provinces.

The AFB reverses the federal government's abandonment of the poor, increasing federal transfers for income support to $7.2 billion, just above the 1995/96 level of funding for the Canada Assistance Plan. The Fund will be boosted again in 1999 by an estimated $700 million. In both years, income support programs will have additional resources because base social assistance costs will decrease as a result of our ambitious job-creation program.

Our National Income Support Fund, a cost-shared federal-provincial program, is based upon the following standards:

- Funding, based on real costs of daily living, must be determined through an open, public process that includes low-income persons, and is regularly updated.
- All who declare they are in need are guaranteed a fair assessment and adequate support.
- Assistance must be needs-based only, and not discriminate on the basis of employability, age, type of disability, or other factors.
- There must be an appeal system with client representation, due process, and reasonable timetables.
- No residency requirements are permitted, and the originating province will pay the first year's support after a client relocates.
- There can be no work or training requirements for obtaining assistance, and it cannot be subject to repayment or garnishing of assets.
- Extraordinary measures not required of other citizens (e.g., fingerprinting and workfare) cannot be imposed.
- Recipients must be allowed to retain their homes and a reasonable amount of assets and earned income.

The fund will have two levels. Level I will provide those in need with income no less than 60% of Statistics Canada's Low-Income Cutoffs (LICOs), and the AFB will raise this level to 75% over the next five years. Level II of the fund will meet special needs, such as those of the disabled, for support services. This funding will cover, for example, counselling, emergency funds, or relocation costs.

The AFB also provides an Enhanced Child Benefit which will provide important financial support to poor families. A year ago, the Liberals announced their national child benefit scheme. Today, it is still being negotiated with the provinces. The proposed scheme would pay $605 for the first child, $405 for the second child, and $330 for each additional child. However, many families receiving social assistance will not receive a net increase in income, because the Liberal child benefits may be deducted from their social assistance.

We regard the government's program as inadequate and discriminatory. Our Enhanced Child Benefit will total some $1,400 per child, rising to almost $1,600 in year two. It will not be deductible from provincial social assistance. Funding for the program will total $4.4 billion in this year's budget, and $5.4 billion in 1999. This initiative should produce a significant reduction in child poverty.

The economic security of children living in poor families will be further improved through an Advance Maintenance System, which guarantees that custodial parents will receive their maintenance support from non-custodial parents. The program will use the income tax system to collect maintenance payments, and pay them out to parents. This will not require additional program spending, but will greatly increase compliance for child maintenance.

IV. The Child Care Investment Fund

While income measures like the Enhanced Child Benefit help to achieve a better quality of life for children, they alone are not enough. Social services and supports, such as child care, are also required. Experts agree that quality child care, particularly in the early years of life, enhances healthy child development. Investment in early childhood education gives maximum return, alleviating the damage done by child poverty. Quality child care is also essential to advancing women's equality, since women still bear the greatest responsibility for raising children and head most single-parent households.

Federal spending for child care has fallen by 33% over the last four years. The AFB's National Child Care Investment Fund integrates existing programs (child care funding formerly covered under the Canada Assistance Plan, Aboriginal Headstart, and others) into one fund, and provides $500 million in additional funding for child care this year, increasing by another $500 million in 1999. Programs will be negotiated between the federal and provincial governments, and Aboriginal peoples.

V. The Housing Investment Fund

Housing needs in Canada are pressing. One out of every four renters and 40% of mother-led lone-parent households are in housing need, living in substandard accommodation, or paying unaffordable rents, or both. There are as many as 250,000 homeless people in Canada.

Non-profit and cooperative housing is the best way to meet these needs. The AFB begins by guaranteeing current federal spending on existing non-profit and co-op housing projects, and proposes that the management of federal housing programs be transferred to these community organizations. In addition to the $1.9 billion currently allocated to the Canada Mortgage and Housing Corporation, $300 million in new funding will be directed towards the construction of 10,000 new non-profit or co-op housing units this year.

An additional $200 million will be targeted to a National Housing Retrofit Program, with priority given to funding community housing project retrofits ($100 million of this funding will be allocated from the Atmospheric Fund and the Infrastructure Fund, described below). The program will create an estimated 3,750 jobs.

Both of these programs are expected to leverage significant resources from other levels of government and community organizations, and will significantly boost the construction industry.

The AFB also establishes a National Information Centre for Housing Alternatives to communicate innovative housing strategies.

VI. The Retirement Fund

Paul Martin's proposed Seniors' Benefit, based on level of income, will replace the Old Age Security and Guaranteed Income Supplement programs, along with the age tax credit and the tax credit for private pension income. In effect, the public Old Age Security (OAS) pension and the Guaranteed Income Supplement (GIS) are to be abolished for a scheme that operates like the present punitive and demeaning welfare system. The Seniors Benefit will discriminate against elderly women by making their pension eligibility dependent upon total family income.

Instead of undermining the economic stability of Canada's seniors, we will improve financial support for the elderly. GIS benefits will be increased by 5%. The OAS payment will be indexed to wages, not prices. This will ensure that benefits maintain a constant relationship to earned income in replacing pre-retirement earnings. These changes will ensure a universal, public basic level of pension protection for all Canadians.

We will further ensure that changes to the second level, the Canada Pension Plan (CPP), will not negatively interact with the first level to allow Canadians to fall between the cracks. We do not support changes to the CPP which reduce benefit levels and tighten eligibility for people with disabilities, as is being proposed by the federal government. We are additionally concerned about the negative impact the proposed CPP reductions will have on workplace pension plans.

Our changes will ensure that all Canadians have basic income protection when they retire, and will not be as dependent on private pension schemes. Many workers simply do not qualify for private pensions, nor can they afford them. An increasing number of citizens in non-standard work have no private pension coverage and little capacity to save for Registered Retirement Savings Plans. The AFB commits the federal government to undertake a thorough review of the tax treatment of private retirement savings to determine changes that would address the income needs of the future elderly, taking into account changing labour market conditions, coverage of workplace pension plans, interaction of the various elements of the system, and a gender analysis of the proposed changes.

The third level of the pension system—tax-subsidized individual pensions—should be more fairly designed. Therefore, contribution room on RRSPs will be limited to $10,800, and the present RRSP tax deduction will be converted into a credit. These changes will reduce tax breaks for individuals earning more than $60,000 a year. Tax dollars saved will be allocated toward enhancing the credit for low-income earners.

The AFB will increase the OAS and GIS pensions by $600 million, thereby decreasing poverty—especially among the 51% of elderly women who live below the poverty line.

VII. The Unemployment Insurance Fund

The Chrétien government has perverted the purpose of the unemployment insurance system, turning a program intended to provide income security against the risk of unemployment into a lucrative additional revenue source for balancing the budget. The fact that unemployed workers now have less than a 40% chance of qualifying for unemployment insurance benefits means that working Canadians are now paying premiums for insurance that they likely won't have access to should they need it. Even for those who are eligible, the reduced duration of benefits means that over a million Canadians exhaust their insurance before they find work again.

These changes undermine unemployment insurance eligibility for all those who do not have full-time, long-term attachment to the labour market: the seasonally employed, and part-time workers, notably women and youth. The Atlantic provinces, Northern regions, and communities with cyclical or seasonal industries have been left without income protection and stability.

The AFB reverses this perversion of the original purpose of the Unemployment Insurance program, but rebuilding the UI system after the massive attacks by this and previous federal governments will take several years. Over the next four years, eligibility will increase to 70% of unemployed Canadian workers, and benefit levels improve to 60% of previous insured earnings. We will add $1 billion to expected UI benefit payments in each of the next two years.

Due to the AFB's emphasis on job creation elsewhere in the budget, this money will be spread among about 100,000 fewer unemployed. Thus an even greater overall improvement in UI benefits should be possible. Targeted job creation will help workers in regions with high rates of seasonal unemployment to requalify for coverage in the program.

We will work toward adjusting the UI benefits and premiums structure so as to discourage overtime and provide incentives for shorter work weeks.

As part of our Equity Participation Foundation, the AFB will fund advocacy organizations for unemployed Canadians to fight arbitrary disqualification from unemployment entitlements and ensure access to training and readjustment programs.

Finally, the AFB will undertake a major review of the persistence of high levels of unemployment in Canada. A Commission of Inquiry will assess the real socioeconomic costs of unemployment.

HUMAN RESOURCES AND TRAINING

Nowhere are the federal Liberal government's policies more shortsighted than in its withdrawal of support and its reduction of scope for education and training. The government's training policies have focused almost exclusively on providing additional training to those with recent attachment to the labour force to improve their short-term employability. This policy ignores Canadians trying to enter or re-enter the labour market for the first time, or re-enter it after a longer break.

By turning training over to the provinces, the government has abdicated its role in ensuring Canadians an equal opportunity to acquire long-term skills for long-term jobs. The fact that Quebec has negotiated special arrangements for resources and provincial control of training is not an excuse for the federal government to hand off training to all provinces recklessly, regardless of their level of commitment to it.

While training is not a substitute for jobs, it should be an entitlement regardless of employment status, and it must be available to those historically under-represented in the labour market: women, people with disabilities, visible minorities and Aboriginal peoples.

The Alternative Federal Budget revitalizes the federal role in training, while continuing to support particular arrangements for Quebec and flexible arrangements for First Nations and other provinces. This is done through the creation of:

- a skills bank establishing universal entitlement to life-long learning;
- a skills renewal fund paid for through an Employer Training Levy, set at 1% of payroll up to a ceiling of 40 hours of training for every worker, and refundable to employers who provide this training in-house (similar to the program in Quebec);
- a Pan-Canadian roster of employment services, linking federal and provincial training and labour adjustment programs and services for all unemployed Canadians regardless of their unemployment insurance eligibility;

- an increase of $200 million for training for social assistance recipients; and
- strengthened infrastructure to support training for life-long employment through the Canadian Labour Force Development Board, to monitor and analyze labour market trends, promote industry sector councils and community training agreements, and to negotiate Pan-Canadian standards.

The AFB will fund Human Resources and Development initiatives at a total level of $4.3 billion. This will include training programs currently funded through the UI program. (The Vocational Rehabilitation for Disabled Persons, Canada Student Loans, and the Children's Special Allowance programs are taken out of this heading in our budget.) Our budget also includes support for the National Youth Job Strategy.

INDUSTRY / RESEARCH AND DEVELOPMENT

The budget for Industrial, Regional, and Scientific-Technological Support Programs will rise in the Alternative Federal Budget to $4.4 billion. New resources will support a $1 billion infrastructure program, and $100 million in support for community economic development initiatives (see the Job Creation section). The core Industry budget—which the Liberal government plans to cut by $500 million in the coming year (on top of the termination of the Canada Infrastructure Works program) will be stabilized in year one of our budget, and increased by 3% in year two. This will improve the research capacity of agencies such as the National Research Council, the Natural Sciences and Engineering Research Council, the Social Sciences and Humanities Research Council, and Statistics Canada. Regional economic development initiatives will also be sustained.

TABLE 3: PROGRAM SPENDING DETAILS ($ MILLIONS)

	1997-98 (LIKELY ACTUAL)*	1998-99	1999-2000
NATIONAL SOCIAL INVESTMENT FUNDS			
Health Care Fund	6,664	9,407	10,500
Post-Secondary Education Fund	2,273	3,137	3,600
Income Support Fund	5,562	7,500	8,200
Child Care Investment Fund	350	896	1,500
Housing Investment Fund	1,863	2,263	2,500
Retirement Fund	22,300	23,497	24,700
Unemployment Insurance Fund	13,200	14,200	15,200
Sub-Total: NSIFs	52,212	60,900	66,200

TABLE 3 (CONT'D)

	1997-98 (LIKELY ACTUAL)*	1998-99	1999-2000
DEPARTMENTAL SPENDING AND OTHER			
Equity Participation Fund		100	150
Disabilities - VRDP	168	198	204
First Nations	4,308	4,808	5,308
Common Security	13,138	12,808	12,628
Agriculture	1,505	1,555	1,600
Industry (incl. Infrastructure)	3,837	4,337	4,600
Environment	517	1,550	1,570
Natural Resources	696	846	981
Fisheries	1,077	1,127	1,161
Transport	1,753	1,753	1,805
Immigration	652	887	913
Human Resources & Training	3,544	4,195	4,321
Justice	3,270	3,275	3,368
Culture	2,524	2,825	3,004
Veterans' Pensions	1,921	1,840	1,840
Equalization	8,300	8,400	8,600
Transfers to Territories	1,100	1,196	1,232
Govt. Services & Other	5,278	6,100	7,615
TOTAL PROGRAM SPENDING	105,800	118,700	127,100

* Actual federal spending in 1997-98 on the CHST and subsidiary health, PSE, and income support programs is allocated between these three categories based on pre-CHST proportions.

DEMOCRACY AND HUMAN RIGHTS

WOMEN'S EQUALITY

Economic hardship is concentrated among women and children, who constitute 70% of Canada's poor. Federal policies have done little to address the reality of gender inequality in Canada; in fact, federal policies have served to deepen it. The wage gap between men and women has begun to widen again, after a period of progress towards equality. Women have lost relatively well-paying public sector jobs, and bear the burden of caring for their families and communities as services are reduced.

The Chrétien government has failed to create a national child care program. The elimination of the Canada Assistance Plan (CAP) and cuts to income support marginalize poor women and children and cause severe deprivation. The federal government has also refused to implement pay equity for women in the public sector, and has introduced changes to public pensions that will hurt women. And it has eliminated the Canadian Advisory Council on the Status of Women, and cut funding for women's organizations and research into gender issues.

The social and economic policies in the AFB are built on the recognition of women's inequality, and a commitment to gender equity. We will reinvest in the social programs so crucial to women's equality. Our job creation strategy is designed to benefit women, employing affirmative action where necessary.

To facilitate women's access to the political process, the AFB will create a special Women In Democracy Fund (modelled on the Fair Share Funding Campaign, "A twooney for every woman and girl child in Canada") to promote women's participation in the democratic process, at a level of $30 million. Targets will be set to increase women's representation in government agencies, committees, public administrative entities, the judiciary, and other bodies. As a first step, an inventory will be taken to determine the current representation of women. In addition, the Equity Participation Foundation (described below) will also support women's advocacy organizations. Funding of $50 million will be allocated to women's centres, shelters and services for combatting violence against women. Finally, the AFB also sets aside resources to implement long-overdue pay equity in the federal public service.

EQUITY PARTICIPATION FOUNDATION

Strong social advocacy organizations are necessary to a healthy democracy and play an essential role in opening public debate about important issues, such as the environment, AIDS, breast cancer, disability, human rights and equity, violence against women and children, poverty, and international development. The withdrawal of public funding for advocacy organizations has forced many to shut their doors or limit their activities, thereby stifling debate on important social issues.

The potential for equity for women, visible minorities, gays and lesbians, the disabled and Aboriginal peoples is jeopardized, and efforts to obtain redress for discrimination and equality are threatened, in the current neoconservative climate. The AFB acknowledges the crucial role of advocacy and activism in achieving social change, and will support this valuable work through an Equity Participation Foundation, which will receive $100 million in funding this year, and $150 million in 1999. The Foundation will provide stable funding for organizations that work to give marginalized Canadians a voice.

RACISM AND IMMIGRATION

The AFB will establish community-based programs to improve the awareness of government and the public about the role immigrants play in the Canadian society and economy, and to combat racism. A Centre of Excellence for Immigration will be created. The Canadian Immigrant and Refugee Centre, a board of community representatives, will provide research and policy advice. A similar Canadian Anti-Racism Centre will be established. Funding for immigration and settlement services will be restored, reversing cuts to training programs, ESL and FSL. The AFB will abolish the immigration "head tax."

CANADIAN HUMAN RIGHTS COMMISSION

Increased funds ($0.5 million) will be given to the Canadian Human Rights Commission, and its mandate will be changed from a complaints-based system to one based on the acknowledgment of systemic discrimination.

A Centre of Excellence for Gay and Lesbian Issues will be established, with start-up funding of $1 million. All federal laws and statutes which discriminate against same-sex couples will be amended to allow equal access to government benefits for gays and lesbians.

CANADIANS WITH DISABILITIES

The popular conception that the needs of disabled persons are met through social programs is incorrect. Almost one-half of disabled persons are unemployed, and far too many live in severe poverty with annual incomes under $10,000. Equality for persons with disabilities demands that the government consider the needs of disabled persons in all aspects of policy. Health and education programs, employment programs, taxation, and other areas of the AFB attempt to achieve this attention to the needs of the disabled.

The AFB restores funding to employment-related programs for disabled persons to $195 million. We also allocate $30 million to improve disabled access to mainstream educational institutions. Grants will be provided for local businesses and municipalities to purchase wheelchair-accessible vehicles.

A Social Audit of services for the disabled across provinces will be conducted, to ensure that minimum national standards are met. Research, through Statistics Canada Census projects, will improve our understanding and awareness of the needs of disabled people across the country.

On the tax side, a refundable Disability Tax Credit (which cannot be deducted from provincial social assistance) is established. A base refund will be available to all who apply, with additional refunds given where receipts for purchased goods and services are provided.

ABORIGINAL PEOPLES

Canada has not honourably or appropriately compensated Aboriginal peoples for the lands and resources which were obtained from them. Far too many Aboriginal people experience unemployment, poor health services, and lack of access to adequate housing. The AFB recognizes that Aboriginal people have never surrendered their powers of self-government. We also recognize an obligation to provide Aboriginal people with the opportunity to enjoy the same standard of living as non-Aboriginal people.

In addition to restoring the cuts to services which resulted from the creation of the Canada Health and Social Transfer, the AFB will provide funding for negotiating and implementing self-government with Aboriginal people ($500 million), in line with the recommendations of the Royal Commission on Aboriginal Peoples, and increase funding for Friendship Centres and Women's Programs within Aboriginal communities. New funding for Aboriginal health is also included in the Health program of our budget.

Other AFB proposals on housing, child care, education, health, income support and employment creation will have a positive impact on the standard of living of Aboriginal people.

ENVIRONMENT AND NATURAL RESOURCES

Recent federal budgets have concentrated on economic growth as the only goal of social and economic policy, neglecting the need for environmental protection. Cuts to Environment Canada (amounting to over $170 million since 1994) and the decentralization of environmental powers to the provinces reveal the federal government's lack of commitment to the nation's environment.

We address the need for environmental protection with a balance of policies: regulation, ecological tax reform, green job creation, and a program of just transition for workers affected by environmental change. We will establish a $1 billion Canadian Atmospheric Fund, on the strength of revenues generated by two "green" tax reforms: a tax on the carbon content of energy fuels, and the elimination of existing tax subsidies for oil and gas exploration. Just over half of the fund will be invested, with the proceeds supporting climate change measures—projects such as energy retrofits, street lighting retrofits, composting programs, and loans to purchase energy-efficient vehicles for public and private vehicle fleet owners.

These kinds of programs have proven highly effective at reducing greenhouse gas emissions; we estimate that these projects will generate up to 15,000 new jobs. The remainder of the Atmospheric Fund will be dedicated to transition funding to support workers displaced from traditional fossil-fuel or chemical industries. In such cases, workers in the affected industries will be protected through income and benefit maintenance, access to new jobs, education assistance, and other support for affected communities.

The AFB also proposes a national program of pollution prevention to deal with pollution and waste. A pilot corporate chemical taxation scheme will lead into the financing of this program. Among the chemicals to be targeted for this tax are mercury, ozone depleters, perclorethylene, dioxins and furans.

The base budget of Environment Canada will be increased to $550 million.

The Agriculture budget will promote sustainable environmental farming practices and support family farming in Canada. We replace the GRIP and the NISA, both of which disproportionately benefit large farming operations, with a new $300 million Family Farm Support Program. An additional $150 million will fund the Beginning Family Farmer and Resettlement Program. These programs will provide income support for existing and new family farms, and help repopulate rural Canada. Rural Community Support Programs, including infrastructure development, housing, and community economic development, are part of the AFB's programs in those particular areas.

The research and inspection capacity of Agriculture Canada will be renewed and redirected with an additional $50 million in funding. This will allow the department to support the development of sustainable farming systems.

The AFB increases Natural Resources departmental spending by $70 million. Our priority is the forestry sector, where the federal government's withdrawal from forestry management has put our forests and the jobs that rely upon them in jeopardy. Due to a 50% reduction in the forestry budget since 1994, federal forest development programs, including reforestation, are now mostly defunct.

We will promote greater sustainability in forest practices through a Forest Investment Fund. This Fund will ultimately receive annual revenues equivalent to 1% of the forest sector's total contribution to our economy (or about $200 million). This funding level will be achieved gradually over the next four years, starting with a $50 million budget this year.

The federal government can also play a role in protecting biodiversity by establishing new protected areas, especially in regions where national parks do not exist to protect the environment. To this end, we establish a $30 million Protected Area Fund. The research budget of the Canadian Forest Service will be restored to $151 million, its 1994 level, over the next two years.

Forestry employment will be increased through the above measures, and through industrial policy initiatives that encourage value-added production.

The Fisheries department budget will be maintained at its 1997/98 level of $1.08 billion, and we will add $50 million in research and conservation funding. Funding for the the Atlantic Groundfish Strategy (TAGS) program will also be maintained. Long-term solutions to the ecological and human crisis facing fishing communities must be found—solutions which put the needs of people and the environment first.

CULTURE

A crisis faces Canada's cultural production, due to massive federal funding cuts, international trade and investment agreements which erode cultural sovereignty, and the concentration of ownership in media and cultural industries. Despite this crisis, the federal government plans to cut cultural spending by $380 million over the next two years, and is pursuing policies such as the Multilateral Agreement on Investment (MAI) which would further limit our collective ability to support the diversity of culture in Canada.

As in previous years, the AFB makes a strong commitment to supporting the cultural sector, and to that end will increase federal spending by $350 million over the next two years. Our reinvestment will include an immediate increase of $125 million to the CBC.

Other measures include the restoration of the tax on split-run magazines, and the Postal Subsidy Program—both measures essential to support Canada's indigenous magazine industry. We also eliminate the GST on magazines and books. Legislation will limit media concentration and encourage worker-owned and cooperative ownership of media through our Community Economic Development strategy. A National Universal Access Fund will be set up to allow affordable public access to new information and communication technology.

As part of our taxation policy, cultural producers will be allowed to average their income over a three-year period, which is a fairer way to tax the income of artists.

CANADIAN FOREIGN POLICY AND COMMON SECURITY

The link between more equitable and sustainable solutions at home and abroad is fundamental to the Alternative Federal Budget. An ethic of global citizenship rejects a vision of Canadian foreign policy based exclusively on short-term commercial and political imperatives, in favour of the goals of sustainable human development and an ethic of global citizenship and partnership. An expansion of trade and investment without guarantees for human rights, labour standards, social well-being and concern for the environment will have substantial costs for human welfare and sustainable ecosystems.

Repeated cuts to Canadian Official Development Assistance (ODA) are ethically indefensible in light of the growing number of people living in poverty around the world. The AFB will restore a positive outlook for sustainable human development by reversing the planned $150 million cut to ODA for the coming year, and by increasing ODA each year for the following seven years, reaching a target of 0.40% of GNP by 2005. Canadian aid programs will be reformed, targeting the needs of the poorest countries and the poorest people.

Aid plays an important role in the struggle to eliminate poverty, but alone it is not enough. Debt forgiveness for the highly indebted poor countries is also essential. Canada will play its part by forgiving outstanding official loans to these countries, at a cost of $800 million over the next three years. We allocate $170 million to this goal this year.

A restructured and more specialized defence force (directed to peacekeeping, search and rescue, and emergency assistance to domestic authorities) will allow for a reduced Defence budget over the next two years. We will also allocate financial and human resources to the Mines Action Fund, in support of the Land Mines Convention of December 1997.

GENERAL AND OTHER

Under the category General Government Services and Other, the AFB will allocate sufficient funding to provide pay equity for the federal public services, as well as some room for improvements in public service wages and benefits.

Working Toward a Fairer Tax System

TAX RELIEF FOR THOSE WHO NEED IT

From its inception in 1995, the Alternative Federal Budget has focused on the macroeconomic and taxation policies needed to rebuild the capacity of the federal government to pay for the public programs we need. We have argued that the main driving forces behind the growth of the deficit in the first place were macroeconomic—high interest rates and high unemployment—and that reversing these policies was the key to an alternative, progressive budgetary direction. Indeed, more amenable macroeconomic conditions since late 1995 (lower interest rates and accelerating growth) have been the main factors in the rapid elimination of the federal deficit.

This sea-change in federal finances has important implications for the AFB's tax policies as well. Reduced interest rates and higher economic growth have already done much of the job of rebuilding Canada's fiscal capacity. And our macroeconomic strategy of sustained low interest rates and economic growth will generate even more fiscal room for rebuilding public programs in the coming years, without running deficits and without increasing taxes.

As a result, we can now begin to focus on improving the fairness of the tax system, without worrying so much about needing to increase the total revenues generated by that system. In past years, we promoted significant up-front increases in taxes (aimed especially at profitable businesses and high-income households) to pay for badly-needed up-front reinvestments in social programs. But this year, since we are starting with a balanced budget and relying on low interest rates and sustained economic growth, we can go a long way towards rebuilding federal programs without imposing major tax increases.

RELIEF WHERE IT'S NEEDED

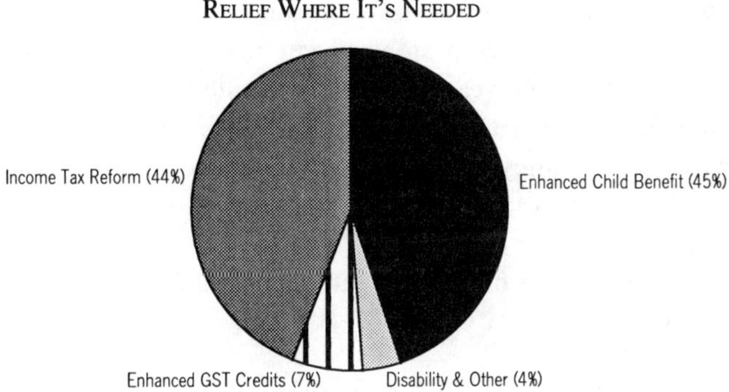

TOTAL TARGETED TAX RELIEF, 1998: $9.7 BILLION

At the same time, however, the growing social emergencies of our communities are so pressing that we feel obliged to do as much as possible in the first year of our program to undo the damage that has been done during the 1990s. We are therefore pledging to immediately increase federal program spending in fiscal 1998-99 back to the same nominal level ($118.7 billion) that prevailed in 1994 prior to the historic spending cuts imposed by Paul Martin in his 1995 budget. This will require a modest one-time increase in the total tax take of the federal government. Beyond the revenues generated by faster economic growth, therefore, the AFB will need a one-year tax increase of $3.1 billion. This tax increase will be aimed especially at super-profitable banks and other interests which have profited immensely from the lopsided economy of the 1990s.

The one-time increase in the aggregate level of federal taxes will be *reversed* in the second year of our budget. For fiscal 1999 and beyond, therefore, we will maintain the ratio of aggregate federal taxes to the size of Canada's economy at exactly the same level—17.5 % of GDP—that was experienced in 1996. With lower interest rates and sustained economic growth, we can indeed rebuild our valued network of public programs in the coming years, without deficits and without increasing taxes.

At the same time as capping the overall level of federal taxes (relative to our economy), we take dramatic measures to improve the fairness of the tax system. This "tax fairness package" is designed in a revenue-neutral way: the revenues gained by closing loopholes for businesses and high-income earners are offset by progressive tax credits offered to low-income households. The AFB contains a total of close to $10 billion worth of tax fairness measures (see figure): tax relief for those Canadians who really need it, financed by closing loopholes and other tax increases for those who can and should be paying more.

In sum, our ambitious program of public service renewal and job creation (including the immediate restoration of program spending to 1994 levels) can be funded with an aggregate tax increase of only 0.3% of GDP, imposed for one year only. The dramatic reduction in the amount of new revenue needed to fund the AFB makes it possible to shift the focus of our tax policy towards providing tax relief for Canadians who really need it. We expect that most Canadians earning less than $60,000 per year will see their federal taxes decline.

The tax proposals of the Alternative Federal Budget are summarized in Table 4.

Components of the Alternative Federal Budget tax program:

- Freeze the overall level of federal taxes in 1999 and beyond at 1996 levels.
- Significantly increase tax credits for families with children, offset by reallocating tax expenditures away from corporations and high-income individuals.
- Provide income tax relief for low- and moderate-income individuals and families, offset by a combination of a tax on wealth transfers (in excess of $1 million), the cancellation of tax preferences for income from capital, and the introduction of two new tax brackets for the highest-income individuals in Canada.
- Create an Atmospheric Fund of $1 billion supported by revenue from a modest carbon tax and the savings from cancelling tax preferences for the oil and gas industry.
- Increase general revenue for one time only in 1998 through a temporary surcharge on bank profits and a one-time increase in revenue from tougher enforcement of existing tax laws.

TAX CREDITS

The Child Benefit will be increased by $700 per child in 1998, to a total of about $1,400, and by another $170 per child in 1999, to a total of close to $1,600. The GST Credit will be increased by $60 per adult. This will provide substantial tax relief for low-income individuals and for families with children well into the middle-income range. This substantial increase in tax expenditures directed towards low-income individuals and families with children will be offset by the proceeds of a sweeping reform in Canada's tax expenditure system.

Beginning in 1998, the AFB will make substantial changes in the tax treatment of capital gains. The special exemptions from capital gains taxation for farms and for small businesses will be replaced by measures better targeted to their objectives. For farming, a rollover of capital gains will be permitted when a farming property is transferred to a family mem-

TABLE 4:
ALTERNATIVE FEDERAL BUDGET TAX PACKAGE (CHANGE IN $MILLION)

	1998-99	1999-2000
TAX EXPENDITURE REFORM:		
Full Inclusion of Capital Gains in Income	+$1,180	
Eliminate Dividend Tax Credit	+$640	
Integrate Corporate & Personal Tax for Small Business	+$346	
CAPITAL GAINS EXEMPTIONS		
Restrict $500,000 farm assets exemption	+$153	
Restrict $500,000 small business exemption	+$548	
Eliminate Capital Gain Freeze, Family Trusts	+$300	
DISALLOWANCE OF CERTAIN DEDUCTIONS		
Meals & entertainment (corporate & personal)	+$305	
Lobbying expenses	+$50	
Salary in excess of 10 times average wage	+$50	
Restrict Eligibility for Scientific Research Credit	+$508	
Restore Non-Resident Withholding Tax to Treaty Rates	+$411	
Introduce Minimum Tax on Profitable Corporations	+$400	
Extend GST to Brokerage & Other Financial Services	+$190	
Restore Tobacco Taxation to Pre-1995 Level	+$495	
INCREASE TAX CREDITS FOR FAMILIES & INDIVIDUALS		
Increase child benefit by $700 per child in 1998, $170 per child in 1999	-$4,400	-$1,040
Increase GST adult credit by $60	-$720	
Increase Disability and Related Medical Credits	-$290	
NEW GST EXEMPTIONS		
Books and magazines	-$49	
Transit passes	-$25	
INCOME AND WEALTH TAX REFORM:		
Wealth Transfer Tax, Estates Over $1 Mill	+$2,925	
Elimination of 3% Federal Income Surtax	-$2,220	
INCOME TAX RATE CHANGES		
Cut bottom rate to 16% from 17%	-$2,050	
Increase top rate from 29% to 30%	+$510	
Add new brackets at $100,000 and $150,000	+$775	
SUB-TOTAL: INCOME & WEALTH TAX REFORMS	+$32	-$1,040
GREEN TAXES:		
$4 per Tonne Carbon Fuel Tax	+$500	
Eliminate Tax Preferences for Oil & Gas Development	+$500	
TEMPORARY REVENUE MEASURES:		
Temporary Surtax on Private Financial Institutions	+$1,500	-$1,500
Enhanced Enforcement of Tax Regulations	+$600	-$600
TOTAL CHANGE IN TAXES:	+$3,100	-$3,100

ber as a going-concern farming operation. In addition, a portion of the capital gain from the sale of farming assets will be eligible for a tax-free rollover into an RRSP. This special RRSP provision will also be available to owners of small business assets.

In addition, capital gains will be made fully taxable (in both the personal and corporate tax systems), ending the 25% tax preference given to this unearned income. And the dividend tax credit will be eliminated and replaced with measures similar to those in the United States for integrating personal income and personally controlled private corporations. As it stands, this tax preference applies only to shares held directly by individuals; it does not apply to shares held by individuals through mutual funds or RRSPs, and hence the vast majority of Canadians derive no benefit from it.

Preferential tax treatment for small business will be limited to the equivalent of that provided to taxpayers in the U.S. tax system; we will ensure that there is no advantage to earning income through a personal corporation rather than directly as an individual.

The deduction from both personal and corporate income for meals and entertainment expenses will be reduced from 50% to zero.

The corporate income tax credit for scientific research and economic development will be restricted so as to reduce its cost to Canadian taxpayers by one-half.

And the provision of Canadian tax law that exempts non-residents from the withholding taxes provided for in our tax treaties with other nations will be eliminated. The effect of this measure is to transfer tax revenue from Canada to other countries.

The GST will be extended to brokerage fees and other financial services, and tobacco taxes will be restored to their pre-1995 levels.

Tax expenditures will be increased in three areas: the GST will be eliminated on sales of books and magazines; the disability and disability-related income tax credits will be increased by 50%; and employer-provided transit passes will be made tax-exempt.

TAX RELIEF FOR LOW- AND MODERATE-INCOME TAXPAYERS

New revenues from a tax on transfers of accumulations of wealth in excess of $1 million will be directed to targeted personal income tax relief. The income tax rate structure will also be changed to promote a more progressive income tax system. Our tax relief package includes the following measures:

- The current 17% lowest rate of personal income tax will be reduced to 16%.

- The current 29% top rate of personal income tax will be increased to 30%.
- Two new tax brackets will be added: 33% of taxable income in excess of $100,000; and 35% of income in excess of $150,000.
- The 3% surtax on federal taxable income will be eliminated.

The combined effect of the income tax rate changes and the elimination of the surtax will be to reduce the bottom rate of tax to 16% from an effective 17.51%; and the middle rate to 26% from an effective 26.78%. The current top rate will be essentially unchanged, rising from an effective 29.87% to 30%. Even for many taxpayers in the current top tax bracket (those earning up to about $75,000 annually), the elimination of the 3% surtax will outweigh the increase in their top marginal rate.

The combined effect of these two sets of measures will be to reduce taxes substantially for low- and moderate-income families and individuals, and to shift the balance in the personal income tax system away from middle-income individuals toward those at the top of the income scale.

TEMPORARY REVENUE MEASURES FOR 1998-9

The bulk of the revenues needed to fund the AFB's program of social reinvestment are provided by ongoing economic growth and lower interest charges. For the first year of our budget, however, modest additional revenues are needed to fund program improvements in the short term. These measures will be limited and targeted, and are designed to ensure that those who have benefited most from the policies of the federal government over the past few years will bear the bulk of the burden. These one-year revenue measures will allow us to restore in a single year the cumulative nominal spending cuts imposed by the Liberals since 1994.

Much of the required $3.1 billion in additional revenue will come from a one-time-only 40% tax on excess profits (profits in excess of a 10% rate of return on equity) of banks and other private financial institutions. This tax will raise an estimated $1.5 billion, and will be imposed only for the first year of the Alternative Federal Budget. The Canadian financial sector continued to pile up record profits throughout the recession of the 1990s, and has profited mightily from the same economic and fiscal conditions (high interest rates, economic stagnation, government indebtedness) that have crippled government programs. This sector can well afford a one-time-only levy to maintain fiscal balance as we rebuild public services.

In addition, the Alternative Federal Budget will begin immediately to intensify the administration of our tax laws so as to draw down the unacceptably high value of unpaid taxes. The most unfair tax is one that is not appropriately collected when it is due, because it penalizes taxpayers who pay their taxes voluntarily and rewards those who cheat. The Auditor General estimated in 1995-6 that $6.6 billion remained uncollected in the personal income tax system alone.

While stepped-up enforcement efforts have stemmed the increase in uncollected taxes, it is unlikely that they have reduced the backlog to any significant degree. And no action has been taken on widespread theft of GST revenues by merchants who collect the tax from their customers but do not remit it to the government. We plan to collect 10% of these outstanding taxes in the first year of our budget. Further collection efforts will be undertaken in subsequent years, but are conservatively excluded from our budget projections.

GREEN TAXES

Finally, the Alternative Federal Budget will also introduce two new tax measures to be used to provide the revenue base for our proposed $1 billion Atmospheric Fund. A tax based on the carbon content of fossil fuels used for the production of energy equivalent to $4 per tonne will provide one-half of the necessary revenues to establish this fund. The tax will be designed to exempt industrial uses of carbon-based fuels as a process input (in steel and cement manufacturing, for example) and to offset the additional impact of energy taxes on residents of northern and remote areas.

The remainder of the necessary funding will be generated by the savings from eliminating special tax measures for oil and gas production. These measures currently bias the tax system in favour of non-renewable energy production.

The introduction of the two green taxes will contribute toward the $3.1 billion in additional revenues required to fund our program spending in fiscal 1998. Unlike the financial institution excess profit tax and the revenues from intensified tax collection, however, both of our green taxes will be retained in subsequent years. For fiscal 1999 and beyond, their $1 billion cost will be offset by the second-stage increase in the child benefit—increasing this benefit by another $170 per child, to a total of almost $1,600. By 1999, therefore, even the introduction of the green taxes does not compromise the overall "revenue neutrality" of our tax package, according to which the overall federal tax rate is maintained at no higher than 1996 levels.

CONCLUSION

Middle- and lower-income Canadians were victimized most by the unfair tax "reforms" of the Mulroney years. They also were hurt the most in the 1991-93 recession. And they have borne the brunt of the massive cuts in public services set in motion by the policies of the Liberal government. The median family income in Canada—before tax—is lower in real terms than it was in 1975. It is small wonder that middle- and lower-income families are asking for tax relief. They need tax relief. But they do not need the tax relief of the Reform Party: one which steals from public programs and gives to the well-off.

Thc 1998 AFB provides tax relief to those who need it most, by rebalancing the tax system so that those who benefit most from our economy pay a greater share of the costs of maintaining it.

COMPONENTS OF THE ALTERNATIVE FEDERAL BUDGET TAX PROGRAM:

- Freeze the overall level of federal taxes in 1999 and beyond at 1996 levels.
- Significantly increase tax credits for families with children, offset by reallocating tax expenditures away from corporations and high-income individuals.
- Provide income tax relief for low- and moderate-income individuals and families, offset by a combination of a tax on wealth transfers (in excess of $1 million), the cancellation of tax preferences for income from capital, and the introduction of two new tax brackets for the highest-income individuals in Canada.
- Create an Atmospheric Fund of $1 billion supported by revenue from a modest carbon tax and the savings from cancelling tax preferences for the oil and gas industry.
- Increase general revenue for one time only in 1998 through a temporary surcharge on bank profits and a one time increase in revenue from tougher enforcement of existing tax laws.

Independent Assessments

of the Alternative Federal Budget

Apart from the intellectual effort and technical expertise that has gone into ensuring that the Alternative Federal Budget is a viable and credible document, we have subjected it to two independent tests. Firstly, we asked Informetrica Ltd. to verify, using its sophisticated computer model of the Canadian economy, whether our budget is consistent and does in fact meet the targets we set. Secondly, we asked a number of economists and political economists from academic institutions and policy research organizations across the country to endorse the general economic and fiscal approach adopted in the Alternative Budget as being both viable and desirable. We reproduce in this section the results of these independent assessments.

The Informetrica assessment covers the first two years of the AFB forecast period; the fiscal years 1998-99 and 1999-2000. It measures the economic and fiscal impacts of the AFB relative to a "base case" that corresponds to the "status-quo" macroeconomic and fiscal outlook of Paul Martin. The assessment finds that thanks to both new federal spending and lower interest rates, we would more than achieve our 4.0% real GDP growth targets in each of the next two years. The AFB would generate some 136,000 *additional* jobs in the first fiscal year (over and above the new jobs that would be created under a status-quo scenario), rising to a total of 255,000 *additional* jobs in the second year. This job creation would be sufficient to meet the AFB's unemployment rate targets--reducing the official unemployment rate below 8% in the first fiscal year, and below 7% in the second. According to Informetrica, the AFB would also have positive effects on household savings and pre-tax business profits. For example, real average household disposable income is forecast to be almost 2 percent higher in an AFB scenario by the second year of our program, compared to a "status-quo" policy case. Informetrica also forecasts significant increases in both labour force participation and in productivity.

We have also revised a very positive endorsement response. As this book went to press, we had received endorsements from 117 economists and political economists. Their names are printed on the following pages.

Mailing Address:
P.O. Box 828, Station B
Ottawa, Ontario K1P 5P9

February 9, 1998

Bruce Campbell
Canadian Centre for Policy Alternatives
#804-251 Laurier Avenue West
Ottawa, Ontario K1P 5J6

Reference: *Alternative Federal Budget, 1998*

Dear Mr. Campbell:

This letter reports our assessment of the CCPA/CHO!CES Alternative Budget proposals for 1998. These are reported as changes to macroeconomic performance from that which should otherwise occur, and in this sense, provides a contrast to the budget proposals that you have indicated you anticipate will be announced by the Government of Canada in the upcoming budget.

On a fiscal-year basis, through changes to expenditures and tax revenues, you have proposed that the fiscal posture of the federal government would provide stimulus to the economy of $8.9 billion in 1998/99, and a further $10.2 billion in the succeeding year. On a calendar-year basis, the increments are $6.6 billion and $10.7 billion in the two years.

Based on the details of your proposed initiatives, we have allocated the changed expenditures in the first year to the following National Account categories (as per cent of total):

transfers to persons - 34%
transfers to other governments - 27%
federal government operations - 35%
capital formation - 3%
transfers to business - 1%.

We have assumed that transfers to other governments would be further recycled by them as transfers to persons (e.g., to finance post-secondary education), or as additional spending for delivery of health care, etc.

Changes that affect the personal tax system are largely redistributive, with little overall fiscal effect in the first year. In the second year, however, there is a net stimulus of $1.3 billion in personal tax reductions. Changes from taxes on nonresidents and on indirect taxes (e.g., the GST and tobacco taxes) impose fiscal drag of approximately $1 billion each year. The large net increase is in taxes on business, with these increased by more than $3 billion in the first year, but less than $2 billion in the second year when the surtax of the first year on financial institutions ends.[1]

For purposes of assessing impacts on the economy that we measure on a calendar-year basis, we have allocated your fiscal-year impacts to each calendar year on a 75/25 basis.

The tabulation below provides summary measures of the effects of the proposed budget changes on general economic activity.

Highlights are as follows:

- including indirect and induced effects, real growth of demands and output in the economy are accelerated by 0.8 per cent in 1998 and by more than one per cent in 1999,
- growth in the number of those employed is accelerated by about 135,000 in 1998, and by a further 120,000 in 1999, yielding a reduction in the unemployment rate of 1.5 per cent in the second year even though some of the formerly discouraged workers are returned to the labour force,
- the balance of the federal government is largely unchanged in 1998, but there is a negative effect in 1999, a year when the consensus would otherwise expect the federal government should be a significant net lender,
- balances of other levels of government are notably strengthened,
- although there is a negative effect on overall government balances in 1999, the debt-to-GDP ratio in that year is reduced relative to what otherwise should be expected,
- real labour income and other sources lead to a significant increase in the income disposable by Canadian households,
- effects on inflation of prices and unit costs of production are modest and limited to first-year impacts.

As in earlier Alternative Budgets, individual elements of the package this year include some bold initiatives, but the overall effect of the proposal is to produce a modest, positive effect on growth and real incomes of households. Although a stronger economy should produce pro-investment consequences, the corporate tax increases do yield a net modest reduction in business capital formation, and a slower growth of the capital stock. Against this effect, which may be argued to have longer term effects on productivity in the economy, it should be recognized that the stock of human capital is being notably strengthened through direct action on education, health of the population, etc., and indirectly, through employment experience.

Yours truly,

C.A. Sonnen,
President.

---

[1] The proposed Carbon Tax has not been included in this evaluation. Were it included, there would be a positive effect on government balances, but a modest negative effect on real economic activity, employment and non-government incomes.

MAJOR INDICATORS, CANADIAN ECONOMY

1998 Alternative Fedeal Budget		1998	1999
Total Real Demand ($86 Mns)		0.77	1.86
Final Domestic Demand		0.63	1.80
Labour Force (000s)		0.00	0.13
Employment		0.96	1.76
Annual Level Effect	(a)	136	255
Unemployment Rate (%)	(a)	-0.88	-1.50
Fixed Investment Effort (% of GDP)	(a)	-0.28	-0.37
Capital Stock ($86 Mns)		-0.12	-0.20
Total Factor Productivity (86=1)		0.22	0.83
Disposable Income per Household ($86)		0.76	1.87
Government Finances			
All-Govt Balance ($ Bns)	(a)	2.0	-4.5
(% of GDP)	(a)	0.21	-0.52
All-Govt Debt-to-GDP (% of GDP)	(a)	-0.86	-0.86
Federal Balance ($Bns)	(a)	0.4	-7.8
Current Account (% of GDP)	(a)	0.07	-0.20
Domestic Savings (% of GDP)	(a)	0.43	-0.25
GDP Deflator (86=1)		0.22	0.12

(a) Level Impact

117 Economists/Political Economists Endorse the Alternative Budget

Sohrab Abizadeh	Economics	University of Winnipeg
Gregory Albo	Political Science	York University
Robert Allen	Economics	University of British Columbia
Sima Aprahamian	Simone de Beauvoir Institute	Concordia University
Isabella Bakker	Political Economist	York University
Fletcher Barager	Economics	University of Manitoba
Karl M. Bennett	Economics	University of Waterloo
Manfred Bienfeld	Public Administration	Carleton University
Errol Black	Economics	Brandon University
Paul Bowles	Economics	University of Northern B.C.
Michael Bradfield	Economics	Dalhousie University
Dave Broad	Social Work	University of Regina
Lorne A. Brown	Political Science	University of Regina
Duncan Cameron	Political Science	University of Ottawa
Maxwell A. Cameron	School of International Affairs	Carleton University
Marie L. Campbell	Human/Social Development	University of Victoria
Robert Campbell	Political Studies	Trent University
Bill Carroll	Sociology	Univeristy of Victoria
Saud A. Choudhry	Economics	Trent University
George Chuchman	Economics	University of Manitoba
Michel Chussudovsky	Economics	University of Ottawa
Michael Clow	Sociology	St. Thomas University
Ken Collier	Professor and Administrator	Athabasca University
James M. S. Craven	Economics	Clark College
Osvaldo Croci	Political Science	Laurentian University
Frank Cunningham	Philosophy	University of Toronto
Kari Dehli	Ontario Institute for Studies in Education	
Ken Dennis	Economics	University of Manitoba
Johan Deprez	Economics	Whittier College
Raj Dhruvarajan	Economics	University of Manitoba
Joseph Dubonnet	Ph.D. Candidate, Sociology	McMaster University
Ross B. Emmett	Economics	Augustana University College
Stephen Endicott	History	York University
David B. Fairey	Director/Labour Economist	Trade Union Research Bureau
Alvin Finkel	Center for State/Legal Studies	Athabasca University
Greg Flanagan	Economics/Political Science	Mount Royal College
Judy Fudge	Osgoode Hall Law School	York University
Herb Gamberg	Sociology	Dalhousie University

Paul Gingrich	Sociology	University of Regina
William Graf	Political Science	University of Guelph
Hugh Grant	Economics	University of Winnipeg
Jonathan Greene	PhD Candidate, Political Stud.	Queen's University
Tom Good	Economics	St.Thomas University
Marjorie Griffin Cohen	Women's Studies	Simon Fraser University
Phillip Hansen	Political Science	University of Regina
Larry Haiven	Industrial Relations	University of Saskatchewan
Terry Heaps	Economics	Simon Fraser University
Roderick Hill	Economics	University of New Brunswick
John Holmes	Geography	Queen's University
Thomas Hueglin	Political Science	Wilfrid Laurier University
Fred Judson	Political Science	University of Alberta
Gregory S. Kealey	History	Memorial Univ. of Nfld.
Bruce Kidd	Physical/Health Education	University of Toronto
Atif Kubursi	Economics	McMaster University
Pradeep Kumar	Industrial Relations	Queen's University
David Langille	Coordinator	Centre for Social Justice, Toronto
Marc Lavoie	Economics	University of Ottawa
Gord Laxer	Director, Parklands Institute	Edmonton, Alberta
Michael A. Lebowitz	Economics	Simon Fraser University
Louis Lefeber	Professor (emeritus)	CERLAC, York University
Mark Leier	History	Simon Fraser University
Wayne Lewchuk	Economics/Labour Studies	McMaster University
Carla Lipsig-Mummé	Ctre Research/Work/Society	York University
Margaret Little	Women's Studies	Queen's University
Jean-Guy Loranger	Economics	Université de Montréal
John Loxley	Economics	University of Manitoba
Vaughan Lyon	Political Science	Trent University
Gayle MacDonald	Sociology/Criminology	St. Thomas University
Judy MacDonald	Social Work	St Thomas University
Michael MacMillan	Political/Canadian Studies	Mount St Vincent University
Rianne Mahon	Public Administration	Carleton University
Stephen McBride	Political Science	Simon Fraser University
Joan McFarland	Economics	St. Thomas University
Susan McGrath	Social Work	York University
Margie Mendell	Political Economy	Concordia University
Manuel Mertin	Economics/Political Science	Mount Royal College
Alex C. Michalos	Political Science	University of Northern B.C.
Douglas Moggach	Political Science	University of Ottawa
Esteve Morera	Philosophy/Political Science	York University
Kenise Murphy Kilbride	Early Childhood Education	Ryerson Polytechnic University
Randle W. Nelsen	Sociology	Lakehead University
W. Robert Needham	Canadian Stuides Program	University of Waterloo
Tom Nesbit	Centre for Labour Studies	Simon Fraser University
Barbara Paleczny	Socio-economic ethicist	School Sisters of NotreDame
Peter Penz	Environmental Studies	York University
Paul Phillips	Economics	University of Manitoba
John Price	History	University of Victoria
Norene Pupo	Sociology	York University
Joseph K. Roberts	Political Science	University of Regina
Gideon Rosenbluth	Economics (emeritus)	University of British Columbia
Amy Rossiter	School of Social Work	York University
Abraham Rotstein	Economics	University of Toronto
Tom Rymes	Economics	Carleton University
Jalil Safaei	Economics	University of Manitoba
Mario Seccareccia	Economics	University of Ottawa
Ardeshir Sepehri	Economics	University of Manitoba

Edward H. Shaffer	Economics	University of Alberta
Andrew Sharpe	Centre for the Study of Living Standards	
Hugh Shewell	Social Work	York University
Harry Smaller	Education	York University
Gerald B. Sperling	Political Science	University of Regina
Brenda Spotton	Economics	York University
Erin Steuter	Sociology/Anthropology	Mount Allison University
Donald Swartz	Public Administraton	Carleton University
Robert C.H. Sweeny	History	Memorial University of Nfld.
Gordon Ternowetsky	Social Work	University of Northern BC
Frank Tester	Social Work	University of British Columbia
Neil Thomlinson	Politics/Public Admin.	Ryerson Polytechnic University
Monica Townson	Consultant	Toronto, Ontario
Eric Tucker	Osgoode Hall Law School	York University
Jesse Vorst	Economics	University of Manitoba
Robert Ware	Philosophy	University of Calgary
Mel Watkins	Economics	University of Toronto
Don Wells	Labour Studies/Political Sc.	McMaster University
David A. Wolfe	Political Science	University of Toronto
Frances Woolley	Economics	Carleton University
Charlotte Yates	Labour Studies/Political Sc.	McMaster University

Analysis of Distributional Impact of the Alternative Federal Budget Tax Changes

The AFB for 1998 contains changes in the tax system and the child benefit that, taken together, result in a significant increase in disposable income for low- and middle-income families in Canada.

The changes proposed in AFB '98 are:

- An increase in the child benefit by $870 per child, from $1,020 per child to $1,890 per child.
- An increase in the adult portion of the GST credit by $60 per adult, from $199 to $259.

A restructuring of the income tax rate system by:

- eliminating the 3% surtax on federal tax;
- reducing the bottom rate of income tax from 17% to 16%;
- increasing the current top rate of income tax from 29% to 30%; and
- adding new rates of 33% for income between $100,000 and $150,000, and 35% for income over $100,000.

Independent Consultant, Richard Shillington, under a contract with the United Steelworkers, analyzed the impact of these proposed changes on Canadians with various family types, using Statistics Canada's Social Policy Simulation Database and Model (SPSD/M). This analysis demonstrates a substantial combined benefit from these changes, throughout the lower and middle ranges of family incomes.

For example, a single-parent family with two children and an income of $25,000 would receive a net benefit of $1,960—a $1,740 increase in the child benefit, from $2,500 to 4,240; a $120 increase in the GST Credit; and a tax reduction of $100.

A couple with two children and a family income of $35,000 would benefit by $2,140—$1,740 from the child benefit, from $2,100 to $3,840, $120 from the GST Credit; and $280 from the tax changes.

Chart:

CHANGE IN CHILD BENEFIT
TWO-PARENT FAMILY
INCOME $50,000

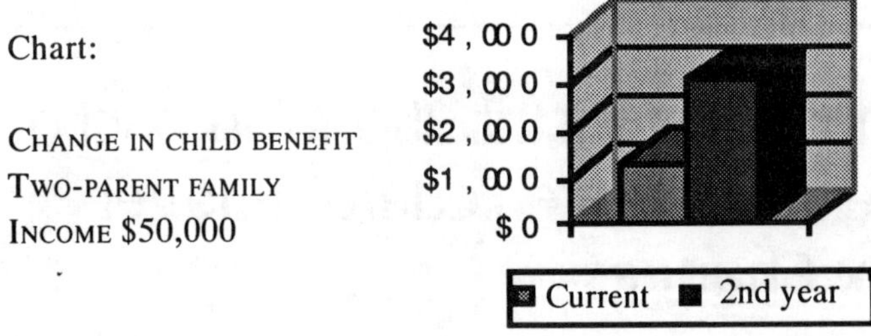

A couple with two children and a family income of $50,000 would see their disposable income increase by $2,250—$1,740 from the child benefit, which increases from $1,318 to $3,058; $40 from the GST Credit; and $480 from the tax changes.

A couple with three children and a family income of $50,000 would see their disposable income increase by $3,100—an increase of $2,610 in the child benefit, from $2,700 to $5,310; a $55 increase in the GST Credit; and a tax reduction of $435.

A couple with no children and a family income of $75,000 would save $500 from the tax rate changes.

Framework Document

ECONOMIC FRAMEWORK
Key Indicators and Goals

CANADA'S ECONOMY: THE GOOD NEWS AND THE BAD NEWS

The 1998 round of federal budgeting should be taking place within a more optimistic macroeconomic context. Canada's real economic growth during 1997 (excluding inflation) was approximately 4%, making it one of the best years of the 1990s. Growth has been powered by low interest rates, ongoing job creation in the private sector, and a consequent surge in household consumer spending and business investment.

After a grim decade of recession, restructuring, and stagnation, Canada's economy is finally showing some signs of sustained life. The benefits of this growth for government finances could be massive: tax revenues rise in step with economic expansion, and so the books are looking a lot better this year for all levels of government.

The great irony, of course, is that this long-overdue and welcome news for most Canadians has set the alarm bells ringing for powerful groups in our society. In particular, Canada's financial industry worries that stronger growth and job-creation herald future increases in wages and inflation. For the owners of financial wealth, inflation is Public Enemy No.1—far worse than the unemployment and stagnation which has so harmed the rest of society. They are demanding that the Bank of Canada clamp down on growth, reining in Canada's economy to what they consider a more "sustainable" 2.5% rate of expansion. This is consistent with their preference that unemployment be maintained in a range between 8 and 9%.

The Bank of Canada has responded to this pressure, raising interest rates four times during the latter half of 1997 by a total of 1.25 percentage points. The Bank of Canada still officially subscribes to the view that unemployment in Canada cannot fall below about 8.5% without sparking off an accelerating cycle of inflation. It must be said, however, that the Bank seems to have been sensitive to widespread public skepticism of its policy of official high unemployment. The Bank has preserved low interest rates longer than the financial community wanted, perhaps signaling that unemployment will be allowed to fall at least somewhat below the official 8.5% target.

The interest rate outlook was further clouded at the end of 1997 by the fall-out from the Asian financial crisis. Financial investors of all kinds flocked to "safe-haven" currencies (such as the U.S. dollar) to wait out the storm, causing major capital flows out of smaller countries such as Canada. The Canadian dollar fell below 70 cents (U.S.) at year-end—to its lowest level in 12 years—in spite of the renewed "confidence" of financial investors in Canada's new-found "fiscal stability." The Bank of Canada therefore came under increased pressure to raise interest rates again, this time to defend the dollar. Higher rates and financial turbulence threaten to derail the much-delayed recovery in Canada's economy; economists were quickly downgrading their forecasts of real growth in 1998 from around 4% to 3% or even less.

Progressives need to keep up the pressure for a more balanced macroeconomic policy, putting top priority on job creation and growth rather than low inflation and financial profitability. And we cannot allow the self-interested actions of currency speculators to derail an economic recovery that was already too late in coming.

The Bank of Canada has raised interest rates despite a deceleration in the inflation rate to less than 1% by the end of 1997, and despite continued weakness in Canada's job market. Recent job creation in the private sector is obviously welcome news: as many as 400,000 net new jobs were created in Canada during 1997, with strong private sector job-creation offsetting continuing job losses in the public sector. But the official unemployment rate remains persistently high: still stuck at 9% by year's end. True unemployment is much higher than the official figure; when we count involuntary part-time employment and the hundreds of thousands of discouraged workers (those who abandoned the labour market altogether during the bleak 1990s), actual unemployment in Canada is closer to 20%.

The questionable quality of many new jobs is another sign of weakness in our labour market. Part-time jobs continue to make up a disproportionate share of all new jobs. Even more worrisome is the incredible growth of so-called "self-employment" in Canada. Over one-half of new jobs created during the current recovery have been self-employed. In many cases, these include marginal home businesses, or nominally self-employed contract workers. Either way, this statistical category continues to hide a great deal of underutilized labour potential.

And despite the robust growth figures recently tallied by our economy, it is far from certain that the current recovery is firmly rooted. Canadian consumers are now more heavily indebted than ever; much of the 1997 growth in consumer spending was financed through new debt (not surprising, considering the impact of continued unemployment and stagnant wages on family incomes), and personal saving has fallen to record low levels. As a result, consumers are still dedicating a high share of their total income (about 8%) to interest charges, despite current lower interest rates.

This means that consumer spending is quite vulnerable to recent and future increases in interest rates. Thus the recent tightening by the Bank of Canada could have a faster negative impact on our economy than most observers expect—especially if Canada's economy is adversely affected by the financial turbulence sweeping Asia and elsewhere.

In summary, the recent improvement in Canada's economy is welcome and long overdue. It will make it much easier for government finance ministers (and for Alternate Federal Budget participants!) to juggle simultaneous demands for a recovery in program spending, reduction of the accumulated debt, and perhaps the reduction of certain taxes. But this recent improvement has not yet gone nearly far enough: labour markets remain vastly underutilized, per capita incomes have barely recovered to the levels of the late-1980s (let alone grown to reflect our increasing economic potential), and social conditions continue to deteriorate despite the recovering economy.

Even worse, Canada's policy-makers are poised to squander the gains that have been made in the last year, thanks to their continued adherence to a discredited model of inflation control, and their continued accommodation of the selfish and destructive behaviour of financiers. Canada's economy needs several more years of vibrant growth and job-creation to repair the damage done earlier this decade; interest rates must be maintained at low levels in order to support this needed expansion.

It will be more difficult, of course, to sustain low rates in an environment of global financial instability. We will need to be prepared to accept a temporarily lower dollar (perhaps even in the 65-cent range) as a consequence of putting top priority on sustaining domestic growth with lower interest rates, rather than protecting the real value of financial assets; but then the lower dollar will help to stimulate exports and further protect domestic employment. We will also need to begin developing the new regulatory and institutional controls and mechanisms that will be required to reimpose discipline and accountability on out-of-control financial markets: limits on foreign investment of tax-subsidized pension funds, support for multilateral efforts to establish a Tobin Tax on international transactions, and the pro-active use of social pools of capital (such as

Bank of Canada debt financing, and the growing CPP reserve fund) to reduce our reliance on the private financiers whose comings and goings have proven so destructive.

THE DEFICIT: THE GOOD NEWS AND THE BAD NEWS

Thanks primarily to low interest rates and accelerating economic growth, the federal budgetary balance is now in much better shape than virtually any observer could have predicted a year ago. Faster economic growth generates more revenue from personal and corporate taxes. Lower interest rates reduce the government's own debt-servicing costs (which totalled $45 billion last year_by far the largest single federal expenditure). Deep program spending cuts shaved another $14 billion from the budget between 1994 and 1996. The final deficit for the fiscal year ended March 31 1997 came in under $9 billion, equal to barely 1% of Canada's GDP. And all the evidence suggests that the federal budget will be balanced in the current 1997-98 fiscal year.

Supporters of the Alternate Federal Budget continue to disagree strongly with the deficit-reduction strategy that has been pursued by the Liberal government since 1995: a single-minded and unnecessary focus on cutting funding for important public and social programs, with consequent painful effects for Canadian society. If it had emphasized lower interest rates and a more expansionary macroeconomic climate, rather than focusing on cutting spending, the federal government could have met its professed deficit timetable without cutting program spending at all.

Nevertheless, the faster-than-expected elimination of the federal deficit is good news for advocates of a more progressive and active role for the federal government in our social and economic lives. As we have argued consistently since the first Alternative Federal Budget in 1995, the issue is not whether or not the deficit will be reduced and the budget balanced: that is a given. The issue is who will pay for this fiscal progress, and what kind of Canada will remain once the budget has been brought back into balance.

We reject the unfair and defeatist principles underlying the Liberal approach—namely, that the pain of deficit-reduction must be borne solely by working Canadians through the erosion of public services, that the vested interests of bond-holders and financiers will be protected throughout this "restructuring," and that there is nothing better that government can do to assist our economic and social development than simply to "get out of the way." But now that the deficit has been eliminated, albeit by perverse means, the case for protecting and ultimately rebuilding public programs has been made all the easier.

Powerful economic forces are now poised to exert huge beneficial impacts on the federal budget. With a balanced budget, the accumulated federal debt will decline steadily and quite rapidly as a share of GDP. Consequently, the dead-weight loss of federal interest payments will decline as a share of total revenues, leaving more spending room for actual, useful programs. Revenues will grow in line with the economy. The bottom-line result will be the oft-discussed "fiscal dividend": an emerging budgetary surplus at the federal level.

The size and duration of the fiscal dividend, however, depends very centrally on whether or not the current relatively vibrant economic recovery is able to—or is allowed to—continue. It has been lower interest rates and rapid growth that powered the rapid improvement in federal finances. If this recipe is undone, either by design (Bank of Canada intervention) or by chance (the aftershocks of Asian turmoil), then the current debate over how to spend that dividend will turn out to have been much ado about nothing.

The Fiscal Dividend: What To Do?

The debate over how to "spend" the fiscal dividend (assuming, of course, that continued economic growth assures its ultimate creation) has broken down into three broad camps: 1) rebuild program spending, 2) cut taxes, or 3) pay down the accumulated debt. Let us briefly consider these three options, in reverse order:

1) Debt Repayment

For the most part, Canada's financial community wants the government to run significant budgetary surpluses which would be used to reduce the outstanding government debt. Contrary to the self-interested pronouncements of financiers, this position does not stem from any fear of government bankruptcy. Financial investors want to preserve the downsized, defensive attitude currently exhibited by government in Canada, even though the immediate fiscal crisis is over. In addition, by beginning to pay off its debt, the government would increase the market value of the outstanding bonds that remain, thus creating a capital gain for the financial investors who hold most of Canada's $600 billion federal debt.

Debt repayment is also Finance Minister Paul Martin's preferred option. Other things being equal, of course, it is usually better for a government to have less debt than more. A smaller debt means less tax revenue is wasted on interest payments, and also somewhat enhances the government's degree of independence from financial markets. However, it is important to remember that the government's real debt burden—

which should be measured in terms of the ratio of debt to the size of Canada's GDP—would fall dramatically, even without any actual debt "repayment." By simply maintaining balanced budgets, in the context of a growing economy, the debt-to-GDP ratio will fall quickly on its own.

The Alternative Federal Budget, therefore, has decided to rule out significant debt repayment as part of its medium-term fiscal plan. We will plan for small nominal budget surpluses of $1 billion per year, starting in fiscal 1999. This allows for some small reduction of the nominal debt (and this decline could be larger in the event that our budgetary targets are exceeded). But the debt-to-GDP ratio will still decline quickly in our scenario, thanks primarily to our commitment to maintain vibrant rates of economic growth for at least another four to five years.

In fact, the debt ratio falls faster in our pro-growth scenario (to an estimated 53.0% of GDP by fiscal 2001) than it does in a status-quo "soft landing" scenario which allows for $3 billion per year of actual debt repayment. This indicates convincingly that the debt-repayment option is no option at all: faster economic growth, not budgetary surpluses, is the crucial variable, yet the same financial interests who are allegedly so concerned about the debt burden are the same powerful forces calling for the deliberate deceleration of our economy for the sake of preserving ultra-low inflation rates.

2) TAX CUTS

Conservative interests would also like to see a significant share of the fiscal dividend devoted to tax cuts. The taxes most often proposed for reduction include personal income taxes and unemployment insurance premiums. As with debt repayment, the goal of conservatives in this strategy is to lock in place the current fiscal handcuffs which have so constrained government social and economic policy initiatives during the past decade. Their starting assumption is that funds allocated by governments are "wasted," while funds spent privately (no matter how frivolously or destructively) are "productive."

The argument that government simply "can't afford" to do more to promote economic equality and opportunity is ringing increasingly hollow, with the approach of the fiscal dividend. But if the funding base for government can be further undermined now through major tax cuts, then the claim of public poverty as an excuse for government inaction would become a perpetual one: government would never have sufficient funds to rebuild a more activist public sector in our society.

Once again, other things being equal, lower taxes are better than high taxes. Nevertheless, there are good reasons why now is not the time to implement significant tax cuts. In terms of job creation and economic stimulus, tax cuts generate much less "bang for the buck" than replacing funding for social programs. Much of the demand stimulus of a tax cut is lost because recipients will save some of their new after-tax income (rather than spending it), while much of the new spending inspired by the tax cut is devoted to imported consumer goods (which create no new jobs within Canada). New funding for public programs, on the other hand, generates a full dollar-for-dollar expansion of domestic demand in a relatively labour-intensive, made-in-Canada industry—and unlike tax cuts, these programs also promote a healthier, more inclusive society.

For this reason, the 1998 Alternative Federal Budget includes no aggregate tax cuts as part of its medium-term fiscal plan. Instead, the overall level of taxation in Canada's economy (measured by the federal tax-to-GDP ratio) will be frozen at its fiscal 1996 level of 17.5%. Within this overall tax freeze, we will take numerous measures to improve the equity and efficiency of our tax system (through higher income taxes on high-income households, selective tax relief for lower-income households, closing unfair tax loopholes, and a major new tax on greenhouse gas emissions). But any new taxes imposed through these measures will be offset by equal tax cuts elsewhere in the system, so that our overall tax package is "revenue neutral."

By reducing the dead-weight loss of public monies wasted on interest payments, and increasing aggregate tax revenues painlessly through faster economic growth, we believe that major improvements to Canada's system of public programs can be financed—within the context of continuing balanced budgets—without any increase in the overall average rate of taxation.

3) REBUILDING PUBLIC AND SOCIAL PROGRAMS

Canada's social safety net has been shredded by the fiscal retrenchment of Canadian governments over the past several years. Program spending by all levels of government in Canada declined from 40% of GDP in 1992 to just 33% of GDP by the spring of 1997. In other words, a full 7% of our total economic production—a sum currently equal to about $60 billion—has been removed, in less than five years, from the real programs and services delivered by the public sector.

At the federal level, program spending declined by $14 billion (or 12%) from fiscal 1994 to fiscal 1996—shrinking from 16% of GDP to 13% of GDP in just two years. Finance Minister Martin plans to spend only $103.5 billion on programs in fiscal 1998, an amount which will then equal less than 12% of GDP. Federal program spending will have declined by one-quarter, in relation to GDP, in just four years—an astonishing withdrawal by government from our social and economic lives. Federal cuts in transfer payments are still cascading down into continued spending cuts in important provincial and municipal programs.

The very nature of Canadian society has been fundamentally altered by this lopping-off of large segments of public or collective activity. Poverty and inequality have increased, despite the economic recovery. The real standard of living has declined for more than half of our citizens, and dramatically so for the poorest among us, the majority of whom are women. Social and regional tensions have grown. Gains made towards gender and race equality have been eroded.

One significant cost of not spending on social programs is that women's inequality is reinforced. The reduction of social spending and the dismantling of social safety nets affect women disproportionately, both as users of services and in terms of the impacts this spending has on enhancing women's overall economic security. To spend or not to spend is not a gender-neutral question.

Funding cuts have particularly targeted the programs that promote the attainment of equality by women—i.e., social assistance, job training, child-care, and community support services—and as such constitute a direct assault on women's equality. Further compounding this assault has been the shift of funding from preventative and supportive programs into more interventionist, crisis-oriented and needs-oriented programs which tend to stigmatize those requiring service or support. These and other pressing social and economic ills are crying out for attention.

Collectively, we could always afford to meet those needs: the claim that the deficits of previous years prevented Canadian governments from doing what was needed was a cop-out. But now, with chronic deficits behind us, and the state of public finances fundamentally improving, we can clearly meet the challenges that face us.

It is for this reason that the 1998 AFB will devote the entire coming fiscal dividend—along with other savings resulting from changes in debt management—to the partial reconstruction of social and public programs. The potential sums of new money will be large: our program will free up approximately $10 billion in new program spending in fiscal 1998, and even more in subsequent years, while maintaining a balanced budget and a frozen average rate of taxation. But they represent only a down payment on the programs and activities that will ultimately be required to repair the social fabric of our country.

Even under our program, federal program spending climbs back only to 14% of GDP by fiscal 2001—still significantly lower than it was in 1995 when Paul Martin implemented his horrendous cutbacks. Our program will seem radical to some, in the context of recent public sector downsizing; but we are not yet even making up for the cutbacks that have been experienced over the past three years.

By emphasizing sustained economic growth and lower interest rates, and devoting the resulting fiscal dividend to the rebuilding of public programs, the AFB presents a vision of how a collective sector of our economy can be rebuilt in a gradual and fiscally responsible manner.

BALANCED BUDGETS: FACT AND FICTION

The Alternative Federal Budget is committed to maintaining the balance in federal finances that we expect to be achieved during the 1997 fiscal year. We agree that large chronic government deficits are not sustainable. And we show that on the strength of lower interest rates and faster economic growth, we can gradually rebuild the important network of public programs that is key to the quality of life in Canada, all with a balanced budget and frozen tax levels.

At the same time we are concerned that the infatuation with balanced budgets that has dominated Canadian politics during this decade may produce an unwise and potentially destructive mindset among Canadians—one that assumes that budgets must remain balanced at all times, come hell or high water. This mindset is reflected in the various "balanced budget rules" that have been enacted or proposed in many jurisdictions in Canada.

The recent popularity of balanced budget laws across Canada will exacerbate social and economic disparities and prevent equity-seeking public initiatives. Balanced budget amendments now exist in five provinces and the Territories. These statutes and laws have important political, economic and legal impacts through their enshrinement of fiscal conservatism.

They constrain governments in their fiscal policy decisions by imposing caps on spending and taxation. In particular, establishing tax limits (as in Manitoba, Alberta and B.C.) restricts the ability to generate new revenues, while increasing the likelihood of user fees. User fees will become easier to implement than taxes, but often have negative distributional consequences.

Balanced budget laws also undermine the crucial role of government spending in stabilizing the economy during private sector recessions. The AFB rejects fiscal limitation laws as the answer to our budgetary problems: those laws blame governments for supposedly acting irresponsibly, when it is in fact markets and the private accumulation of power that need to be regulated in the broader interests of society.

This extreme approach is wrong: balancing the budget, and keeping it balanced, is an important goal. But it must be weighed against other equally important goals, particularly in the event of an economic slowdown. If Canada's economy slows too much in the wake of higher interest rates or global financial turbulence, the much-vaunted fiscal "dividend" could disappear entirely, replaced by renewed deficits. In this case, more spending cuts would only make matters worse. Budgets cannot be kept in balance during a recession without making that recession even deeper—and that would truly reflect mixed-up priorities on the part of our economic policy-makers.

The ultimate measure of sound fiscal policy is the government's debt ratio. We all agree that the federal debt ratio must first fall and then be sustained at some lower level; in fact, it falls faster under the Alternative Federal Budget than expected under Paul Martin. But the debt ratio can be kept stable, while still allowing for occasional deficits during years of recession. For example, if the government balanced its books during half of the economic cycle, while sustaining modest deficits during the years of recession and initial recovery, the debt ratio would be maintained as a constant share of GDP. The Alternative Federal Budget is committed to maintaining a balanced budget for several years—a feat which should be amply possible as long as economic growth is sustained. But we do not want this commitment to be interpreted as an endorsement of the balanced budget "extremism" currently fashionable among Canada's conservatives.

ECONOMIC ASSUMPTIONS, FISCAL PROJECTIONS, AND TARGETS

To conclude, the 1998 Alternative Federal Budget will be based on the following economic and fiscal "building blocks."

MACROECONOMIC STRATEGY

Interest Rates: We will instruct the Bank of Canada to maintain short-term interest rates in the same range (between 3% and 3.5%) as was experienced during the first half of 1997, for at least another two years. In subsequent years, short-term rates will rise with inflation to maintain real (after-inflation) rates of about 1%. We will also instruct the Bank of Canada to increase its "target band" for inflation to a range between 2% and 4%. (It goes without saying that we are assuming the cooperation of the Bank of Canada with our macroeconomic policy direction, and would be willing to take the necessary institutional measures to ensure that co-operation.)

Economic Growth: On the strength of sustained low interest rates and significant increases in federal government program spending, we expect that real economic growth in Canada could maintain its current 4% pace for at least another three years.

Debt Management: We will refinance 2% of the existing outstanding federal debt through the Bank of Canada (at commercial interest rates) in each of the next five years.
Inflation: We expect a gradual and moderate acceleration of inflation from about 1% at present to 3% (the middle of the Bank of Canada's new target range) by fiscal 2000. In the event of faster-than-expected inflation, various ameliorative instruments may be invoked—including restrictions on commercial lending by private banks, slower debt refinancing through the Bank of Canada, and (if necessary) increases in interest rates.

FISCAL AND SOCIAL TARGETS

Deficit Target: We will maintain a balanced budget in fiscal 1998 and after. A $1 billion contingency reserve fund will be included in fiscal 1999 and after.
Debt Target: We aim to reduce the federal debt-to-GDP ratio to less than 60% (equal to the European Community's Maastricht target) no later than fiscal 2000, and we will continue to reduce the debt ratio in following years.
Tax Target: We aim to maintain the overall level of federal taxation at approximately its 1996 level (17.5% of GDP) throughout our fiscal plan.
Unemployment Target: We aim to reduce the average official unemployment rate by one full percentage point per year, from 9% at present to no higher than 5% by fiscal 2001. At the same time, we allow for a gradual recovery of the labour force participation rate from below 65% at present back to its pre-recession high of 67.5% within five years.
Poverty Target: We aim to reduce the average poverty rate in Canada by 1.5 percentage points in each year, from about 18% at present to 12% (6 points lower) by fiscal 2001. We expect that two-thirds of this improvement will automatically accompany the strengthening labour market in our expansionary macroeconomic strategy. The other third will be accomplished on the strength of our pro-active anti-poverty measures.

Social Economy

Sharing values or sharing value?

Federal documents indicate concern among policy-makers about poverty and social exclusion, as well as the erosion of symbols of national identity. The government hopes to shore up social cohesion by promoting common values and helping the third sector or social economy (especially volunteers and charitable organizations) create "social capital."

This is reminiscent of the 19th century. Unbridled capitalist development devastated communities, making millions destitute. Then, too, philanthropists set up charitable institutions to palliate these social ills. But they never addressed the true problem—the unregulated expansion of the market economy. On the contrary, their goal in strengthening social cohesion was to foster a stable business climate.

Today, neo-liberals regard the social economy as a vehicle of privatization and workfare. But most organizations in the social economy are active in one geographical area, have small budgets, and few assets or employees. The social economy relies heavily on direct government financing, as well as on the physical and social infrastructures (income security programs, hospitals, schools, community centres, libraries, parks, playgrounds) that the social state builds and makes available to all citizens. As the social state withers, so too will the social economy.

In the current context of markets being deregulated and states restructured, the third sector on its own can offer no salvation. At best, it can patch up some of the damage done by structural adjustment. What sort of social cohesion can it achieve in the midst of a widening rift between business and workers, and between rich and poor? Which values are to be shared—the individualistic values of neo-liberalism? The patriotic values of sharing the pain of deficit reduction?

Yet the 19th and 20th centuries have produced alternative, co-operative models, consisting of mutual aid, self-help and self-defence by the working class and the poor: friendly societies, co-operatives, trade unions, loan circles, etc. These are the basis of a different economy, based on the values of reciprocity, solidarity, mutual aid, collective ownership, and democracy.

The deepest need, though, is not for shared values, but shared value, i.e., shared wealth. Here the grassroots, solidarity-based economy has much to offer, not just in terms of working to share wealth, but in terms of helping to redefine the nature of wealth.

There Is More to Work than Wages—There Is More to Wealth than Money

There is more to life than working for an employer, just as there is more to life than being a consumer. Not all work is done for a wage. The economy is not limited to buying or selling. Wealth means a lot more than property; it also includes health, knowledge, culture, a clean environment. The mixed economy encompasses more than just commodity exchange and state redistribution; it also includes networks of reciprocity and domestic labour.

As time-use surveys show, Canadians devote a large, and often the greater, part of their waking time to *unpaid* work—whether it be the domestic labour of raising children and maintaining a household, or volunteer activities outside of the home. Statistics measuring such activities are few. However, Statistics Canada reported in late 1995 that, if unpaid work were remunerated, it would be worth anywhere between $234 billion and $374 billion. The unpaid work accomplished was estimated as the equivalent of 13 million jobs, i.e., about the number of jobs now in the paid workforce. At least two-thirds of unpaid work was carried out by women.

Recognition that such activities are actually work and generate a major part of national wealth has been slow in coming. The Canadian government made a commitment to integrate unpaid work into policy decisions at the UN Conference on Women in Beijing in 1995. Status of Women Canada is devoting some effort to research on unpaid work. But there is some concern that the federal government is ultimately only looking for ways to entrench women's responsibility for unpaid work and to make it more palatable, now that the demise of the Canada Assistance Plan has created the conditions for its increase.

For most Canadians, wages remain the chief means of acquiring the necessities of a civilized life. Poverty and affluence are closely correlated with participation in the paid workforce, with the number of hours worked and with the number of wage earners in a household. These factors in turn are correlated with a person's occupational category and gender.

Working for a wage is also the condition of access to the best public income-security programs for those who are out of work or retired. Only those who have had paid employment qualify for social insurance (EI, CPP/QPP, etc.), as well as a range of possible private social benefits partly or entirely funded by their employers: insurance, health plans, and so on. For those who work for no wages in the household economy and voluntary sector, however, social security coverage consists of residual, paternalistic, targeted programs, such as welfare.

Non-market activities tend to be ignored and neglected in our society. For most Canadians, only paid employment confers the status necessary for full integration into the mainstream of society. "Unemployment" — not participating in the paid labour force — means impoverishment, isolation and exclusion. But even the living standards afforded by wage labour are growing increasingly precarious or inadequate for more and more Canadians.

Furthermore, cuts to public social services have meant that more and more socially necessary work is being shifted from the paid public sector to the unpaid domestic sphere. Women especially are being asked to invest far more labour in caring for children, elderly and sick relatives, with no compensation.

THE ROLE OF THE SOCIAL ECONOMY

Firstly, citizens should not be penalized or impoverished because they have devoted themselves to caring for the young, the sick, the elderly or the disadvantaged, instead of producing profits for an employer. Social security programs must compensate the opportunity cost of unpaid caring activities or volunteer work.

Secondly, however, families, and especially women, must be protected from having to be the main or only *producers* of services that the state no longer can or wants to offer—e.g., looking after sick relatives for whom there is no place in hospital, or being compelled to do volunteer work in schools and hospitals because of staff shortages. Public services—health care, education, transportation, libraries, and so on—must be strengthened (see the "Social Infrastructure" measures in the *Employment* section).

The social state came about largely because of the failure, both of the market and of voluntarism and charity, to cope with citizens' needs in modern industrial democracies. Only the state could mobilize and command the resources necessary to provide collective goods in a regular, reliable, accessible, fair, democratic, efficient, and professional manner. Democratic government was best placed to minimize paternalism and class-based or racial prejudice on the part of the service-providers. Access to services is a right of citizenship, not a privilege or a favour.

Advocates of the free market claim that it offers individuals the freedom to choose the goods and services they prefer. Those who believe in a strong public sector rightly point out that such freedom is an illusion for all but the wealthy. But the public sector itself is not without need of reform. Citizens are too often placed in a passive situation as mere *consumers* of public services designed and managed by invisible or opaque institutions. Public sector workers are too often the pawns of regressive policies and management practices. Public services need to be democratized through the empowerment of those who provide and use them.

A complementary progressive option is for workers and consumers in the personal social services to form non-profit and co-operative networks to meet their needs for home care, child care, health care, community transportation, culture, recreation, environmental protection, workers' and consumers' co-operatives. To be successful, such ventures most often require financial support from the state. (In some countries, indeed, many of these services are directly provided by the public sector. In others, they are provided by co-operative and non-profit enterprises as complements to state programs.)

In resorting to self-help and co-operation, rather than the pursuit of profit, workers and consumers create new networks of reciprocity among themselves. In doing so, they define their needs themselves—the need for what they lack and the need for new ways of fulfilling that need. They *jointly construct the supply and demand* for personal social services, rather than having these services imposed on them.

To meet Canadians' contemporary needs, then, the 1998 Alternative Budget is committed to a strategy of combined social and economic development uniting the public sector and the social economy (see the *Employment* section). The essence of such a strategy is that it unites the goals of income generation and redistribution with that of building social networks of co-operation and mutual assistance.

Setting up a universally accessible, affordable, high-quality child care program would, for example, create thousands of jobs in the construction industry, the public service and post-secondary educational institutions, as well as in child care facilities themselves. It would also make it possible, of course, for many parents to enter the paid labour force or to increase their labour force participation (see the *Employment* section).

But such a child care system would naturally do far more than create jobs or enhance paid labour force participation. It would improve child-rearing for both parents and children by establishing a system comprising day care centres, but also resource centres, drop-in centres, toy and book libraries, support from public health nurses, and so on. By contributing to building networks and common identities, such initiatives strengthen neighbourhoods and communities in ways that go beyond the provision of an income, however important that is.

SOCIAL ECONOMY INVESTMENT PRINCIPLES

Within the context of a strong public sector, volunteering, co-operation, self-help and mutual assistance, the basic values of a social economy, are essential contributions to a thriving society. The Alternative Budget sets out the following principles as a basis for federal funding. The social economy must:

- be the site of well-paying, lasting jobs;
- respect the primacy of people and labour over capital;
- promote local initiative;
- emphasize goods and services that meet the needs of the community that produces them;
- ensure the democratic participation of workers and citizens in the decisions that affect them, including the management of enterprises;
- in no way facilitate or encourage the privatization or elimination of public services;
- in no way be used as a substitute for the public or broader public sectors;
- not be used as a vehicle for workfare;
- be subject to all legislation affecting labour and employment; and
- ensure equal participation and remuneration of men and women.

The state must provide infrastructures and social services; it must ensure that adequate and appropriate financial and technical resources are available to make development sustainable.

Policy measures

The 1998 Alternative Federal Budget commits the federal government to—

- promote sustainable development, including non-profit and co-operative community economic development (CED) projects (e.g., housing retrofits);
- introduce measures to bring about a reduction in paid working time (see Job Creation section);
- introduce new tax measures, including tax deductions to corporations that give employees time off to volunteer;
- encourage the development of third sector services that complement public services in such areas as transportation, home care, child care,

literacy, housing, environmental work (public education, energy conservation, etc.), human rights, services for women, cultural and artistic projects and enterprises;

- ensure adequate funding of social economy enterprises and projects; in particular, rebuild and strengthen the physical, financial and administrative infrastructures which the public sector provides for third sector activities including such public institutions as libraries, community centres, sports and recreation facilities, schools and community health centres; the federal government must do this by working in partnership with the provinces, as many of these activities comes under provincial jurisdiction;
- strengthen Canada's credit unions;
- initiate a review of charitable status and the non-profit sector in general;
- support grassroots projects that emphasize democratic workers' participation—e.g., CED, workers' co-ops (see the proposals for CED in the Employment section);
- track unpaid work over time, as health and social services are reduced and restructured.

Ottawa, Quebec and the Provinces

1. Three distinct types of society have emerged in Canada over the course of this century: English Canada, Quebec and the First Nations. Each of these nations has its own sense of national identity, tied to a specific tradition of social rights. Today, each believes that its national identity and social welfare can best be defended by an order of government accountable to its members. The thing is that each sees a different order of government achieving this.

Aboriginal peoples aspire to Aboriginal orders of government founded on their own traditions of self-government. The people of Quebec have always regarded the National Assembly of Quebec as the bulwark of their language, culture and collective social development. Over the past half century, English Canadians have identified the federal government as the guarantor of their rights and identity.

These differing visions have often collided, fuelling constitutional disputes. For example, since the 1940's the federal spending power has been the main instrument for ensuring Canada-wide minimum standards for the social programs that are so intimately bound up with English-Canadians' sense of national identity. Yet, there has been a widespread consensus in Quebec among sovereigntists and many federalists that the federal government should not take advantage of its spending power to intrude into areas such as social policy, which the constitution places under provincial jurisdiction. According to this consensus, the federal government should transfer some of its taxation power to Quebec, enabling it to raise its own money to run its social programs as it sees fit.

Over the past twenty years, federal-provincial arrangements have not granted Quebec the autonomy and spending power required to fulfil the national goals generations of Quebeckers have pursued. Yet those arrangements have also thwarted the expansion of social rights for English-Canadians, by limiting the federal role in building a comprehensive welfare state. This mutual frustration was made manifest by the result of the referendum on the Charlottetown Accord: Quebeckers rejected the Accord because they felt it granted the federal government too much power, while Canadians in other provinces voted against the pact because they felt it gave too much away to the provinces.

Most English-Canadians believe in a strong role for the federal government. Yet, over the last twenty years a strong belief in the equality of all the provinces has also arisen among them. Both of these attitudes are part and parcel of the new nationalism that has developed in English Canada. This sense of national identity has been greatly bolstered by the 1981 Constitution Act, with its emphasis on equal rights and the homogeneous status of all the people of Canada as Canadian citizens.

While many English Canadians have been willing to acknowledge the distinctiveness or uniqueness of Quebec, many are deeply suspicious of anything that might hint at "special treatment" for Quebec. Such attitudes have encouraged the view that the solution to Canada's impasse lies in limiting federal powers and granting all the provinces the same powers as Quebec. While the overt premise of this view is that Quebec should be treated like other provinces, its gist is in fact that all the provinces should be treated as though they were Quebec. The problem is that this erodes the social citizenship of Canadians outside of Quebec by diminishing the federal power that has been its guarantor — yet it does not fully grant to Quebec the powers and distinctiveness it claims.

2. Against this background, the last few years have witnessed severe fiscal restraint in public services, institutions and social programs at all levels of government. While officially designed to tackle the public debt crisis, these austerity measures have been part of a concerted plan to restructure the Canadian state.

This restructuring process is based on the claim that payroll taxes, minimum wage laws, unionization and social programs have created market "rigidities," raising the cost of labour and discouraging investment. The "reckless" spending associated with the welfare state is alleged to have come home to roost in the form of catastrophic public debt. In the name of "sound public finance" and "competitiveness," there have been massive public spending cuts, an end to universal social programs, and privatization of many government enterprises and services. This attack on the welfare state has occurred throughout the world economy, taking the form of "Thatcherism" in the UK, "Rogernomics" in New Zealand, or the "Common Sense Revolution" in Ontario. In the Third World it is known as "structural adjustment."

As part of this process, the federal government has withdrawn or retreated from areas such as housing and labour market programs. It has implemented significant regressive changes to programs such as health care, post-secondary education, social assistance and social services, the costs of which it shared with the provinces. The federal government used its spending power in the past to impose its leadership in social policy. In an era of diminished federal spending, the provinces are seeking a much greater say.

These changes have helped shape the way Canadians view federal-provincial relations and social programs. On the one hand, belief in the solidarity between regions and provinces has been shaken. Austerity has fueled competition and resentment, contributing to support for workfare and other repressive measures against the less fortunate, as well as to hostility towards people of other ethnicities, regions or countries.

On the other hand, many progressive-minded people feel and express great dissatisfaction with the federal government's power to cut program spending and eliminate standards unilaterally under the guise of being fiscally responsible. It is possible to see a strong social union as essential to equality and nationhood, without by that token being tied to one vision of the specific roles the federal and provincial governments should play.

3. The Alternative Federal Budget continues to subscribe to the historic view of progressive English Canada that the federal government should play a leading role in economic, social and cultural policy. Thanks to its spending power, the federal government can play a leading role in creating and developing national cultural institutions, enforcing national standards for social welfare coverage, and building a strong, independent national economy. There is no doubt, also, that in the current context, the demands for devolution of powers to all the provinces bolster and facilitate the efforts of right-wing forces bent on dismantling national social programs.

Yet, attributing such a leading role to the federal government runs counter to the position expressed by every Quebec government since 1945, whether of federalist or sovereigntist persuasion. Establishing the national institutions and notions of individual citizenship desired by English Canada should not infringe on the expression of Quebeckers' national identity and social rights. English Canadians' social rights could in fact be more secure if Quebec's uniqueness were recognized substantively, rather than merely symbolically, in Canadian political institutions. The key issue for English Canadians should not be the accommodation of Quebec's uniqueness, but the way that uniqueness is accommodated.

The 1996 AFB sought to address this impasse over social policy jurisdiction by stating that: "Until there is a resolution of the Quebec-Canada relationship, our approach to federal-provincial fiscal relations recognizes the need for special arrangements with Quebec which may not be open to the other provinces." This was our position in 1997 as well and it remains so in 1998.

Regardless of whether the resolution of the Quebec-Canada relationship results in a restructured federation or in separate nation-states, the need for a social dimension to the relationship remains, if only because of the high degree of economic integration. We suggest that the solution to the impasse lies not in complete across-the-board devolution, but in recognizing that Quebec, but not the other provinces, has primacy in its jurisdiction over social policy and the right to opt out of joint federal-provincial programs in this area; and for the rest of Canada, recognizing joint federal-provincial responsibility with a federal leadership role in funding social programs, as well as setting and enforcing national standards.

We also believe that it is essential to have common standards. This could be achieved through a social charter which would reflect our common social values and be based on the UN Covenant on Economic, Social and Cultural Rights.

Trade and Investment Agreements

The approach of the Alternative Federal Budget to trade and investment agreements is very different from that of the current government. We reject its efforts to expand trade and investment through initiatives such as the Team Canada trade missions without reference to human rights, core labour standards, social well-being and concern for the environment.

In particular we oppose the extension of some of the most damaging aspects of the North American Free Trade Agreement (NAFTA) through the Multilateral Agreement on Investment now being negotiated within the Organization for Economic Cooperation and Development (OECD) in Paris.

Not only would the MAI extend the reach of NAFTA's investment rules to all member countries of the OECD (and later to other countries which are to be invited to sign on), but it would also make NAFTA's investment rules more restrictive.

The MAI would be worse than NAFTA in the following respects:

1. The MAI's definitions of investment and investor are more inclusive and most decisively extend this agreement's scope.
2. The MAI covers sub-national governments, including provinces and local governments, in an expanded way.
3. The reservations for social services (health care and education) are confined to the federal jurisdiction, and therefore all aspects of health care and education under provincial jurisdiction are placed under the sweeping changes initiated by the MAI.
4. The MAI extends the principle of national treatment (which means that foreign investors must be treated as favourably as domestic investors) beyond NAFTA's scope. It would prohibit performance requirements, such as demanding job creation or purchase of local inputs by investors who receive assistance from all levels of government.

We emphatically reject the MAI, and, as we affirmed last year, we are committed to the renegotiation of those parts of NAFTA that are most prejudicial to genuine economic and social development, beginning with the investment chapter.

In seeking the renegotiation of NAFTA, we are not turning our backs on our neighbours to the south. On the contrary, we will continue to build alliances with social movements throughout the Americas to realize an alternative development compact based on equity and reciprocity.

Many participants in this Alternative Federal Budget also participate in the Common Frontiers initiative. Our alliance is based on relationships between civil society groups who oppose the neo-liberal model favoured by corporate interests.

In May of 1997, Canadian trade unions and social organizations pledged to work together with colleagues from Mexico, the United States, Chile, Brazil, and the Inter-American Regional Organization of Workers (ORIT) for trade agreements that would promote genuine, sustainable development for all the peoples of the hemisphere, rather than a Free Trade Area of the Americas (FTAA) modelled on NAFTA.

In light of U.S. President Clinton's failure to achieve fast track authority from Congress to negotiate an FTAA, the peoples of the Americas now have an opportunity to consider other options. Accordingly, we will take initiatives to distance our trade policy from the model favoured by the U.S. government and transnational corporations. In particular, we will actively pursue independent relations with South American nations, especially the Mercosur trading bloc encompassing Brazil, Argentina, Paraguay and Uruguay, with a view to striking strategic alliances for negotiating agreements that differ substantially from the neo-liberal model enshrined in NAFTA.

We premise these renewed relations on the need to enhance the regulation of private investment through the exercise of sovereign national powers and through international agreements.

Rather than impose the neo-liberal model on all nations, regardless of their degree of development, we recognize the urgent need to respect economic pluralism in international trade and investment agreements. Hence our vision of a continental trade and development agreement recognizes each nation's unique development strategy, allowing for national sovereignty in essential areas without regressing into destructive protectionism.

Rather than consigning environmental standards and labour rights to ineffective side deals, we will make the enforcement of core labour rights and respect for the environment integral to any agreement. We shall also work with civil movements in other countries to ensure that these standards are enforced.

We reject the race to the bottom that is occurring under the neo-liberal model enshrined in NAFTA. Instead we will support improvements in wages and working conditions within our trading partners.

This Alternative Federal Budget again endorses regulations on investments flows to contain speculative, fly-by-night capital. In addition to endorsing the Tobin tax to slow down speculation on the money markets, we will explore other measures such as those used by Chile to regulate portfolio capital. Chile requires foreign portfolio investment to remain within the country for a minimum period and requires foreign investors to deposit a portion of their assets with the country's central bank.

Unlike the current Canadian government, which tried to persuade the Chileans to abandon these measures during the negotiation of the Canada-Chile free trade agreement, we will negotiate amendments to NAFTA to allow such measures and encourage other countries to emulate the Chilen measures.

Taxation

The years of deception about the real causes of Canada's fiscal crisis are over. So are the exaggerated claims about the rate at which the deficit could be eliminated.

The extent to which the crisis was manufactured as a rationale for the Liberals' breathtaking shift to the political right has been revealed. The federal budget will be balanced in the 1997-8 fiscal year—this fiscal year—a full two years before the date targeted originally by the government. Moreover, the revenue data reveal that Finance Minister Paul Martin could easily have met his original target with no spending cuts whatsoever.

Because economic growth and lower interest rates have gone a long way towards restoring the fiscal capacity lost in the recession of the early 1990s, our proposed program can be financed, and fiscal targets more than met, without any increase in the share of Canada's GDP going to taxation.

This means that, in formulating the AFB's taxation program, we no longer have to focus on rebuilding Canada's fiscal capacity. We can, instead, shift our focus to issues of fairness —restoring some of the balance in the system destroyed by Brian Mulroney's lavish tax breaks for the rich and powerful, and using the increased revenue to provide badly-needed tax relief to ordinary Canadians.

The aim of this year's Alternative Federal Budget tax policy is to restore balance to the tax system, and to counterbalance the inequitable distribution of the benefits of economic growth in Canada.

Targeted and strategic increases in tax for those who can well afford to pay will be balanced against tax reductions for low- and moderate-income Canadians.

The goal is to produce the fairest tax system that we can, within the constraints that Canada faces in an increasingly integrated international economy.

We address inequitable gaps in Canada's tax system, and recycle the additional revenue into tax reductions targeted to low- and middle-income taxpayers.

There are a number of important gaps in our tax system:

- Income from capital is taxed at lower effective rates than income from employment.
- Canada is one of the few countries in the OECD that does not levy a tax on transfers of large pools of wealth between generations.
- Canada's system of tax-delivered subsidies to corporations has been cited even by the International Monetary Fund as excessively generous.
- The profits of Canada's major banks and other financial institutions are well above the average for the economy, and well above what would be expected in an industry that benefits from significant regulatory protection.
- Canada's system for integration of business and personal income taxation is much too generous and delivers little in the way of economic benefit.
- Canada loses hundreds of millions of dollars in potential revenue through exemptions to the non-resident withholding tax in excess of those provided for in tax treaties with other nations.
- The benefits provided for in the current RRSP system are biased heavily in favour of the highest income earners in Canada.
- Canada has no effective "green" or environmental taxation.

TAXATION OF INCOME FROM CAPITAL

The core of the taxation strategy of the Alternative Federal Budget for 1998-99 will be a series of measures designed to restore balance to the tax system by increasing taxes on capital and income from capital. It will do so carefully and strategically. In this increasingly integrated world economy, no country can make tax policy without reference to its impact on capital mobility. As much as we accept the reality of these limits on Canada's policy flexibility, however, we do not believe that Canada should be passive in response to these threats to the fairness of our tax system. Canada should be at the forefront of nations pressing for an international agreement on the taxation of income from capital. Such an agreement is needed to ensure that corporations and wealthy individuals are not able to cherry-pick among jurisdictions the most favourable tax rules.

ELIMINATING TAX PREFERENCES

Nearly 30 years after the Carter Commission made the phrase "a buck is a buck" famous in its recommendations for a tax system that treated all sources of income the same way, regardless of their source, a buck in Canada is still not a buck.

Capital gains income is taxed at an effective rate that is 25% lower than the rate of tax paid on wage and salary income. Capital gains on farming assets and small business assets are exempt from tax entirely, to a maximum capital gains exemption of $500,000. Dividend income receives preferential treatment through a system of credits.

We see no case based on fairness for giving preferential tax treatment to unearned income. The general 25% exclusion should be eliminated.

In the same category is the 25% exclusion from tax of the proceeds of employee stock options. This is a clear giveaway to the most highly paid executives in Canada, and cannot be justified under any circumstances.

WEALTH TAXATION

Canada is virtually alone in the OECD countries in not having a wealth tax of any kind. Only Australia and New Zealand share with Canada the distinction of not taxing wealth in any form. In effect, this country is a tax haven when it comes to wealth taxation.

Most countries with wealth taxes raise between 0.3% and 0.75% of GDP from these taxes. The United States, for example, raises about 0.3% of GDP in the form of wealth taxes. At a minimum, we would expect that Canada could generate at least the same percentage of GDP from wealth transfer taxation as the United States. With a more aggressive approach to tax design and administration, perhaps modelled on the German system, we would anticipate that Canada could generate revenue of between 0.4% and 0.5% of GDP.

SMALL BUSINESS TAXATION

Canada's preferential rate of taxation for earnings of Canadian-controlled private corporations is extremely generous by international standards, and far too generous under the current economic and fiscal circumstances. The issue arises in two areas. First, the definition of what is "small" in business taxation is much broader than is the case in the U.S., for example. In the United States, $75,000 is the tax system cut-off for small business tax treatment. In Canada, it is $200,000. Second, whereas in Canada income earned by an individual through a corporation is taxed at a lower effective rate than the same income earned directly as an individual, in the U.S. the first $75,000 of such income is taxed as if it were earned by the individual directly. Special tax treatment is limited to rules that eliminate double-taxation of income earned through a corporation.

These special preferences have been highlighted as particularly generous by the International Monetary Fund. Department of Finance data on tax expenditures show that these preferences cost Canadian taxpayers over $2 billion a year in lost revenue. We believe that the economic benefits associated with small business development can be realized with tax-based incentives much closer to international norms.

CORPORATE TAX CREDITS AND DEDUCTIONS

Consistent with our belief that public industrial policies have an important role to play in shaping Canada's future economic destiny, we support the use of tax incentives as one of a number of industrial policy instruments available to governments.

At the same time, however, we believe these tax-system-delivered subsidies should be treated as tax expenditures. At a minimum, this requires disclosure, accountability, annual approval, regular review and value-for-money audit—the same standard that applies to all other areas of public spending.

The basic criterion for continuing with a tax expenditure can be summed up in the following straightforward question: Would the provision be considered acceptable and justifiable if it were provided through an otherwise identically designed direct grant program?

After the reduced tax rates for small business and manufacturing and processing, the most significant tax expenditures in the corporate tax system are the provision for deduction of depreciation for tax purposes at rates in excess of economic depreciation; the fast write-off for Canadian exploration and development expenses; the scientific research and experimental development tax credit; and the elimination of taxes on the Canadian income of many foreign companies. The AFB will propose ways of reducing the tax revenue losses from these five measures.

Other corporate tax expenditures that need to be addressed include meals and entertainment deductions, lobbying expenses deductions, and the overseas earnings of life insurance companies.

Reducing or eliminating these tax expenditures will go a long way towards eliminating the phenomenon of profitable corporations paying no corporate income tax.

Some of these exemptions, credits and deductions, of course, are worthy of support. Such provisions can play important roles in industrial policy and in environmental policy. However, they can also be stacked so as to eliminate the tax liabilities of profitable corporations, to make it possible for profitable corporations to pay no tax. That is not the intended result of using the tax system as an instrument of economic and social policy. That is why we support the implementation of a corporate minimum tax that would override special tax preferences, so that every corporation that makes a profit pays corporate income tax.

EXECUTIVE SALARIES

The huge and widening gap between average wages and salaries in Canada and the salaries and bonuses paid to corporate executives at the top end of the scale is of real concern to many Canadians. They frankly have trouble understanding how any executive could be "worth" the high six- and seven-figure salaries that are becoming commonplace in Canadian big business. And they wonder how countries like Japan and many European countries manage to survive with ratios of top salaries to average wages much smaller than those found in Canada.

We cannot prevent corporations from paying these salaries. But we can make our disapproval clear by denying corporations a tax deduction for salaries in excess of what is considered a reasonable relationship between executive salaries and what average working people earn.

A SURTAX ON BANK PROFITS

Most Canadians have been shocked that Canada's chartered banks managed to earn steadily increasing profits throughout the most difficult recession to hit this country since the 1930s. In 1997, the six largest chartered banks reported profits in excess of $7 billion.

The banks owe their privileged position in our economy to public regulation, which protects their status as one of a very limited number of institutions permitted to take deposits from the public. When that privileged position results in the earning of profits far in excess of normal rates of return in the economy, a public policy response is required.

We would establish an excess profits tax, applicable in the first instance to financial institutions. Excess profits would be defined as that portion of an institution's rate of return on shareholder equity that is in excess of the average rate of return for all corporations in the non-financial sector of the Canadian economy.

A MORE PROGRESSIVE PERSONAL INCOME TAX SYSTEM

NEW TAX BRACKETS FOR VERY HIGH INCOMES

While we accept in general the argument that Canada's top marginal tax rates have to be monitored carefully in relation to those in other countries, we believe that there is room in the current system for an increase in marginal tax rates applicable to very high income individuals.

New federal tax brackets will be added to the current system for those earning very high incomes. This will still leave regular top marginal tax rates at reasonable levels, and will generate a substantial amount of additional revenue.

AN END TO SURTAXES ON THE POOR

Lower-income Canadians have paid more than their share of the price for Canada's fiscal crisis in the form of reduced services and curtailed entitlements. In our view, it is unacceptable that these individuals should be required to pay a surtax on their federal taxes as well.

RRSPS - WHO BENEFITS? WHO PAYS?

The special tax treatment accorded to retirement savings is by far the most significant tax expenditure in the personal income tax system, with a cost in foregone revenue of nearly $22 billion in 1993; $16 billion after taking into account tax paid on withdrawals.

The Mulroney era reforms of the system of tax assistance for retirement saving increased contribution limits significantly and tied those limits more closely to income. Increasing the maximum RRSP contribution has been of great benefit to people with higher incomes who can save 18% of their income, but have offered little to working people. The skewed distribution of the tax subsidy for retirement income delivered through the RRSP system is well documented. For example, in 1993, over 46% of RRSP contributions were made by the top 12.5% of tax filers. Because the deduction for contributions is worth more, the higher your income, the distribution of the tax subsidies is even more heavily weighted towards the top end.

The benefits from the tax-subsidized retirement system— both RRSPs and pension plans—are heavily skewed in favour of people with high incomes. For taxpayers with incomes over $100,000, average tax-subsidized retirement saving (RRSP contributions plus Pension Adjustments) in 1994 was $12,662, and 80% of taxpayers in that income group either belonged to a pension plan, or contributed to an RRSP, or both. People in that income range made up only 7.7% of taxpayers.

In the $40,000 to $50,000 income range, 80% of taxpayers participated, but the average contribution was $5,191. Only 18% of taxpayers had incomes above $50,000. In the $20,000 to $30,000 range, the average contribution was only $2,335 and only 25% of taxpayers participated.

Data made available in 1996 for the first time have cast further doubt on the role of RRSPs in providing for retirement income. According to Statistics Canada, between 1990 and 1994, Canadians under age 65 withdrew $16.6 billion from RRSPs and used a further $4.4 billion in the Home Buyer's Plan. Those withdrawals were disproportionately from middle- and lower-income tax filers, raising serious questions about the role of the RRSPs in the retirement income system.

Tax assistance for retirement saving is paid for though general taxation. We are all paying for the generous improvements Brian Mulroney made in the tax position of high-income savers.

There are a number of problems with the current system. The maximum pension—and therefore the maximum RRSP equivalent— eligible for tax subsidy is far higher than the maximum pensionable earnings under the Canada Pension Plan. Assistance is delivered in the form of a deduction, rather than in the form of a credit. The result is that higher income taxpayers get a larger tax subsidy for the same amount of retirement savings than do lower-income taxpayers. And the conservative assumptions used in determining the RRSP equivalent to a pension plan mean that RRSPs are treated more favourably than pensions.

The data provide a clear and disturbing picture of the role of RRSPs in Canada's retirement income system. Low- and moderate-income individuals are saving too little for retirement; and the subsidies delivered by the tax system go disproportionately to those who need them the least. The Alternative Federal Budget will restructure the RRSP system to direct a greater share of tax support to lower- and moderate- income people. RRSP limits will be reduced to make them equivalent to pension limits in the current economic environment. And the tax subsidy will be converted from a deduction to a credit.

The Alternative Federal Budget will also close a major tax loophole that permits funds deposited in Registered Education Savings Plans to be transferred to RRSPs if the funds are not used for education.

CIGARETTE AND TOBACCO TAXES

The federal government has already moved part way towards reversing its tobacco-tax-reduction policy with the recent increases in tobacco taxes. Completing the reversal of this policy by reinstating tax levels at their pre-1994 level would be an important further step in putting Canada's anti-smoking policy back on track.

Environmental Taxation

Environmental consumption taxes will be an important part of the 1998 AFB, and are discussed in detail in the section of this framework document dealing with environmental issues. But the final Alternative Budget will reflect both an assessment of their potential for environmental gain and their impact on income distribution.

Other areas of environmental tax policy activity will include tackling the issue of subsidies to the oil and gas industry in the income tax system. The aim would be to level the playing field between renewable and non-renewable energy production.

Rather than propose new tax expenditures for environmentally friendly industries, the AFB will eliminate provisions of the Income Tax Act that provide incentives for non-renewable resource extraction.

As part of the Alternative Budget's climate change initiative, the Alternative Federal Budget will develop an Atmospheric User Charge based on a carbon tax, with a rate set so as to raise approximately $500 million per year. The tax will exclude uses of carbon in industrial process (in steel-making and cement manufacturing, for example) and will be designed to protect residents of northern and remote areas who have disproportionately high energy costs.

The increased revenue from both the Atmospheric User Charge and from the elimination of tax subsidies for non-renewable resource extraction will be directed towards a national Atmospheric Improvement Fund.

GST Policy Changes

The GST will be removed completely from books and magazines. (The application of the GST to Canadian magazines and books has turned this country into one of the world's highest-taxed jurisdictions for reading material.)

The harmonization of provincial sales taxes with the GST will be eliminated immediately. (This harmonization, as it has been carried out in Atlantic Canada, has reduced the fiscal capacity of provincial governments and resulted in a significant transfer of the consumption tax burden from business taxpayers to individuals. The AFB will cancel the agreement to harmonize the GST and provincial sales taxes in Atlantic Canada, and terminate any negotiations currently under way for harmonization in other parts of Canada.)

The GST rate for the 1998 AFB will reflect our analysis of the most appropriate way to provide benefits to low- and moderate-income individuals and families.

In the longer term, there are a number of possible options for reform. The GST could be replaced by a European-style value-added tax. Such a tax could build in higher rates of tax on luxury items and lower rates on necessities, so as to make the impact of the tax less regressive.

The rate structure could also be adjusted to reflect environmental objectives, e.g., by taxing (re)used products or products made from recycled materials at a lower rate, or by taxing toxic substances at a higher rate. The general rate of tax could also be reduced as finances improve and social programs are renewed.

GST reform could also be addressed in the broader context of the division of taxing responsibilities between the federal government and the provinces and territories. One option would be for the federal government to vacate the sales tax field entirely, in exchange for an expanded role in the taxation of capital and income from capital.

Such an exchange would give provinces exclusive jurisdiction over a tax base which it is relatively easy for provincial governments to defend, in exchange for a tax base which is much more easily defended by the federal government.

FINANCIAL TRANSACTIONS TAXES

TAXATION OF INTERNATIONAL CURRENCY TRANSACTIONS

We remain committed to the goal of re-regulating the capital market. We call for measures to reduce our general social vulnerability to the power and mobility of financial capital.

To achieve this goal, we will work with other nations to establish a Tobin tax on international currency transactions. Such a tax, named after its Nobel Prize-winning originator, economist James Tobin, would tax all international currency transactions at a rate of approximately 0.25%.

The primary purpose of such a tax would be to act as a disincentive to international currency speculation. It would also give more leeway for countries to adopt autonomous monetary policies by opening up a gap between domestic and international interest rates.

It has been estimated that, even after allowing for tax avoidance and changes in patterns of transactions and providing for an exemption for official transactions, a Tobin tax at a rate of 0.25% would raise $US300 billion a year.

To be effective, however, a Tobin tax would have to be levied by all of the major players in the international financial economy. The problem of tax havens could be addressed by levying punitive rates of tax on transactions involving such havens, but the refusal of even one of the major industrialized countries to participate would destroy the effectiveness of the tax.

We anticipate that most countries would want to participate in an international Tobin tax regime. When the topic was raised by Canada at the Halifax G-7 meeting several years ago, it generated a great deal of interest, and a number of studies are currently under way.

If an international currency transactions tax were to be established, Canada's share of the revenue, based on our current share of the international market, would be about $7.5 billion a year. As has been proposed by most advocates of such taxes, we would favour reserving a substantial proportion of the revenue raised by such a tax for international development support.

DOMESTIC FINANCIAL TRANSACTIONS

Should Canada have a domestic financial transactions tax?

In recent years, there has been considerable discussion of the potential for a domestic financial transactions tax in Canada as a replacement for the GST.

We do not propose a general tax on financial transactions in the 1998-99 Alternative Federal Budget. Our research has shown that the revenue potential for a financial transactions tax falls far short of that required to replace the GST, and has raised questions about the distributional impact of such a tax. It has also raised questions, which we have not been able to answer to our satisfaction, about its impact on the monetary system in a renewed regime of monetary regulation.

Tax avoidance could be massive and difficult to predict. All taxes are subject to avoidance. Financial transactions taxes would be particularly vulnerable to avoidance. By their very nature, a financial transaction can be moved easily to another jurisdiction, changed to a form of transaction or contract that is not subject to tax, or disguised as a non-taxable transaction.

Financial transactions taxes much more modest in scope (and revenue potential) exist in a number of jurisdictions, most notably Japan, Switzerland, and Britain. These taxes typically apply small fees to various types of stock market transactions and generate nominal revenues in the range of 0.05 to 0.1% of GDP. There seems to be no valid reason why a modest tax of this kind should not be introduced in Canada.

A tax on trades in equities at rates similar to those in other countries would raise about $190 million, according to a review of transactions taxes by the Library of Parliament.

Another approach would be to address a major gap in the base for the goods and services tax by including financial services (other than interest payments) in the base of the GST. The tax would apply, for example, to the commissions and fees charged by investment brokers.

Making the Tax system More Progressive—Providing Tax Relief for Low- and Moderate-Income Families

The measures presented above address major gaps in our tax system that undermine our fiscal capacity, and enable many high-income individuals and corporations to get away with paying far less than their fair share of the cost of providing public services in this country.

They also generate substantial additional revenue. In the first two Alternative Federal Budgets, any additional revenue generated from our tax package was needed to meet our targets for public services renewal and deficit reduction. In the 1997-98 AFB, we were able to plan for substantial tax relief in the last two years of our budget planning cycle because of the impact of economic growth on the revenue base of the federal government.

This revenue base, however, has grown considerably in the past three years. It is now large enough to fund public services renewal over our planning cycle and meet debt and deficit targets without any increase in taxes as a share of our economy. This year's AFB will not increase taxes as a percentage of GDP.

As a result, the revenue generated from our fair tax package can be used, in its entirety, to provide tax relief for those who need it most: low- and moderate-income individuals and families.

The question is: how best to provide that relief? In designing this year's AFB, we have a number of choices. We could reduce the GST rate. We could reduce UI premiums. We could cut income taxes across the board. Or we could increase one or more of the tax credits in the personal income tax system.

Our analysis shows clearly that the most effective ways to provide tax relief are: for middle-income families, to make the income tax system more progressive; and for lower-income families and individuals, to enhance the value of refundable credits— credits in the income tax system based on family composition which are paid to the taxpayer whether or not the taxpayer otherwise has any tax liability. Tax credits, for example, are far more effective as a way to deliver tax relief to families with children than any other tax measure.

EMPLOYMENT

Job Creation

THE CONTINUING JOBS CRISIS

The Chrétien government has repeatedly promised a "jobs and growth" agenda. But the deficit was eliminated through massive, job-killing cuts to social programs and public services, rather than from the revenue growth and reduced reliance on income support programs that would have come from the creation of more well-paid and secure jobs in a growing economy. Through their spending cuts, the Liberals have put a major brake on job creation. At the same time, by cutting training, research and development and industrial and regional development programs, the government has largely abdicated its responsibility to support and shape job creation in the economy. This agenda has left the jobs crisis still largely unresolved, despite the benefits of recent economic growth and job creation.

The Bank of Canada is expected to raise interest rates over the coming months in a deliberate attempt to slow the pace of job creation. Massive fiscal restraint—-largely driven by direct federal spending cuts and cuts in federal transfers to the provinces, compounded by provincial cuts—-has also had a significant negative impact on job creation. These cuts are expected to continue into 1998.

The national unemployment rate is still well above the cyclical low of 7.5% reached in 1989. Unemployment rates in all provinces east of Ontario remain well into double-digit levels, and the same is true of many rural areas in other provinces. The official youth unemployment rate, currently near 17%, is far above the 11.2% youth rate in 1989.

The labour force participation rate at 64.9% last fall, is significantly lower than the 67.5% rate in 1989. This indicates that there are still many "discouraged workers" who will return to the labour force if and when more and better jobs are created. Average real wages are stagnant, and real wages are falling for most workers.

Given these grim realities, a top priority of the 1998 AFB is to set overall targets for job creation and a steady fall in the unemployment rate.

There is a need to change and shape the dynamics of the market-driven job creation process. It is not enough simply to stimulate stronger economic growth through macro-economic policy, important though that is. We must also make sure that economic growth helps us achieve our social goals, and this involves policies to favour job creation in public services and the not- for-profit sector. Growth must also be made compatible with our environmental goals, and this involves policies to create jobs in "green industries." We must ensure that jobs are created for groups with particularly pressing needs—-such as the designated affirmative action groups, young people, the long-term unemployed, and residents of high unemployment communities.

We also want to make sure that we lay the foundations for a more innovative and productive economy capable of generating the skilled, high-paid, secure jobs which working families need. All of this requires significant increases in public investment and in public regulation of the market. Accordingly, the Alternative Budget seeks to promote social investment and community economic development.

Finally, job creation must also involve reduction and redistribution of working time.

PUBLIC INVESTMENT — CREATING JOBS AND MEETING LONG-TERM NEEDS

In 1998-99, the Liberals plan to cut about another $2.5 billion from federal government programs. Much of the impact will fall on job creation programs. For example, the Canada Infrastructure Works Program will be phased out, and science and technology and regional development programs will be cut by about $400 million. Previous spending cuts have eaten deeply into federal government investment in physical and social infrastructure, and federal investment in housing has been all but eliminated.

With the deficit now behind us, it is time to reinvest in areas which create more and better jobs, while meeting important social objectives.

A public investment program is a much more powerful vehicle for job creation than a broad tax cut because it can be targeted to areas which are job intensive and make heavy use of Canadian made materials and services. Public investments also lay the basis for higher growth in the future.

Accordingly, the AFB commits the federal government to provide up to one-half of the funding for a three-year federal-provincial/ territorial-municipal/ broader public sector investment program in environmental and social infrastructure and not-for-profit housing.

- The federal commitment for each of the next three years,is to be divided equally between environmental infrastructure, social infrastructure, and not-for-profit housing. Because projects would be relatively labour- intensive, this would generate some 150,000 to 200,000 additional jobs over each of the next three years (not counting indirect and spin-off impacts).
- Projects will be proposed by provincial and municipal governments and by public sector and not-for-profit agencies. The "third sector" of the economy will be explicitly included, and expansion of third sector will be a major goal of the program.
- These programs will be explicitly designed to create reasonably well-paid jobs for workers who are now marginalized. Proposals submitted for funding under these programs will have to clearly identify the employment and training dimensions of the project.
- A major effort will be made to train and to employ social assistance recipients in order to provide a voluntary and decently paid alternative to "workfare," and in order to reduce the net cost of the program to governments.
- Clear targets will be set for the employment and training of women, visible minorities, persons with disabilities, and Aboriginal people.
- Priority will be given to projects which provide jobs to young people who have left the educational system with limited qualifications—a group which has been largely excluded from Liberal youth programs—and to the long-term unemployed.
- Priority will also be given to projects proposed from communities experiencing very high rates of unemployment.

Environmental Infrastructure

A key goal of the AFB is to shape the economic growth process to help us achieve our environmental goals. Growth must be made much more labour-intensive, less materials- and energy-intensive, and less destructive of the natural environment. This means that economic activity and job creation should be provided through public investment in areas which directly promote our environmental goals.

In the environmental component of the public investment program, the AFB priorizes the following areas, in consultation with other levels of government and not-for- profit agencies:

- Capital investments in bike paths, public transit, commuter rail systems, and inter-urban rail systems in order to reduce commuting by automobile and energy consumption. Reducing daily use of the automobile also produces more liveable and less costly urban environments.

- Capital investments in water, sewage and waste reduction, and recycling facilities.
- Retrofits of public buildings in order to achieve higher standards of efficiency in the use of energy and water while creating jobs.

Social Infrastructure

Investing in public services generates more jobs and better jobs, while helping us achieve our social goals.

The AFB will therefore increase federal transfers to the provinces for shared cost programs, reducing the squeeze on provincial and municipal governments, as well as on educational and health services.

- A social infrastructure investment program will also be introduced as part of the public investment program to develop community based, not-for-profit child care, social services, elder care services, services against violence against women, and other community programs designed to meet the needs of women. Since community and women's groups require core funding, not project-based funding, monies disbursed from this program will take the form of core funding.

Housing

The third component of the public investment program will be construction of social and co-op housing by municipal non-profit housing corporations, community-based housing associations and First Nations, and retro-fitting and rehabilitation of low-income housing.

SOCIAL INVESTMENT

The Alternative Budget recognizes the need to shape the investment and production decisions of the corporate sector if we are to build an economy which sustains and creates well-paid, secure, highly skilled jobs. The pressing tasks of national, regional, and community economic development should not be left to the corporations alone.

The AFB therefore commits the federal government to establish National Capital Investment Funds to provide long- term, relatively low interest loans and/or equity to Canadian-based companies contemplating investments which would secure and create good, permanent jobs. This initiative would incorporate the existing Federal Business Development Bank.

These Funds will be financed through compulsory long-term deposits by the banks, insurance companies, and other financial institutions, which are making huge profits while failing to provide needed risk capital to Canadian companies, co-operatives, and community development corporations. Total assets of the banks, trust companies, and insurance companies exceed $1,000 billion, so even a very modest required deposit would generate very significant resources, while having only a modest impact on conventional lending for mortgages and consumer and business loans. Such deposits would pay modest rates of interest. Pension funds will be encouraged to invest, with a competitive rate of return being guaranteed by the federal government.

The Funds will be set up at arms-length from the federal government, with board representation from business, labour, other key social actors, and all levels of government.

4) COMMUNITY ECONOMIC DEVELOPMENT (CED)

Community economic development programs facilitate the growth of local ventures that employ local people and produce goods and services that meet local needs. The intent is to create jobs rather than to maximize the return on capital and, most importantly, to develop the capacity, potential and resources of communities, particularly those that have been marginalized. (See the Community Economic Development section.)

Such programs now exist, on a small scale, in some provinces and in some cities. But there has been little or no concerted national effort in CED since the 1970s. Community economic development has been closely associated with the idea of building more integrated and more sustainable local economies through the creation of local linkages which lower dependence on outside suppliers.

The inclusion of not-for-profit agencies and other CED initiatives in the infrastructure programs proposed in the AFB would stimulate such activity. In addition, the AFB makes these proposals:

- Federal and provincial governments will actively encourage community organizations to establish community development corporations.
- The AFB will establish a CED initiative with the following two components: 1) a pool of capital to support CED enterprises, the control and distribution of which will be based in the community; Capital Corporations will be created, with boards representative of and accountable to the community; and 2) stable and consistent funding for CED education; a CED education program will train community-based CED Co-ordinators, sponsored by the communities."
- Community Reinvestment: A portion of all funds loaned out by branches of banks, trust companies and other deposit-accepting institutions will go to community economic development ventures, including co-operatives.

- Chartered banks and trust companies will be required to comprehensively disclose data on loan applications, lending, and loan loss rates to measure their performance with respect to lending to small business, women, visible minorities, First Nations, and borrowers in lower-income neighborhoods.
- Investments by individuals in Community Economic Development Corporations will be made RRSP-eligible.

5) RE-DISTRIBUTING WORK TIME

Despite productivity growth in many parts of the private sector, the hours of work have been steadily increasing for many regularly employed workers in the form of unpaid overtime for salaried workers (particularly in public services) and paid overtime for hourly workers. In the first three months of 1997, almost one in five (18.6%) of workers worked overtime, averaging almost nine hours.

Redistributing work time from the "over-employed" to the unemployed and the underemployed clearly must be part of an overall job creation strategy, since it would also improve the quality of life for working people. By increasing the number of jobs we can derive from a given rate of economic growth, work time reduction also serves environmental goals.

Most work time issues are best negotiated between employers and workers and their unions, but the federal government could help by establishing an office to monitor work-time arrangements and to encourage negotiated workplace arrangements which create jobs through the redistribution of working time.

For 1998, the AFB commits the federal government to allocate funds to subsidize negotiated work-time reduction and redistribution agreements which create new jobs.

Governments also have a role to play in setting basic rights and standards. The federal government should make the Canada Labour Code—-which covers about 10% of all workers—-a model statute by reducing the standard work week in the federal jurisdiction to 36 hours, by giving workers the right to refuse overtime, by limiting total overtime hours to 100 hours over the course of a year, by giving workers the right to return to a job after taking an extended parental or educational leave, and by requiring employers to provide equal pay and benefits to part-time workers.

Provincial governments must be actively encouraged to adopt similar standards, and both levels of government must also make a determined effort to stamp out the evasion of employment standards by employers of temporary, contract, and home workers.

Enhancing access to leaves and improving the conditions of part-time work would encourage some workers-—particularly those in well-paid jobs—-to reduce their hours of work on an ongoing or temporary basis, thus freeing up work time for others.

Other initiatives include 1) adjusting private pension plans to facilitate early retirement and "phased-in" retirement that would allow older workers to work shorter hours with no loss of pension; 2) facilitating educational and training leaves by making workers taking such leaves eligible for UI-paid benefits, and 3) allowing more workers to self-finance such leaves by reducing their pay over a prior period.

For us, working time includes hours spent doing paid market work, as well as unpaid work of economic value. This unpaid work includes activities such as child care, housework, and volunteer work. Canadians spend more time in unpaid work than in paid work. And, according to Statistics Canada, a great gender imbalance in total workload exists, with men predominantly engaged in paid work, and women's largest contribution being in the unpaid non-market sector. Women's total workload (paid and unpaid) continues to be greater than men's. Any attempts to redistribute work time must take these imbalances into account.

6) Investments in an Innovative, sustainable and Productive Economy

Left to their own devices, corporations will not make the long-term investments in research and development, in skills and in new technology which are needed to build a more productive Canadian economy—an economy which is less highly exposed to international competitive pressures to drive down wages and social standards.

"Free trade" and leaving it all to the market have not produced the promised "positive restructuring" of the corporate sector which is needed to secure future prosperity. Yet the Liberals ave dramatically slashed the public sector investments which have, in the past, helped offset private sector failure and helped to build successful, Canadian-based companies.

Departmental spending on industrial, regional, and scientific and technological support programs were cut by 28% (1994-95 to 1997-98) and Human Resources Development programs have been cut by 40%, with much of the reduction falling on training programs. Support for academic research and higher education has also been deeply cut, along with the federal government's own research efforts in gender analysis, agriculture, natural resources, the environment, and industry.

The AFB therefore proposes that the federal government:

- significantly increase federal investment in research and in technology diffusion through a major expansion of the highly successful IRAP program of the National Research Council, and through increased support for the research and outreach programs of the Departments of Environment, Energy and Natural Resources, and Agriculture;

- increase grants to university and technical institute based programs delivered through the government's granting councils; additional funds should be earmarked for increased funding of graduate and post-graduate research and for the expansion of the Networks of Centres of Excellence program which has been highly successful in developing integrated research programs in areas of strategic importance to the social and economic development of the country.

The AFB also commits the federal government—

- to scale back no-strings-attached tax breaks for business R and D in favour of results-based, repayable loans such as those extended under the Technology Partnerships Program which assist companies to make long-term, risky investments at relatively low cost to taxpayers;
- to encourage companies in the same sector to work together to build Canadian strengths—for example, through joint, sectoral-based R and D, technology diffusion, marketing, and training initiatives;
- to continue and expand federal financing for sector- based, joint business—labour training programs directed towards building the skills base of the Canadian labour force; and
- to introduce joint federal-provincial-territorial- broader public sector procurement councils to co-ordinate and plan orders and to channel a greater share of public sector purchases of health care equipment, computers, software, and other sophisticated goods and services to Canadian-based companies.

Community Economic Development

The Canadian economy continues to experience jobless growth—more wealth being created by by less labour. The Liberal government, contributes to this phenomenon of jobless growth by slashing government services. Yet the government also feels some pressure to respond to the high-profile poverty and social decay that are a result of its policies. One approach to "solving" the resulting economic crisis, favoured by both the federal government and the business community, is called "Community Economic Development" (CED).

CED as currently practised by the federal government, however, is an economic end in itself. Such an approach appeals to the government largely because of its relatively lower rates of pay and unionization, and because it is an efficient way of training people in the community so that they may easily become absorbed into the labour market.

This approach to CED—for example, in the form of government-guaranteed business start loans—continues to put the interests of business first. The initiatives that result do not address in any real way the root causes or tragic consequences of poverty and community decline. The government's most basic principle—so fundamental that it is never even discussed—is to support and maintain the current capitalist system. It works—and will continue to work—toward this end by supporting private-sector economic development, and by denying resources to those community development enterprises that challenge the established free market order.

In contrast with the above approach, the AFB sees CED as a powerful tool for social and political change. It supports CED as part of a broad social movement which strengthens community capacity, encourages grassroots organizing, cultivates the development of alternative visions for economies and the ways workplaces are structured, lessens community reliance on state and business support, and moves toward a truly democratic society—one that includes community control over the means of production. This form of CED stands as one of the most effective and realistically achievable ways to reduce exploitation by capital and the state.

A more progressive model of CED develops economic institutions that are based in and accountable to the community. It fosters the development of non-traditional, more democratic forms of organization, and is designed to keep more resources within the community that generates them.

The AFB's conception of CED can usefully be seen in historical context. It fits in some ways into the social economy (see the Social Economy section) as part of a tradition of what Eric Shragge calls "community intervention" in the economy, in which working class people act in solidarity to create community-based economic enterprises. Examples of these include cooperative enterprises, mutualist associations, and consumer cooperatives. Such institutions generally placed the interests of community above those of business, and were not merely designed to stoke the economy by stimulating private enterprise.

In a capitalist economy, wealth is produced by labour, and yet most workers never control the wealth their labour creates. Quite simply, the wealth is siphoned off in a variety of ways. In the same way, disadvantaged communities suffer not just because of the low level of wealth being generated by the community, but because these resources so quickly leave, primarily in rent and profits.

CED enterprises, on the other hand, are designed to keep resources within the community, to build self-sustaining economic infrastructure, and increase community self-reliance.

CED enterprises have very real positive influences on the lives of people in the community. Workplaces that employ non-hierarchical or collective structures, for example, provide an opportunity to learn skills and participate in decision-making to people who otherwise have been systematically disempowered. Housing co-operatives can charge fairer rent because there is no landlord or property owner taking the largest share.

In keeping with the AFB's view of CED as part of a larger movement for social justice and community empowerment, the key tenets in our CED policies are as follows:

- The need to preserve and protect the autonomy of CED organizations, to minimize the pressures from the state and market to adopt traditional capitalist practices.
- The need to foster within the CED movement a vibrant political culture with clear awareness of its social and economic vision and prac-

tices. This is crucial to avoid further isolating communities that are supposed to be helped by CED initiatives, and would be accomplished by preserving community independence and by education.

- The importance of the direct involvement of people from the community wherever possible. This principle rests on the belief that no one is better suited to make decisions than those who are most affected by them. If CED and community empowerment are to mean anything at all, this principle must be respected.
- A commitment to real democracy in workplaces, organizational structure and process, and internal decision-making. In other words, it is possible for CED enterprises such as worker-owned collectives to eliminate exploitation and inequality in the workplace.
- Special emphasis on and support for Aboriginal CED initiatives. Traditionally, Aboriginal communities have had a preference for and imaginative ideas about community-based initiatives, and yet these communities have received little support from lending and funding bodies.
- Strong financial support for CED enterprises that embody the above principles, as well as a strong educational and training component. This education component must be based in the community, taking advantage of the knowledge already possessed by many people, and designed to institutionalize this sharing of information, as opposed to imposing it from outside.

CED presents a formidable challenge to private ownership and capital accumulation, and so CED enterprises will feel contradictory and destructive pressures to the extent that they are forced to rely on financing from business and a capitalist state. In order to preserve the autonomy and independence of CED initiatives, the AFB will introduce a variety of models for providing funds to CED organizations. It will create a pool of capital, the control and distribution of which would be based in the community. For example, capital corporations with boards representative of and accountable to the community could be created, and would eventually replace government funding agencies.

Such boards and similar organizations would have an important secondary impact, in that they would encourage the involvement of community people in the process of determining their own economic future, and in developing and debating alternative economic visions. If CED activities become a central part of a politically active community, they will give communities the clout to act on their social and political demands.

The ultimate goal is to have the local community consider the development potential and consequences of all activities taking place in the community, and to have the power to influence these activities to the degree that the community will be affected. There exist now a variety of models for such education, but most are either voluntary or financially precarious. The AFB will provide stable and consistent funding for CED education. Some of this funding will pay for the training of community-based economic development coordinators. Such coordinators will be sponsored by the community, and will help to develop community capacity from within. In other words, the educational model will be bottom-up, not top-down.

Communities that are currently disadvantaged will remain that way as long as they do not have control over their own resources or the political influence that such control would give them. The AFB includes CED initiatives as part of an acknowledgment of the links between the economic development of communities and their social and political growth. Moreover, it is consistent with the principle that decisions can and should be made by those who are most affected by them.

Youth Unemployment

The effects of the youth unemployment crisis are by now well known. The official unemployment rate for young people remains about 17%, with the real youth unemployment rate estimated at over 25%. Since 1990, the labour force participation rate of young people has dropped by 10 percentage points, bringing it to a 25-year low.

Those young people who can find work are increasingly employed in part-time, short-term and low-waged jobs. The poor labour market conditions that afflict young people now last longer, with many workers in their late 20s and early 30s working in the kind of service-sector jobs traditionally associated with teenagers and students.

Young people are also increasingly finding work only in non-standard jobs (temporary, part-time, multiple jobs, self-employed). The rate of young women in these jobs increased from 49% to 64% from 1989 to 1994 alone.

The effect on youth incomes of lower labour force participation, higher unemployment and increasingly part-time and temporary jobs has been dramatic. Over the last decade, real median incomes of young people have declined substantially. These conditions refute the notion, sometimes heard, that youth can expect to earn incomes comparable to those of an earlier era, once a kind of "waiting period" to get into a real job is over. The overall trend is towards a lower wage economy, and young workers are the "shock troops" of this transition.

To add insult to injury, young people are frequently blamed for their own circumstances. Responses to the youth job crisis continue to be focused on young people's "need" for a little more training, some time on the Internet, a better resumé, pre-employment programs, or a bit of unpaid or low-waged work experience. These responses do little more than position young people to compete in a labour market that simply does not provide enough jobs for those who need and want to work.

Existing federal government youth employment initiatives are, for the most part, directed toward summer jobs, short-term work experience programs, small loans for youth starting their own businesses, or top-ups for private companies to hire youth on short-term contracts. Most of them are geared towards post-secondary students and graduates--who have the lowest levels of youth unemployment —and offer little for less-privileged youth.

The size, scope, length and targets of these programs are too low to make any significant impact on the problem of youth unemployment.

The overall impact of youth unemployment is having a devastating effect on Canada's future. Today's youth are the first generation since World War II to believe their economic circumstances will be worse than those of their parents. If present trends continue, there is every reason to think they are right.

ALTERNATIVES

In January 1993, 10 months before the Liberal opposition won the federal election and formed the government, it released a report entitled "Agenda for Youth." That document called for strong measures to address the "grave crisis" facing Canada's youth. "The federal and provincial governments must be committed to act in partnership with all Canadians to develop a concerted plan for young people in Canada," stated the report. "We cannot absolve ourselves of responsibility for the poverty, unemployment, marginalization, and powerlessness of youth. Nor can we look to others to provide relief from the appalling social conditions faced by many young Canadian women and men."

Stating that "the future of Canada's youth is at stake," the Liberal House and Senate committee put forward a "widc range of measures to cope with deep-seated problems." The Liberals knew then, as we still know today, that there are alternatives.

A NATIONAL YOUTH JOB STRATEGY

One of the strongest recommendations of the Liberal report "Agenda for Youth" was that the problems youth faced could not be resolved without addressing larger economic problems. "No one has benefited from the ill-advised strategy of simply setting market forces to work," stated the report.

A central part of the national youth job strategy is addressed in the Alternative Federal Budget's job creation targets. Young people are not out of work because they are mismatched with the labour market's needs; rather, youth unemployment is a direct fallout of sustained double-digit unemployment. While job strategies directed toward young people will address the immediate needs under the youth unemployment crisis, a national job strategy will ensure that there are jobs for them to move into.

Youth Benefit From Social Programs

In "Agenda for Youth," the Liberals criticized the Mulroney government for cuts to program spending. "There is a palpable sense that the federal government's earlier commitment to full employment has been superseded by policies which amount to a form of social Darwinism," stated the report. "Reductions in government expenditures--and in the willingness to accept responsibility--in education, training, social assistance, and job creation, have occurred as the Canadian economy struggles to become increasingly global. The obstacles to youth have increased, both in scope and scale."

Cuts to program spending, however, did not stop when the Liberals took office: on the contrary, they accelerated. The cuts have not hurt youth any less under the Liberals than they did under the Progressive Conservatives.

A crucial part of turning around youth economic insecurity is reversing public spending cuts. From public school budget reductions to rising tuition fees, cuts to education have an enormous impact on youth and their ability to obtain meaningful, well-paying jobs, and to graduate without massive debt. Cuts to the social safety net, such as those to EI and welfare, not only increase youth economic insecurity, but also force young people to keep any job they can get, regardless of whether it is suitable, fair or providing a decent wage.

As a part of addressing the youth unemployment crisis, funding to social programs must be restored and stabilized.

Increased and Stabilized Funding to Existing Programs

Despite widespread and drastic cuts, some of Canada's federal youth programs remain in place. Existing programs with a proven record will have their funding increased to former levels, and have their funding stabilized for a minimum of three years.

A major new initiative as part of the federal government's youth job strategy

There is more than enough work to be done in Canadian society today to give every out-of-work young person a job, whether it be protecting the environment, developing adequate housing, participating in community development, caring for children who lack adequate day-care, or providing services to seniors who want and need to stay in their homes, saving vital health care dollars and improving the quality of life for seniors.

Other initiatives put forward directly by youth range from promoting Canadian culture to building alternatives to environmentally destructive transportation methods to developing technological expertise. Job growth in the general labour market will open opportunities for young workers. Youth can participate in the economy by working in small business, or starting their own.

The focus of the national youth job strategy will be a new program to finance youth-run community projects that address tangible community needs and create jobs for young workers. While the program is broad-based, its central component is to address the youth jobs-deficit by putting young people to work addressing the country's social deficit.

The new program introduced in this year's AFB will target youth aged 16-29, who will develop their own proposals for community-based projects, both single-job initiatives and group projects. The program will emphasize the need to involve young people of diverse backgrounds and ethnicities. Program funding will be available on both a short- and long-term basis, with regular "goal-post" evaluation and ongoing program support. Exploration grants will also be available to allow young people to support themselves adequately while studying the feasibility and needs of their proposals.

Youth will be expected to develop long-term plans and identify specific outcomes, both in their project's contribution to the community, and the long-term economic security of the participants. A priority will be placed on building links and mentorships with community non-profit groups, schools, labour, and business. Young people will also be encouraged to seek provincial and private funding partnerships.

The projects will be structured to avoid acting as a simple wage-subsidy that benefits only private sector employers, and to avoid displacing public sector workers.

The program will be phased-in over three years, beginning with an immediate, broad-based consultation process with young people and those who work with them. This process is intended to identify current programs that can be enhanced, and to develop the framework for the new program. Pilot projects will be commenced in the first year, reviewed and expanded in the second, and fully implemented in the third year. The initiative will aim to employ the equivalent of 50,000 full-time, full-year young people.

Federal Training Policy

The federal government has an important role to play in the development, administration and funding of labour market training and adjustment policy. Under the current government and its predecessors, however, training policy has been set within a narrow range of priorities, determined for the most part by the requirements of employers. Like education, training is at risk of being driven solely by demands for "employability."

For most people, this translates into working longer hours, in increasingly precarious employment forms, for less pay, while absorbing the costs associated with government privatization and cutbacks in programs and services. Working people have been encouraged to take responsibility for investing in their own skills development and job creation from their own pockets. It doesn't take long to see through the smoke and mirrors to find the flaw in this panacea: working people, women, the poor and youth are bearing the brunt of the government's cutbacks. Meanwhile, corporate Canada reaps unprecedented profits.

The labour force has been polarized between a two-tiered system of occupational training: the top tier of formal recognition for structured and accredited occupational training, and the bottom tier of 'employability measures', including short-term, minimal basic skills training and workfare. This system serves to entrench the employment trends of casualization and precarious employment that prevails in a deregulated labour market.

Canada continues to lag behind the majority of OECD member states, ranking 19th out of 20 OECD countries on direct investment in employer-sponsored workplace training. In fact, only 28% of the population receives any form of training, according to the 1997 Adult Education and Training Survey conducted by Statistics Canada. (Note: The AETS measured training participation rates for 1994 and reported the results in 1997.] Of these, 38% were in the employed workforce (39% full time and 33% part-time). Only 23% of unemployed people received any form of training. And only 13% of those people not in the labour force received training of some sort (these include 'discouraged workers,' as well as young people and others trying to get their first job or return to the labour force after an extended absence).

The AFB commits the federal government to countering these trends. Training is not a substitute for good jobs. Labour market training must be accompanied by concrete measures designed to achieve and maintain environmentally sustainable economic growth and development. Training is a basic entitlement to which people must have access regardless of employment or other status.

NATIONAL TRAINING STANDARDS

Development of a system of National Training Standards must be our first priority. In the federal government's drive to dismantle universal programs and deregulate the labour market, program design and delivery have increasingly reflected free market ideology and values. Equity and access principles have been eroded, if not abandoned. For these reasons, the AFB immediately undertakes, through the Canadian Labour Force Development Board, the development of a negotiated system of National Training Standards. These Standards will adhere to the principles outlined below, and will inform all subsequent training agreements governing the transfer of public funds between and among labour market partners.

Key Principles:

i) All training must be accredited, sequential and transferable.

ii) Training must be targeted to the four designated equity groups: women, people with disabilities, visible minorities and Aboriginal peoples. Access to and participation in all training services must reflect the principles and priorities of employment equity. The AFB would restore the Designated Group Policy.

iii) Training activities must include and reflect curriculum developed to counter racism, sexism, and homophobia. Curriculum designed to encourage critical thinking and critical problem-solving provides the basis for progressive standards in adult education and training activities. Finally, curriculum must incorporate labour education, including health and safety, workplace and community diversity and employment standards.

iv) Training programs and services must include provision for supplementary allowances and child care.
v) Occupational training must reflect the current standards of the occupation, to ensure relevance and portability.
vi) Participation in training must not be linked in any way to compulsory participation in any wage-subsidy or work-for-welfare scheme.

These basic standards will enable the federal government to work with the key labour market partners, including labour, business, equity groups and other levels of government, in the design and delivery of relevant labour market training and adjustment services.

The AFB also restores and enforces the prohibition against workfare originally included under the provisions of the Canada Assistance Program. Access to labour market training and adjustment services is an entitlement of all people within federal jurisdiction and is not tied to income support eligibility provisions of either provincially-administered social assistance or federally-administered Employment Insurance.

POLICY MEASURES FOR AN IMPROVED TRAINING STRATEGY

The AFB sees a revitalized role for the federal government in the following policy and program areas:

- a skills bank establishing general entitlement to life-long learning, including basic skills training and skills upgrading for all Canadians;
- a skills renewal fund to facilitate workplace-based training for all working people, paid for through an Employer Training Levy, set at 1% of payroll to a floor of 40 hours of training for every worker;
- a comprehensive roster of employment services to link federal and provincial training and labour adjustment programs and services for unemployed working people, regardless of EI-eligibility—paid for from general revenues, not tied to income support;
- infrastructure development in the form of additional funding to expand the work of the Canadian Labour Force Development Board in four key areas: monitoring, labour market information, sector councils, and community training agreements.

THE SKILLS BANK: TOWARD AN INTEGRATED SYSTEM OF LIFELONG LEARNING

The Skills Bank will make available a basic entitlement to a total of 5,000 learning credits against which individuals can draw at any time throughout their working life. Learning credits will be drawn down in the form of accredited training courses administered through any one of the following: government-to-government training agreements, direct purchase option, provincially administered training and education programs, and workplace training.

The Skills Renewal Fund

The Skills Renewal Fund is an initiative designed to imporve employer-sponsored participation in labour market training. The fund will administer revenues derived through an employer training levy, and made available to employed workers through a variety of mechanisms, including sector councils, joint workplace training committees, and through public, labour and community-based training agencies.

The AFB endorses the long-standing demand of the Canadian Labour Congress and provincial labour federations and affiliates for the introduction of an employer training levy. The levy will be set at 1% of total payroll to ensure a basic standard of 40 hours structured and accredited training for all employees. Where appropriate, matching sector council funding can be drawn upon to cover costs associated with infrastructure development and innovative research in occupational analysis and development, assessment tools and training delivery methods. Training trust funds will continue to be administered separately through negotiated collective agreement provisions, but could be combined with Skills Renewal Fund initiatives. Training initiatives include labour-based education programs.

Employment Services

Access to employment insurance under the current EI Act has been reduced to levels we consider to be dangerously low. Thousands of unemployed and under-employed women and men are denied access to necessary services. This is not a sustainable option over the longer term, and must be corrected through the provision of comprehensive employment services through a revitalized network of Human Resource Centres.

Training is an integral component of a broader set of employment services. For those who have lost their jobs, who are seeking to enter the work force for the first time or to re-enter after an absence, employment services must be made available through fully-staffed Human Resources Centres. In this program, access to employment services will not be limited by EI-eligibility.

Technological tools, in the form of computerized job banks and job search mechanisms cannot replace the work of Canada Employment and Immigration Union members. Direct one-on-one job search counselling, vocational counselling and related assistance remains absolutely essential for those having to deal with the crisis of job loss and the prospect of subsequent unemployment.

Community-based centres and workplace-based action centres are also important vehicles for the provision of a comprehensive roster of employment services, including training and adjustment services like vocational counselling, vocational and occupational assessment, training referrals and related supports. Local planning initiatives with HRDC and training delivery agents can include multi-party provisions for employment services to enhance access, including to designated groups. However, the AFB will not support any measure designed to contract-out or privatize HRC functions.

Federal HRCs have, in the past, played an important role in an integrated local labour force development network, providing referrals and counselling for people seeking training and adjustment services, and linking with workplace- and community-based initiatives. These functions--and the jobs that accompany them--will be restored under the AFB.

DEVELOPING THE SYSTEM INFRASTRUCTURE: STRENGTHENING THE CANADIAN LABOUR FORCE DEVELOPMENT BOARD

Previous attempts to develop a comprehensive system of labour force development boards met with limited success. Nonetheless, the AFB recognizes that the absence of a national board creates an unacceptable vacuum for all labour market partners. A central labour force development board, working with HRDC, can conduct and foster important work in a variety of key areas in a truly multi-partite environment based on consensus and shared commitment.

The AFB will increase the funding commitment of the federal government to the work of the CLFDB by regularizing its funding relationship to the board as an arms-length agency with autonomous powers for decision-making, charged with four principal areas of responsibility: 1) monitor transfers to provinces and direct purchase option [restored under this AFB] to ensure compliance with national training standards and equity guidelines; 2) labour market information; 3) sector councils to administer training levy and training trust fund allocations for employed workers; and 4) community training agreements to administer training and adjustment services for the unemployed and those wishing to enter or re-enter the labour force.

The AFB will encourage provincial governments to return to a system of multi-partite labour force development boards, ensuring full and transparent accountability and co-determined decision-making in the design, development, funding and delivery of training and adjustment activities. These boards will provide vehicles through which cost-shared federal and provincial training activities can be administered.

STARTING OVER: BUILDING BLOCKS FOR A VIABLE TRAINING SYSTEM

LITERACY, BASIC SKILLS AND ESL/FSL

Many Canadians are disadvantaged by limited literacy and communication skills. For one in five people, literacy levels are well below those needed to participate in the political, social and economic life of our communities and workplaces. Many people require second language instruction in English and French.

Basic skills training, language training and technological literacy are the foundation from which we must develop occupational skills. The AFB will directly restore funding for English/French as a Second Language by removing the residency time limits imposed by the current labour market language training/language instruction for newcomers to Canada. That is, ESL/FSL instruction must be made available to all requiring it, regardless of length of residency in Canada and/or citizenship status. The AFB, in consultation with the National Literacy Secretariat, will launch a national literacy/numeracy campaign to ensure that basic literacy/numeracy skills development is a core component of all labour market training and adjustment activities. The AFB will ensure adequate funding to community-based and workplace-based training in each of these core skills areas.

FINANCING MECHANISMS

Access to training has become increasingly tied to EI-eligibility. The AFB maintains that people must be able to take training regardless of their EI or employment status. Training must bc paid for through general revenues and not tied to the EI account. At the same time, unemployed workers and people seeking access to the labour market will require some form of income support, administered through the EI system. The AFB will therefore negotiate into its federal-provincial training agreements adequate income support provisions for people who are not eligible for income support through the EI program.

Training purchase allocations must be established and administered to reflect national and local labour market conditions. Training agencies, including colleges, union-based and community-based agencies, must be enabled to operate within local and regional labour market parameters. Current restrictions, consigning training deliverers to servicing only the narrow HRDC catchement area, preclude comprehensive local planning based on forecasted labour market activities at the local, regional and national levels over the medium and long term. The AFB will direct HRDC to lift the unnecessary limitations imposed on training deliverers in the name of decentralization, and will instead require HRDC to work with labour market partners through mechanisms like the CLFDB and local labour force development boards to develop comprehensive purchase-of-training plans based on accurate labour market information.

CONSTITUTIONAL OPT-OUT

The AFB will provide an opt-out consideration for Quebec, pending agreement to provisions on social and economic equity, universal entitlement, and prohibitions against workfare. In recognition of the central role of the federal government with respect to national labour market conditions, however, the AFB maintains the federal and provincial roles by restoring and strengthening a national infrastructure in labour force development and labour market training and adjustment services.

Unemployment Insurance

The number of unemployed receiving Unemployment Insurance (UI) benefits has plummeted over the past seven years—from 89% in July of 1990 to less than 50% in 1996, and to fewer than 43% at the present time.

By the time Paul Martin had brought down his first budget in February 1994, the previous Tory cuts had reduced UI coverage to 63%. Bill C-12, the latest UI legislation implemented in January 1997, together with Martin's 1994 cuts, will reduce coverage to only about one-third of the unemployed.

Even without the C-12 changes, the higher entrance requirement and the massive cuts to the length of the benefit has already reduced coverage to one-third of the unemployed in Ontario. In British Columbia, UI coverage has fallen to 45%. Several Canadian provinces now have lower protection than some U.S. states.

Shortening the benefit period has left over a million claimants exhausting their benefits before they find another job. Martin, in his first budget, reduced the length of the benefit period to half of what it was in 1989. Most claimants had their benefits cut by 10 to 16 weeks in that budget.

Coverage dropped sharply in 1997, now that the minimum work requirements are measured in hours. Whereas previously a week of work was a week in which individuals worked for more than 15 hours, the new entitlement formula bases work-weeks on a 35-hour week.

The higher entrance requirement and shortened benefit period have cut benefit payouts by $8 to $10 billion a year. Every UI bill passed in the 1990s cut the benefit rate—from 60% of weekly earnings to 57% in 1993 and to 55% in 1994. Bill C-12 cut the benefit rate for more than three-quarters of weekly earnings of the claimants. In some cases the effective rate is as low as 25% of weekly earnings.

Claimants making more than $39,000 a year who were claimants in previous years will have benefits clawed back. Some construction workers, and other workers who are vulnerable to seasonal conditions and to the boom-and-bust of the business cycle, will be punished for layoffs that have nothing to do with their current conditions of layoff.

THE IMPACT

- Child poverty will increase because the parents of many thousands of children will be without income for several months. In the case of seasonal employment, the benefit cheque will hardly be sufficient to pay for food.
- Thousands of women who re-enter the labour force, particularly those who take part-time jobs, will not qualify for regular benefits if they are laid off or go on maternity leave.
- Thousands of laid-off young people will fail to qualify for protection under new rules requiring 26 weeks of work, averaging 35 hours a week.
- Thousands of workers in seasonal industries will have their weekly benefit cut in half.

  Bill C-12 will have a devastating effect on hundreds of communities and entire regions of the country. Atlantic Canada and the northern regions of every province with seasonal industries will have little or no protection against the loss of earnings due to layoff.

THE UI SURPLUS AND GOVERNMENT DEFICIT

The cumulative surplus in the UI Account at the end of the 1997-98 fiscal year will exceed $13 billion—even with the premium rate reduction to 2.7%. By the end of the 1998-99 fiscal year, the cumulative surplus will be $20 billion. Benefits payout will again drop much lower than Martin predicted in any of his budgets.

AFB PROPOSALS

While the Alternative Federal Budget contains a number of specific proposals, our main concern is with that of the cumulative account surplus and benefit entitlement. It is important, however, in making our AFB proposals, that we have a clear understanding of the history and purpose of unemployment insurance in Canada.

The Unemployment Insurance Act was proclaimed in Canada in 1940 in response to the social and economic conditions between the period from 1919 to 1939. In order to establish an Unemployment Insurance program, the federal government sought and obtained agreement from the provinces for a constitutional amendment giving them the authority for such a scheme.

A number of important provisions were incorporated into the U.I. Act of 1940, including the following:

- that workers would be covered against the risk of job loss;
- that the program would be financed through the payment of premiums by workers and employers; and
- that the federal government would contribute to the plan, initially one-fifth of the aggregate program costs.

This last point was extremely important in that the federal government through its contributions acknowledged that its fiscal and monetary policies might influence the rate of unemployment. Withdrawal of federal financing, increased demands on the program for training purposes, chronically high unemployment, and a desire to reduce UI premiums in order to remain internationally competitive, as well as a preoccupation with debt and deficit reduction, continue to threaten this integral income support program.

A program which once achieved near universality has become eroded to the point where fewer than 40% of Canada's unemployed workers can hope to collect UI benefits. Yet, as 1997 drew to a close, the federal government announced a modest UI premium reduction, while employers continue to eye the UI surplus and call for a massive reduction in premiums.

In light of this surplus and ongoing threats to the Unemployment Insurance program, the central AFB recommendation is that coverage be restored to 70% of Canada's unemployed, and that the benefit rate be restored to 60% of previous earnings. This could be accomplished by maintaining the 1997 UI premium rate while still being able to balance annual program revenues and expenditures.

The 1998 Alternative Federal Budget will:

- restore Unemployment Insurance coverage to 70% of Canada's unemployed;
- maintain UI premiums at 1997 levels ($2.90/$100 of earnings for workers and 1/4 that amount for employers;
- restore the UI benefit rate to 60% of weekly earnings from the current variable formula;
- repeal the divisor and intensity rules, which are confusing and blatantly punitive to seasonal workers;
- ensure that the federal government maintains responsibility for training, and oppose the federal withdrawal from labour market training;
- ensure that UI training benefits are considered entitlements, that rational criteria be developed for training decisions, and that UI claimants have a statutory right to appeal training decisions;

- that older workers or those workers with a lengthy labour force attachment be given extended UI benefits to pursue training, and that an entitlement formula be developed such as one week's paid training leave for each week worked;
- structure benefits and premiums to discourage overtime and encourage and provide incentives for shorter working time;
- impose penalties on employers who fail to provide workers with sufficient notice of layoff;
- provide more funding for employment services—labour market information, counselling, etc.—for workers who are displaced through downsizing and business relocations, often resulting from free trade and increased globalization;
- provide funding to community-based organizations which represent UI appellants before Boards of Referees (appellants who are unrepresented win less than 25% of their appeals, compared with success rates over 60% for represented appellants); and
- establish a Commission of Inquiry to examine the real cost of unemployment, including its scope, magnitude, demographics, and its impact on health, community and social structures.

BENEFICIARIES AS % OF UNEMPLOYED

Year	%	Year	%
1987-88	81.2%	1993-94	62.5%
1988-89	86.2%	1994-95	56.4%
1989-90	87.0%	1995-96	51.6%
1990-91	85.7%	1996-97	45.7%
1991-92	79.4%	1997-98	40.9%
1992-93	73.4%		

NATURAL RESOURCES

Environmental Protection

The environment is rarely given the importance it deserves in social and economic policy-making. The reasons include a failure to see environmental issues as a fit object of social activism, when in fact environmental degradation is a human health issue affecting the work environment, community health and ecological integrity alike. The environment affects the air we breathe, the water we depend on, the food we eat, the soil our children play in; it's about chemicals, poisons, and carcinogens in our community.

Even at the level of an amenity, the environment is important for us: the beauty of nature is (among other things) an amenity for us to enjoy. Degrade the environment and we not only deny this enjoyment to the next generation, but we impoverish our own social existence as well.

Recent federal government budgets have relegated the environment to a distant secondary status. The government fails to see that the environment is in effect the basis for all economic activity. Destroy the environment and you destroy the economy.

Humankind and its societies are entirely dependent on the global environment—the biosphere. Without a healthy biosphere, no society can exist. The Alternative Federal Budget therefore views a healthy environment as a central policy goal. Just as past AFBs have defined social concepts such as fairness, equity, universal health care and education, so now we begin to define ecological concepts such as limits to growth, the carrying capacity of the Earth, the Genuine Progress Indicator, regulations and economic measures to control the scale of our activities. Thus another fundamental goal—a healthy, life-supporting environment—becomes integrated into economic and social policy.

Though the polls tell us that environmental values are high on the public agenda, these are not good times for environmental progress. Within

Canada, the federal government is bent on the decentralization and devolution of environmental powers, in the name of "harmonization." The globalized economy also puts much stress on "harmonization," in the name of international standards, but really as a codeword for the destruction of national environmental regulation and the powers of governments to protect the national environment.

The concept of public ownership and control has long been one of the cornerstones of Canadian natural resource conservation and management. As public institutions in other sectors of Canadian society—such as hospitals and schools—are being undermined by laissez-faire market principles, the public administration of natural resources is undergoing a similar attack.

Examples of recent efforts that are inconsistent with a socially progressive and environmentally sound economy include the pressure to privatize publicly owned and managed fish stocks, attempts to loosen public control over Crown land, and the injection of commercial interests into the national parks system and the management of wildlife populations.

These trends are what could be called the "commodification of nature"—nature as a commodity to be bought and sold only in terms of its private market value. The lessons of Canadian history are that unfettered markets lead inevitably to degraded habitat and depleted animal populations.

A successful effort to protect the national environment would result in a huge amount of green job creation. For instance, environmental protection measures and the resulting green industries have created over 110,000 jobs within 4,000 companies over the past 25 years in Canada. This trend can only continue with the maintenance and enhancement of environmental regulatory programs at the federal and provincial levels. "Environmental regulations create jobs."

The Rational Energy Program prepared by the Canadian Climate Change Network (CANeT) projects that an aggressive program to reduce greenhouse gas emissions through energy efficiency improvements and increased use of alternative energy sources will produce a net increase of 1.5 million Canadian jobs over 15 years. This job creation occurs primarily in the areas of retrofitting of buildings, construction, energy efficiency measures, alternative energy sources, and service industries/social services. This reflects the employment potential of alternative energy sources.

It has been calculated that it takes 100 workers in a nuclear plant, or 116 workers in a coal-fired plant to generate 1,000 gigawatt-hours of electricity per year. Yet 248 would be employed in a solar thermal facility, or 542 in a wind farm, to generate the same amount of electricity. At the same time, investments in energy efficiency have been shown to create more than four times as many jobs as investments in new emergy supply, because energy efficiency improvements are labour-intensive and produce energy bill savings that can be spent in the community to create local economic activity and jobs.

The 1998 AFB is informed by the underlying considerations of environmental sustainability, and cover five main issue areas: natural resources, energy, pollution and waste, nature conservation and consumer issues.

Policy should be guided by the following principles:

1. primacy of prevention;
2. the precautionary principle: (when in doubt adopt the least harmful strategy);
3. just transition: (protect workers adversely affected by policy);
4. weight of evidence;
5. the critical load principle: (don't exceed the threshold of pollution that would inflict damage on the environment);
6. cradle-to-grave and life-cycle analysis of environmental impact: (consider all phases of the production process);
7. best available technology;
8. sustainable use: (don't over-exploit renewable resources; conserve and develop substitutes for non-renewable resources);
9. full-cost accounting: (pricing of the so-called environmental externalities); and
10. the polluter-pays principle.

On the "instruments" of environmental policy, the 1998 AFB adopts the following strategy:

1. that regulation, within a mix of instruments, is always the preferred policy option;
2. that where "green taxes" are to be adopted, taxation at the "front end" of the production process is to be preferred;
3. that green taxes should be "loop taxes" or dedicated revenue—dedicated to resolving the issues, especially the employment issues, which are the occasion for levying the tax in the first place;
4. that green taxes should reflect the principles of ecological tax reform and should, at least in part, be offset by reductions in other taxes; and
5. that green taxes internalize "externalities" as part of the cost of doing business.

These proposals, with the emphasis on regulation, form the rationale for the restoration of the budget of Environment Canada in order to carry out a national regulatory program.

The central focus for the 1998 AFB is a mix of policies: regulation, ecological tax reform, green job creation, and a program of just transition for workers affected by environmental change. It makes two concrete proposals: one for a National Atmosphere Fund that would provide municipal governments with resources to design and implement local greenhouse gas emission reduction strategies (with a large green-job-creation potential); and the other a pilot corporate chemical taxation scheme to finance a national pollution prevention program.

In both these schemes, ecological taxation is used to help finance "just transition" schemes. The idea of "just transition" is to address the workplace effects of major environmental change, such as the banning of a high-volume feedstock chemical, or a move away from coal in energy olicy. In such cases, the workers in the affected industry are protected by way of full income and benefit maintenance, access to new jobs, educational assistance, and support for affected communities.

The 1998 AFB proposes the removal of subsidies to the resource sector and the nuclear and petro-chemical industries. In the area of energy use, the 1998 AFB implements a modest carbon tax to contribute to a $1 billion National Atmosphere Fund. This Fund, in essence, provides loans to municipal governments that will support the development and implementation of actions to reduce greenhouse gas emissions at the municipal level.

Municipal governments will be expected to repay these loans from the savings generated as a result of investments made with the Fund. It is hoped that these monies will also help leverage additional amounts from provincial governments, municipal governments, and the private sector.

Municipal governments can use the Fund to provide loans for greenhouse gas emission reduction measures within both municipal operations and the community as a whole. The interest earned from the Fund can be used to provide grants to cover project development costs and small community initiatives to fight climate change.

While the full $1 billion will initially be available to municipalities, $430 million is ultimately earmarked to support "just transition" for workers displaced by actions to protect the climate. This portion of the Fund will be used for these purposes, as required.

The 1998 AFB represents only the first step in the development of a Canadian Action Plan to reduce greenhouse gas emissions. Over the coming year, the AFB will examine a range of fiscal measures, including a more substantial carbon tax implemented as part of a broader ecological tax reform, to help Canada meet its emission reduction commitments. In addition, the AFB will examine the resources needed to fund a more comprehensive set of climate change measures, including:

- new fuel economy standards for automobiles;
- energy-efficient standards for buildings;
- tax incentives for investments in energy efficient and renewable energy sources; and
- increased direct support for research, development and commercialization of energy efficient and renewable energy technologies.

These efforts will be reflected in the 1999 AFB through a much more detailed and comprehensive package of measures to help Canada meet its international obligations to protect the climate.

The 1998 AFB also proposes a national program of pollution prevention to deal with pollution and waste, and a pilot corporate chemical taxation scheme as a lead into the financing of the national program. Among the chemicals to be targeted for this tax are mercury, ozone depleters, perchlorethylene, dioxins and furans. The projected revenue from this tax on chemicals is $1 million.

To amplify the foregoing environmental priorities, a "Green Alternative Budget" based on the Genuine Progress Indicators concept will be drafted to complement next year's AFB.

Agriculture

The wheat economy in the Prairies, the cod fishery in Atlantic Canada, and the lumber industry in British Columbia have something in common. The are all renewable resources that are being converted into their opposite. The cod fishery is fished out, soil erosion and land degradation continue, and clear-cutting is denuding the landscape and probably altering the climate.

The tendency of these primary industries and those who exploit them to deplete their human resource—people—is legendary. Capital-intensive production and the demands for ever greater returns on invested capital are destroying the very resources which generate the corporations' profits—and in the process also destroying the livelihood of those who work in these primary industries.

In the case of farming, it is now an open question whether or not the industry can actually be sustained. Canada's thousands of small and medium-sized family farmers are continuously being undermined by large-scale industrial farm production based on high capital investment and cheap labour, especially in poultry and livestock, but to some extent in all segments of farming.

On the one hand, this is not a good way to produce food. It leads to unemployment and declining communities; the food itself is often of poor quality; it destroys a way of life and erodes cultural and economic diversity; it may yet drive another nail in the coffin of democracy. As a nation, are we reaching the point where succeeding generations will have neither the will nor the knowledge to farm?

On the other hand, whether Canada ends up with family farming or industrial farming, the lives of those who actually do the work, and the living conditions of their families and their communities, must be defended. And we can be sure they will not be defended by the powerful corporations that run the global marketplace.

It is time for Canadians, especially those who are not farmers, to decide how and where they want their food produced, and what they want farm production and farm communities to be like. During the past decade at least, the Canadian government has been unabashedly encouraging the trend to large-scale industrial farming. Although some marketing boards have hung on from a time when family farming was politically favoured, in other ways the government has encouraged restructuring (the euphemism for getting small farmers out of the business), cut back on research and inspection (since large farms connected to agribusiness don't need them, anyway), encouraged rural economic development and value added (the euphemism for supporting agribusiness and turning rural Canada away from farming), and focusing its support programs on commodity production and the global markets. From a family farmer's perspective, it has not worked. But can it?

The 1998 AFB aims to balance a federal agriculture program based on global commodity market sustainability with one that sustains farming and rural life as a national policy.

AFB POLICY PROPOSALS

1. Remove GRIP and NISA: The 1998 AFB will eliminate and replace these programs. NISA clearly favours large and well- established farmers who are able to generate savings which are then matched by government.
2. Introduce a Family Farm Support Program: This will replace GRIP and NISA. It supports farm family income. It is based on a formula that will account for market forces, input costs and transportation. It cuts out income derived from commodities marketed through marketing boards. (This may turn out to be too harsh, since the margins for these commodities may also become very low. But program will ensure that farm families cannot become unduly wealthy by working both systems, the FFSP and marketing boards.) Cost for 1998 - $300 million.) [Here we have the dilemma mentioned above. Perhaps it is time to simply put in place a guaranteed income system, not just for farm families but for all families in primary production, and indeed for all Canadians. It would be adapted to each sector so as to accommodate the unique needs of families in that sector and to ensure fairness across sectors. For agriculture, it would probably look essentially like the FFSP which the AFB has proposed.]
3. Institute a Beginning Farm Family and Resettlement Program: The 1197 AFB supported beginning farm families by making available to them low-cost loans on capital investment. Such a program works,

sometimes well, when the new families are the sons and daughters of existing farm families who typically get lots of help—financial, labour, and knowledge—from their relatives. Even so, they have a steep learning curve during which their incomes drop perilously low. The 1998 AFB expands this program by providing them with special income support while they are getting started. Beyond that, we need a broader effort to repopulate rural Canada. Several counties in Ireland and others have tried such resettlement programs with success. This program would settle non-farm families initially with established farmers, with a view to facilitating farm transfer, or the establishment of the new farm family on another viable farm.

4. Restore the inspection capacity of Agriculture Canada.
5. Redirect the research capacity of Agriculture Canada: Turn research to the development of environmentally sustainable, small-scale family farming systems.
6. Launch a Surplus Food Disposal Program: It is often the case that Canadian agriculture produces food commodities in excess of effective demand. This "surplus" is disposed of below the cost of production, often without careful or systematic consideration of the needs of the hungry, both in Canada and abroad. But these needs are real. The growing importance of Canada's food banks and the Canadian Foodgrains Bank attests to the extent of hunger and malnutrition. The combination of surplus farm production with hunger and malnutrition is a contradiction that is unacceptable. Further, Canada's international rank as a foreign aid contributor has actually been declining in recent years. The 1998 Alternative Budget will correct this anomaly by undertaking a program of grants to domestic food banks and Canadian aid agencies such as the Foodgrains Bank to systematically purchase "surplus" commodities for domestic and foreign use.

This program is not meant to be a price support measure, although it would obviously add to the stream of revenues received by some Canadian farmers. Nor is it intended to dump our food surplus into developing countries in such quantities and at such low prices that it would undercut and endanger the livelihoods of farmers in these countries. It is meant, rather, to assist in famine relief and other food shortage emergencies abroad, and to address the problems of hunger and malnutrition at home. Everyone should have a right to adequate food, and Canada should sign on to international initiatives to guarantee food security to people everywhere.

7. Provide Rural Community Support Programs: Rural communities must be attractive places to live and raise families, perhaps no more but also no less attractive than urban communities. The AFB else-

where contains proposals for the delivery of programs to defend and enhance our communities. They include infrastructure development, the provision of adequate housing and community buildings, as well as community co-operative and economic development.

8. Rail transportation must be re-regulated to slow down and rationalize the process of rail line abandonment, to facilitate the development of short line rail companies, and to coordinate this with road construction and maintenance.
9. Agricultural labour will have to receive greater protection from revised and improved labour codes as industrial farming systems advance. This must include revisions that facilitate the unionization of agricultural workers.
10. Environmental protection will have to be enhanced through improved research on environmental hazards entailed in farming and how to avoid them, and through tougher environmental laws and review processes. "Right to farm" legislation and related policies which exempt farms from national labour and environmental standards should definitely be avoided.
11. The Role of the Canadian Wheat Board: The CWB has been weathering a sustained attack from the grain trade, the government of Alberta operating in the interests of livestock firms, would-be commodity brokers, a gaggle of misguided farmers and their organizations, Washington and some U.S. grain interests, and at times even cooperatives. The CWB must be defended. In grain production it is an important protector of small and medium-scale family farming. And it is a flagship in the family of Canadian marketing boards.

The CWB's powers and structure are currently being redefined in law, but the changes won't correct one of the Board's main weaknesses. The Board sells grain directly to domestic millers and foreign buyers, although it does use multinational grain merchants as agents of the board from time to time. On its other side, while the Board buys directly from farmers, the grain handling and transportation system relies completely on the private trade and cooperatives. But these are the very firms that would like to usurp the Board's powers and extract even greater profit for themselves though also buying, selling and blending grades.

The 1998 AFB will extend the CWB's powers so that it can not only buy grain directly from farmers but also physically make the on-farm purchases, undertake the shipping and handling, and so compete directly with the private firms, including the railways, that now enjoy oligopoly—or, in the case of the railways, monopoly—powers in that service area. There would be no cost to the federal Treasury from this proposal, since the CWB can fund the additional activities and equipment from its ongoing operations.

Forestry

By almost every measure, forestry is one of Canada's pre-eminent industrial sectors. It accounts for 3% of Canada's GDP. Forest products are one of our most important exports, amounting to more than $41 billion in 1995, and resulting in a $34 billion balance of trade surplus in 1995. Direct employment is 369,000 jobs, and including indirect employment this sector employs more than 880,000 Canadians. Some 340 local communities in Canada are economically dependent on the forest industry. Heavily unionized, the forest industry in 1995 provided $10 billion in wages and salaries to its workers.

Given the importance of this industry for the Canadian economy, any relevant economic strategy for Canada must include a forest strategy as one of its fundamental pillars.

Heavily unionized, the forest industry provided $10 billion in wages and salaries in 1995.

Forestry is also the single most important sector that shapes Canada's environment. Forty-five per cent of Canada's land base is forested, and in provinces like B.C.(65%), Ontario (65%) and Quebec (62%) the majority of the land is forest. The future of these forests will in large part determine the "green" character of Canada, not least the fate of more than 200,000 species of plants, animals and organisms which account for two-thirds of all the species found in Canada.

THE FEDERAL WITHDRAWAL FROM FORESTRY

Against this background, the sudden and dramatic withdrawal of the Canadian federal government from forest sector policy and development is deeply troubling.

The 1997-98 budget of Natural Resources Canada was at just 50% of the 1994/1995 level. The entire forestry budget is a mere $98.1 million. This is a decline from $117.9 million in 1996/1997; from $218 million in 1995/96; from $243.2 million in 1993/94; and from $245.8 million in 1992/93.

In the most recent National Research Council estimates, forestry did not even rate a separate section. Forestry programs are treated as subsets of the ministry's larger purpose to serve corporate clients. The National Forest Service still exists, but it is almost invisible within NRC and has virtually no role in forest policy or strategy in Canada.

The major casualty of the federal withdrawal from forestry are the forest development programs which were instituted in the 1990s in response to increasing harvests and under-stocked forest lands. Federal/provincial forest development programs (FRDA I and FRDA II), which between 1980 and 1995 funded most of the reforestation activities in Canada, are now defunct.

The current federal role in Canada's forest industry is reduced to support for research and preparing various reports. In effect, the federal government has removed itself from any meaningful role in the direction of Canada's largest industry.

THE REAL STATE OF CANADA'S FORESTS

While the forest harvest in Canada has remained stable since the Liberal government was elected, replanting and silvicultural activities have suffered as a result of the ending of FRDA. The number of seedlings planted in Canada in 1995 (most recent data) is at the lowest point since 1986. The area of land reforested is at the lowest point since 1987.

Spending on intensive silviculture (pruning, thinning, fertilization, etc.) has declined substantially in seven provinces, remained somewhat stable in B.C., and increased only in Saskatchewan and Quebec. Over the term of the present Liberal government, total investments in forest management in Canada have declined in relation to harvests, to GDP contribution, and in absolute terms.

The State of Canada's Forests report comforts Canadians with the assurance that harvest levels are within the Annual Allowable Cuts (AACs) in each province. However, current AACs are not necessarily a measure of sustainable forestry. For example, the recent review of AACs in B.C. has seen allowable cuts in large parts of the province drop dramatically.

The industrial wood harvest in Canada has increased by 56% since 1970. In some provinces, harvests will continue to grow. In the major forest economy provinces, harvest levels are now generally stable or face decline due to overcutting. However, there are now much greater demands on forest lands than in 1970. Today's forest must be managed for diverse values, especially to maintain bio-diversity. Protected areas are a fundamental feature of a modern forest industry. The federal government and most provinces have set a target of protecting 12% of representative eco-regions. According to the State of Canada's Forests Report, 7.6% of Canada's total land and fresh water base was protected in 1995--and about half of these protected forests are considered "strictly protected" and excluded from industrial activity such as logging and mining.

A NEW FEDERAL ROLE

Canada needs a new and profoundly different forest strategy. In this sector particularly, market forces must be regulated and constrained in the interests of sustainable development. Meeting environmental imperatives in forestry, however, does not at all imply reduced employment. The Canadian forest industry under-performs by international standards in the area of job creation. Environmental action, such as new forest practice codes, can also enhance employment. Strategic investments in silviculture and value added production are also employment generators.

To meet these goals, the federal government must re-enter the forestry field. A federal role need not duplicate provincial stewardship of resources. However, as past experience proves, shared programs with the provinces can be a powerful tool for encouraging investment in the forest resource.

There are two overarching purposes for a federal role in forestry. First, the economic centrality of forestry to Canada's export industries (forestry products constitute 17% of Canada's total exports), balance of trade, and fiscal stability (without the *net growth* in forestry exports of over 7% annually over the past decade, Canada would have experienced a $4.5 billion balance of trade deficit in 1994).

Second, Canada's forests are properly characterized not by province, but by species and eco-zones. Sustainability of species and inventory of timber must be assessed from an eco-zone perspective, within which several provincial jurisdictions may operate. There is a vital national role to ensure that the environmental impact of forestry in each zone is monitored and that effective action to ensure sustainable forestry is in place across provincial borders. Canada's National Forestry Database identifies 15 terrestrial eco-zones in Canada, each with its distinct climate, geology, soils, vegetation, animal and forest species.

FEDERAL POLICY GOALS AND BUDGET INITIATIVES

The Alternative Federal Budget defines the federal role in forestry in terms of the following four policy objectives.

Policy 1: to promote greater sustainability and economic benefits of Canada's forest resources through a forest investment fund.

Canada's forests are a renewable resource, provided that renewal takes place through investments in the resource. Although many questions remain outstanding about the productivity and character of second-growth forests, there is an overwhelming consensus among foresters that investments in the resource through intensive or incremental silviculture will enhance both the growth and yield of second-growth forests.

It is time for the federal government to re-enter the forest development business through partnerships with the provinces and with industry based on shared government and industry expenditures.

The federal contribution to forest development should reflect the forest sector's contribution to GDP. One per cent of forest sector GDP in 1995 (latest available data) was $202.27 million. This amount would be a good starting point for the federal contribution to a Forest Investment Fund, created through new federal/provincial forest development agreements. The forest investment fund should be directed towards enhanced forestry or intensive silviculture which improves forest growth and yields.

Because of relatively low stumpage rates and royalties on forest resources in most provinces, provincial contributions to a Forest Investment Fund can be generated from forest activities, without adding costs to provincial budgets. Increased stumpage rates in the provinces (except B.C., which has existing rates more than double those of any other province as a result of its Forest Renewal Plan) could produce revenues that match the federal contribution.

Policy 2: to set enhanced employment targets achieved by strategic investments in the land base, and by industrial policy to encourage value added production.

Forest investment is a direct job creator, now and in the future. B.C.'s forest renewal program estimates that $396.4 million in investments in land-based programs in 1997/1998 will create 6,661 direct person years of employment.

With matching provincial revenues generated through increased stumpage rates in the provinces, similar results for a new Canadian Forest Investment Fund would create 7,000 new direct jobs across Canada.

Policy 3: to enhance bio-diversity protection through new protected areas in representative eco-regions of Canada.

The 1995/1996 State of Canada's Forests Report contains an annual report on protected areas as the first indicator of conserving biodiversity and forest sustainability. The report, prepared by the World Wildlife Fund, addresses the federal government's specific responsibilities and notes that the national parks system is 56% complete. Of 39 forest eco-regions in Canada, 22 are represented in the national parks system; 17 regions remain unrepresented. The National Forest Strategy commits the federal government and the provinces to complete a network of protected areas representative of all forest eco-regions by the year 2000.

The federal government should establish a two-year Protected Area Fund to complete the federal government's commitment to forest biodiversity. This fund should be adequate to cover the costs of acquisition of land, compensation of third parties where necessary, labour adjustment for affected workers, and park development and management.

Policy 4: to support environmental and forest science research.

Forest science research is the only remaining vital role for the Canadian Forest Service. However, this too is in decline as a result of Liberal budgets. In 1994 the research budget of the Canadian Forest Service was $151 million, but this was reduced to $102 million in 1995, and to $92 million in 1996.

Research is critical to a sustainable future for Canada's forest sector, as the industry makes a difficult transition to second-growth forests. Inventory is especially important in measuring the sustainability of our present harvest levels and future projections for allowable cuts.

At a minimum, the AFB will restore federal research capacity and negotiate federal provincial agreements to fund a country-wide inventory program.

SOCIAL POLICY

An Overview

The war on the deficit has been won. The federal budget will be balanced by the end of the 1997-98 fiscal year. If the Bank of Canada doesn't choke off economic growth by raising interest rates, there will be a growing budgetary surplus which could total $50 billion in just five years! We should all be celebrating. Right?

Wrong! The "fiscal dividend" resulting from a balanced budget and future surpluses has not been achieved without great cost to the majority of Canadians: poor families and individuals, children, unemployed workers, the survivors of public and private sector downsizing, seniors, women, people with disabilities, Aboriginal peoples, visible minorities, youth, immigrants and refugees, women in the federal public service denied their rightful pay equity settlement, gays and lesbians denied basic human rights, and low- and middle-income Canadians whose wages stalled or declined while public services were reduced or eliminated.

On the other hand, a fortunate few—-bankers, bondholders and shareholders—-have become immensely richer as their profits and dividends soared, bolstered by minimal taxes and the availability of lucrative tax loopholes. They have profited, as well, from the mass layoffs of private sector workers, from the privatization of public agencies and the contracting-out of public sector jobs, and from the deregulation of key national services such as transportation and communications. Corporate CEOs have enjoyed huge salary increases and bonuses.

The war on the deficit, in short, has cost most Canadians dearly while heaping exorbitant rewards on a privileged minority.

THE LEGACY OF THE WAR ON THE DEFICIT

INCREASED POVERTY AND GROWING INEQUALITY

The contrast between winners and losers is stark. More than five million Canadians now live in poverty, 1.4 million of them children. Over half of single women 65 and older are poor. On average, the incomes of our 1.1 million poor two-parent and single-parent families with children are close to $9,000 below the poverty line. The average income of single-mother families is just $14,998. Such a large income gap means that poor families inevitably suffer severe deprivation and hunger. At last count, over 2.5 million Canadians depended on food banks to survive.

INCIDENCE OF POVERTY

	1989	*1995 ('000)*	*Increase*	*Increase (%)*
Persons, Total	3,770	5,205	1,435	38
Children Under 18	1,016	1,472	456	45
Single Individuals	1,243	1,520	277	23
Single Women	785	875	90	11

Source: Statistics Canada. Income distributions by size in Canada, 1995, Catalogue no. 13-207-XPB.

During the eight-year war on the deficit, 456,000 more children and 963,000 more adults in Canada have been plunged into poverty. What kind of "victory" over the deficit can be claimed when one in every five of our children have been subjcted to such cruel and debilitating treatment during their formative years? We know that poverty jeopardizes poor children's health status, their ability to do well in school, their life expectancy, their chances of reaching their full potential and becoming contributing members of society. What a Pyrrhic victory when we consider all the anxiety, fear, insecurity, grief and stress borne by parents and individuals in the daily struggle a life of poverty entails.

ASSAULT ON THE PUBLIC SECTOR AND NATIONAL SOCIAL PROGRAMS

Governments at all levels fought the deficit war, in part, by laying off staff, and by privatizing and contracting-out public sector work. Between 1992 and 1996, 121,000 public sector jobs were eliminated in

Canada, with serious implications for those affected, and indeed for the economy as a whole. Public sector jobs have traditionally been a good source of secure and well-paid jobs, particularly for women. Laid-off public sector workers who manage to find jobs in the private sector are quite likely to be employed in small or medium-size businesses or to be self-employed, which usually means lower wages and fewer benefits. Rather than good public sector jobs supporting economic growth and jobs in communities, the loss of these jobs inevitably undermines local economies.

The war on the deficit supplied the excuse for an assault on the national social programs and public services which had helped to raise living standards and promote social cohesion. Federal cuts to health care, education, social assistance, public pensions, unemployment insurance, and other public services have started to erode the social and economic well-being of Canadians. Individuals, families and communities have been forced by massive government cuts in program funding to shoulder a heavier burden of social responsibilities. This burden rests most heavily on women, who tend to be care-givers, and has increased their unpaid work.

Our national system of public health care has been put at risk by severe funding cuts and by the CHST legislation currently in place for future federal transfers. As the federal share of health funding declines in proportion to total health care spending, provincial and territorial governments will feel little compulsion to abide by the national standards in the *Canada Health Act*. Without corrective action, it seems nothing will prevent a complete privatization of the system.

Privatization is already well advanced in some parts of Canada. At least one province seems determined to permit a two-tier health system based on the ability to pay. Giant U.S. health care corporations are preparing to carve out a huge chunk of public health care dollars. The insidious free trade agreements—- NAFTA, the AIT, and the MAI—-are paving the way for the eventual looting of our public health care system.

The federal government has maintained the 20-year monopoly patent protection for the manufacturers of brand-name pharmaceutical drugs, claiming that our international trade agreements have tied its hands. Evidence to the contrary has been ignored. Being at the mercy of the brand-name pharmaceutical industry will perpetuate skyrocketing costs for new drugs, and this alone has the potential to destroy Canada's public system of health care.

The federal government has also put its war on the deficit above the health and safety of Canadians by eliminating the Drug Directorate branch of Health Canada. This branch, through its independent scientific research, assured Canadians that the drugs being prescribed for them were safe and met the claims of pharmaceutical manufacturers. The government has not seen fit to reinstate these labs, effectively allowing the brand-name pharmaceutical industry to regulate itself.

The federal government has also abandoned any serious commitment to affordable, high quality post-secondary education. Rising tuition fees and unsustainable debt loads are fast pushing higher education beyond the hopes and dreams of many low- and middle-income Canadians. Education RRSPs and student loans are unavailable for most young people and their families who occupy the lower income strata, nor will they be helped by the one-time Millennium Scholarship Fund.

Drastic changes to the original Unemployment Insurance system have ensured that fewer and fewer unemployed workers will qualify for UI; and those who do qualify will receive lower benefits for a shorter period of time If they have the misfortune to work in seasonal employment, their benefits will be even lower. Only 40% of unemployed workers are now eligible for UI, despite having paid insurance premiums for this protection while working.

ASSAULT ON BASIC HUMAN RIGHTS

Rather than an assault on poverty in Canada, there has been an assault on the poor themselves. Just as the government made it harder to qualify for UI, so it put in place the Canada Health and Social Transfer which eliminated the federal-provincial cost-sharing agreement for social assistance. In doing so, the government has recession-proofed social assistance policy. When the next recession hits, Ottawa will not be required to share in the rising costs of welfare as unemployment inevitably rises, even though its monetary and fiscal policies may have caused the recession, as was the case in the early 1990s.

In addition, the CHST did away with all conditions for the receipt of federal funding for social assistance except the residency condition, presumably so that the poor can be free to roam the country looking for those low-wage jobs they have been led to believe might lift them out of poverty. Contravening crucial international laws and covenants which Canada has signed, including the Declaration of Human Rights and the International Covenant on Social, Economic and Cultural Rights, the federal government has legitimized workfare through the CHST, with especially harmful effects on women. Workfare increases women's vulnerability to sexual harassment and exploitation, while reducing the time they have available to care for their children.

In fact, the CHST has disenfranchised all Canadians from the basic social and economic rights of citizenship guaranteed in international law. It is nothing short of a complete rejection of the fundamental principles of social and economic justice.

Obviously, a concern for human rights was not going to be allowed to detract from the war on the deficit and the attacks on social programs, on workers, and on the poor. On the contrary, self-serving politicians had the gall to blame the poor and the unemployed for their own plight.

Homelessness is on the rise. At least 25% of Canadians who rent accommodation pay unaffordable rents, as do 40% of single-mother families. More than a million Canadians are in need of core housing. By the government's own estimates, as long ago as 1992 half of the housing units on Aboriginal reserves were deemed unsuitable for human habitation, and drastic shortages continue to exist.

In response to the crucial need for adequate, affordable housing, the federal government cut funding for new non-profit and co-operative housing in both 1992 and 1993. In 1996, it abandoned its financial responsibility in this area by offloading the administration of federally-sponsored social housing. As the current agreements run out, so do federal funds.

CHANGING THE NATURE OF THE CANADIAN FEDERATION

The massive restructuring of these programs and services has profoundly restructured the very nature of the social union itself. The central role of the federal government to promote equality and protect the basic rights of citizenship has been all but abandoned.

As the federal government offloaded its financial responsibility for health care, education, social assistance, and labour market programs onto the provinces and territories, they in turn understandably demanded greater control over these programs, on the grounds that the one who pays the piper should call the tune. Their demands include severe limits on federal spending power, the development of "guiding principles" for social programs rather than conditions or national standards, an end to the unilateral federal enforcement of national standards, particularly the standards in the *Canada Health Act*, and a clearer separation of constitutional responsibilities for these programs.

The core principle underlying the provincial/territorial blueprint is that the federal government ought to be just one of 13 equal partners around the constitutional negotiating table. In short, the decentralization of social and labour market programs means a decentralization of the federal role in these areas.

In the 1997 Speech to the Throne, the federal government capitulated to that view, promising that it would not launch new social programs in the area of provincial jurisdiction without the consent of the provinces. The last First Ministers' Conference solidified this federal commitment.

This fundamental change in the federation is taking place without full public debate or understanding of the implications, even though it likely means that the federal government will never again be able to initiate a national program on its own or build on a provincial initiative without the consent of all or most of the provinces and territories. If this had been the case in the past, we would not have Medicare today.

Moreover, turning away from national standards enforceable by the federal government inevitably means that Canadians will no longer have access to reasonably comparable programs and public services, no matter where they happen to live in the country. While this goal had not yet been fully met, it remained until recently a key objective worth pursuing. Its loss clearly precipitates a downward spiral of social protection in the key areas of health care, education, and social assistance.

CHANGING CANADIAN VALUES — TURNING AWAY FROM EQUALITY

There has been a sea-change in the core values which underpin Canadian social policy. This is not to say that the thinking underlying social policy at the government level has ever been truly progressive. It hasn't; but Canadians have come to believe that national social programs embody the core values of caring, sharing, and collective responsibility which help to advance public policy in the direction of greater equality.

It is certainly true that, over the years, government transfers, social programs and public services have helped cushion the harmful effects of low incomes and deprivation on many Canadians. Unquestionably, our levels of poverty would have been much higher in the absence of Medicare, the OAS and CPP, and Unemployment Insurance.

But the direction of social policy since it has come under the influence of the Department of Finance undermines these important programs and the values which they embody. In cutting social programs, allegedly to cut the deficit, the following claims have been widely publicized. They sum up the Chrétien government's approach to social policy:

- income support ought to be targeted to the poorest of the poor;
- each individual is responsible for his or her economic and social circumstances, rather than the state being responsible for the collective well-being of society;
- the individual should be "free" to purchase the quality of health care he or she can afford;
- immigrants and refugees reduce job opportunities for "real" Canadians, as do equity programs;
- social programs such as UI and social assistance are disincentives to work;

- those who are unemployed or dependent on social assistance are somehow intrinsically less worthy than those who are not;
- the voluntary sector and charitable organizations are better suited than governments to assist the victims of the corporate agenda; and
- no one on welfare should have more income than the lowest wage provided by the private sector.

This approach to social policy—the current federal government approach—is based on the belief that citizens have no right to economic and social security outside the marketplace. In other words, basic human rights flow from participation in the market, not from rights of citizenship, and thus cannot be universally applied. From this twisted viewpoint, the dismantling of the welfare state has not been solely or even primarily motivated by a desire to reduce the federal debt, but by a desire to implement a market-driven neo-liberal ideology. It has also fostered the distorted view that people in need of social assistance are lazy parasites, when in fact the great majority of them—especially single mothers bringing up children—are making very important contributions to society.

Social policy "reform" by the Chrétien-Martin regime has been a deliberate attempt to shrink the social wage; to promote a greater dependence on the marketplace for income; to divide the poor into "deserving" and "undeserving" categories; and to use high interest rates, high unemployment and low unemployment insurance benefits—and the hunger, misery and insecurity these measures spawn—to force workers into lower-paid jobs or workfare.

This combination of reduced social protection, a minimal role for government in the economy, and a lack of commitment to full employment makes for a bleak future indeed. It is a future blighted by even more poverty and inequality. It is the exact opposite of redistributing income and wealth as a means of achieving social and economic justice. Government rhetoric about the arrival of good times to come, now that the "fundamentals" are right, rings hollow when it is obvious that no real effort is going to be made to address the failure of the labour market to meet the economic and social needs of a growing number of Canadian families and individuals.

THE AFB APPROACH

Public debate now centres on what to do with the "fiscal dividend," in the form of expected budgetary surpluses. The fundamental issue here is tax cuts vs. increased spending. Those on the right want the surplus to be used to cut taxes. The AFB recognizes that the main focus must be on restoring investment in the tattered social fabric of the country and on measures that will improve the social and economic well-being of the majority of Canadians through a more equitable distribution of income and wealth.

This is the framework within which the 1998 Alternative Federal Budget has been developed.

The AFB is committed to a public policy of "zero tolerance for poverty." Poverty reduction targets will be put in place to eliminate poverty in Canada within 10 years. In accordance with the United Nations World Summit for Social Development, a plan of action will be introduced to meet these poverty reduction targets. This plan will include the AFB job creation program, strategic investments in key national social programs, and progressive tax reforms.

An Anti-Poverty Commissioner will be appointed and directed to make an annual report to Parliament on the government's anti-poverty initiatives, as well as its success or failure in meeting the poverty reduction targets. In accordance with the United Nations Fourth World Conference on Women in Beijing, the Anti-Poverty Commissioner will be authorized to require the undertaking of gender impact analysis studies on public policies and programs, and to have these studies released into the public domain.

To fulfill Canada's international commitments contained in key United Nations declarations and covenants to which we are signatory, the following specific measures will be taken:

- The National Income Support Fund will be cost-shared and national standards will be put in place founded on the principle that the right to adequate income is a basic human right. Key among these standards are a prohibition against workfare, a universal right to appeal the denial of assistance, and levels of assistance tied to the cost of living across the country.
- Targets will be set to increase women's representation in government agencies, committees, public administrative entities, the judiciary, and other bodies. As a first step, an inventory will be taken to determine the current representation of women.
- To facilitate women's access to the political process, a special Women In Democracy Fund will be established to provide training and resources to enable more women to participate in the democratic governance of the country. (The 1998 AFB supports the broad-based National Women's Group Campaign called the Fair Share Funding Campaign with the motto "A twooney for every woman and girl child in Canada" to promote women's participation in the democratic process. In addition, the Equity Participation Fund begun last year will provide a stable source of funding which will contribute to this goal and to the goal of giving marginalized Canadians a voice in the po-

litical process, and to advocacy groups which raise public awareness on important equity issues.)

- Funding will be restored to women's centres, shelters and advocacy groups, and services for combatting violence against women.
- Increased funds will be given to the Canadian Human Rights Commission, and its mandate will be changed from a complaints-based system to one based on the acknowledgment of systemic discrimination. In this way, the principle that all human rights are universal, indivisible, interdependent, and interrelated will be recognized.
- With the participation of women's groups, social advocacy groups, and the labour movement, a co-ordinated plan will be developed in accordance with the Beijing Platform of Action. This plan will include recognizing the importance of women's unpaid work and tracking such unpaid work over time.
- In recognition of the role Canada played in developing an international commitment to recognize housing as a right during the UN Habitat II conference, a plan will be developed to restore the federal presence in ensuring access to affordable and adequate housing. Key elements include the Housing Investment Fund, a National Housing Retrofit Fund, and measures to increase the stock of non-profit and co-operative housing. Housing advocates will participate in the development of this plan.
- The pay equity settlement owed to federal public employees is a priority in this budget.

As previously mentioned, the slash-and-burn mentality has led to a backlash of increased racism and blatant discrimination for many Canadians, particularly for gays and lesbians. New initiatives will be undertaken to extend human rights to these Canadians. A Centre of Excellence for Gay and Lesbian Issues will be established, with appropriate funding, and all federal laws and statutes which discriminate against same-sex couples will be amended to allow equal access to government benefits for gays and lesbians. A Centre of Excellence for the Contribution of Immigrants to Canada will also be established.

Other AFB National Social Investment Funds remain in place for health, education, child care, post-secondary education, and retirement income. The National Advanced Maintenance Child Support will continue. The 1998 AFB continues to focus on investing in the social needs of all Canadians and their families. As such, the 1998 AFB contains measures directed to issues of concern to Aboriginal Canadians, those with disabilities, and new Canadians, both immigrants and refugees. In light of the ongoing and even increasing concerns about AIDS, additional funding will be given to the National AIDS Strategy.

After lagging behind the provinces and territories, the federal government increased the federal minimum wage to equal the prevailing minimum wage in the provinces where its workforce resides. This was a step in recognizing that the federal minimum wage was ridiculously inadequate. However, the federal government needs to take more of a leadership role based on the principle that income from work, particularly full-time work, ought to provide a living wage, i.e. a wage above the poverty line. The AFB will establish a Task Force on the Minimum Wage in Canada with a mandate to assess the impact of minimum wages on jobs, competitiveness and the contribution of the minimum wage to living standards. This Task Force will also examine the U.S. experience with workfare and its impact on public sector jobs, poverty, and minimum wages.

Finally, as noted in the section Ottawa, Quebec and the Provinces, we recognize that Quebec (but not the other provinces) has primacy in its jurisdiction over social policies and the right to opt out of joint federal-provincial programs in this area; while, for the rest of Canada, we recognize joint federal-provincial responsibilities, with a federal leadership role, in funding social programs as well as setting and enforcing national standards.

Poverty

The Economic Council of Canada has defined poverty as "insufficient access to certain goods, services, and conditions of life which are available to everyone else, and have come to be accepted as basic to a decent, minimum standard of living."

Although it has been 30 years since the Croll Senate Committee's comprehensive plan for eliminating poverty in Canada, the numbers of unemployed and working poor remain unacceptably high. By 1996, poverty rates had risen to 17.9%, with 5,294,000 people living below Statistics Canada's Low Income Cut-Off lines.

The National Council of Welfare estimated that the poverty gap—the increased income necessary to reach an acceptable living standard for all—had grown to $16.3 billion.

A huge problem clearly remains, and these numbers alone can only hint at the appalling extent of human misery that continues to blight Canadian society.

Historically, poverty has risen and fallen with the economic cycle and the rate of unemployment, but, despite the recent economic "recovery," the number of low-income Canadians continues to increase. In 1993, the United Nations Committee on Economic, Social, and Cultural Rights declared that, despite Canada's immense wealth, "there seems to have been no measurable progress in alleviating poverty over the last decade, nor in alleviating the severity of poverty among a number of vulnerable groups."

Government policies that have kept wages low and unemployment high, while creating more income and wealth for a privileged minority, have increased inequality in our society. Macroeconomic policy leading to private sector restructuring and layoffs, massive cuts to social spending, and widespread layoffs in the public sector, have had the combined effect of increasing the number of people in need, while depriving them of adequate support.

CUTS TO SOCIAL ASSISTANCE

On April 1, 1996, the Canada Health and Social Transfer (CHST) replaced the Canada Assistance Plan, and placed social assistance funding in the same envelope with health care and post-secondary education. Lost with the CAP were requirements that the provinces and territories give assistance to all those "in need," with a guaranteed right of appeal.

While condensing funding into a single block, the federal government also reduced the total amount provided. Federal cash transfers fell 33.5% between 1993-94 and 1997-98, from $18.8 billion to $12.5 billion. Unemployment benefits have been cut as well, and the proportion of unemployed eligible for support has fallen from 89% in 1990 to less than 50% in 1996. Amid a culture of "welfare bashing" and "scapegoating" of the poor, the provinces have used the flexibility afforded by block funding to cut their welfare rates even more drastically than health care and education.

In violation of the UN Covenant on Economic, Social, and Cultural Rights, social assistance benefits have been reduced all across Canada—by a shocking 21% in Ontario and 17% in Alberta. Even more of the cutting, however, has been done by limiting eligibility for social assistance and restricting recipients' power to appeal, in order to decrease caseloads.

Special needs benefits, dental care, free prescriptions, and other support services have also been reduced or eliminated. And most disturbingly, regressive measures that treat recipients like criminals, such as workfare and fingerprinting, are becoming more prevalent.

A FEDERAL RESPONSIBILITY

We must reverse the trend toward increased poverty and the abandonment of those in need. Ensuring that everyone has the resources for adequate living, and for raising healthy children, is fundamental to the health and sustainability of our communities. At a time of dramatic societal transition, the reorganization of the family, a shift in the labour market to part-time and casual work, and rapid technological change, government has a responsibility to support those disadvantaged by such changes, and help build a new sense of community.

Our social programs were designed to create a national sense of shared social citizenship, and are part of our identity as Canadians. It is essential that the federal government play a strong role in maintaining social programs and setting national standards, instead of implementing fiscal and monetary policies that perpetuate unemployment and increase the demands on social assistance. It is unreasonable for the federal government to expect the provinces and territories to bear all of the costs of its anti-inflation and anti-deficit policies.

ECONOMIC AND SOCIAL DEVELOPMENT

Income support provides citizens with the minimum needed for sustainable living in a modern society. But, in addition to financial support, programs and services are required to help disadvantaged Canadians participate fully in society. An income support fund must be accompanied by adequate social services and child care, comprehensive (un)employment insurance, and funding for advocacy. Ensuring there is ample affordable housing, preserving universal publicly-funded health care, and improving access to education are all essential parts of the AF's blueprint for a healthy society.

Poverty cannot be eliminated solely by economic growth, since growth benefits only those who can take advantage of it. Economic policy must be guided by social goals; it must create new opportunities for those in disadvantaged regions, and promote sustainable development. Community economic development that produces local jobs and services local needs remains a priority, particularly support for public and not-for-profit sectors.

The AFB's labour measures and job-oriented fiscal policy will improve the economic circumstances of the poor by facilitating the creation of meaningful, well-paying jobs. Clearly, the minimum wage is too low, with 25% of poor children having a parent with a full-time job that does not provide an adequate income. A reasonable minimum wage, lower unemployment, social development, and adequate income support are crucial to eliminating poverty—an approach that combines compassion, social justice, and common sense.

THE NECESSITY OF INCOME SUPPORT

Income support should not be viewed as charity. It is a way for society to provide people with the minimum income needed for sustainable living in a modern society. In addition to financial support, programs and services are required to help people regain their self-sufficiency. This is the modern version of the informal family and community support systems that existed in the past, but that could never guarantee support for all.

The motivation for accepting responsibility for the disadvantaged must come from a combination of compassion, social justice and common sense. Income support helps those in need, but it also helps all of us to live together in peace and mutual respect.

THE NATIONAL INCOME SUPPORT FUND

The Alternative Federal Budget proposes that the federal and provincial governments jointly develop a National Income Support Fund, which would constitute a "floor" of financial support below which no Canadian can fall.

Part of the responsibility of governments is to redistribute some income from the more fortunate citizens to the less fortunate. This helps to create a more stable economy and promotes prosperity that is more sustainable.

The Alternative Federal Budget recognizes that the well-being of all Canadians is important to the health and prosperity of our country. In order to ensure such universal well-being, the federal, provincial and municipal governments must establish a common set of principles and standards to govern the delivery of income support and the programs and services that accompany it.

The following minimum standards will be established as a requirement for the federal portion of the fund:

1. Funding, based on real costs of daily living, must be determined through an open, public process that includes low-income persons, and is regularly updated.
2. All who declare they are in need are guaranteed a fair assessment and adequate support.
3. Assistance must be needs-based only, and not discriminate on the basis of employability, age, type of disability, or other factors.
4. There must be an appeal system with client representation, due process, and reasonable timetables.
5. No residency requirements are permitted, and the originating province will pay the first year's support after a client moves away.
6. There can be no work or training requirements for obtaining assistance, and it cannot be subject to repayment or garnishing of assets.
7. Extraordinary measures not required of other citizens (e.g., fingerprinting) cannot be imposed.
8. Recipients must be allowed to retain their homes and a reasonable amount of assets and earned income.

Income support will be provided at two levels. Level 1 establishes the income floor, which would provide a base of financial support to both families and individuals in need at an amount equal to no less than 60% of Statistics Canada's Low-Income Cut-Offs (LICOs) for the 1998-99 fiscal year. The welfare rates in some provinces, of course, already exceed this minimum level, and should, if anything, be raised even higher. But in other provinces—New Brunswick, for example—welfare payments are as low as 25% of StatsCan poverty levels, so for them a 60% floor would be a substantial improvement. Over five years, the floor will be raised to 75% of the LICOs.

Level 2 of income support will provide additional funding to restore the financing of social services that have been reduced or eliminated by the provinces and to meet the special needs of families and individuals, such as the extra costs due to disability or ill health. The second level of income support will also be used to help fund the provision of related services such as counselling, relocation assistance, emergency funds, etc. A standard schedule of available services for those persons who must use the Income Support Fund would be negotiated.

FUNDING RESPONSIBILITIES

In 1998-99, the federal and provincial governments will enter into negotiations with a view to establishing the fiscal arrangements for Levels 1 and 2 of the Income Support Fund. It is recommended that both levels be cost-shared, with the appropriate percentages to be determined, so as to ensure that there is no off-loading of responsibilities between governments. The Fund will therefore be counter-cyclical. There will be a phasing-in of compensation for the three provinces which had CAP transfers "capped" before the introduction of the CHST.

This year, in response to reductions in provincial welfare rates across the country (particularly for single employables) as a result of the end of the Canada Assistance Plan and the introduction of the CHST, the AFB will increase funding by the federal government for direct income support.

The additional money will be provided to all provinces that agree to the development of the Income Support Fund, adhere to its standards, and implement the guaranteed first level of support at 60% of the LICOs (as well as a commitment to increase the floor to 75% of the LICOs within five years). No additional cuts to welfare rates can be made, and the extra dollars must be allocated to those persons whose incomes are currently below 60% of LICOs.

The Income Support Fund will not be sustainable over time unless there is a concomitant push to raise minimum wage rates in all of the provinces. The AFB strongly urges the provinces to take this progressive step, and in the meantime raises the minimum wage in all sectors and industries that come under the federal jurisdiction. This will deal with any real or perceived "disincentive," and ensure that jobs are available at living wages so as to reduce the need for accessing the Income Support Fund.

The National Income Support Fund will be implemented by using a multi-year strategy to include increases to the first level of funding, as well as renegotiating the second level of funding on a five-year basis, after evaluation of the outcomes.

The process of designing and developing an income support program must include the participation of people who are currently receiving income support.

Accountability will be an important feature of the National Income Support Fund. Full disclosure of the use of all funds will be required, and must be done in such a way as to ensure that the confidentiality of the Fund's recipients is not compromised.

The National Income Support Fund will be integrated with other components of the Alternative Federal Budget, such as Child Care, the Enhanced Child Benefit, Employment Creation, and Training and Post-Secondary Education.

THE CHILD BENEFIT

The AFB is committed to raising all persons out of poverty. Unfortunately, the extent of the poverty problem in Canada is such that it would take a number of years before the AFB, even implemented in its entirety, would raise all persons above the poverty line.

Given that reality, and given the fact that the needs of a growing number of poor and modest-income families with children are going unmet, the AFB is proposing that an enhanced Child Benefit be implemented to provide direct and immediate relief to families with children.

The design of such a Child Benefit is critical, since it could be misused as a tool to ensure that parents have little choice but to be forced into low-wage work. Wage supplementation for poor parents with children can become such a tool.

Following is a list of conditions that will be respected in the development of an appropriate Child Benefit:

- Any new program must recognize the important contribution made by parents to society as a whole.
- Additional revenues will be required if we are to begin to alleviate child and family poverty; it is not possible to begin to alleviate the problem by simply "redirecting funds" from other vulnerable groups. such as the disabled, single employables, or poor families without children.
- An enhanced Child Benefit program needs to be coupled with a comprehensive strategy to raise minimum wage rates. Any new Child Benefit program must not be used as a tool to reduce alleged "work disincentives" when the real disincentive for families is the lack of

good-paying jobs.

- An enhanced Child Benefit can be considered as a down payment only; alleviating child and family poverty requires an overall strategy that would include other program areas such as housing, child care, an advanced payments system, training, post-secondary education, and job creation.
- The benefit and the eligibility threshold must be indexed to inflation.
- The benefit cannot be deducted from provincial welfare payments.
- A low-income parent with pre-school children should have the right to choose to stay at home to raise his or her children or to go out into the workplace, with the corresponding supports that are required to do so.
- The federal government must assume primary responsibility for the income security needs of families with children, just as it does for senior citizens.
- The amount of the benefit should be sufficient to have a significant impact on raising poor families out of poverty.

The enhanced child benefit will increase the current level of support being provided to children with families. The value of the support will be reduced by a proportion of family income over and above a certain threshold.

The value of the benefit will reduce to zero for higher income families, but a non-refundable tax credit will assure that all families receive public recognition for the social contribution of parenting.

The AFB supports the work Campaign 2000 has done in addressing the issue of child and family poverty and stressing the responsibility of government to alleviate this crisis.

CHILD SUPPORT ENFORCEMENT

The 1998 Alternative Federal Budget introduces a National Advance Maintenance Child Support System. This would guarantee that children and their custodial parents have the income they need under the new Child Support Guidelines announced by the federal government in its 1996 budget—without delay, frustration, and the diversion of time and energy from the challenging responsibilities of parenting.

Without adequate enforcement measures, custodial parents and children are left at the mercy of the support-paying parent for the provision of an adequate income. The existing federal family support enforcement is so weak that children and custodial parents can be left destitute for years while waiting for payments that, even if received on time, are still in many cases inadequate.

In conjunction with the enhanced Child Benefit and other anti-poverty measures contained in the 1998 Alternative Federal Budget, the Advance Maintenance Child Support System (AMCSS) ensures that custodial parents have the income necessary for child support.

The AMCSS will be national in scope, and administered by a national agency, complementing reforms already under-way for a National Tax Collection Agency. The federal government will pay out the required child support payments, using the same administrative mechanisms as those used for the comprehensive child benefits.

The new federal-provincial taxation agency will be the vehicle to recover the payments from non-custodial parents anywhere in Canada. This would ensure much higher compliance rates and remove much of the uncertainty from custodial parents for income security.

Such an Advance Maintenance Child Support System will not reduce eligibility for other income assistance programs.

The 1998 AFB includes the start-up funding for this approach and challenges the federal government to take responsibility for the well-being of children and families, instead of waiting to pay the enormous social costs of neglect later.

Housing

More than two years ago, at the United Nations Conference on Human Settlement (Habitat II) in Istanbul, Canada committed itself to continued recognition of safe, adequate housing as a distinct, separate and legal human right, and agreed to work toward the full implementation of that right. Although Canada played a pivotal role in developing the strongly-worded Habitat Agenda, Canada—unlike most other industrialized nations—still has no national action plan to implement it.

Canada is a paradox: economic comfort enjoyed by most Canadians in contrast to the misery and economic deprivation reserved for a growing part of the population. After the Second World War, it was taken for granted that the national government was committed to providing housing for all Canadians. In that context, the Canada Mortgage and Housing Corporation (CMHC) was the cornerstone of that policy through its various private and public sector strategies.

Housing needs in Canada are growing. In 1991, according to the CMHC, nearly 1.2 million low-income Canadians (one in eight households) were in core housing need—paying more than 30% of their gross household income for shelter, or living in homes that were otherwise inadequate or unsuitable. Today, although official figures have not yet been released, the number is undoubtedly much higher.

At least one in four renter households and 40% of mother-led lone-parent households are in housing need. Seniors are also disproportionately represented among those paying unaffordable rents.

Aboriginal housing requires a major infusion of resources. In 1992, according to the government's own estimates, only half the 70,000 housing units on Indian reserves were adequate or suitable for human habitation. According to the CMHC, in 1991, over 63,000 Aboriginal households living in areas off-reserve were in core housing need. The high level of crowding in remote and northern Aboriginal housing off-reserve reflects extreme housing shortages in these parts of the country.

In urban areas, the high costs of shelter make housing unaffordable for a great many. To meet the current and anticipated needs of Canada's Aboriginal peoples, at least 9,000 units per year should be built or renovated.

The rise of homelessness is also rapidly reaching crisis proportions, as evidenced by the sharp increase in the number of people using or seeking shelters. The face of the homeless is also changing as families with inadequate incomes or shrinking social assistance payments find they can no longer meet their rental payments. Young people unable to find work are also found in growing numbers in emergency shelters. Unofficial estimates now put the number of homeless in Canada at between 130,000 and 250,000.

How did our housing situation deteriorate so badly? Canada's social housing programs used to be the envy of the developed world because they effectively harnessed local communities to meet the need for decent and affordable housing. Within the framework of an adequate social safety net, such housing was seen as essential to maintain the attractiveness and vitality of our urban centres, for living and learning, and for investment.

Countries that do not provide adequate housing for those with low incomes quickly find themselves with rapidly growing concentrations of poverty in their cities, along with increased homelessness and hunger. Low-cost housing either disappears or deteriorates. In the end, the major cities in these countries become less appealing places in which to work and live, or to invest in.

Today, Canada clearly faces such a social breakdown. And only the federal government has the resources—and the experience—to enact the housing policies needed to avoid that grim fate.

A Renewed Federal Role

Within the context of a renewed federation, the Alternative Federal Budget supports three broad policy initiatives. They reflect a continued federal presence in enabling communities and individuals to care for themselves through the strengthening of the non-profit and cooperative housing sectors. They reflect a clear national interest in protecting and strengthening Canada's affordable housing resources. And, just as importantly, they reflect a sense of "nationhood"—that Canadians should have equal access to decent and affordable housing, no matter where they live.

PROTECTING OUR INVESTMENT

First and foremost, existing non-profit housing assets must be protected. No matter how federal housing programs are administered in the future, the AFB commits the federal government to guarantee current expenditure levels for existing non-profit and cooperative developments, so that lower-income families will not risk losing their homes or housing-related subsidy as a result of administrative change. Moreover, the AFB ensures that any social housing which is sold will be replaced, at least unit for unit, with new, well-located, non-profit housing.

The AFB proposes a system of sectoral management in which non-profit and cooperative non-governmental organizations administer federal non-profit and cooperative housing programs. Both the *Canadian Housing and Renewal Association* and the *Cooperative Housing Federation of Canada* have presented detailed proposals on sector-based administration. Significant cost savings could be achieved in administration and operation, while retaining full accountability to Canada's taxpayers.

LINKING SOCIAL AND ECONOMIC POLICY

Secondly, the linkages between housing and health, immigration, child poverty, children's performance at school, social and family disruption, labour market mobility, public security, and corporate investment in Canada warrant the adoption of joint strategies to consider housing concurrently with social and economic development strategies. Housing is a key determinant to how much money has to be spent in Canada's health care system.

Nationally, approximately 35% of total social assistance funding—$5.2 billion—is now spent to cover the housing costs of social assistance recipients. It is not clear that this money is being effectively spent or that welfare recipients and the governments supporting them are getting good value for dollars spent. Too often, the Canadian housing marketplace provides very little choice to low-income households. Too many now must: spend large amounts of their income for shelter—money needed for food, clothing and other necessities; live in crowded conditions; choose shelter which is in poor condition; and live in places far away from work, shopping and services.

Leadership in coordinating joint strategies—an essential role for the federal government—should include establishing national standards to reduce regional housing disparities and, in the end, improve the housing conditions that many Canadians face.

The CMHC's pan-Canadian Direct Lending Program, which taps national economies of scale to provide lower-cost capital (and hence saves money on housing charge subsidies) should continue.

RESEARCH AND INFORMATION SHARING

A renewed federal role also lies in research and information sharing. The CMHC's research programs have played a critical role in our ability to learn from one another, and these programs should be substantially strengthened.

There should be a strengthened strategy to communicate innovative housing ideas across the country. The strategy should address a method and mechanism for information development, information clearing and exchange. Such a network would go a long way to levering the involvement of many more players in the affordable housing area, particularly at the community level.

A National Information Centre for Housing Alternatives should be established. Such a centre is needed now that the transfer of responsibility to address the administration of social housing has taken place in some jurisdictions and thus preventing the CMHC from playing the same role at the community level as it has in the past, given that many of its local offices have been closed.

A NATIONAL PLAN FOR AFFORDABLE HOUSING

To ensure that many more Canadians can be affordably housed, the AFB calls for renewed programs to build and maintain alternative non-profit and cooperative housing. Clearly, Canada's affordable housing needs cannot be met without senior governments playing a significant role. A reasonable annual target is the creation of 15,000 new affordable units developed through the non-profit and cooperative sectors.

The AFB proposes the creation of a non-profit housing foundation with:

- a mandate to encourage and support the development of affordable housing; and
- a dedicated non-profit housing fund to provide repayable loans or equity contributions to eligible non-profit and cooperative sponsor groups.

It will require an annual federal government grant to be funded by dividends produced through the commercialization of the mortgage insurance fund, savings in the existing minister's social housing budget, along with a new annual commitment of approximately $300 million. The foundation will create 12,000 to 18,000 new affordable housing units yearly, in partnership with community groups, which would receive support from the private sector, municipalities, provinces and territories.

In this way, the foundation will lever equity contributions and other resources from provinces, municipalities, the private sector, churches, service clubs, seniors' organizations, existing non-profit and cooperative housing groups, and other community groups.

Research has clearly demonstrated that, in the long term, these enabling strategies will be much less expensive than private sector rent supplements, and will bring significant equity to the table to stretch housing dollars further.

Second, a National Housing Retrofit Program will be established to ensure that important programs such as the residential rehabilitation assistance program can continue to revitalize communities and upgrade substandard housing. This program will initially be targeted to non-profit and co-operative projects in need of renewal, with $50 million per year to be spent on this program.

There are welcome employment spin-offs from these initiatives. Each 10 new housing starts generates 22 person- years of direct and indirect employment and induces the generation of a further six person-years; $1 million spent on renovation creates 21 person-years of employment through direct and indirect means and a further six through the induced multiplier effects on the economy.

Rental housing starts have been declining steadily since 1987 and are now insignificant, despite a growing need for such accommodation. This decline is largely due to the cancellation of social housing programs, coupled with almost negligible starts is the deteriorating condition of the rental stock, much of which was built in the 1960s and '70s.

By stimulating the production of new rental stock, these programs will provide housing to Canadians who need it, create a significant number of well-paying jobs, and help boost our stagnant rental-unit construction industry.

Child Care

Today in Canada, there is a broad consensus among experts in child development, social policy-makers and practitioners that public investment in children during their early years is vital to our collective future. This consensus enjoys firm public support for governments to initiate measures designed to provide health and social assurances for children. Even the federal Liberals' Speech From the Throne argued on September 23, 1997 that "a country that invests in its children successfully will have a better future."

In spite of this consensus on the importance of early childhood, federal cuts to child care spending over the last four years have *de-invested* millions of dollars from a sector that is a cornerstone for securing a social policy infrastructure in Canada. A country with good child care policies can fulfill multiple social and economic goals. Many of these goals have been recommended by various government task forces and studies, including most recently the National Forum on Health and the National Crime Prevention Council. Today there is agreement on three basic points:

- Healthy development in the early years sets the stage for readiness to learn, lifelong good health and well-being, and competent citizenship.
- Early childhood education occurs during the stage of life when the learning curve is highest. Therefore, investment at this time is likely to yield the greatest returns.
- Multiple social goals can be attained through sound childhood policies, including aiding parents in labour force attachment, alleviating some of the effects of child poverty, furthering women's equality, and fostering healthy child development.

Across the country, child care and other services for children share the common features of shrinking resources, insecure political support, and uneven access for parents. Since the Canada Health and Social Transfer was implemented on April 1, 1996, billions of dollars in federal transfer payments for services have been withdrawn. For children, the "new social union" has meant considerable disruption in the provision *of* child care services to their families, as well as increasing disparity in families' access to child care services.

Overall federal spending on child care services suffered a 33% cut ($105 million) over the last four years. In Ontario, omnibus legislation is *expected to* have dramatic negative effects on the province's education system and social services. Yet there is at least one bright spot; in Quebec there has been a policy commitment to children and families through a comprehensive strategy that includes changes to family allowances, paid parental leave, child care, and kindergarten. It is expected that these changes will phase in a universal fee of $5 per day, beginning with $4 to six-year-old children.

We also have a general agreement that income supports alone will nor suffice to meet all the needs of families with children. The major commitment to children in the 1997 federal budget was a tax measure in the form of the National Child Benefit; the promised next step was accompanying support services. The impetus to add building blocks to the National Child Benefit System will likely result in the design of a National Children's Agenda. It is vital that the N.C.A., currently under development at both federal and provincial levels of government, address the multiple needs of all children and their families today. Highly targeted measures will only serve to marginalize programs and possibly stigmatize children living in low-income families. This agenda should be designed to realize the following goals:

Maximize public investment: By comparison to other industrialized countries that have enacted early childhood policies as matters of national importance, Canada lags behind. Although our public spending on children's services in Canada adds up to billions of dollars annually, it will not produce the highest yields attainable without an integrated policy framework.

Integrate programs: The existing patchwork of policies for children is linked to the ways we have compartmentalized our knowledge of the early years. This has produced targeted and fragmented policies that threaten to marginalize children considered "at-risk" or living in low-income families. A comprehensive framework of early childhood education and care will help to assure that both the educational needs of children and their parents' access to family supports such as high-quality child care will be realized more evenly across Canada.

National principles: This comprehensive policy framework will succeed if it is based on principles similar to those in the Canada Health Act:

universal, affordable and available); comprehensive (a variety of service models planned at the community level); high quality (well-regulated and publicly-funded); and accountable (not for profit).

There is a consensus among experts on child development, social policy analysts, many politicians, and community advocates that income supports alone will not result in positive outcomes for children in Canada. It is fortunate that there is an abundance of research on the early years of human development that supports the argument for social investment in this stage of life.

Most recently, both the National Forum on Health and the National Crime Prevention Council found that the development of early childhood strategies was essential for the preventative and health and justice goals of these groups. In 1998, two national studies are expected to produce conclusions that reflect both the service erosions in child care and the need for coherent child care policies. Additionally, an economic analysis of the costs and benefits of high quality child *care is* expected to demonstrate that the market has failed to provide adequate child care for Canada, and only strong public investment will compensate and produce the social and economic benefits a national child care strategy can realize.

This investment need not start from scratch. There is currently a patchwork of early childhood programs with varying goals: regulated child care, kindergarten, Community Action Programs for Children (CAP-C), Aboriginal Head Start, Aboriginal and Inuit Child Care Initiative, the Child Care Expense Deduction, Dependent Care Allowances, and several others. Funding and administration of these programs crosses sectoral and jurisdictional boundaries. The National Children's Agenda holds the possibility of integrating these various measures with enhanced funding of under-funded areas in an early childhood policy framework designed to meet the needs of an industrialized nation.

As we approach the millennium, children in Canada have few assurances that governments will begin to redress the reduced transfers in social spending since the CHST was implemented. Women and children who have borne the brunt of these cuts especially require a strategy that addresses multiple social goals. The National Children's Agenda would provide an opportunity for governments in Canada to develop a Millennium Project for Canada's Children that would address the following areas:

- labour market policies, including a strategy for the creation of full-time, well-paying jobs that would recognize the importance of women's earnings for families' well being;
- income security, for example expanding and indexing the child benefit;

- healthy child development strategy, which includes comprehensive early childhood education and child care services that are accessible for all children;
- designated social investment funds;
- annual reporting on the well-being of children and youth, and a child advocate in every province and territory.

CHILD CARE INVESTMENT FUND

The Alternative Federal Budget commits the federal government to open negotiations with the provinces, territories and Aboriginal peoples to establish a cost-shared Child Care Investment Fund combining the current cost-shared expenditures with new child care funding.

This fund will require the support of a federal policy framework based on principles that ensure high-quality services for children from coast to coast, compatible with provincial/ territorial/Aboriginal jurisdictions, and the need for appropriate local strategies to provide planning and service delivery.

The Child Care Investment Fund will be based on the principles outlined above. Negotiations for the use of this fund will be based on these principles.

Post-Secondary Education

Access to post-secondary education in Canada needs to be dramatically improved. Accessibility does not simply entail increasing enrolment figures. Increased accessibility means providing resources to allow students from all socio-economic backgrounds to attend a post-secondary education institution. It also means enabling students to successfully complete their programs and to graduate without a debilitating level of debt. Access to post-secondary education is the freedom to obtain—and the ability make use of—an education, without mortgaging the student's future.

Between 1993 and 1997, the federal Liberals cut $2.29 billion from post-secondary education. During the same period tuition fees increased by 45%. Post-secondary education enrolment has declined for all students from 1994 onward, with the enrolment level of part-time students decreasing the most. Rather than choosing what is best for them, students are compelled to make education and training decisions based solely on finances.

To improve access, tuition and ancillary fees must be immediately frozen, a universally accessible national system of grants based on need must be implemented, and deferred grants must be offered for those already suffering under high debt loads.

TUITION FEES

Tuition fees increased rapidly during the recent recession, coinciding with high unemployment, stagnant household income, and diminished savings. Tuition fees rose by 62% in real terms between 1990 and 1995. In contrast, average family incomes fell by 5%, and the average employment earnings of the 20-to-24 age group working full time declined by 21%.

As a result, individuals do not have the required resources to afford a post-secondary education. Students currently spend approximately $3 billion a year in tuition fees. Average Canadian tuition fees are the third highest of all the Organization for Economic Co-operation and Development (OECD) countries, after Japan and the United States.

The following member countries of the OECD do not charge any post-secondary education user fees: Austria, Czech Republic, Denmark, Finland, France, Germany, Greece, Hungary, Iceland, Ireland, Mexico, Norway, Portugal, Sweden, the Netherlands, Turkey, and the United Kingdom. Other non-OECD countries with national economies which are weaker than Canada's also charge no up-front user fees for post-secondary education, including Cuba, Brazil, Costa Rica, and the Dominican Republic.

Canada has a long history of providing tuition-free post-secondary education to war veterans, to members of the Canadian Forces, to Status Indian peoples and Inuit people and to convicts within the prison system. The province of Newfoundland had free tuition up until the early 1960s, and, under the Employment Insurance Act, college courses were paid for the "re-training" of unemployed people.

In May 1976, Canada signed the United Nations' International Covenant on Economic, Social and Cultural Rights. Part III of Article 13, *Right to Education*, section 2(C) reads: "Higher Education shall be made equally accessible to all, on the basis of capacity, by every appropriate means, and in particular by the progressive introduction of free education." In 1995, Canada signed the Beijing Platform for Action, which commits the signatories to "provide the required budgetary resources to the educational sector".

It is high time that Canada lived up to its international commitments.

POST-SECONDARY EDUCATION ACT

The very fact that university tuition fees for Nova Scotia are double the fee level in Québec, and that student loans are not portable across provincial borders, point to the acute need for national standards for post-secondary education. A Post-Secondary Education Act would outline the responsibilities of the provincial/territorial and federal governments, establish standards, enact enforcement mechanisms, and determine funding formulas.

The need for standards and the removal of barriers is important for all Canadians, especially for those groups that have historically been under-represented, among them Aboriginal students, students from lower-income backgrounds, and rural students. The federal government would play a primary role in establishing and enforcing national standards, which would ensure a *high quality, publicly-funded and publicly-administered, fully accessible, comprehensive and portable system of post-secondary education in Canada.*

NATIONAL STANDARDS

- Public Administration: A post-secondary education system that is nationally planned and governed on a not for profit basis.
- Accessibility: Post-secondary education will be available to all individuals with the capacity and desire to be educated and/or acquire skills, irrespective of their background; post-secondary institutions will be free of all user fees. A system of national grants will be available to students in need.
- Comprehensiveness: A public education system designed to ensure a complete range of options: university, community colleges, professional and vocational training, distance education, and continuing and adult education.
- Transferability: Credits acquired will be transferable between all institutions in the country; all barriers between different types of institutions and provinces will be eliminated. This will not involve the complete standardization of curricula.
- Mobility: All residency requirements for eligibility for student grants and awards will be eliminated.

To expedite the negotiations, a National Advisory Council on Post-Secondary Education and Research will be established. This council will be headed by a federal Minister and would bring together representatives from the education and research communities, students, constituency group representatives, faculty, support staff, administration and government. The councilors will be democratically elected or selected by their peers.

The Council's mandate will be to ensure that post-secondary education, student assistance, and research continue to meet the needs of the community. The Council will ensure that the national standards do not trigger a race to the bottom, to the lowest provincial or territorial standard. The Act will not apply to Québec, but separate negotiations will be undertaken on the transfer of funds, based on the foregoing standards.

FEDERAL TRANSFER

On April 1, 1996, the federal government implemented the Canada Health and Social Transfer (CHST), which combined federal transfer payments for post-secondary education and health (EPF) with transfers for social assistance and social services provided under the Canada Assistance Plan (CAP), creating one block fund. Not only did the federal government combine the payments, but it also reduced them and eliminated almost all of the national standards found in previous programs.

In 1980, university operating funds received $6.44 in government grants for each dollar collected in tuition fees. By 1995 this amount had fallen to $2.97. The cash transfer was intended to serve as an equalizer between the "have" and "have-not" provinces. Since the CHST decreases the cash portion and leaves mostly tax points, the have-not provinces will see their ability to properly fund education, health care, and social assistance programs decrease even further.

A Post-Secondary Education Fund is needed which would be a distinct cash transfer for post-secondary education separate from health care and social assistance.

A NATIONAL SYSTEM OF GRANTS

Financial need is impeding the educational achievement of a significant number of young people, which works at cross-purposes to our national interest of economic revitalization and democratization. The average debt load for a student borrowing from the Canada Student Loans Program was $17,000 in 1996 and is predicted to climb to $25,000 by 1998.

The present formula of student loans, interest relief, loan remission and income tax credits, which was designed to accommodate massive cuts in government funding, has burdened students with ever-increasing debt loads. The funds spent on these programs would be more effective and more equitable if they were direct transfers of funds to the provinces and institutions under the Post-Secondary Education Fund and direct grants to students.

A National Grants Program will ensure that every student, regardless of geographic origin, language of study or socio-economic background, will have equal access to financial assistance. Provisions must be made to address the costs for students living on their own, students with dependents, part-time students, students with special needs, such as those with disabilities, or those residing in regions with a high cost of living.

A student aid program is ineffective if it does not address the factors which prevent students from attending school, or result in students either dropping out before completing the program, or becoming financially indebted to the government, family, and/or the financial institutions for one, two or three decades. A National System of Grants will improve access for those students most in need.

EMPLOYMENT PROGRAM FOR STUDENTS

One in five students could not find work last summer. The average summer unemployment rate for returning students between the ages of 15 to 24 for the 1997 summer months was 19.7%. The majority of students who did find jobs could only find part-time jobs. Youth (non-student) unemployment rates are consistently double that of the 'adult' rate.

Young Canadians need a post-secondary education to enter the workforce, and they need summer and part-time employment to be able to afford an education. Job creation initiatives should be linked to employment targets, towards which the federal government should work with the same fervor it did to reach its deficit reduction targets.

What students expect from job creation programs is to be employed in a meaningful work experience with decent wages. Students should not be expected to volunteer their time and knowledge in order to gain job experience. To create these kinds of jobs, the obsession with low inflation and high interest rates must be abandoned. This would provide the proper economic environment for small and medium businesses to invest, and create new jobs.

Direct hiring and direct spending by the federal government is the most beneficial and effective method of job creation. Students and youth need a comprehensive job creation strategy involving summer employment programs, in-school paid co-op placements, first jobs and internship programs.

THE LIBERAL INITIATIVES

Two of the most recent initiatives of the federal Liberals are designed more to promote themselves than to deal with the issues at hand.

The Liberals' concept for funding research, the Foundation for Innovation, is contingent on direct corporate funding. This dependency on corporate funding undermines the very idea of critical independent research. While Canada's investment in research and development has been widely criticized for being far below the international norm, developing a new bureaucracy will not solve the problem.

The existing research granting councils are capable in their administrative abilities, but they lack the funding required to promote and nurture research. Funding for the granting councils must therefore be restored.

As for the Millennium Scholarship Fund, waiting for several more years for new stipends for students does nothing to address the long-standing crisis of high student debt and is merely condemning the present generation of students to debt bondage to the banks.

The Fund will be based on merit, which does nothing to enlarge access to post-secondary education. It is not only high achievers who are in financial need. The Millennium Fund must be established immediately and provide awards based entirely on need.

What is at stake is our ability to make the right decisions as a society. Each day our world grows increasingly complex, forcing us to come to terms with rapid technological changes and often-conflicting societal values. As long as we believe in the ideal of a democratic society, we must strive to give all Canadians the education required to make sophisticated judgments about the future of our country.

Ultimately, that is what underlies our vision of a truly accessible, high-quality post-secondary education system.

Health Care

Canadian support for the five principles of the Canada Health Act remains very high, with a general belief that public payment for insured services implies both public ownership and control of those services.

The Constitution Act of 1867 assigns no explicit legislative jurisdiction over health care, reflecting the view at that time that health was an individual, not governmental, responsibility. A century later, attitudes had changed, and Canadians identified both health and access to health care as public concerns requiring national leadershipand a strong federal role.

Canadians want committed leadership and financial support from the federal government for health care. In a March 1996 public survey by Ekos Research Associates, nearly 80% of those polled said they wanted the federal government to either maintain or increase its role in the health care sector, while fully 89% said Ottawa and the provinces should work together to improve the health care system.

In the same survey, only 6% of those polled said they preferred that private business be given responsibility for health care, compared to 71% who wanted governments to retain that role.

In another survey by the same company, 84% rated equal access to health care for all Canadians and the quality of health care services as the most important aspects of the system, while 60% rejected "queue jumping" by individuals able to pay for services.

Yet the course chosen by the federal government in the last ten years is leading in the opposite direction. The private sector is expanding its role in insuring and providing services across Canada, while both federal and provincial governments are decreasing their regulatory and financial involvement. Access is being threatened as services are excluded from coverage on public health plans, forcing many low-income Canadians to pay a higher percentage of their income for health care than those with larger incomes are.

Early discharge policies in the hospital sector is contributing to a rapid growth of non-hospital services such as home and private nursing care, which in most provinces are outside the arena of insured services. Consequently, annual private sector per capita expenditures have increased from $441 in 1987 to nearly $800 in 1997. Concern about the future of the Canada Health Act—the federal legislation that creates and maintains national standards (universality, comprehensiveness, accessibility, portability, and non-profit public administration)—is rising for three main reasons:

1. Cuts to federal government financing: Since 1986, cumulative cuts to federal transfers to the provinces for health have reached almost $36 billion. With the Canada Health and Social Transfer (CHST), federal support for health continues to be eroded, and cutbacks in social program funding are exacerbating factors which influence health, including increased poverty, unemployment, homelessness, hunger and family breakdown. The cuts are imposing a heavier burden on women, who usually assume the care-giving responsibilities when people are sent home from hospital early, and professional home-care is not available.

Provinces have responded to the withdrawal of federal support for health by de-listing services and drugs from health plans, or by refusing to insure new therapies and services that enable individuals greater autonomy and self-control.

Individuals face costs in the thousands of dollars to access these services, drugs or medical devices. As Canada's population grows and ages, the need for uninsured services, from home care to home infusion therapy, will continue to rise, further increasing financial barriers to medically necessary health care.

2. Privatization: As provincial governments continue to cut health spending, there is a shift away from publicly-funded and non-profit care to for-profit payment and provision. Government spending cuts create a negative ripple effect throughout the economy: fewer services are listed on public health plans; costs are shifted to employers whose supplementary health payments are rising by 18% to 20% per year; and individuals and families, particularly those employed by small- and medium-sized businesses, are being forced to shoulder more and more of the cost for necessary medical care.

In addition, public funding cuts are leading hospitals to narrow the scope of their "core business". Uninsured outpatient services are being privatized and hospitals are contracting the corporate sector to provide a broad range of so-called non-core services, including diagnostic and nutritional services, and medical records management. To generate needed revenue, many hospitals are forming partnerships with large corporations to establish profit-making health companies.

3. Growing inequality: Privatization of both the payment and provision of health services is creating or supporting existing inequities across the country. A growing number of health care services and products threaten to become inaccessible to all except the most wealthy.

Reaffirmation of a legislative and clearly defined federal responsibility for health care, along with increased federal-provincial cooperation, are urgently needed. Federal funding must be seen first and foremost as an enabler—in the same way that federal participation in infrastructure programs, for example, enables provinces to build wharves or highways—while reinforcing the ability of the federal government to maintain national standards.

PRIVATIZATION

Overall health care costs are falling in Canada. From a peak of 10.1% of GDP in 1993, total health care spending fell to 9.1% of GDP in 1996. But this came entirely from public spending cuts. In real per capita dollars, combined public and private spending has been decreasing since 1992. Government spending on health care dropped last year for the first time since the birth of Medicare, with a concurrent increase in private spending:

- Canada now is 17th among 28 OECD member countries in public spending on health care; it is fourth in overall public and private spending.
- Total health care expenditures continue to rise, up from $72 billion in 1994/95 to $75.2 billion last year. But public expenditures dropped slightly, by 0.5% to $52.5 billion, while private-sector health care spending rose by 5.5 % to $22.6 billion. [Figures rounded out don't add up to $75.2 billion.]
- Over the last 20 years, private spending has risen from 23.6% of total spending to 30%, while the public share has fallen to only 70%. Private spending on health care now exceeds total federal government spending. Only 20% of dollars spent on health come from the federal government, compared to 42% in the mid-1970s. The public-private split is expected to reach 60%-40% by 1999.
- We are spending less on hospital care, but more on drugs. In 1975, 45% of all health dollars went to hospitals. By 1994, this had fallen to 37.3%. On the other hand, in that same period, the cost of pharmaceuticals rose from 8.8% of expenditures to 15%. Drug costs have grown at an average rate of 4.5% per year. This is mostly out-of-pocket consumer spending.

As employers and private insurers pay a growing portion of the health care bill—for drugs, long-term care and home care, among other services—control over the decisions affecting health and access to health care is shifting as well. The Canada Health Act, limited to insured physician and hospital services, is leaving the door open to profit-making corporate providers, some of which are owned by or "partnered" with private insurers.

Health care in Canada is a $75 billion market, and U.S.-based transnational corporations, armed with free trade agreements, threaten to dominate the provision of services, with the support of some provincial governments, most large employers, and large sections of organized medicine.

For-profit companies, including InterHealth Canada, MDS Inc., SmartHealth and HealthStreams Technologies, are benefiting from government participation in joint ventures, lucrative contracts with ministries of health, outsourcing arrangements with hospitals, generous tax breaks for venture capital investors, access to Medicare payments, and direct grant allocations. Fighting privatization clearly will take political will and commitment.

The AFB will:

- establish a National Health Care Fund. The Fund will provide stable, increased federal cash funding for health care, at pre-CHST levels. Starting from the 1995-96 funding level as a base, cash funding will grow with the economy, at the three-year floating average per capita GDP increase. Regional equity will be guaranteed through a national baseline per capita entitlement and cash transfers equalized according to provincial tax revenues.
- develop legislation defining and restricting public- private partnerships and joint ventures, including requirements that such arrangements must demonstrate a clearly-defined public benefit.
- establish an arms-length body to collect and publicly disclose information on the for-profit sector in health care—including financial and investment records, international activities, and contracts with public bodies—and to monitor the effects of free trade agreements, including the Agreement on Internal Trade, the FTA, NAFTA, the MAI and the World Trade Organization.

HEALTH CARE DELIVERY

Canada's health care delivery system is framed by the principles of the Canada Health Act. But, while the Act establishes that provinces must publicly-insure physician and hospital services, it does not, in fact, govern non-insured services, i.e., those services delivered by non-physicians outside of the hospital sector. Nor does it preclude public payments to for-profit providers of insured services. Consequently, an uneven patchwork of for-profit and not-for-profit delivery has emerged across the country.

The framework for publicly-insured health care in the C.H.A. is outdated and inadequate. Funding health care provision through an insurance mechanism has failed to protect and maintain Canada's non-profit system of delivery. It also undermines the creation of more affordable non-institutional alternatives to the current institutionally-based "medical model." Public insurance has failed to accommodate changing definitions of "medically necessary," and lags behind medical and scientific research regarding the treatment of chronic ailments and new therapies. Home care, rehabilitation, respite care, pharmacare, and other types of care which fall outside the scope of public insurance plans are growth sectors, as any review of demographics clearly shows.

Studies indicate that tax-based health systems typically absorb two to three percentage points less of Gross Domestic Product (GDP) than social insurance models, and tend to be more fully integrated at the community level. Canada, which has a tax-based system, is the exception to this rule: the use of insurance funding mechanisms and fee-for-service payments to physicians prevents us from maximizing the cost savings and efficiencies that characterize all other tax-based models.

Insurance funding also undermines the development of an integrated community health centre model for basic health care. The term "integrated health care delivery" has been seized upon by the U.S. corporate sector to describe a merger of payers and providers, whether those payers are workers' compensation or health insurers, and whether those providers are pharmaceutical or rehabilitation companies. In this scenario, health care integration is facilitated by the use and manipulation of information systems tracking patients' use of prescribed drugs, medical products and services, an information highway leading to restrictions on patient choices, the loss of autonomy and privacy, and the emergence of corporate-managed care.

Canadians must design an integrated system in the public sector, governed by federal criteria, with community input and control—a system that is also responsive to special needs, such as those of women, people with disabilities, and immigrants who do not speak either of the official languages. Such a system would provide a broad spectrum of primary health, social and related services available in one location in each community; cooperative multi-disciplinary teams to deliver care; an emphasis on prevention, health promotion, education services, and community development; and salaried remuneration of health care professionals.

Hospitals' staff will be trained and maintained at adequate levels to meet the needs of patients with higher levels of acuity, while community-based care-givers will have access to education and skill development to meet the needs of their patients.

The AFB will:

- establish a public review of alternative funding methods for health care in Canada, including a cost analysis based on the application of the five principles of the Canada Health Act to a publicly administered, funded and controlled non-profit system of service delivery;
- initiate a comprehensive study to determine the comparative costs of a tax-based public health insurance model and a tax-based public health delivery model;
- include public administration and management of all publicly-funded institutions, such as hospitals and community health centres, as a criteria for federal funds;
- create a Canadian Council on Health, with a focus on prevention strategies, the Council also to develop national goals for population health, monitor national health trends, and issue an annual Report Card on Health;
- ensure that health care in outpatient and non- institutional settings is publicly funded and provided;
- require that home care, meeting the needs of both the patient and the at-home care-givers, be provided as a public (as opposed to insured) service to all Canadians, and develop specific strategies to address the needs of disabled people whose standards of living can be dramatically altered by access to home care and other necessary services; and
- develop a national strategy with broad public input to ensure that the potential benefits of information technology accrue to Canadians, with measures to prohibit the use of patient records for commercial purposes. (Corporations with a vested interest in information technology, including consulting, information systems and telecommunications firms, will not participate in the process. Patients will be able to audit access to their records, while control over access will reside exclusively with individuals. Adequate firewalls will be erected to protect patient information, which will be maintained in public institutions. In addition, the strategy will recommend ways to protect Canadians from cross-border movement of patient information.)

NATIONAL DRUG STRATEGY

Canadians need a National Drug Program reinforced by other measures to prevent inequities in drug coverage between provinces, increases in drug costs resulting from the lack of a national strategy for new and existing drugs, and the maintenance of restrictive trade practices inherent in drug patent legislation.

The AFB strategy will ensure access to drugs and drug delivery mechanisms as a right under the Canada Health Act, providing standardized drug coverage to all Canadians. It also will address the underlying supply-side factors in escalating drug costs, such as excessive pharmaceutical profits.

The AFB will introduce a National Drug Plan to provide a universal drug program over the next several years. The program will be developed in consultation with provincial governments, and its cost will be offset by the following measures:

- the repeal of Bill C-91 and a review of Canada's drug patent policies. Rising drug costs are a consequence, in large part, of restrictive trade practices protecting patented drugs from fair competition by generic and alternative manufacturers. This places an extreme financial burden on individual consumers and governments. Reinstitution of compulsory licensing potentially will save $4 billion over 10 years, while abolishing patents on some pharmaceutical products, such as blood, and generic brand preference legislation may provide longer-term benefits to Canadians.
- the centralization of drug purchasing in one agency for federal and provincial governments. Bulk purchasing is widely-used by U.S. insurers and employers as a practical method to lower prescription drug costs, and is long overdue in Canada. The AFB will empower the agency to establish a lower "market value" on drugs to contribute to a reduction in drug prices, and to introduce a tendering process on bulk purchases. Limits will be placed on pharmaceutical advertising, sales promotion, and similar activities. The agency also will be able to initiateinvestigations under a strengthened Combines Act to determine whether the acquisition of pharmacy benefits managers by pharmaceutical companies violates anti- combines regulations.

The AFB also will:

- restore the budget of the Health Protection Branch to 1993/94 levels of $237 million and re-establish the drug research bureau and food safety labs whose dismantling endangers the protection and health of Canadians. The recommendations of the Krever Inquiry will be applied across the entire Branch, not just the Bureau of Biologics.
- establish a public inquiry into the failure of the Branch to uphold the Food & Drug Act.
- review and monitor relationships between hospitals, on the one hand, and Contract Research Organizations (CROs) and pharmaceutical manufacturers, on the other, to protect vulnerable patient populations from being ill-used during the drug research and experimentation process. The role of CROs in Canada will be examined to ascertain whether they are necessary, given the increased authority of the Health

Protection Branch proposed in the 1997 AFB.

- vest in the Canadian people all "patentable discoveries" by universities in receipt of public grants to develop new or improve existing drugs.

AFB AND THE NATIONAL AIDS STRATEGY

The funding for the National AIDS Strategy has remained constant throughout Phase II and is projected to be continued at roughly these levels throughout Phase III. Not only are the levels inadequate, but they are also decreasing in real terms.

The summary findings of a study on the economic impact of HIV and AIDS indicates that the combined direct and indirect costs to the Canadian economy of each case of AIDS is in excess of $750,000. It also indicates that in Britain, where a consistent emphasis has been placed on education and prevention, the prevalence of HIV infection is significantly lower.

Factoring in the capacity for community-based organizations to effectively utilize increased funding, the AFB will:

- propose an immediate increase in funding from $42.2 million for 1998 to $50 million, and thereafter annual increases of $25 million. At the end of five years, the funding for the National AIDS Strategy would be $150 million, significantly higher than current levels, but very small when compared to the potential cost to the Canadian economy of inadequate financial support.

ABORIGINAL HEALTH

When the Royal Commission on Aboriginal Peoples released its report, the federal government delayed responding for a year and a half to the Commission's recommendations. Yet the appalling inequality in the health status of Aboriginal peoples is an urgent matter within these communities: Aboriginal babies die at twice the national average, and life expectancy is seven to eight years lower for Aboriginal people than for other Canadians. Infectious and chronic illnesses are much more prevalent in the Aboriginal community, exacerbated by racism and high rates of poverty and unemployment.

The Commission recommends a new strategy for health and healing, which deals with the root causes of ill-health, provides local control over health and social services for Aboriginal people, and stresses the importance of Aboriginal culture and traditional and spiritual healing perspectives.

The AFB will commit the government to the implementation of the recommendations dealing with health in the Royal Commission on Aboriginal Peoples.

Four central recommendations are to be implemented immediately:

1. reorganization of services under Aboriginal control;
2. training for Aboriginal people to provide services;
3. adaptation of mainstream services; and
4. community infrastructure to deal with housing, clean water, and waste management.

Retirement Income

Public pension programs will undergo major changes over the next few years. The government has already implemented significant changes in the Canada Pension Plan and it has announced the abolition of Old Age Security and the Guaranteed Income Supplement, along with the age tax credit and the tax credit for private pension income. Within the next few years, these four programs are to be replaced with a non-taxable income-tested Senior's Benefit.

Canadians have been led to believe that our aging population had made these changes a matter of urgent necessity. The debate on pension reform has been permeated by an atmosphere of crisis, which has made it easier for some to mount an attack public pensions and for the government to push through cutbacks in public pension programs with little opportunity for public input or discussion.

The approach to retirement incomes policies is in marked contrast with what the government saw as a priority when pensions were last at the top of the public policy agenda about 15 years ago. The framework for what came to be known as the "Great Pension Debate" was described in the 1979 report of a federal government task force on retirement income policy as a "response to a growing concern among many groups about the current and future well-being of Canada's elderly." This time around, the emphasis is almost entirely on "the rising costs of our public pension system," which the Finance Minister claims Canadians believe "are placing their pensions at risk."

Changes to public pensions are being made solely to reduce the costs of these programs, regardless of the consequences for future seniors. Unless a number of key issues are addressed, progress in reducing poverty among the elderly may well be reversed, and Canada will face the possibility that the incomes of future seniors will fall well below those of the non-elderly.

NO CONCERN FOR WELL-BEING OF FUTURE SENIORS

There has been no consideration of how the changes to public pensions might affect the financial security of those who will be retiring in the future. Neither the original government Information Paper issued in February 1996, nor the final agreement on changes to the CPP issued in February 1997, contained any discussion of the impact of the CPP changes on the financial security of those who will become seniors over the next few decades.

It is inevitable that, as the elderly form an increasing percentage of the population, a higher proportion of Canada's total output of goods and services will have to be devoted to its older citizens. More of our national resources will have to be directed to the elderly—whether through the public sector or through the private sector. But recent policy on retirement incomes appears to be based on an approach that seeks to reduce the role of public pensions in Canada's retirement income system and looks to Canadians to make up the difference for themselves through their own private savings.

Ironically, however, these so-called "private" arrangements for retirement savings receive huge tax subsidies, paid for by all taxpayers—including those with low incomes who do not benefit from the private retirement income system.

INADEQUACIES OF CURRENT SYSTEM HAVE BEEN IGNORED

There is compelling evidence that, if we are concerned about the well-being of future seniors, we should be looking at strengthening public pension programs, not cutting them back. Under the existing retirement income system, significant segments of the elderly population still have low incomes. For example, while the incidence of low income among elderly families (defined as families where the head is aged 65 or older) is now lower than that of non-elderly families, 51% of unattached women aged 65 or older have incomes below Statistics Canada's low-income cut-offs. And more than half the income of current seniors—65% of the income of women and 47% of the income of men aged 65 or older—comes from public pensions and other government transfers. Recent cuts to public pension programs have ignored the situation of current seniors.

NO ANALYSIS OF LABOUR MARKET TRENDS

The debate on pension policy has also ignored recent labour market trends which will have a significant impact on the ability of Canadians to provide a retirement income for themselves. For example, government documents produced during the current round of CPP reforms have emphasized the fact that most women are now in the paid labour force and earning pensions in their own names. But about 40% of women (and 27% of men) in paid employment are working in non- standard jobs—including part-time, temporary, part-year or contract work, own account self-employment or multiple jobs.

Workers in non-standard jobs are unlikely to have workplace pension plans because they do not have a long- term, ongoing employment relationship withone employer. And because their jobs are often insecure and poorly paid, they are likely to find it particularly difficult to save through RRSPs.

These labour market trends have serious long-term implications for pension policies. But there has been no analysis of the implications of the proposed changes to public pension programs in light of these labour market developments.

No Consideration of How Elements of the System Interact

Nor has there been any consideration of how changes to public pension programs interact with other parts of the pension system. While the government has announced its intention to abolish OAS and GIS in favour of an income- tested Seniors' Benefit, it has also implemented changes to the CPP without any consideration of how those changes may interact with the new Seniors' Benefit, or vice versa.

For example, women who receive reduced CPP pensions may not be able to claim the new Seniors' Benefit to make up the difference, because eligibility for the Seniors' Benefit will be based on family income.

As well, the proposal to switch to the new Seniors' Benefit has ignored the important role that OAS now plays in replacing pre-retirement income for lower-income workers, many of whom are women. For a typical woman worker working full-time for a full year and earning about $29,700—the average earnings of women in full-time paid employment in 1995—OAS represents about 16% of her pre-retirement earnings. With CPP at 25% of average earnings, public pensions would replace 41% of re-retirement earnings for this worker.

However, under the new Seniors' Benefit, married women will no longer be able to count on OAS for part of their replacement income needs in retirement, because their eligibility for benefits will depend on their spouse's income. Since CPP retirement pensions will effectively be reduced under the changes now being enacted, the interaction of changes in these two public pension programs is likely to seriously undermine women's economic autonomy and financial security in old age.

No Gender Analysis

In fact, many of the changes in public pension programs now being implemented would have a much greater impact on women than on men, but there has been no credible gender analysis of the changes. The federal government made a commitment at the International Women's Conference in Beijing to undertake a gender analysis of all proposed policies as they are developed. Yet the Information Paper issued in February 1996 outlining proposed changes to the CPP had no acknowledgment of gender issues at all.

In fact, virtually all the proposed changes listed in that paper would have an adverse impact on women—from limiting the inflation indexing of CPP retirement pensions to restricting the CPP dropout provisions; from limiting surviving spouse benefits to reducing the retirement pension. There was no official recognition of these adverse effects on women whatsoever.

Refocusing the Debate on Retirement Income Policies

Public policy on retirement incomes must be re-focused and must address a number of key issues. First of all, it is essential that concern about increased costs of public pensions is balanced by a concern for the well-being of the future elderly. To ignore the impact that changes to the retirement income system will have on the incomes of the future elderly is a recipe for disaster, especially since the current pension system still results in significant segments of the elderly population ending up with incomes below the low-income cut-offs.

As well, Canada needs a comprehensive and coherent retirement incomes strategy which emphasizes the well-being of future seniors. Policy must move away from simply cutting costs through piecemeal changes to the system and towards a more careful consideration of how the different parts of the retirement income system interact and what impact changes will have on incomes of the future elderly. It goes without saying that a thorough gender analysis of all policy proposals must also be undertaken.

Within the public part of the pension system, a conscious decision needs to be made about the proper balance between OAS, GIS and the CPP. If a new Seniors' Benefit is to replace the current OAS and GIS, as well as the two tax credits aimed at seniors, attention must be paid to the balance between this part of the system and the CPP.

Another key part of the analysis must be how to achieve a better balance between public and "private" pensions. The government is under heavy pressure to increase tax support for private savings in RRSPs, while at the same time cutting back on public pension programs such as OAS and CPP. But there has been no consideration of the impact such a policy direction might have on the incomes of future seniors, either. Given the developments outlined above, it would almost certainly increase the risk that more seniors in the future will end up with sub-standard incomes.

With a focus on the well-being of future seniors, tax support for workplace pension plans and RRSPs needs to be reviewed to determine if it would make more sense to curb tax support for private arrangements in favour of improving public pension programs.

CHANGES TO THE CANADA PENSION PLAN

The first round of changes to the CPP came into effect on January 1, 1998. Contribution rates are to be increased by 73% over the next six years, with the intention of generating a fund that could be worth about $120 billion by the end of that period. The fund is to be invested in the stock market. The government claims that investment returns on the fund will supplement contribution revenues so that contribution rates never have to go up again.

A combined employer/employee contribution rate of 9.9% of contributory earnings will be reached by 2003 and held at that level indefinitely.

At the same time, a number of changes are to be made on the benefits side, effectively reducing retirement pensions; making it more difficult to claim disability pensions; reducing the combined benefit claimed by individuals—overwhelmingly women—who have their own retirement or disability benefit as well as a surviving spouse pension; and freezing at current levels the year's basic exemption from contributions of the first few thousand dollars of earnings.

CHANGES STILL BEING CONSIDERED

Among the changes just implemented is a provision to review the operation of the CPP every three years instead of every five years. The next triennial review will get under way at the end of 1999. Calls to abolish the CPP completely and replace it with a system of mandatory RRSPs will undoubtedly be revived over the next two years leading up to the next round of CPP changes.

As well, federal and provincial finance ministers have agreed to discuss several specific measures, including further changes to surviving spouse benefits; mandatory sharing of CPP credits between spouses on an annual basis as they are accumulated; raising the ceiling on contributory earnings; and phased retirement, already implemented in the Quebec Pension Plan, whereby workers would be able to reduce their hours of work but continue to contribute to the CPP as if they were still working full-time.

DEALING WITH PENSION REFORM IN THE AFB

While changes to the CPP are a matter for negotiation between federal and provincial finance ministers, changes to the first tier of the retirement income system may be made by the federal government acting alone, since these programs are funded from general tax revenues. No legislation has yet been tabled to implement the proposed Seniors' Benefit. The proposal has been criticized from all sides. We believe it should be abandoned.

Accordingly, the Alternative Federal Budget will maintain OAS and GIS as separate programs, possibly funding them through a Retirement Income Fund.

Benefits to seniors will be increased.

An increase in GIS would benefit poorer seniors directly, but a weakness of this approach is that it discourages reliance on other sources of retirement income because these sources, including the CPP, are taxed back at 50 cents on the dollar. This is the very same problem for which the proposed Seniors' Benefit has been criticized.

The existing OAS clawback will be eliminated. It treats income from social programs as a subordinate class of income for tax purposes. If the federal government believes that incomes above the level at which the OAS clawback applies are not necessary, then incomes from all sources—and not just those from OAS—should be subject to a surtax.

OAS will remain as a taxable benefit, but moving to a system of deduction of income taxes at source will reduce gross program expenditures and produce a one-time-only positive fiscal impact. It will be fiscally neutral over the long term and it will not change the after-tax situation of retirees.

In addition, as we recommended in the 1997 AFB, indexing of OAS will be changed so that benefits are indexed to wages rather than prices. This will ensure that OAS benefits maintain a relatively constant relationship to average wages and salaries, thereby allowing the OAS program to play a relatively constant role in replacing pre-retirement earnings.

We eliminate the age credit and the pension income credit (which is available only for income from private retirement savings arrangements) and redirect the money saved to the enrichment of OAS.

For the past two years, the AFB has proposed that RRSP contribution room be limited to $10,800. We reiterate that position in the 1998

AFB. The measure will affect only those people with incomes of $60,000 a year or more.

In addition, the AFB commits the federal government, over the next year, to undertake a thorough review of the tax treatment of private retirement savings to determine further changes that might be made to address the income needs of the future elderly, taking into account changing labour market conditions; coverage of workplace pension plans; interaction of the various elements of the system; and a gender analysis of the proposed changes.

In particular, consideration will be given to whether the objective of tax assistance to retirement savings which allows individuals to replace 70% of pre-retirement earnings is still appropriate; whether the ability to shelter 18% of earned income from taxation through contributions to a workplace pension plan or RRSP should be reduced; whether the ability to carry forward unused RRSP contribution room indefinitely should be revoked or modified; and whether the deduction for RRSP contributions should be converted to a credit.

MOVING TOWARDS EQUITY

Women's Issues

The new market-driven economic world order which the Canadian government fully endorses has hurt women in many ways—as workers, as mothers, as care-givers. Their struggle for true equality has been halted and then reversed by the last four "bankers' budgets" that Finance Minister Paul Martin has brought down, especially by the deep and painful cuts to social programs on which women in particular depend.

A government's economic policies are not—indeed, cannot be—gender-neutral. The finance minister's spurious "gender-analysis" of his budgets have no purpose other than to try to placate "angry feminists." But, try as he might, he can never hide or sugar-coat the harsh reality that every federal budget he has introduced has been detrimental for the majority of women and their families.

Women generally have a greater need than men for social and public services, for health care, social housing, and grants programs. Most women also rely more on public pensions than do most men.

The wage gap between men and women, which had been getting smaller up to the 1990s, has actually been widened once again by the effects of government policies in this decade. The gap would be even wider now if men's incomes had not also been curtailed by the mass lay-offs, wage freezes, and other neo-liberal measures that have been implemented in both the public and private sectors.

It is women, however, who have been the hardest hit by the Chrétien government's economic policies; and this is not mere speculation. The government's own statistics attest to this fact.

We live in a world where women control only 10% of the world's economy, own only 1% of the world's land, yet perform over 66% of the world's work. And Canada is no exception.

With the deep cuts to education, to health care, to social assistance, to pensions and other social programs, as well as to public sector jobs, women have been penalized in two important ways: they have lost relatively well-paying public sector jobs, while being burdened with an increase in their unpaid work as parents, as homemakers, and as care-givers. It is primarily women who pick up the slack in cities and towns devastated by cutbacks, thereby increasing their share of social responsibility and social development at the community level.

Women and children comprise 70% of the people living in poverty in Canada. Over 57% of all families living in poverty are single-mother families. The federal government itself contributes to women's economic inequality by refusing to implement pay equity legislation in the public service.

The impact has been hard on nearly all women, but especially so on those with inadequate incomes. Poverty among young women, older women, women with disabilities, and Aboriginal women are disgracefully higher than for other groups. So are the unemployment rates among young women, women of colour, Aboriginal women, immigrant and refugee women, and women with disabilities.

Women's agencies and programs have been targeted for the worst cuts, and the backlash against women's groups is being fuelled by right-wing politicians, academics, media commentators, and other regressive forces. But there is an even more sinister side to this assault. When we take into account the cuts to public and social services, the attacks on the public pension system, the travesty of a child benefit scheme the government claims to be planning, along with the cuts to women's programs funding, a picture emerges of a government policy that is based on a blatant denial of women's economic equality.

The buzz words of "family values," "building strong families," and being "committed to combating child poverty" are all being misused to undermine women's economic empowerment and to turn back the women's equality agenda.

By now, it should be clear to all of us that children live in poverty because their mothers and families are living in poverty. Pretending to be concerned about child poverty, and not about the poverty of their families, can only be construed as an insult to all women and a rejection of women's equal place in Canadian society.

If the government were truly concerned about child poverty, we would have a national child care program by this time, and well-funded universal and accessible social and public services.

The cuts to women's programs funding are really curbs on women's ability to participate in the country's social, economic and political affairs. It is mainly through these programs that women's groups are able to frame policy positions and lobby for more adequate and equitable government actions.

The government cannot continue to recite the mantras of "fiscal responsibility," "trade liberalization," or "slaying the deficit dragon" as excuses for postponing and effectively denying women's equality. This is the hard reality that this government has sought to conceal in the soothing rhetoric of its budget exercises.

Neither an equality-based Canada nor a progressive social union can be achieved unless the principle of women's equality is reflected in federal and provincial budgets. Women's equality has many benefits:

- it reduces violence against women;
- it gives women economic equality; and
- it promotes women's political and social equality.

All of these components work together to ensure that women's human rights and full participation are guaranteed in the social union.

Several measures proposed in the 1998 Alternative Federal Budget—to be found in the major economic, fiscal, taxation, employment and social policy sections—specifically address women's issues and needs. They are designed not only to stop the attacks on women's equality that have marked federal government budgets in the 1990s, but to resume the march towards true equality that these inequitable budgets have so callously interrupted and undermined.

Equity Participation Foundation

In a truly democratic society, an effective means of ensuring access to public debate and the political process is through strong, healthy social advocacy organizations capable of generating the necessary social and political analyses. Such organizations play an important role in the democratic process by raising critical issues, ranging from the environment to health concerns such as AIDS and breast cancer, to disability, to human rights, to equity issues, to violence against women and children, to poverty, to international development issues.

Advocacy organizations represent the diversity and complexity of today's world, and give voice to Canadians who would otherwise be marginalized or excluded from the political process.

There has been a concerted effort in recent years to diminish the effectiveness of advocacy organizations by labelling them as "special interest groups," as if the advocacy they do is self-serving and of value only to a small minority of Canadians. Critics have gone so far as to claim that such groups have captured government agendas and that their lobbying efforts undermine democracy. The propaganda campaign against advocacy organizations has given governments a rationale for reducing and eliminating funding for these organizations.

The withdrawal of public funding has meant that many organizations have had to shut their doors. Those that remain have had their effectiveness and potential reduced as a result of staff reductions and overextended staff and volunteers. This will have the effect of stifling progressive debate on public issues. In addition, an unhealthy backlash flourishes in the fear generated by the loss of jobs and economic security.

As governments retreat from their role as arbiters of fairness, equity, and regulation, as has the federal government, it is ever more important to ensure that community organizations, including equity activist/advocacy groups, have the capacity to promote public debate.

For example, the decision of the government to delay the eradication of poverty; the elimination of national standards for welfare; the imminent privatization of social housing, prisons, the health care system, and other social trusts; the reduction in services to the disabled; the cuts to, and in some cases the elimination of, women's program funding; the cuts to and elimination of programs and services to immigrants and refugees—all are examples of key issues affecting the quality of people's lives which need to be kept on the public agenda.

Equity for women, visible minorities, gays and lesbians, the disabled, and Aboriginal peoples is on the wane. Social activists worked for years to raise public awareness of equity issues, yet efforts to obtain redress and equity are being overturned at an alarming rate in the current neoconservative climate.

There must be renewed commitment to support the non-profit and volunteer sectors, and strengthen their ability to lobby and provide leadership and direction for strategic action in the future.

Accordingly, the AFB sets up an Equity Participation Foundation which will provide stable funding for organizations that work to give marginalized Canadians a voice, provide needed services to disadvantaged groups of Canadians, and/or provide a voice for progressive public policies.

The Foundation will be empowered to fund, among other things, collective actions and organizing on behalf of people who experience discrimination and economic injustice.

Canadians With Disabilities

According to the most recent census information from Statistics Canada, about four million Canadians live with some type of disability which affects their capacity to carry out activities of daily living. As a group, these citizens are often marginalized from fully participating in the mainstream of Canada's economy and society. Almost half of Canadians with disabilities are unemployed and an unacceptably high number live on less than $10,000 per year. Most experts believe that the number of Canadians with disabilities will increase over the next decade or two, because of our aging population.

The current status of people with disabilities is largely misunderstood by politicians, bureaucrats, and the general public. It is widely believed that Canadians with disabilities are somehow "looked after" by social service agencies, whereas in fact they are massively unemployed, a vast majority live in poverty, and many remain isolated from their communities because of numerous barriers that prohibit participation.

While federal and provincial Ministers of Social Services have identified people with disabilities as a priority concern, disabled Canadians continue to experience reductions in service, fewer jobs, and continued discrimination.

Canadians with disabilities who have found employment often receive very low wages and are often employed in short-term jobs which do not address their long-term economic needs. The Alternative Federal Budget will make the economic improvement of people with disabilities a priority.

TRAINING AND EMPLOYMENT

Employment remains the critical issue for Canadians with disabilities. The 1996 federal budget announced the creation of the Opportunities Fund of $30 million per year for three years. While welcome, this fund is actually $15 million less than what was being spent just a few years ago under the Canadian Jobs Strategy Program. The AFB will restore the funding of employment-related programs for people with disabilities to the previous levels of $45 million. In addition, a portion of Aboriginal and Youth employment initiatives will be allocated for youth and Aboriginals with disabilities, and a process will be put in place to track this expenditure.

In addition to the above special initiative, the AFB will also increase access by people with disabilities to mainstream training and employment services by allocating funds from general government revenues to address this population's needs. This funding will be used to help both individuals with disabilities get jobs and to support organizations controlled by persons with disabilities to educate employers, as well as to develop job readiness programs for persons with disabilities.

This measure will respond to the existing unacceptable problems resulting from the need for most people requiring labour market services to be eligible for Employment Insurance. By providing funds from general revenues to meet the needs of Canadians with disabilities, the AFB will be improving the employment opportunities of disabled citizens.

TAX REFORM

The 1996 federal Task Force on Disability Issues recommended a number of tax measures to offset additional costs of disability. Some of these were responded to in the last federal budget. The AFB will expand on federal government tax support to Canadians with disabilities by introducing a refundable disability tax credit, after negotiation with the provinces to ensure that this refund is not treated as income by the provinces and deducted from social assistance. We will establish a base rate refund for all individuals who qualify, plus a refund for receipted items from an approved list of refundable expenses.

We will work with the disability community to ensure that all federal tax initiatives do not result in any reduction of support services provided at the provincial level. Tax reform will continue to be a vehicle used by the AFB in addressing disability issues; but, being a very blunt instrument, it will not be the only mechanism we use.

National Standards and Development of a Social Audit

Strengthening national standards and accountability systems for social program spending is an urgent concern for Canadians with disabilities. The AFB will respond to the need for national standards for Canada's social programs to ensure the mobility of all Canadians, including those with disabilities. We will re-establish standards that ensure all Canadians have access to similar programs and services.

Further, we will support a mechanism for determining how dollars transferred from the federal government to the provinces are spent. A Social Audit process will be funded to measure, both quantitatively and qualitatively, the comparability of social services in each province.

Provincial and federal governments have recently indicated their support for developing a set of measurable "outcomes" in relation to child poverty. The AFB will introduce a Social Audit mechanism for all citizens, including those with disabilities.

Supporting the Health Care and Independent Living Needs of Canadians With Disabilities

The Alternative Federal Budget will strengthen the health status of disabled Canadians by introducing a national pharmacare program, as recommended by the National Forum on Health Care. This will greatly enhance the quality of life of millions of Canadians with disabilities who currently spend a significant percentage of their often limited incomes on pharmaceutical drugs which are necessary because of their medical condition.

The second major initiative will be the improvement of home care services across the country through a national Home Care Program. This program will be designed according to Independent Living principles developed by Canadians with disabilities. Elements of these principles will ensure that the program will be universally available without a means test, that funds will be targeted to the individual, and that funding for necessary equipment will be provided.

Housing

Access to affordable and accessible housing is a priority concern of people with disabilities across Canada. The federal government must play an important role in developing housing options for people with disabilities. The AFB will commit the federal government to maintain a role in the area of social housing for people with disabilities by allocating monies targeted to stimulate the development of suitable and affordable housing for Canadians with disabilities.

TRANSPORTATION

The Alternative Federal Budget will introduce a federal program delivered by the Department of Transportation to provide grants to small businesses (e.g., taxi firms) and local municipalities to purchase wheelchair-accessible vehicles for transportation systems for people with disabilities. A similar program existed a few years ago, but has since been cut. We will re-establish such a financial aid program to ensure that the transportation needs of people with disabilities are being maintained and improved throughout Canada.

In addition, we will create a funding program to support inter-city bus operators to offset costs associated with making their fleets accessible to travellers with disabilities.

FEDERAL CENSUS ON CANADIANS WITH DISABILITIES

The Alternative Federal Budget will allocate funds to do more census work on the quality of life and needs of people with disabilities. We will provide funds to enable Statistics Canada to maintain an up-to-date database on disabled Canadians. This is a critical issue because, without adequate statistical information, governments at all levels cannot properly respond to the economic and social issues affecting Canadians with disabilities. These data are also vital for monitoring the effectiveness of employment equity measures undertaken by all levels of government.

ORGANIZATIONAL FUNDING

The Alternative Federal Budget recognizes the value of organizations of citizens with disabilities. Such organizations coordinate their views and aspirations, and they provide necessary research advice to all governments on the complex issues concerning disabled Canadians. Since a healthy democratic nation must have participation from all sectors of society, monies will be allocated to fund organizations controlled by persons with disabilities. Funding will be provided for core programs, as well as for innovative demonstration projects developed by organizations of people with disabilities.

Racism and Immigration

The history of Canadian immigration policy is one of racism and exploitation. Immigration has been used as an integral part of Canadian economic and social policy for centuries. Every group of new immigrants has been allowed into Canada to satisfy a specific need, from the use of Chinese immigrants to build railways and Eastern Europeans to farm the Prairies, to the use of Italians to meet the employment needs of the construction industry. At the same time, every new wave of immigrants has been treated with hostility and suspicion.

> *"In 1991 49% of Canadians polled indicated that 'too many' refugees were being admitted into the country. [As well the public makes some distinction between refugee groups which they prefer to come in lesser numbers: refugees from the Middle East appear to be the least welcome."* Holton and Lanphier, 1992, pp. 6-7

Gradually, new generations of immigrants from Europe have integrated into the social, political and economic life of Canadian society. The same, however, cannot be said of People of Colour from the South (Asia, Africa and Latin America), who have always been thought of and classified as "immigrants," no matter how many generations their families have been in Canada. This classification carries with it some loaded prejudices, chief among them that it is all right to deny social and economic benefits to anyone looked upon as an immigrant of colour.

The current backlash against immigrants from the South is not restricted to Canada. The federal government is emulating immigration policy in the United States (Proposition 187) and other Western countries. This policy favours whites from Europe and wealthy immigrants. In the United States, Great Britain and Europe, immigrants and refugees from the South are subjected to harassment, beatings, incarceration and deportation.

Rarely discussed is the hypocrisy of Canada's and other Western countries' international economic policy regarding immigration and refugees. Our support of right-wing international financial institutions and world bodies, such as the International Monetary Fund and the World Bank, makes us complicit in the devastation of social and economic infrastructures in Africa, Latin America and Asia.

Many of the men and women who seek refuge and a new life in the North are escaping unbearable social, political and economic conditions brought about by the economic policies forced on their countries of origin by financial institutions from the North. Many bring with them highly specialized skills in research, medicine, technology, business and other sectors, further penalizing their countries of origin through a severe "brain drain" to the North.

To gain support of the general Canadian public for restrictive immigration policies, right-wing political parties, extreme right coalitions and anti-immigrant interest groups have strategically exploited people's fears about their economic and family security.

The more extreme right-wing groups create the opportunity for "less" extreme groups and political parties to legitimize anti-racist policies. In turn, traditional Canadian political parties attack the policies of the Reform Party as being too extreme, all the while advocating discriminatory immigration policies of their own, such as the head tax adopted by the Liberal government.

As a result, there is a trend in Canada towards the acceptance of anti-immigrant xenophobia as a legitimate response to unfounded but popular arguments about economic and personal security.

SANITIZED XENOPHOBIA: THE ECONOMIC ARGUMENT

Canadians are being told by right- and extreme right-wing groups that immigrants are taking away their jobs and costing them too much in social benefits. They are also being told that Canada does not have the capacity to settle and integrate refugees, immigrants and their families. Leading this campaign at the political level is the Reform Party of Canada and the Ontario and Alberta Conservative governments.

It's a fact. A recent report of The Canadian Council of Refugees analyzed government statistics and revealed a decrease of 7.9% of refugee arrivals in 1994, down from 14.5% in 1992, which is further down from the 1980s average of 17.9%.

The strategy to link immigrants and refugees with declining access to long-term job security is dividing working people in Canada, Europe and the United States. Working people now look the other way when Canada closes its door to working class immigrants and refugees of colour, but opens it to immigrants from the investment and entrepreneurial class (with whom Canadian workers have little in common), on the promise that every Canadian will benefit from the wealth they create.

> *"The first Canadian study to state that on balance, immigrants may create more jobs than they take' by John Samuel in 1986 was corroborated by the Economic Council of Canada in 1991."*

The fact that no one can provide any evidence that working class immigrants and refugees take away jobs from Canadians doesn't seem to matter. Nor does the fact that there is plenty of evidence to show that the only jobs immigrants "take away" are the lowest-paid, most insecure jobs. Canadians are hardly ever presented with the well-documented proof of the substantial contribution of immigrants to our economy, and to our social and cultural well-being.

The result has been changes to federal immigration and refugee policies that have a disproportionately negative impact on immigrants and refugees of colour, such as the $975 head tax for each adult immigrant and refugee who applies to become a permanent Canadian resident, the $500 landing fee, and proposed legislation requiring sponsored immigrants to post a $10,000 bond to guarantee they will not use social assistance.

There has been a dramatic decline in refugee landings in Canada over the last few years. In 1996, 17,479 refugees out of about 23 million worldwide were landed in Canada. This reflects 7.9% of the total immigration, the lowest percentage in 15 years.

The IRB (Immigration and Refugees Board) is now reduced from three to one adjudicator to hear refugee cases. This is an arbitrary and unilateral approach to dealing with such cases. Clearly, the handling of the immigration and refugee situation in this country by governments has the effect of stigmatizing and demeaning these people in our midst. Popularized in our culture are the myths that most refugee claims are bogus; that Canada accepts too many refugees; that Canada has no obligation to accept refugees.

New identification requirements will undoubtedly result in the deportation of refugees from Somalia, Afghanistan and other countries with no central governments to issue identification papers. The federal government is also considering other reprehensible proposals: a requirement for immigrants who have their sponsorship claims "challenged or refused" on the grounds that they are not related to their sponsors, to pay for and submit to a $1,000 DNA blood test; and denying children born to refugees and immigrants automatic rights to citizenship.

FAMILY REUNIFICATION UNDER ATTACK

In recent years, a large number of immigrants have come from countries of the South under the family reunification classification. Right-wing critics claim that family reunification constitutes "unproductive immigration." Recent changes to immigration policies have made it much more difficult for people to qualify under this classification and thus the number of immigrants and refugees from Africa, Asia and Latin America has dropped.

The limitations to the family reunification classification reveal systemic biases that discriminate against immigrants and refugees from the South. For example, the narrow definition of what constitutes a "nuclear family" is Euro-centric. It excludes many of the members who traditionally make up the extended families in Africa, Asia and Latin America.

In addition, the immigration policy grants only one member of the "traditional" newcomer family independent status, usually the male. Yet most women who migrate are contributors to the family income before and after immigration. This sexist bias ignores women's skills and educational and work experience, and structurally contributes to family inequalities by legally defining women as having "dependent" status.

RESTRICTIVE SETTLEMENT POLICY

Since the 1980s, Canada's immigration policy on settlement and integration has become increasingly racist and narrow. Although the positive role immigrants of colour have played in Canada's development clearly outweighs the cost of settlement, governments have reduced funding to support and settlement services for newcomers and refugees. The emphasis has instead shifted to a "law and order" agenda. Cuts to support and settlement services include:

- training programs from Unemployment Insurance;
- access to social assistance programs; and
- access to ESL and FSL due to government cutbacks in transfer payments to the provinces.

In the workplace, Canadian institutions and employers continue to support the inherent racism in the accreditation process by failing to recognize the previous educational and work experience of individuals from the South. Many are required to re-take graduate level courses in order to enter graduate school, or take expensive examinations even if they have professional degrees and extensive experience. These requirements are designed to limit the intake of foreign graduates.

THE LAW-AND-ORDER AGENDA: CRIMINALIZING IMMIGRANTS OF COLOUR

The adoption of a law-and-order agenda on immigration has effectively criminalized the immigration process, leading to a patchwork of legislation and policies aimed at policing immigrants and refugees. The Department of Immigration has put such a high priority on this agenda that it now spends a disproportionate amount of money on policing and enforcement compared to settlement programs.

Legislation aimed at appeasing right-wing groups has created a poisoned environment for newcomers to Canada, and it reflects an increasing anti-immigrant sentiment and overt racism in cities across the country, ranging from the resurgence of fascist, far-right groups, hate propaganda, racist telephone hotlines and Internet groups, to the right-wing recruitment of young people in our schools and numerous beatings, rapes and harassment of immigrants and refugees across this country. The fact that there was no public outcry when Premier Harris of Ontario publicly stated that Somali refugees were using their welfare cheques to fund warlords in Somalia is indicative of the growing pervasiveness of racism in Canada.

Pressure from the Reform Party and its right-wing allies has succeeded in shifting the Liberal government's focus of immigration and refugee policies to security, criminality and enforcement. One example is the "Just Desserts" (Bill C-44), introduced after a Black man, a landed immigrant from Jamaica, shot a woman in a Toronto restaurant. This bill gives police the intrusive authority to search the mail and homes of newcomers suspected of criminal activities, thus promoting the policing and criminalization of immigrants and refugees.

Other measures include increased policing at settlement centres, new agreements between Canadian and American police services to share information on newcomers, and internal surveys to determine the attitudes of Canadians towards certain "ethno-racial" groups.

The AFB's Measures

- A Canadian Immigration and Refugee Centre will be established, fully staffed and reporting to a board of directors comprised of community appointees. Its mandate will be to provide a) research on immigration and refugee issues; b) information on the positive contribution of immigrants and refugees; and c) policy advice to government departments and agencies.
- A Canadian Anti-Racism Centre will be established, fully staffed and reporting to a board of directors comprised of community appoint-

ees. Its mandate will be to provide a) research on racism issues; b) information on People of Colour, such as the impact of government social and economic policies on the People of Colour community; and c) information on policy and the delivery of programs.

- The head tax will be repealed, and funding for immigration and settlement services will be reinstated.
- Immigration and refugee policy will be examined with the view to eliminating systemic bias along racial and class lines.
- A Centre of Excellence will be established to study the contribution immigrants have made to Canada.

Aboriginal Issues

Much of Canada's wealth comes from the lands which were obtained from the Aboriginal peoples. Canada has not honourably or appropriately compensated Aboriginal peoples for those lands and resources and for the wealth which Canadians continue to benefit from every day It is time to set matters right and to formalize the relationship between Aboriginal peoples, Canada and the provinces. The debt to Aboriginal peoples is owed by all Canadians. As a national issue, it is also a moral, legal and financial federal responsibility.

A renewed relationship between the Aboriginal peoples and the rest of Canada must be based on respect and become one of equals sharing commonly owned resources. Aboriginal peoples did not surrender their powers of government when and if they surrendered their lands, and so they retain inherent rights of self-government. It is time to recognize the rights of self-government of all Aboriginal peoples.

Not only must Aboriginal peoples be invited to participate in the government of this country as equals, but they must also be guaranteed equality of condition. The social conditions in which most Aboriginal people find themselves in this country are intolerable, and it is imperative that we work together to find solutions.

The Alternative Federal Budget generally endorses the approach of the Royal Commission on Aboriginal Peoples issued in 1996. The policies pursued by previous AFBs have already implemented many of the recommendations of the Royal Commission. We have ended the government's practice of cutting funding to Aboriginal programs, restored funding in many areas to earlier levels, and set aside monies for negotiating and implementing self-government with First Nations. With this AFB we continue with those policies and provide the necessary additional funding.

We also implement the recommendation of the Royal Commission that the federal government take a lead role in the renewal of the relationship between all Aboriginal peoples and Canada: First Nations, Metis, Non-Status and Inuit. We accept that this renewal should be guided by mutual respect and cooperation, and should take place on the basis of an acknowledged right of all Aboriginal peoples to self-government. This will require that we set aside sufficient resources in this Alternative Federal Budget to begin negotiations towards establishing a forum which will facilitate meaningful self-government. Consistent with our position in previous AFBs, we leave it up to the Aboriginal peoples themselves to decide the details of the renewed relationship.

In this Alternative Budget, we set aside sufficient funds for implementation of the renewal of the relationship with aboriginal peoples to ensure that aboriginal peoples are able to attain an equal and fair position in Canadian society within 20 years as suggested by the Royal Commission.

In fact, our recommendation will achieve this goal sooner given that the Royal Commission has as its base funding, the levels in place in 1996. Given that we have not incorporated the cuts to aboriginal programs of the federal governments in the past four years, our starting point is the higher funding levels of 1994.

FIRST NATIONS ISSUES

TRANSFER TO FIRST NATIONS OF ADMINISTRATION OF GOVERNMENT SERVICES

Most, if not all, First Nations are ready at this time to take control of the administration of services and programs delivered by government. Some services have already been transferred or are in the process of being transferred: education, health, and others. This process should continue as negotiations towards self-government proceed.

In the past, the federal government has decreased and limited funding available to First Nations during the process of transferring the administration of programs and government services. This should not be permitted to continue. In fact, it should be recognized that transfers will initially require higher levels of funding than delivery through federal or provincial ministries, so as to allow First Nations to gather and develop the expertise and infrastructure necessary for the exercise of self-government, as well as acknowledging the demographics and other realities, such as servicing their constituents who reside outside their territories.

With the transfer of administrative powers to First Nations, the need for the Department of Indian Affairs will lessen and it will ultimately cease to exist. For this to happen smoothly, appropriate education and training needs must be met.

FIRST NATIONS SELF-GOVERNMENT NEGOTIATION

A full and equal relationship between First Nations, Canada and the provincial governments cannot be settled once and for all solely with cash payments and the entrenchment of limited First Nations rights. Rather, it will require ongoing discussions, negotiations and adjustments such as are normal between federal and provincial governments today

As they emerge, First Nations governments must be assured of adequate and stable funding. It is necessary, therefore, to provide budget resources for a thorough review of constitutional and fiscal matters related to self-government, and to allow for a forum where First Nations, federal and provincial governments can decide on how First Nations government is to be funded.

FIRST NATIONS TREATY SETTLEMENT

An inevitable consequence of formalizing relations with First Nations will be the settlement of outstanding obligations to them. Many First Nations are still owed lands and monies from existing Treaties signed in good faith in the past. These obligations must be met in full.

In addition, a number of First Nations have never entered into a formal relationship with Canada. These First Nations must be invited to enter into Treaty with Canada. The Treaty settlement process must be acknowledged and accelerated with adequate funding and compensation.

FIRST NATIONS SELF-GOVERNMENT IMPLEMENTATION

There is no single model for First Nations government. First Nations are culturally and politically diverse and so, too, will be their governmental institutions. It will be necessary to work with individual First Nations as they move towards taking up full powers of self-government. To this end, monies will be set aside to begin negotiations with First Nations, establishing framework agreements, setting the parameters for negotiations, and establishing mutually acceptable details.

Negotiations will proceed as First Nations are ready to enter into the process, alongside Treaty settlement or other negotiations if necessary. Each First Nation will decide for itself when it wishes to enter into the process and may also decide how the negotiations are to proceed. First Nations may negotiate individually or in groups.

NON-STATUS, METIS AND INUIT ISSUES

It is indisputable that, in Canadian constitutional law, the Inuit fall within federal jurisdiction. We accept the reasoning of the Royal Commission on Aboriginal Peoples that the federal government also has responsibilities towards the Metis peoples and to Non-Status Aboriginal Peoples. These responsibilities arise through S.91(24) of the Constitution Act and through the federal government's lead role in colonizing Aboriginal lands.

We accept that the federal government has duties of a fiduciary nature to all Aboriginal peoples, not just to First Nations.

We acknowledge that provincial and territorial governments also have some obligations towards Aboriginal peoples. We believe that the intricacies of the relationship between federal, provincial and Aboriginal groups, organisations and governments should be negotiated rather than referred to the courts. We believe that the historical and constitutional makeup of Canada gives the federal government the lead role in facilitating negotiations between Canada, the provinces and Aboriginal peoples. To that end, the Alternative Federal Budget will set aside extra funding to establish negotiations between Canada, the provinces and Aboriginal peoples.

The off-reserve, Metis, and Non-Status peoples will be invited to participate in negotiations to establish the parameters of their governing institutions. These discussions will proceed in accord with the wishes of the Aboriginal peoples. Off reserve, Non-Status and Metis peoples may negotiate their future relationship on a community, regional or national scope. As part of its fiduciary obligations to Aboriginal peoples, it is the responsibility of the federal government to ensure meaningful provincial and territorial government participation in negotiations. We note that self-government arrangements for Inuit people are already well-advanced.

URBAN ABORIGINAL ISSUES

Urban Aboriginal peoples at present are not well served by the existing governmental structures. We accept the suggestion of the Royal Commission that urban Aboriginal peoples be encouraged to develop their own governmental structures within urban settings. Urban Aboriginal Peoples may wish to move to self-government as unique communities in their own right, or they may wish to participate in concert with umbrella organizations such as First Nations governments or the Metis organizations.

Certainly, clear formal linkages between urban structures and First Nations/Metis/Inuit and provincial/territorial governments will be essential as various government models are implemented.

It is up to Urban Aboriginal Peoples to decide the appropriate forum for negotiating self-government arrangements. Adequate new funding will be made available for the negotiation of urban Aboriginal self-government.

Aboriginal Peoples: Interim Measures

It may be several years before these issues are fully addressed and Aboriginal peoples take up their rightful role in Canada. Through the intervening years, the federal government will take the lead role in ensuring the improvement in the quality of lives of all Aboriginal peoples. Until self-government is implemented, the federal government will remain responsible for the delivery of many governmental services to First Nations.

There will be no cuts in governmental services delivered by the federal government to Aboriginal peoples.

Aboriginal peoples today fare less well than other Canadians, in terms of life expectancy, health, education, employment, quality of housing, and exposure to violence. These conditions must not be allowed to persist. Social conditions in all Aboriginal communities must be improved with all speed to a level equal to those of other Canadians.

The current plans of government with respect to social programs and other expenditures threaten to make living conditions for all Aboriginal peoples much worse than they are already We take a different approach. There are no cuts to Aboriginal spending in this Alternative Budget. On the contrary, initiatives elsewhere in this Budget (in housing, employment creation, child care, taxation, and transfers to low-income households) should have a large, direct, beneficial impact on all Aboriginal peoples. In addition, there will be a significant increase in funding of First Nations health care facilities, with particular emphasis on preventive medicine.

New funding will also be made available to the Aboriginal peoples for economic development, and community development initiatives.

In these ways, we hope to significantly reduce the social inequality between Aboriginal peoples and the rest of society.

This Alternative Budget will also reverse announced cuts to the Aboriginal Economic Programs, since it is the lack of economic development that is partly responsible for the abysmal living conditions of Aboriginal people. Additional funding will be made available to Aboriginal Friendship Centres.

Finally, concerted efforts will be made to support and strengthen the development of Aboriginal culture. Native Citizens' Programs will be reinstated, as will funding for the Northern Native Access Program and the Aboriginal-Women's Program.

COMMUNITY—AT HOME AND ABROAD

Urban Issues

THE FINANCIAL SQUEEZE ON LOCAL GOVERNMENT

Local governments across Canada are contending with a financial squeeze created by the policies of federal and provincial governments. These policies have put local governments in an untenable position: they have more responsibility for meeting the needs of their citizens, but fewer resources to fund even existing programs and services.

Both senior levels of government have relied primarily on spending cuts and decentralization of responsibilities to solve their fiscal problems.

Measured as a share of the economy, government spending has declined dramatically in the 1990s. Federal spending (including debt interest) rose to 24.1% of GDP at the height of the recession (1992) and has since fallen to 21.3% of GDP in 1996. Provincial spending (also including debt interest) has followed an almost identical pattern, peaking at 24.3% of GDP in 1992 and falling to 20.9% in 1996.

The most dramatic cuts have occurred since 1994, when the economy began growing again but federal and provincial budgets were cut in absolute as well as relative terms. On average, total federal spending fell by 0.2% annually between 1994 and 1996. Provincial spending fell by an average of 0.3% a year during the same period.

In contrast, federal and provincial revenues have remained fairly constant during the 1990s. In both cases, revenue growth has closely followed the economy, slowing down in the recession of the early 1990s, then picking up since 1994. Consequently, there has been little change in revenues when measured as a share of the economy: federal and provincial revenues have fluctuated by less than 1% of GDP during the 1990s.

Cuts to transfers have been a favoured target for spending cuts by both federal and provincial governments. In other words, both senior levels of government have transferred a large part of the cost of deficit elimination to the next lowest level of government.

Federal cash transfers to support provincial health and social programs have been cut by 33% in the two years since the CHST was implemented. Total federal transfers, which include minor transfers to local governments as well as non-discretionary transfers to provinces such as equalization payments and the Quebec abatement, were cut by an average of 4.3% annually from 1994 to 1996. Employment insurance has also been a target for spending cuts: premium payments fell by 11.2% annually during the same period. By forcing jobless people onto social assistance, EI cuts also transfer costs to the provinces. In contrast, federal spending on goods and services was cut by 0.9% annually from 1994 to 1996.

Cuts to provincial-municipal transfers have been less dramatic, although there are significant differences between provinces. Overall, transfers to municipalities grew rapidly in the early 1990s, driven by rising social assistance costs in Ontario, Manitoba and Nova Scotia (where municipalities fund a portion of welfare costs). By 1994, municipal transfers were virtually stable. In 1996 they were reduced by 2.8%. Provincial spending on goods and services has followed a similar pattern, falling by 2.3% in 1996—significant cuts in real per capita terms.

These figures show that cuts to provincial-local transfers have been proportionately smaller than cuts to federal-provincial transfers. They have also been more consistent with cuts to other areas of spending than is the case at the federal level.

However, the capacity of local governments to absorb their transfer cuts and simultaneously assume devolved responsibilities is much more limited because provinces have access to more diverse and more robust alternative sources of revenue.

Local governments in every province are prohibited from running deficits in their operating budgets. Borrowing is allowed only for capital purposes, and only in accordance with provincial regulations. Consequently, any shortfall in revenue must be offset by spending cuts, and there are often few options other than cutting services.

Local governments are also constrained in their ability to offset transfer cuts with alternative sources of revenue. Provincial legislation restricts their revenue base property taxes and a variety of minor taxes and charges.

The capacity of property taxes to provide additional revenues is limited because, unlike income taxes, revenues do not increase in direct proportion to growth in the value of the tax base. While new construction does add to property tax revenues, an increase in the value of existing property does not automatically generate more revenue. Municipalities must impose rate increases or reassess property values in order to realize more revenue from any increase in the value of existing property. And, because the property tax is a very visible tax, it carries with it severe political limitations. Few municipal politicians dare propose rate increases these days; and property owners are quick to appeal their assessments, often participating in concerted campaigns by ratepayer organizations.

It should also be noted that Canadian property tax levels are high in comparison to other industrialized countries. In 1995, property taxes equalled 3.25% of GDP, compared to a G-7 average of 1.97%. While 16 other OECD countries had higher ratios of total taxes to GDP, Canada's property tax ratio was the highest in the OECD. (Canadian Tax Highlights, October 21 1997, page 75.)

These constraints are evident in the National Accounts data. Since the recovery began in 1994, local government revenue from taxes has increased by only 1.4% a year, while revenue from all other sources has declined. During the same period, annual increases in personal income tax revenues have been 5.1% at the federal level and 6.0% at the provincial level.

Property taxes and other sources of municipal revenue are not adequate to offset the reductions in provincial transfers. With no lower level of government on which to pass on the costs, municipalities must cut their own services. In 1996 total municipal spending declined by 2.3%.

DECENTRALIZATION AND DISENTANGLEMENT

The squeeze on municipal finances has been made more severe in provinces where significant new responsibilities have been devolved to municipalities without new resources to pay for those services. Even where devolution has not occurred, costs of existing municipal responsibilities are increasing due to demographic changes, social impacts of federal and provincial policies, and environmental concerns.

Efforts at disentanglement are also changing the responsibilities of municipalities in most provinces. In general, provincial governments are attempting to extricate themselves from detailed regulation of municipal affairs and reduce provincial government involvement in the delivery of municipal services.

One means of disentanglement has been to reduce conditional grants to municipalities proportionately more than cuts to unconditional grants. This change in funding structure reduces provincial government liability for funding of urban services such as public transit. It also increases municipal discretion in spending provincial transfers, at the same time that the transfers are being diminished.

Another means of disentanglement underway in several provinces involves changes to the legislation that defines municipal authority and powers. To varying degrees, the legislative reforms replace specifically prescribed municipal powers with broader powers within defined areas of municipal jurisdiction. These changes are represented as steps toward municipal "empowerment," and do partially respond to longstanding demands from some municipal organizations for "natural person powers" in place of powers only where specifically prescribed in provincial legislation.

However, none of the legislative reforms appear to provide municipalities with significant new revenue-raising capacity. Even in Alberta—-where the reforms have been underway longest, and the provincial government claims to community empowerment have been loudest—-municipalities are reporting that they require provincial approval to exercise the important powers, and have unreasonable borrowing limits.

Although any generalization is complicated by significant differences between provinces, municipalities are generally assuming greater responsibility for how they manage their affairs without acquiring additional authority and resources to support these responsibilities.

URBAN ISSUES, NATIONAL INTERESTS

While municipalities are the constitutional responsibility of the provinces, there are several reasons for giving some priority to urban issues in the AFB.

1. The CHST and other federal cuts have contributed to the latest wave of cuts in provincial transfers to local government; corresponding federal action is needed to undo the damage of these policies.
2. The state of Canada's cities affects the national economy as an increasing share of economic activity takes place in urban areas.
3. Urban governments are most directly involved in providing services with important environmental consequences, such as transportation and public transit, water and sewage treatment, and recycling and solid waste disposal.
4. Racial minorities and off-reserve First Nations peoples are largely concentrated in urban areas, and racial inequality and conflict is most visible at the local level, so initiatives at this level are needed to build a more just, diverse society.
5. Because job opportunities, unemployment levels and labour participation vary widely between urban areas, employment initiatives are likely to be most successful when they are tailored to local economic and labour market conditions.

A more general reason for giving priority to urban issues is based on the belief that revitalizing local government is key to restoring public faith in the political process. When people participate in running their local communities, they contribute to a more vital and healthy national political life.

Opinion polls consistently show that Canadians strongly support locally-provided public services. However, there are signs of widespread and perhaps growing disaffection with local electoral politics. In Ontario, there has been massive public protest against the province's arbitrary reforms, but the recent municipal elections saw much higher than usual numbers of candidates acclaimed to municipal council. In 20 rural Newfoundland communities, not one resident even wished to be acclaimed to the local council during elections in the fall of 1997. Not surprisingly, Canadians in many communities are reluctant, despite their support for local public services, to take on onerous responsibilities without adequate resources and authority.

There are no signs that the changes of the 1990s are revitalizing democratic participation at the local level. It seems more likely that the opposite is occurring: that fewer Canadians are willing to participate in governing their communities. If this is the case, the consequences for Canadian democracy as a whole are not good.

OPTIONS FOR THE ALTERNATIVE FEDERAL BUDGET

What follows are suggestions for two different approaches to addressing urban issues in the AFB.

The first not-so-ambitious approach identifies initiatives that the federal government could take independently. As several of these initiatives involve policy areas which are being addressed by other AFB working groups, the approach would be partly an exercise in repackaging these initiatives.

The second much-more-ambitious approach would require the federal government to work in partnership with provincial and local governments. This "creative entanglement" agenda would require integration with AFB proposals across the policy spectrum, including taxation and social policy.

REPACKAGING

This approach recognizes that the employment creation and social investment initiatives included in past AFBs would greatly benefit our major urban centres and relieve much of the pressure on local government. It works with other policy groups to make some additions to these proposals and suggest ways of presenting them in the budget to give more emphasis to the benefits for urban areas.

Urban policy areas and initiatives already being considered elsewhere in the AFB include: housing, social economy, public transportation, and infrastructure. Urban policy areas which could be further developed include:

- water and sewage treatment: to give emphasis to its environmental significance as well as an area that requires infrastructure investment and therefore has potential for job creation;
- public health: more investment in preventive health services and disease prevention; important overlap with environmental concerns.

These initiatives could be included in other sections of the AFB, e.g., infrastructure and health, respectively. With this approach an urban issues section would include some text about the need to invest in our cities, then reference these initiatives as part of an urban agenda.

CREATIVE ENTANGLEMENT

This approach would be directly counter to the momentum that "disentanglement" policies have gained at both the federal-provincial and provincial-local levels. The overriding aim would be to rebuild the financial and institutional framework needed to support new partnerships between federal, provincial and territorial governments.

It recognizes that most Canadians want to see their governments working together. It also recognizes that the social policy renewal exercise involves only limited and contingent collaboration between federal and provincial/territorial governments, despite all the talk about a new era of partnership in building the social union. The basis for partnership has been significantly dismantled by the CHST, Employment Insurance cuts, and devolution of labour market policy, housing, and other programs.

The "creative entanglement" agenda would rebuild the framework for partnership between federal and provincial/territorial governments, and it would give municipalities access to more power and authority than they currently have.

Some elements of this agenda (which require further development) could include:

- Tax-sharing: agreement among federal and provincial governments to give local governments some access to income and/or sales tax revenue.
- Protection from offloading: federal and provincial governments agree to a principle that any transfer of responsibility is accompanied by a transfer of adequate revenue; this could be implemented through a co-ordinated budgeting process (see following item) or through an

arms-length commission charged with determining the costs of government measures.

- Co-ordinated budget process: create an institutional framework in which provinces, local government organizations, labour and employer organizations openly negotiate the parameters of the federal budget with the federal government, including macroeconomic assumptions and monetary policy; Paul Martin has made the federal budget process slightly more open, but no less arbitrary, by announcing all the major budget measures in advance; an institutional framework would open the process up and build in consideration of regional implications; Denmark could serve as a model.

This approach has consequences beyond urban policy, and thus requires further development and discussion at the steering committee.

Rural Issues

The neo-liberal agenda has arguably had more severe impacts on rural areas with small and scattered populations than on the major centres such a Toronto, Montreal, Ottawa and Vancouver. The CBC cuts, for example, hurt Newfoundland (where over 50% of its services were slashed) more than anywhere else in the nation.

The shift from local industry to export-oriented big business, the move to massive corporate tree farms from smaller locally-owned farms, the move to a large factory ship and dragger fishery away from the small-boat family-centered inshore fishery, the move to agri-business away from the family farm—all these impact more on rural Canadians than those who live in the larger urban centres.

These initiatives are drastically changing the character of rural Canada. Small towns everywhere are losing population, losing infrastructure, and losing most of the economic enterprises they previously had. Newfoundland's outports, prairie farming towns, bush towns in the north, and Aboriginal communities are all suffering in the present climate.

Just as government policy and the Canadian Constitution were intended to achieve equalization among the provinces, so too is there a national interest in maintaining stable rural areas. The AFB contains many provisions which will work to address the disadvantages suffered by rural Canadians. Here are some others:

1. A COMMITMENT TO ADEQUATE AND AFFORDABLE ACCESS TO TRANSPORTATION THROUGH SUBSIDIES AND TAX RELIEF.

It is accepted that Canada was unified as a nation by the building of coast-to-coast railways in the 19th century and by the completion of the Trans-Canada highway in the 1960s. We believe that a contemporary application of these initiatives is to ensure that all areas of the nation have affordable transportation links with all other areas.

It should be no more difficult (or prohibitively costly) for a resident of Inuvik or St. John's to travel to, say, the nation's capital, Ottawa, than it is for a resident of Toronto. We believe, therefore, that the federal government should support and where necessary subsidize transportation links to the more remote regions of the country.

The ferry links between mainland Canada and the island portions of the provinces should remain under government control, and travel on them subsidized. The ferry links between Newfoundland and Nova Scotia, between Newfoundland and Labrador, and between Vancouver Island and the mainland of British Columbia should be treated as integral parts of the Trans-Canada Highway system and maintained and subsidized to the same extent as the road portions. There should be minimal user fees charged for the use of these ferries.

We believe also that remote northern communities should receive tax benefits to support adequate passenger and freight services. In those areas where road or rail travel is possible—for example, in the Prairies—a national transportation program should establish and support both adequate bus and rail services for all.

2. A NATIONAL RURAL INFRASTRUCTURE PROGRAM; TAX AND OTHER SUPPORTS FOR COMMUNITY COOPERATIVES AND OTHER SMALL BUSINESSES; AND SUPPORT FOR LOCAL PROCESSING AND MANUFACTURING.

For those rural towns and villages which have already suffered severe impacts on their infrastructure and which are experiencing out-migration, programs will be established to preserve existing infrastructure and where necessary to develop new structure.

This will include preferential tax treatment for community cooperatives and small local businesses. We will also develop tax and other incentives for local processing of raw materials and natural resources.

These measures will benefit small rural communities across the country, including Newfoundland's outports, rural Prairie towns and northern bush towns by encouraging the development of resource-related small manufacturing infrastructure.

3. CONTINUED DECENTRALIZATION OF GOVERNMENT OFFICES.

The AFB will also continue to decentralize government services. With access to high-tech electronic communications systems, there is less reason to continue to consolidate the administration of government in the major cities. The creation in rural areas of stable employment in the delivery of government services will do a great deal to stop out-migration and continued erosion of community infrastructure.

The AFB believes that the depopulation of rural areas can and should be halted. With these programs and with other measures noted elsewhere in the AFB, we shall have made a start in this direction.

Culture: The Crisis Continues

In past years, the Alternative Federal Budget emphasized that Canada's arts and cultural industries are intrinsic to our sense of nation, to the cultivation of a shared identity, to the expression of our diverse heritage, and to a prosperous economy.

Recognizing the critical role the cultural sector plays in Canada, the AFB has put forward a series of budgetary and policy proposals designed to strengthen the arts and cultural community. These initiatives included restored funding for Canada's public broadcasting system, subsidies to assist Canadian magazine publishers, the creation of a national content development strategy to promote Canadian content in film and broadcasting, support for multiculturalism and aboriginal programs, and the introduction of a national universal access fund to encourage broader participation in the emerging information networks.

Unfortunately, the federal Liberal government has plotted a different course for the cultural sector, one that threatens the continuing health of our cultural community. The situation facing Canadian artists and creators today is nothing short of a crisis—a crisis that has its roots in three interrelated developments.

First, public funding for culture and the arts, at all levels of government, has continued a steep decline. At the federal level, direct and indirect cuts have amounted to over $1 billion since 1984. Despite the current "fiscal dividend" now enjoyed by the government, cultural spending as a whole is still scheduled to fall. Total cultural spending, according to the Department of Heritage's main estimates, will drop another 15% from 1996-97 to 1999-00. If no new funding is allocated, by 1999-00 cultural spending will be 25% lower than it was in 1994-95.

Funding cuts, however, are not the only danger faced by Canada's cultural community. Through international trade and investment agreements, the federal government is abdicating its responsibility and right to develop public policies which nurture and promote Canadian culture. This was made clear earlier this year when the World Trade Organization struck down tax measures Ottawa had used to protect Canadian magazines from "split-run" American publications. The ruling, which also forces the government to eliminate postal subsidies for Canadian titles, has dealt the magazine industry a potentially fatal blow.

Meanwhile, the government is intent on further eroding Canada's cultural sovereignty by negotiating the Multilateral Agreement on Investment (MAI) which, if signed, could strike down virtually every measure Canada has taken to protect and promote our artists and creators.

Finally, as cuts in funding and the rollback of existing cultural policies have made it more difficult for Canadian voices to be heard, the problem has been aggravated by the increasing concentration of ownership of the media and cultural industries into fewer and fewer hands. The press, broadcasting, publishing industry, and new information networks are in the control of a handful of corporations and individuals. Government action is clearly needed if we are to ensure that our media and cultural industries reflect the true diversity of Canadian political and social life.

1. REVERSING THE DAMAGE

In its 1997 election document, Red Book II, the Liberal Party promised the following measures regarding the cultural sector if elected to a second term:

- an increase of $25 million a year for five years for the Canada Council;
- $15 million a year for five years for loan guarantees for multimedia productions;
- $15 million a year for four years for publishing support through the newly created Canadian Publishing Development Corporation;
- $10 million to commission works of art for the new millennium; and
- $5 million a year for four years to provide Voluntary Sector Network Supports for access to computer equipment, the Internet, and training.

If these promises are kept, cultural spending could rise by up to $70 million in the next fiscal year. Even if that happens (and there is good reason to doubt Liberal election promises), it will do little to reverse the serious damage that has been done. Nor will it seriously make up for the further reductions planned. Over the next two years, total cultural spending is scheduled to be reduced by another $380 million.

Equally troubling is that, despite the existence of a "fiscal dividend," the Liberal government appears unwilling to reverse the cuts made to the

CBC's parliamentary appropriation. Reductions in the CBC's budget initiated by the Liberal government will total $400 million by the end of 1997-98 fiscal year. To put that into perspective, on a per capita basis the CBC's current funding today is 47% lower than it was in 1984-85.

Restoring funding to the CBC is important to Canadians and to the cultural community as a whole. Cuts to the CBC's budget have had a ripple effect throughout the cultural sector, since the CBC has traditionally been the largest employer of artists in Canada.

In contrast to the Liberal cuts, last year's AFB made a strong commitment to Canada's cultural sector. In fact, if the 1997-98 AFB had been implemented, an additional $707 million would be available for Canada's cultural community in the coming fiscal year.

The AFB 1998 will reverse the cuts to cultural spending, including reversing the $400 million in cuts to the CBC's budget since 1994. The short-term goal of the AFB will be to restore cultural spending to at least its 1994 levels ($2.906 billion) by 1999-00.

2 International Trade Agreements and Canada's Cultural Sovereignty

Faced with the enormous competitive advantages enjoyed by the large U.S. cultural industries, Canada has developed a series of measures and policies designed to ensure that our voices are not overwhelmed by an avalanche of American cultural products. Canadian content requirements, foreign ownership restrictions, and funding programs aimed at developing Canada's own cultural industries have all been developed to create a space for our artists and creators.

Despite these measures, Canada is still the most open market in the world for cultural products. But while we may believe in the free movement of ideas, information and entertainment, we also want to see ourselves reflected in what we watch, hear and read. The basic objective of cultural policy in this country has to be that of ensuring that Canadians have this basic choice.

International trade agreements, however, are undermining Canada's cultural sovereignty and threatening to eliminate our own unique voices. In particular, the proposed Multilateral Agreement on Investment (MAI), which the current Liberal government supports, could affect virtually every cultural policy, program, and agency in Canada. Some of the current policies which are vulnerable include: i) restrictions on foreign ownership, ii) funding programs now limited to Canadian individuals and firms; and iii) Canadian content requirements;

Contrary to the course set out by the current federal government, the Alternative Federal Budget finds the MAI unacceptable for Canada's cultural community. It must be categorically rejected. Instead of putting our cultural sector at greater risk, our budget asserts the three basic principles of cultural sovereignty that will define our approach to cultural policy:

1. A nation has the right to define what it means by culture.

The role of government must be to develop policies that promote the nurturing of creativity, the preservation of the multicultural heritage of peoples within a nation, the expression of diversity, and the accessibility of all citizens to a nation's creative content.

2. A nation has the right to develop and implement public policy instruments at all levels of government in order to assure the continued creation, preservation, promotion and accessibility of culture to all its citizens.

By adopting this position, the AFB remains committed to maintaining those budgetary measures that support Canada's cultural producers even if they contravene international trade and investment rules.

In particular, we propose that the AFB maintain support for Canada's magazine industry by:

- continuing to impose a tax on split-run magazines restoring funding to the Postal Subsidy Program. (For 125 years, postal subsidies have provided preferential postage rates for Canadian magazines and has been a critical support for the industry).
- eliminating the GST on Canadian magazines and books.

3. Media Ownership Concentration

Government cuts and the rollback of existing cultural policies under "free" trade agreements are seriously undermining Canada's cultural infrastructure. Meanwhile, private ownership of the media and cultural industries is increasingly being consolidated within fewer corporations and individuals.

In order to counter this trend toward greater media ownership concentration, the AFB implements the following measures:

- In cooperation with Industry Canada and the Competition Bureau, legislation will be developed to set specific limits to how many media holdings any one individual or corporation can control, and to provide funds to encourage alternative forms of ownership (e.g., worker-owned, co-operatives, non-profits, community-owned, etc.)
- Funding will be provided to develop a National Universal Access Fund, financed in part by government and in part by Internet service providers, to promote affordable public access to the new communications networks and to promote the dissemination of Canadian content on those networks.

4. A NATIONAL CONTENT DEVELOPMENT STRATEGY

Government cutbacks, trade agreements, and the concentration of ownership in the cultural and media industries have all contributed to a narrowing of the range of Canadian voices that get heard in the cultural arena. More than ever, we believe there is a need for the federal government, in close partnership with the cultural community, to design and implement a National Content Development Strategy to foster the development of creative talent in this country. This strategy will involve:

- providing a renewed mandate to the CBC/SRC, Telefilm Canada, the National Film Board, the CRTC, and the Canada Television and Cable Production Fund to develop Canadian film and video, as well as multimedia products;
- providing a renewed mandate to the Canada Council and the National Arts Centre to develop and promote Canadian talent in literary, visual, media and performing arts;
- raising the level of investment in Canadian film and television production required for private broadcasters;
- providing more support for Canadian independent film producers by improving their access to the Canada Television and Cable Production Fund;
- establishing a secure, stable and multi-year funding arrangement for all cultural agencies;
- implementing recommendations 5.7, 5.8, 5.10, 5.11 and 5.12 of the Information Highway Advisory Council that will ensure a strong Canadian presence in the content carried on the new communications networks; and
- affirming the right of all governments in Canada to promote and sustain the arts and cultural industries.

6. TAX FAIRNESS FOR CULTURAL WORKERS

According to Statistics Canada, the cultural sector directly and indirectly employs more than 1.1 million Canadians and is one of the fastest growing sectors in the economy.

Cultural workers, however, are on average amongst the lowest paid employees in the work force. Artists and writers, because of the nature of their work, often experience wide fluctuations in their income from year to year. One consequence of this is that they are taxed at a high marginal rate one year, even though their average income over several years remains low.

To ensure that cultural workers are not unduly taxed because of wide income fluctuations from year to year, the AFB implements an income-averaging measure for income tax purposes. Cultural workers will be taxed at a rate based upon their average income over several years.

Canadian Foreign Policy— A New Vision

The accelerating integration of the world's economies is increasing instability and inequality everywhere. The financial crisis in Southeast Asia demonstrates that even rapidly expanding economies reach the limit of their capacity to absorb capital and invest it wisely, with destabilizing effects on global capital markets and trade relations. As occurred in the aftermath of the Mexican crisis of 1994-95, "stabilizing" Asian economies and bailing out financial institutions will have a profound impact on the poor. It will also sharply reduce opportunities for the middle class and may ultimately lead to political crises.

The Asian "meltdown" also suggests that Canadians cannot seek solutions to economic and social problems in isolation. A progressive agenda for change in Canada must have strong links with like-minded groups in other countries who also resist simplistic "free market" solutions and who are seeking mutual strategies for alternative paths to equitable and sustainable development.

The link between more equitable and sustainable solutions at home and abroad is fundamental to the perspective of the Alternative Federal Budget.

Our goal is sustainable human development which requires empowering local communities to shape their own local economies, to protect their ecosystems, and to meet their own needs.

We commit ourselves to the participation of civil society, South and North, in shaping economic and social policies. We commit ourselves to an ethic of global citizenship and partnership.

This vision rejects a Canadian foreign policy based exclusively on short-term commercial and political imperatives. The government's efforts to expand trade and investment through initiatives such as Team Canada trade missions without reference to human rights, labour standards, social well-being and concern for the environment, will have substantial costs for human welfare and sustainable ecosystems in the longer term.

The 1998 AFB takes a number of foreign policy initiatives to implement this vision, to bring coherence to Canadian policies abroad, and to lay the groundwork for global conditions necessary to realize domestic policies for social equity and sustainability.

Our agenda for change includes:

1. renewed growth for Canadian official development assistance programs, targeted to achieve sustainable human development;
2. retooling Canadian defence forces to contribute to global common security;
3. implementing rapid and comprehensive debt remission for the poorest countries;
4. the democratic reform of United Nations structures, agencies and financial institutions, all falling under the direct mandate of the UN charter and the Declaration of Human Rights; and
5. renegotiation of trade and investment agreements to assure more democratic control over investment decisions within Canada and abroad to promote genuine, sustainable development for all the peoples of the hemisphere. (Our detailed proposals on this issue may be found in the Trade and Investment Agreements section.)

REFORMING FOREIGN AID

The Development Assistance Committee (DAC) of the OECD, in its official report of Official Development Assistance (ODA) for 1996, revealed Canada's worst performance in 30 years, with Canadian ODA of $2.4 billion falling to 0.31% as a proportion of our GNP. As a measure of generosity (against an internationally agreed target of 0.7%), Canada's rank among the 21 donor countries dropped to 11th position in 1996, a far cry from 6th spot a year earlier, and our long-standing position next to the Nordic countries.

Such a precipitous fall in Canadian ODA, more than 40% between 1991/92 and 1998/99 (when the effect of inflation is removed), has tarnished our reputation as a nation willing to share its relative wealth with the poorest nations and poorest people. The current government continues to recognize the target of 0.7% of GDP, but only "when Canada's fiscal situation allows it." Yet, despite the elimination of the federal deficit two years ahead of schedule, there has been no commitment to rescind the $150 million cut in ODA planned for 1998/99.

Such continuing cuts are ethically indefensible in light of the growing number of people living in poverty around the world. The United

Nations estimates that 1.3 billion people are living in absolute poverty on less than $1 a day, with an astounding 3 billion—two-thirds of the developing world's population—living on less than $2 a day.

This Alternative Federal Budget restores a positive outlook for sustainable human development. It does so by a) rescinding the planned $150 million cut for 1998/99 for the International Assistance Envelope (IAE) in the Federal Budget; and b) setting out a specific budgetary framework for renewed growth of Canadian ODA until it reaches 0.40% of our GNP in 2005/06.

Some have suggested that private investment flows to developing countries, now more than four times the US$55.8 billion in aid contributions, will consign aid to the margins of global development. But a mere 12 countries receive 73% of these flows, more than 50% of which have been highly volatile investments in stocks and bonds. Private capital is no substitute for targeted aid programs. Sub-Saharan Africa, for example, received less than 3% of the private flows in 1996.

Inequalities between and within countries are growing at an alarming rate. The 1997 UNDP Human Development Report highlighted a widening gap in income between the richest 20% of the world's population and the poorest 20%. For every dollar of income received by the poorest 20%, the share of the richest 20% has more than doubled, from $30 in 1960 to $78 in 1994. What is even more alarming is that this share has increased by 28% in a mere three years, during a time of accelerating globalization and unprecedented investment in open economies.

Aid is an important catalytic factor in the struggle to eliminate poverty. But aid alone is insufficient. Achieving sustainable human development depends on aid resources working coherently and strategically with policies that promote respect for human rights, gender equity, and more equitable trade and economic relations between and within countries.

The 1997 AFB proposed a policy framework for international cooperation and for the elimination of poverty through targeted ODA. We reaffirm this framework that meets basic human needs for those living in poverty (primary health, primary education, clean water, etc.) and that expands the rights of those who have been politically, economically, and socially excluded.

CANADIAN DEFENCE AND COMMON SECURITY

The December 1997 signing of a Convention by 121 countries banning the production, stockpiling, sale and use of anti-personnel landmines is a major achievement for an activist foreign policy agenda promoted by Defence Minister Art Eggleton. Its accomplishment is no small measure of the ability of citizens' organizations around the world to mobilize people and involve governments in creating a more secure world for everyone.

The landmines initiative does not end with the December signing. The 1998 Alternative Federal Budget is committing significant human resources and new financial resources over five years to the Mines Action Fund, available to appropriate skilled organizations, with particular assistance to domestic agencies in the affected countries. These funds will ensure that the Convention is quickly and universally ratified, that compliance with its terms is effectively monitored (encouraging non-governmental organizations to play a strong role), that programs are in place for the rehabilitation of victims of landmines, and that a high priority be placed on investment in research, training, and personnel for the rapid removal of landmines. They are contributed over and above our commitments to increase Canadian ODA.

Canada's potential contribution to common security must be more than the sum of individual initiatives, however important each may be. Canada's domestic and multilateral responsibilities require an affordable new mandate for Canada's defence forces that focuses on their strategic contributions to common security. The AFB achieves this goal by shifting from multi-purpose, combat- capable, air, land and sea forces towards a military focused on peacekeeping, control over Canadian land, air space and water, coordinated search and rescue operations, and assistance to civilian authorities (their help was invaluable during the 1997 Winnipeg flood and the 1998 ice storm in Eastern Canada).

Restructuring and retooling the capabilities of Canadian military forces will make these forces increasingly relevant to a foreign policy devoted to common security. The more limited mandate will direct reduced resources for defence spending to the training and equipment requirements needed to carry out the mandate effectively. Project Ploughshares, a Canadian peace and disarmament organization sponsored by Canadian churches, suggests that a more specialized Canadian military would cost approximately $7.5 to $8.0 billion, realizing an annual saving of $2.5 billion over prior budgets that could be directed to a broader common security agenda. In contrast, the Department of Defence estimates the 1997/98 costs for peacekeeping, where Canada has already made very significant contributions, to be a mere 2.7% of its budget.

Axworthy's indication that a next target for Canadian diplomacy will be to reduce the production, sale and stockpiling of conventional small arms is to be applauded and supported. In line with this objective, the AFB will focus government attention on strengthening current Canadian restrictions on the transfer of military commodities, banning transfers to those countries where systematic human right violations occur, to those countries engaging in various forms of armed conflict, and to countries that do not report dealings in international arms to the UN Arms Registry.

A similar diplomatic initiative on nuclear disarmament would yield even greater security and savings. The AFB endorses an international NGO campaign, "Abolition 2000," to persuade the nuclear countries of the world to commit to a scheduled program for eliminating nuclear weapons.

Debt Remission

Canada can make a meaningful contribution to accelerating debt reduction for the highly indebted low-income countries. The 1998 AFB proposes several initiatives that will release considerable financial resources for education, health, and other basic human needs investments by the poorest countries.

The World Bank identifies 41 highly indebted poor countries (HIPC). The total external debt of these countries, mostly official bilateral and multilateral rather than private, rose from $55 billion in 1980 to $215 billion by 1995, a sum more than twice their total export earnings. Of the 41, 32 are from Sub-Saharan Africa. Unsustainable debt burdens are not just cold financial data, but, as OXFAM has demonstrated, "behind this dense fog, the debt crisis wears a human face".

African countries now spend four times as much on servicing their debt as they do on health care. A bankrupted Mozambican treasury can ill afford to provide even half of its 16 million citizens with access to basic health care, and 10 million now go without access to safe drinking water.

The 1998 AFB will undertake a Canadian debt initiative that will forgive all outstanding Canadian official debt with the 41 highly indebted poor countries. Almost all Canadian ODA debt with poor countries has been forgiven during the past decade. What remains is Cdn $1.2 billion owed mainly to the Export Development Corporation and to the Canadian Wheat Board (and most of this debt is owed by four countries: Honduras, Kenya, Cameroon and Cote d'Ivoire). Estimates for the cost of forgiving this debt is between $700 and $850 million. We will write off this debt over the next three fiscal years, at a cost of approximately $170 million in 1998/99 and $320 million in each of the next two fiscal years.

While included in Canada's ODA for these years, this amount will be in addition to the annual budget for the International Assistance Envelope. Treatment of this debt will be similar to that accorded to Egypt between 1992/93 and 1995/96. Following the Gulf War, a total of $238.8 million worth of Egypt's official debt to Canada was written down. This amount was reported as part of Canada's Official Development Assistance for those years, as an amount in addition to the International Assistance Envelope.

We will also mobilize support at the multilateral level for accelerated treatment of the debt of the poorest countries under the Highly Indebted Poor Country (HIPC) Initiative. This World Bank/IMF Initiative is now bogged down, with Canada's G-7 partners, Japan, Germany and the United States, reportedly holding up progress. Even if the Initiative were to proceed as planned, only six out of 41 highly indebted poor countries, at best, will see any benefits before 2000. The framework itself is highly flawed.

We will be promoting a 1997 Commonwealth initiative by the British government (the Mauritius Mandate) to accelerate debt relief for all eligible countries in the HIPC Initiative. In addition, we will push for the following measures:

1. Creditor nations must go beyond current HIPC and Paris Club arrangements. We will commit Canada to press for writing off all outstanding debt of the severely indebted low-income countries to the World Bank and the IMF. (US$36.2 billion at the end of 1996). This can be accomplished through the sale of approximately US$7.6 billion in IMF gold stocks to cover debt owed the IMF and the use of reserves and loan loss provisions to cover commercial loans owed to the World Bank. However, it will also require a special replenishment of the International Development Association (IDA) as these concessional loans are written off. Since these IDA credits are on concessional terms, we anticipate that the net present value and hence the cost of remitting the US$29.9 billion owed by SILICs to the IDA will be much less than the face value of these loans. Since we do not know when this debt remission will occur or the eventual cost to Canada of replenishing the IDA, we have not included any spending estimates for this item in this budget.
2. Debt relief provided by the current HIPC Initiative will be additional to aid, and must go beyond writing off debt that was not being paid, anyway.
3. Poverty assessments will be incorporated into the HIPC framework and will be central to determining the level of debt relief under the current plan. These assessment should not be used as a call for more performance and extra social conditionality to the burden of the debtor. Eligibility and debt forgiveness plans should be delinked from current IMF conditionality.

REFORMING MULTILATERAL INSTITUTIONS

To achieve a coherence in global policies to secure our common future, the AFB will seek a rebalancing between support for United Nations agencies and that accorded to international economic institutions.

The UN agencies offer a higher degree of democracy, accountability and transparency, but suffer from severe and chronic underfunding.

The economic institutions, the International Monetary Fund (IMF), the World Bank, the World Trade Organization (WTO), and the Organization for Economic Co-operation and Development (OECD) have more influence than UN agencies but function with too much secrecy, too little public accountability, and undemocratic voting structures. For example, the developed countries (as defined by the World Bank) control 62% of the voting power in the World Bank and the IMF. Thus the economically powerful prevail over the impoverished.

As stated in last year's AFB, we will use all Canada's leverage to promote the democratization, transparency and accountability of these institutions. We support citizen involvement in the review of the structural adjustment programs that the World Bank and IMF impose on debtor countries.

In our initiative to achieve significant debt reductions for low-income countries, we will insist that the World Bank and the IMF not make debt relief conditional on strict adherence to orthodox structural adjustment programs. We are dismayed that, instead of offering genuine debt relief, the IMF proposes to use revenues from sales of its gold stocks to fund its Enhanced Structural Adjustment Facility (ESAF). Loans from that facility, however concessional their repayment terms, carry an unacceptable degree of structural adjustment conditionality. Debt relief should not be tied to current forms of IMF conditionality. Instead we would replace structural adjustment programs (SAPs) which are geared to debt repayment and greater international integration with adjustment programs geared more to the revival of production for local markets.

To this end, we shall participate in the Structural Adjustment Participatory Review Initiative in which 300 non-governmental organization will collaborate with national governments and the World Bank to review past experiences and propose new policy initiatives. Furthermore, we will pursue the reform of the international financial institutions that will rebalance voting rights, giving more voting power to the less developed countries which represent the vast majority of humanity but now have only a minority voice in these powerful institutions.

Economists' Round Table

January 20, 1998

THE ECONOMICS OF BALANCED BUDGETS: CHALLENGES AND OPPORTUNITIES

This Round Table was convened as part of the Alternative Federal Budget consultations. A number of leading economists were invited. Also invited to make presentations were representatives from the major political parties. Only New Democratic Party Leader Alexa McDonough responded. The Round Table lasted for more than 5 hours and was televised in its entirety on the Canadian Parliamentary Channel (CPAC). Due to space constraints, we have reproduced here an edited version of the presentations from invitees.

PRESENTATION BY JIM STANFORD,
VISITING FELLOW, CANADIAN CENTRE FOR POLICY ALTERNATIVES, AND
ECONOMIST, CANADIAN AUTO WORKERS

Our round table is entitled "The Economics of Balanced Budgets" because we want to take stock of the dramatic change in the fiscal landscape in Canada, a dramatic change generated by the quick achievement of balanced budgets at the federal level and now in most provinces. Balanced budgets were achieved much faster than virtually anyone would have expected in Canada, including the architects of those deficit reduction plans.

Now, as sponsors of the Alternative Federal Budget over the past few years, we of course disagree with the means that were used to achieve that position of balance in the government sector in Canada. We continue to believe that the deep program-spending cuts and the social dislocation they caused were not necessary—that, with lower interest rates and continued economic growth, we could have eliminated the deficit, even according to Paul Martin's original deficit reduction timetable, by simply freezing program spending.

Nevertheless, what's done is done, and now here we are, at a position of fiscal balance. The federal budget almost certainly will be balanced in the current fiscal year, and obviously that opens up some opportunities for some new and much more pleasant directions in fiscal policy than the belt-tightening that we have experienced through the 1990s. But at the same time, this rapid achievement of fiscal balance also raises some concerns.

In the first place, there are important economic issues that have not been resolved by the attainment of balanced budgets. Deficits and the need to eliminate them may have dominated headlines through much of this decade, but simply eliminating deficits does not solve all of our problems. The way we try to maintain balanced budgets may in fact create new problems.

Now, the participants in the AFB, of course, have their own views on some of these issues, especially on things like how we should spend the fiscal dividend, and you will hear from us on that point. But at the same time, we also want to hear from a range of views, to challenge ourselves, to engage with others with differing perspectives, and hopefully to broaden the debate over the fiscal situation at the federal level. That is the idea behind the roundtable today.

Obviously, we have a certain perspective on the federal budget, one that emphasizes social solidarity and the need to preserve public programs in Canada. We have, I think, emerged over the last few years as a leading and credible voice for that point of view, and I regret that the business economists we invited to participate in our discussion have chosen not to engage with us—although they represent private firms, with private interests, and they can choose to do that.

To help offset the relative lack of dark-blue suits around the table, and without really stating a particular view, I do want to raise six questions about balanced budgets.

Question 1. The issue of debt reduction. Debt reduction is posed as one of the three points of the triangle of options that we face in Canada about what to do with the fiscal dividend. Paul Martin, of course, is trying frantically to position himself exactly in the middle of that triangle, saying: "I support all three at once." What about the debt reduction point on that triangle? If we are going to reduce the debt, the question is: do we want to do if fast or do we want to do it even faster?

The point that I think has often been missed in discussing debt reduction is the idea that, with balanced budgets and continued economic growth, Canada's federal debt burden—measured as it should be, as a share of our economic potential—will fall quickly even if we do not devote a single loonie to actually paying down the debt.

If you assume that nominal GDP continues to grow at about 4.5% a year—and that is the sustainable rate of nominal growth according to the Bank of Canada's view, 2.5% real and 2% inflation (2% being the middle of their target range)—the debt burden will decline by 15 percentage points in just five years, even with simply balanced budgets.

On the other hand, if we devoted a $5 billion annual surplus to paying down the nominal debt, the fall in the debt burden would not be that much faster. In Figure 1, we see two scenarios for debt reduction in Canada. It shows the actual climb in the federal debt burden over the past two decades, and then scenario A assumes balanced budgets in 4.5% annual rate of nominal GDP growth. Scenario B allows for $5 billion of explicit debt repayment each year. There is not a lot of difference between A and B.

FIGURE 1

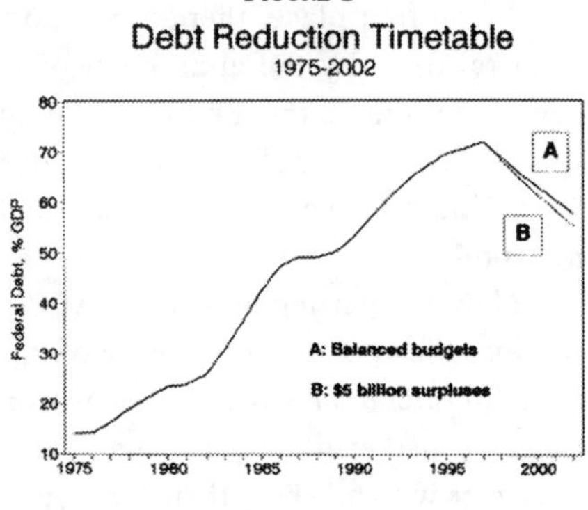

I am waiting for someone to tell me that the difference between A and B matters to Canadians, matters to financial markets, would have any real impact on our macro-economic well-being. Yet that $5 billion annual surplus that would have to be set aside to achieve B instead of A is costly to Canadians.

Question 2: Do we want to balance the budget in the long run or do we want to stabilize the debt burden? Obviously, it is the accumulated debt, not the deficit incurred in any year, that matters for things like the interest burden, the financial stability of the economy, and so on. We all agree the debt burden needs to come down. 70% is too high. We do not yet agree on how far it has to fall, but once it does fall to a more sustainable level, it is important for us to recognize that occasional deficits can be incurred during recessionary years, while still maintaining the debt burden at that stable and sustainable level.

Figure 2 shows just a very simple simulation of a typical eight-year business cycle, where you have one year of recession that shows 0% nominal GDP growth. That would be equivalent to a 1.5% or 2% decline in real GDP. Then you have a couple of years of slow recovery and then you have five years of growth at the Bank of Canada's sustainable rate. You could run significant deficits in those first two years, equal to 4% of GDP, then gradually eliminate the deficit as the economy picks up steam,

FIGURE 2

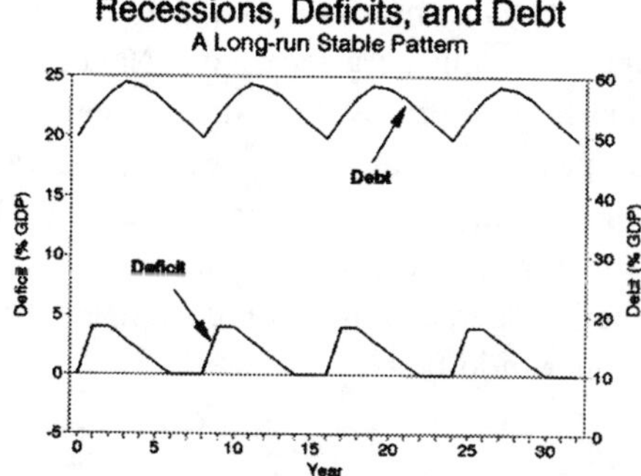

balance the budget for only three years of eight, at the peak of a cycle, and still have stability in the debt burden.

So the notion that we have to balance budgets, year in and year out, is wrong. Obviously, we cannot run large structural deficits year after year after year. That is unsustainable, now that those structural deficits have been eliminated. But we are concerned that the ideology of balanced budgets and maintaining balanced budgets and all the simplistic analogies to your household spending-budgets have created a situation where it will become difficult for Canadian governments to incur a deficit if the economy does go into recession. And that would be a mistake.

FIGURE 3

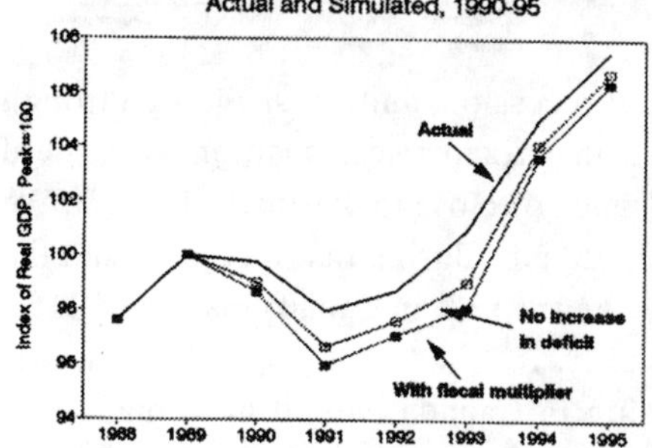

Figure 3 shows graphically the simulation that was just mentioned. You can run significant deficits for a couple of years of moderate recession, gradually eliminate the deficit, balance the budget during boom years, and the debt ratio cycles in a stable pattern at about 50% of GDP.

That leads to Question 3: Should we indeed try to balance the budget in a recession? We genuinely hope this is a hypothetical question at this point. If Canada's economy does slow down as a result of the Asian crisis, the financial aftershocks of it, or higher interest rates in Canada, or the great unknown—say, consumer behaviour in response to all of that uncertainty—well, that will be terrible for Canada because we need several years of good growth for households and for governments to get back what we have lost so far.

Nevertheless, responsible government has to be prepared for the possibility that such a slowdown may occur, if not this year, then perhaps one or two or three years from now. And I think that we have to be up front and say, despite the powerful consensus that has been built in Canada about the need to eliminate deficits, that government must be prepared to run deficits during a recession.

The automatic stabilizer function of government has obviously been eroded in Canada, thanks to cuts in the income-security programs that typically kick in as unemployment rises during a recession. Nevertheless, I think the fiscal balance is still quite pro-cyclical. It has been the strong economic growth over the past year that has helped the federal government eliminate its deficit so quickly. And another recession will undo some of that recovery. Our worry is that governments would then still insist on maintaining a balanced budget, and that would significantly worsen the recession that Canadians would face.

Go back to the 1990-1991 recession in Canada, as reflected in Figure 4. We did not start with a balanced budget, obviously. We had a large structural deficit going into that recession. But suppose the government had said: "We are going to fix the deficit. We are not going to let the deficit get any worse than it was." But if they had fixed the deficit at the levels it reached as it went into that recession, and cut spending through the recession in order to maintain that fixed fiscal position, we would have had a real GDP decline in Canada of close to 4% instead of 2%. We would have lost an additional 200,000 jobs during that recession and the unemployment rate would have peaked at 13% in Canada instead of 11%.

FIGURE 4

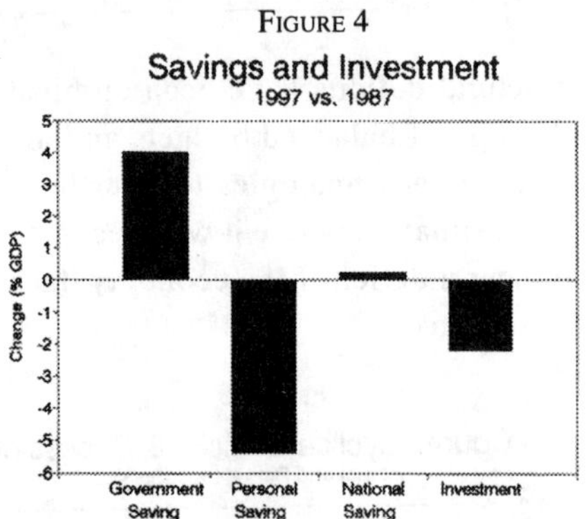

So the balanced budget mentality, if it had been applied in that extreme way during the last recession in Canada, would have made that recession much worse. And that is a lesson we have to make sure our policy-makers understand and make sure Canadians understand as the current business cycle continues to run its course.

Question 4: Does government saving imply national saving? The argument was made many times during the campaign to reduce deficits that, if we stop this fiscal bleeding within the public sector, the national savings balance will improve and we will have more money to invest in real economic expansion and job creation in Canada. Well, the net government saving position has improved dramatically. The government sector now in Canada is a net saver. But the decline in the savings of private households in Canada has been even more precipitous during that same period of time.

Now, some might argue that those are coincidental but unrelated events. I am not so sure. The federal deficits and the provincial deficits have been eliminated in large part by withdrawing billions of dollars of purchasing power from Canadian households, both in cuts to transfer payments to persons, as well as in cuts to public-sector employment and wage levels. And a decline in billions of dollars in purchasing power for private Canadians must inevitably be reflected, to some extent, in a decline in personal savings.

Aggregate national savings, ironically, have been virtually unchanged during this incredible recuperation of public-sector finances. And that means there is no extra money to invest in future economic growth. The idea that eliminating the deficit will create the financial conditions for faster rate of growth, as well as more investment and more innovation in Canada, I think, is not coming to be. What we will really need ultimately are pro-active policies designed to increase household incomes so they will have money to save and to directly increase investment. It may not be a shortage of savings that is slowing down investment, after all. It may be something else.

FIGURE 5

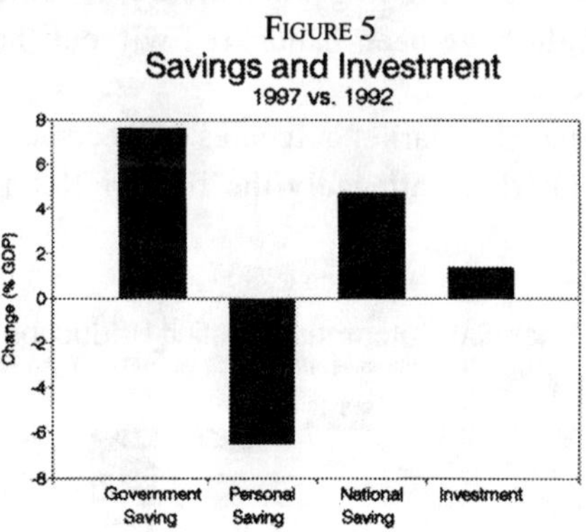

Figure 5 shows the situation in Canada in the first half of 1997, compared to 1987, a decade ago. I consider 1987 to be a roughly similar point in the business cycle to where we are at now. In that year we were five years into an expansion. Now we are six years into expansion. But the expansion of the 1980s was much stronger. So I think it is a roughly comparable position in the business cycle.

The government saving position has improved by 4 points of GDP. Personal saving has deteriorated by 5 points of GDP. That is an even faster change in a very important fiscal balance. National saving is unchanged. And despite the investment boom that is now being experienced—"investment boom" being a relative term—investment now, as shown in Figure 6, is actually smaller as a share of GDP than was the case in the late 1980s.

Question 5: This is one of those rhetorical questions where the answer is obvious, especially given what has happened in global financial markets in recent weeks. Do balanced budgets imply financial stability? The argument was made that we have to eliminate deficits in order to improve the confidence of financial investors, bring down interest rates in Canada, and insulate us from the financial storms that sweep the global markets. And clearly balancing the budget is going to have little if any effect in those areas. We did get a decline in interest rates last year—

or starting in late 1995, actually—that was very significant and very important. In retrospect, it seems that that was not a long-run financial reward for swallowing tough medicine. It was, instead, pro-active counter-cyclical behaviour by the Bank of Canada, attempting to offset the negative macro-economic effects of the deep cutbacks.

FIGURE 6

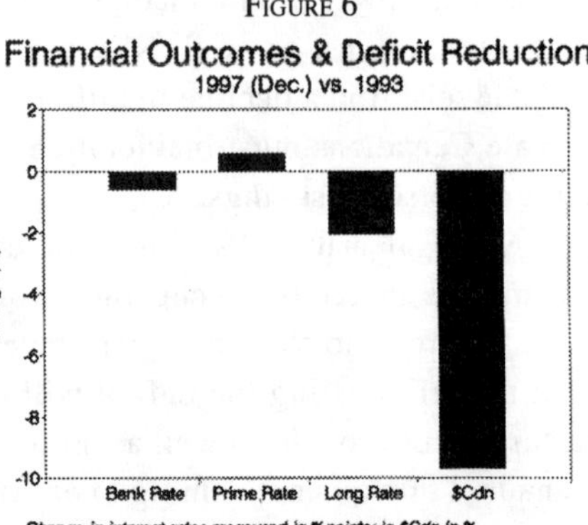

In fact, interest rates have come back up quickly. Real interest rates in Canada, relative to our inflation rate, are still high. Given that we are a small country, with a small currency, in a deregulated financial system, when financial investors start running for those safe harbours, we are going to get hammered, I would guess, virtually as hard as we would have been hammered without the tough medicine we swallowed.

In Figure 7, we compare the financial market outcomes of December 1997 to those in 1993, the year in which allegedly the financial constraints facing Canadian governments were coming to bear. The federal deficit was huge, the debt burden was ballooning, concern about government bankruptcy was growing, pressure from the financial markets on government was intense. Now we have dealt with all of those things, where do we stand in relation to where we were at that pre-crisis point in time in 1993?

FIGURE 7

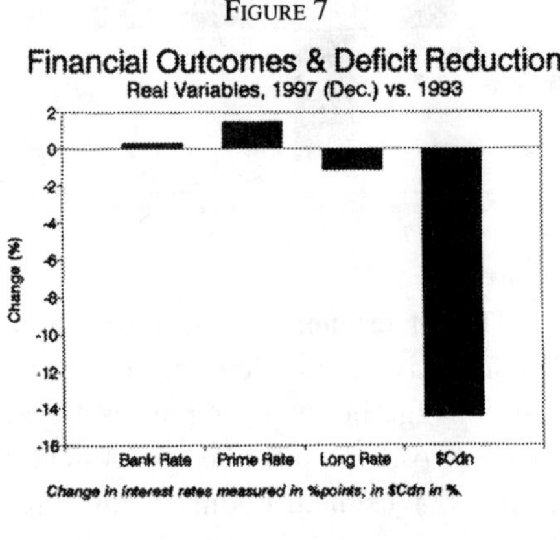

In nominal terms, short-term interest rates are about the same. They are about half a point lower than they averaged during 1993. The prime rate is about half a point higher than it was on average in 1993. The long rate has come down almost two points. The Canadian dollar has depreciated by about 10% since 1993. If you look at those same variables in real terms, short-term interest rates are actually higher than they were in 1993. So I am still waiting for my financial market dividend for the tough medicine that I have swallowed.

FIGURE 8

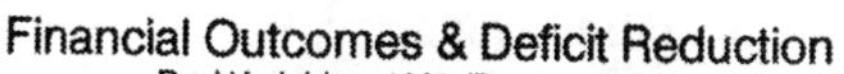

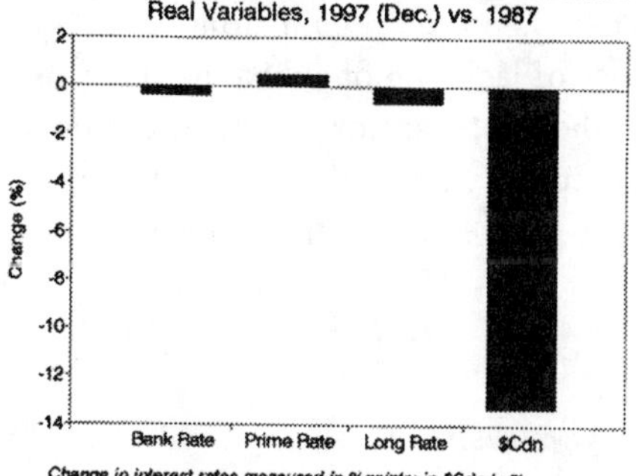

As indicated in Figure 8, the decline in the long rate in real terms is modest, less than a point. The decline in real terms in the Canadian dollar is a 15% depreciation, when you consider the fact that our inflation rate has been significantly lower throughout this period than has been the case in the United States.

Over a longer time horizon, seen in Figure 9, when you compare the situation now to a decade ago, in real terms, you see virtually no change in interest rates across the yield curve now versus 1987, despite this huge change in public finances. So the argument that high interest rates in Canada were the result of public deficits, as opposed to being the result of a pro-active choice in monetary policy—I think that argument is increasingly less credible, especially in view of the very steep decline in the Canadian dollar.

FIGURE 9

Room for Social Reinvestment

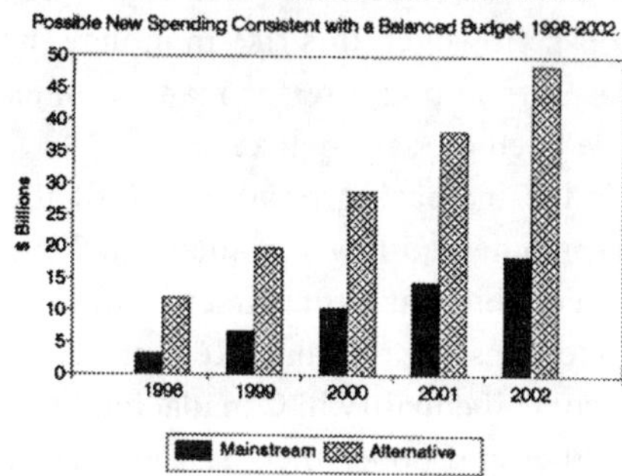

Finally, one last rhetorical question: Question 6: Can a balanced budget be a humane budget? The answer is clearly yes. Ongoing economic growth, provided we get it, combined with the erosion of the debt burden as a share of GDP, is opening up a huge amount of room for social reinvestment, while maintaining balanced budgets, and, indeed, maintaining tax levels. The notion that we need to run deficits or increase taxes in order to pay for a humane society is clearly wrong now. Even if you accept the mainstream macro-economic constraints—2.5% real growth, 2% inflation—we have got room for $20 billion in new social-program initiatives on an annual basis, phased in over the next five years.

Now, that would only partially undo the damage that has been done so far in the 1990s, but that would still be a major step forward. In an alternative forecast, where you pro-actively tried to increase that rate of growth, tolerated more inflation and lower interest rates, you are looking at more than twice as much spending. We think that, in our Alternative Federal Budget outlook, we could increase federal program spending by

$45 billion dollars over the next five years, while still maintaining a balanced budget and not touching the overall tax rate.

There is no need for greed. There is no fiscal gain from being inhumane. Our position is that the excuse of lack of money that has been used to justify restraint and cutbacks in the public sector is not valid. I do not believe it was ever valid, but it is especially not valid now, and so we are going to be looking for Canadian governments to start repairing some of that damage.

PRESENTATION BY FRANCES WOOLLEY,
ECONOMICS DEPARTMENT, CARLETON UNIVERSITY

Three fundamental economic changes in the Canadian economy have led to increased support for tax cuts. The first is a decline in many people's real incomes caused by a combination of stagnant earnings and rising taxes. The average real earnings of men working full-time have not risen since the mid-1970s. Before-tax family incomes have risen for some families because of the huge increase in the labour force participation of married women, combined with a modest increase in women's earnings (about $4,000 between 1975 and 1994). However, this rise in money income has come at the cost of increased time pressure for many women and men, and part of these gains have been eroded by taxes.

The second economic change is the increasing polarization of the labour force. The gap between high-income and low-income Canadians is increasing. This rise in earnings inequality has been offset in Canada (unlike the U.S.) by government tax and transfer programs. Redistributive policies have managed to stabilize income inequality in Canada, but have done so through higher taxes on middle- and upper-income Canadians, and, it seems, at the cost of eroded support for the overall tax system.

The third economic change is the cumulative impact of the government debt. In 1995-96, the federal government spent almost $48 billion on debt charges, or 33 cents in debt charges for each dollar collected in government revenue. If people feel that they get less than a dollar's worth of goods and services for their tax dollar, it is because they do. Almost one-third of tax revenue collected goes to service the debt.

Given this fiscal and economic climate, it is not surprising that there is support for tax cuts. Tax cuts can benefit the rich, but they can also make the tax system more progressive. If taxes are to be cut, which taxes should they be?

The most pro-rich cuts are reductions in the personal and corporate income tax. I have attached some figures and a chart prepared by Frank Vermaeten, Irwin Gillespie and Frank Vermaeten (1995) showing the average rate of personal and corporate income according to family income group. These figures show that the effective personal income tax rate rises steadily from those with the lowest incomes to those with the highest incomes. Corporate taxes show a slightly different pattern. Since holdings of corporate assets are heavily concentrated at the very top of the income distribution, only the very rich pay any significant amount of their incomes in corporate income taxes.

These results depend heavily, however, on the assumed incidence of the corporate income tax. If the corporate income tax is passed on to workers in the form of lower wages or to consumers in the form of higher prices, it will be much less progressive than shown here.

I have done some calculations to illustrate the effects of two possible changes in the federal personal income tax structure: elimination of the federal income surtax, and a more generous treatment of RRSPs. Based on the federal government's Taxation Statistics for 1995, elimination of the federal income surtax would cost $2.4 billion. The benefits of this action would, however, be highly skewed. People with incomes under $30,000 would benefit by less than $100, with benefits rising to $243 in the $50,000-to-$60,000 income range, about $740 in the $90,000-to-$100,000 income range, and over $8,400 for people with incomes over $250,000, as shown in Table 1.

A more generous treatment of RRSPs has almost as skewed an impact. For people with incomes under $30,000, the average RRSP contribution per tax return was under $1,000 (admittedly many of these people may be retired or unemployed, hence not eligible for RRSPs); this average contribution rises steadily as income increases, reaching a maximum of over $11,000 for people earning over $250,000. For RRSPs, in contrast to the individual income surtax, there is a difference between the average size of contribution and the average amount per retum, reflecting the large number of people, especially at low income levels, who do not make any RRSP contributions.

Yet there is room for compassionate tax cuts. The progressive tax reduction measures I would advocate are, first, fully indexing all components of the income tax system, but especially the goods and services tax credit and the child tax benefit. Of the close to $3 billion the federal government spends on the goods and services tax credit, almost all goes to families with incomes under $30,000.

Over half of the money paid out in child tax benefit goes to families with incomes under $25,921 (figures taken from Taxation Statistics, 1995). At present, these benefits are indexed only to reflect increases in the cost of living over and above 3% per year. This means that the real value of these tax credits are slowly eroded each year—an unconscionable increase in the tax burden placed on those who can least afford it.

, I would advocate reducing Unemployment Insurance and sion Plan premiums. As the work done by Frank Vemmaeten, spie and Amdt Vemmaeten has found, these benefits hit mid-e eamers the hardest. Once earnings rise above the maximum insura[illegible] eamings, no further premiums are paid, so CPP/QPP and UI premiums are a smaller portion of income for higher income earners.

It might be argued that cuts in UI and CPP premiums are not possible because premiums must cover the cost of benefits paid. However, the unemployment insurance program funds an increasing number of training and other job-related services which could more equitably be funded out of general income tax revenue.

The Canada Pension Plan faces serious problems in the future. However, considerations of inter-generational and intra- generational equity limit the extent to which the CPP should be balanced through increases in premiums, rather than reductions in benefits, or from general income tax revenue.

Finally, I would advocate decreasing the GST. Because higher- income Canadians save a greater portion of their income, the GST taxes a greater percentage of income away from lower-income Canadians. Again drawing on the study by Vermaeten, Gillespie and Vermaeten, I would argue this would be a progressive tax cut.

There are fundamental economic reasons—stagnant eamings, rising taxes, polarization of the labour market, and the high percentage of govemment spending going to debt charges—which have created and will continue to create a movement towards lower taxes. If taxes are going to be cut, it is better to cut some taxes than others. Reductions in personal income taxes, and particularly the federal income surtax and the RRSP provisions, are the most pro-rich tax cuts. Full indexation of the income tax system, especially indexation of refundable tax credits, reductions in Ul and CPP premiums, and a reduction in the GST are the most progressive tax cut measures.

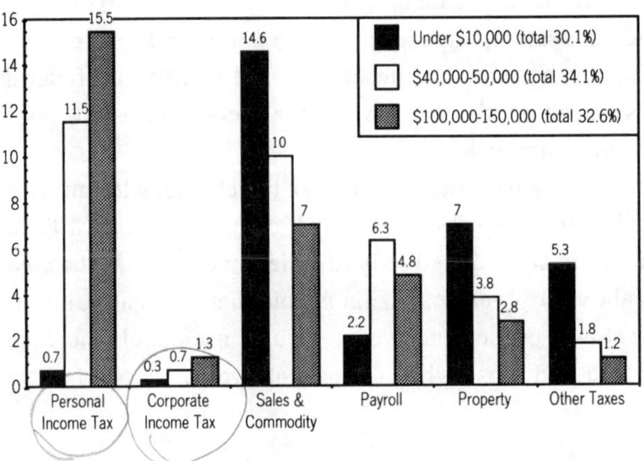

TAX BURDEN BY INCOME

TABLE 1
FEDERAL INCOME SURTAX, 1995

Individual Income ($'000)	Average amount paid per payor	Average amount paid per return
$1-10	8	1.13
$10-$15	20	10.58
$15-$20	37	31.65
$20-$25	58	61.82
$25-$30	79	77.24
$30-$40	117	115.94
$40-$50	180	178.85
$50-$60	244	243.36
$60-$70	309	308.51
$70-$80	414	412.39
$80-$90	574	571.03
$90-$100	743	739.83
$100-$250	1,176	1,167.27
$150-$250	1,133	2,393.96
$250+	8,460	8,410.17

TABLE 2
RRSP CONTRIBUTIONS OF INDIVIDUALS IN 1995

Individual Income ($'000)	Average Size of contribution	Average amount per tax return
Loss & Nil	3,371	13.33
$1-10	1,129	44.18
$10-$15	1,523	147.81
$15-$20	1,870	372.10
$20-$25	2,152	630.44
$25-$30	2,344	867.76
$30-$40	2,906	1,386.64
$40-$50	3,630	2,088.59
$50-$60	4,292	2,756.89
$60-$70	5,174	3,593.28
$70-$80	6,539	4,821.84
$80-$90	7,943	6,046.92
$90-$100	9,061	7,004.05
$100-$150	11,149	8,650.04
$150-$250	13,274	10,192.94
$250+	15,165	11,315.14

PRESENTATION BY ARTHUR DONNER, ECONOMIC CONSULTANT

I have decided to foresake the macro-economic issues and touch on two issues that I believe are very important, and obviously have financial and economic implications. One is the financing of health care in Canada, and the other is working-time and the distribution of work, which can have an impact on some of our longer-term unemployment problems.

With regard to the financing of health care in Canada, my remarks were prepared in collaboration with Gail Donner, who is Associate Dean of Education at the University of Toronto. We were both struck by the response that Tom Kent received from his critique of what has been strangling the financing of medicare in Canada. I quote Mr. Kent: "For the past 20 years, Medicare has been sustained by the public will. For this Medicare, we owe no thanks to the present generation of federal policitians. It survives despite them." Basically, I want to take off briefly on some of those points.

The big problems facing Medicare in Canada clearly are linked to fiscal cutbacks, the provincial threats to opt out of the federal transfer system, the erosion of the five underlying principles of Medicare. All these trends, in my mind, are shifting us towards a two-tier health-care system that I do not think Canadians truly want. I believe the public is right to be concerned about the shift towards a two-tier health system. We know from other jurisdictions, whether it be health or education, that, once you debase the public sector program, it tends to lose middle-class support, and a withdrawal of middle-class support could be the death of Medicare as we know it.

There are proponents of a two-tier health care system, both on the provider side and the consumer side. One of the rationales is that this is the only way we can deal with what they perceive to be an underfunding of the system. Well, the National Forum on Health suggests that there is really enough money around, but the real problem is the organization and the distribution of the monies that are there. The federal government has not taken a position on whether or not there is adequate overall funding. But whether or not you believe that there is in totality sufficient funding, there is little doubt in many people's minds that somehow the system is drifting in a two-tier direction and perhaps for some is deteriorating.

We can trace many of the problems to federal government cutbacks. We do not blame any one particular government. This is a process that started back in the 1980s. The original publicly-run health care system was geared to 50-50 cost-sharing between the feds and the provinces, who, of course, have full jurisdiction over delivery of the program. But the federal government has continuously compromised their commitment to health care, despite claims to the contrary. Of course, this has changed the underlying distribution of who is financing it.

The latest version of the transfer payments for health come under the Canada Health and Social Transfer Program (CHST), through which funding has declined sharply. Ottawa has recently placed a floor in the CHST, promising that CHST funding will never be allowed to drop lower than $12.5 billion annually. Now, at the same time that the system is under real financial stress, there are proponents, such as Kent and others, who want to see the system expand into areas such as drugs or children's health. I think all those objectives of expanding the system are laudable, but only if we provide adequate financing. I think what we need is a sixth principle for Medicare, and that sixth principle is a guarantee of adequate and sustainable financing.

The federal government's fiscal situation is clearly stronger today, and I think there is some room for the federal government to get back into the business of health care funding. But it should be noted that the current government, like its predecessors, dislikes Medicare transfer payments for one very important political reason: They get no credit and no respect. The fact is that it is the provinces, not Ottawa, that actually deliver the program, no matter to what extent Ottawa provides funding. So the provinces tend to get most or all the credit. And it was largely because the federal government's contributions were not recognized that Ottawa has pulled back. Which is very unfortunate. My own view is that it is absolutely essential that the federal government get back into the health care funding business.

The accompanying tables provide a quick overview of the financial shifts that have occurred in the 1980s and 1990s. Table 1 looks at total house expenditures and health expenditures per capita and relative to GDP. The key point is that these are total health expenditures, both public and private, and they also include expenditures by departments that go beyond health but are clearly health-related. As we all know, during the 1980s economic boom, we saw very steep increases in nominal health expenditures. Clearly those rates of increase were not financially sustainable, The cutbacks started in the 1990s, at both the federal and provincial levels. You can see that, according to these figures from the Canadian Institute for Health Information, nominal rates of increase in health expenditures for 1997 are estimated to increase about 1.5%. This is without taking inflation into account, and I should point out that we do not have good information about health care inflation as it might be reflected in the Consumer Price Index (CPI). But I dare say that, if you took the overall CPI, in real terms, even with these small nominal increases in real terms, health expenditures have actually been been decreasing.

Table 2 looks at the four largest provincial governments. Here you can get the sense that the cutbacks in health care spending have been somewhat uneven. Alberta was the earliest to cut back in normal dollar terms in a very massive way, starting around 1993, 1994 and 1995. And, despite all the criticisms of the Ontario government, in fact, in absolute dollar terms, it has not cut back health care. In other words, nominal health spending by the Ontario government has been fairly flat. Of the four largest provinces, only B.C. seems not to have had major reductions in health-care spending. On a per capita basis, the cutbacks are even worse.

The percentage allocations in Table 3 give an indication of the developments since 1975. Essentially, the federal government contribution to overall health care finances declined. No surprise. The provincial share has been rising. Once again, not surprising. The private sector share also has been increasing. Behind these shifts in shares is the major fiscal pressures at the federal level and at the provincial levels. This, we would contend, has made the financing of Medicare much more fragile. I also would argue that the provincial cutbacks in medical care spending can directly be traced to the federal cutbacks in the CHST and the caps that were imposed on the transfer payments to the larger provinces.

Finally, Table 4 indicates that health-care transfers, which are not earmarked but part of the CHST funding, are very uneven on a per capita basis because they are subject to caps in the wealthier provinces. For example, Ontario, which has 37.5% of the population, only received 32.5% of the per capita transfer. I do question the wisdom, when we do have equalization programs, of using the CHST as another kind of equalization program, because clearly, in this case, it has impacted negatively on Medicare.

What is needed to restore federal government credibility is a lot of federal government money. Some of you have probably noticed that the federal government clearly is signalling that it wants to become more involved in health care financing. But they are going directly to individuals, directly to institutions. They are not going through the provinces. We think that is a mistake. We can understand why the federal government may resist wanting to have the provinces deliver programs; but, after all, it is a provincial jurisdiction and I think the provinces do need their involvement.

Secondly, we believe that Ottawa should be appointing a blue-ribbon panel to publish an annnual report card on how each province is doing with respect to health care.

Finally, to gain further leverage in credibility, the federal government simply has to resume a larger share of overall funding. Tom Kent's idea of having the federal government earmark funds directly for children's health is intriguing. Personally, I do not believe it will fly at this particular time, because, once again, it will seem as if the federal government is funding a program that has been delivered at the provincial level. Most important, we believe that the federal government should unscramble the CHST egg and resume earmarking funds directly to health care spending, as it did in the past.

Now turning to the working-time issue, I was fortunate several years ago to chair a federal government advisory group on working time and the distribution of work. This advisory group made some very important recommendations, but so far no government has seen fit to really run with them.

There is an area that we did not make a recommendation on, but, being a tax issue, I would like to see the Alternative Federal Budget consider it. That is the area of levelling the playing field between new job hires and overtime or long hours worked. I would contend that the playing field, for a variety of reasons, has become extremely unlevel.

A lot of people have quarrels with the CPP or with unemployment insurance. I can understand the quarrel because there has been an argument that these taxes are job killers. But also the design of the tax, the design of many of these programs, are also job killers. And we can redesign these programs in a budget-neutral fashion so that the incentive given to employers will not be an incentive to work the existing person longer and longer hours, but one that will promote a shift towards hiring a brand new person.

TABLE 1
TOTAL CANADIAN HEALTH EXPENDITURES - 1975-1997

Year	*Total Health Expenditures*		*Total Health Expe. per capita*		*Health Expenditures as a % of GDP*
	($000,000)	annual change (%)	($)	annual change (%)	
1975	12,260.8	-	528.28	-	7.1
1976	14,103.7	16.0	599.71	13.5	7.1
1977	15,501.8	9.9	651.44	8.6	7.1
1978	17,172.4	10.8	714.44	9.7	7.1
1979	19,292.6	12.3	794.89	11.2	7.0
1980	22,408.3	16.1	911.15	14.7	7.2
1981	25,449.1	18.0	1,052.21	16.6	7.4
1982	30,912.9	18.9	1,226.61	15.5	8.3
1983	34,158.1	10.5	1,342.23	9.4	8.4
1984	36,819.9	7.8	1,432.58	6.7	8.3
1985	40,058.1	8.8	1,544.16	7.8	8.4
1986	43,583.0	8.8	1,663.23	7.7	8.6
1987	47,057.2	8.0	1,772.42	6.6	8.5
1988	51,084.7	8.6	1,899.43	7.2	8.4
1989	56,347.8	10.3	2,058.04	8.4	8.7
1990	61,256.1	8.7	2,204.20	7.1	9.1
1991	66,564.5	8.7	2,367.15	7.4	9.8

TABLE 1 (CONT'D)
TOTAL CANADIAN HEALTH EXPENDITURES - 1975-1997

Year	*Total Health Expenditures*		*Total Health Expe. per capita*		*Health Expenditures as a % of GDP*
	($000,000)	annual change (%)	($)	annual change (%)	
1992	70,156.6	5.4	2,457.99	3.8	10.2
1993	71,791.8	2.3	2,480.11	0.9	10.1
1994	73,115.2	1.8	2,499.19	0.8	9.8
1995	74,491.8	1.9	2,515.31	0.6	9.6
1996f	75,479.2	1.3	2,519.03	0.1	9.5
1997f	76,535.9	1.5	2,528.47	0.4	9.2

f - forecast
Source: Canadian Institute for Health Information, News Release

---

TABLE 2
PROVINCIAL GOVERNMENT TOTAL HEALTH EXPENDITURES, SELECTED PROVINCES, 1975-97

Year	Quebec	Ontario	Alberta	B.C.	10 Provinces Plus Territ.
1975	2,531.2	3,143.5	894.9	928.3	8,710.4
1980	4,607.8	5,164.5	1,510.2	1,933.8	15,795.8
1985	7,516.8	9,747.9	3,035.1	3,203.1	28,148.9
1990	10,211.3	16,022.6	4,080.0	4,965.1	42,097.1
1991	11,050.4	17,821.5	4,318.7	5,526.4	45,859.5
1992	11,506.5	18,664.4	4,578.2	6,034.9	48,014.0
1993	11,681.8	18,558.5	4,518.6	6,456.4	48,390.1
1994	11,789.0	18,576.4	4,273.1	6,656.3	48,583.5
1995	11,745.9	18,689.9	4,029.0	6,801.9	48,650.2
1996f	11,531.6	18,643.4	4,033.9	6,956.9	48,572.9
1997f	11,358.5	18,898.9	4,008.4	7,108.9	48,614.6
% change					
1990	6.7	7.9	5.9	12.8	8.1
1991	8.2	11.2	5.9	11.3	8.9
1992	4.1	4.7	5.0	9.2	4.7
1993	1.5	-0.6	-1.3	7.0	0.8
1994	0.9	0.1	-5.4	3.1	0.4
1995	-0.4	0.6	-5.7	2.2	0.1
1996f	- 1.8	-0.2	0.1	2.3	-0.2
1997f	-1.5	0.3	-0.7	2.2	0.1

f - forecast
Source: Canadian Institute for Health Information, News Release

Table 3
Per Capita Provincial Government Total Health Expenditures, Selected Provinces, 1990-97

Year	Quebec	Ontario	Alberta	BC	10 Provinces Plus Territ.
1990	1,454.48	1,549.37	1,596.00	1,504.53	1,514.80
1991	1,560.66	1,701.92	1,660.23	1,635.12	1,630.84
1992	1,606.77	1,753.12	1,728.98	1,735.74	1,682.21
1993	1,613.82	1,715.91	1,682.29	1,806.19	1,671.68
1994	1,617.41	1,698.48	1,573.56	1,813.84	1,660.66
1995	1,599.55	1,684.18	1,463.98	1,807.65	1,642.74
1996f	1,560.81	1,656.84	1,446.07	1,804.58	1,621.06
1997f	1,527.97	1,638.03	1,419.98	1,802.74	1,603.95
% Change					
1990	5.6	5.9	3.8	9.7	6.5
1991	7.3	9.8	4.0	8.7	7.7
1992	3.0	3.0	4.1	6.2	3.1
1993	0.4	-2.1	-2.7	4.1	-0.6
1994	0.2	-1.0	-6.5	0.4	-0.7
1995	-1.1	-0.8	-7.0	-0 .3	-1.1
1996f	-2.1	-1.1	-1.9	-0.1	-1.1
1997f					

f - forecast
Source: Canadian Institute for Health Information, News Release

---

Table 4
National Health Expenditures by Source of Funding, 1975-94

($ billions)	1975	1980	1985	1990	1994
Federal - direct	0.4	0.6	1.1	2.0	2.6
Federal-transfers (cash only)	3.4 (3.4)	6.9 (3.8)	11.2 (6.4)	14.8 (7.3)	15.9 (7.9)
Provincial (incl. tax points)	5.3 (5.3)	8.9 (12.0)	16.9 (21.7)	27.3 (32.8)	32.2 (40.1)
Municipal & workers comp.	0.3	0.6	1.0	1.4	1.4
Total public	9.4	17.0	30.3	45.5	52.1
Private	2.9	5.5	9.7	15.5	20.4
Total	12.3	22.4	40.0	61.0	72.5

Source: National Health Expenditures in Canada, 1975-94 (1996)

PRESENTATION BY ROY CULPEPER, PRESIDENT, NORTH-SOUTH INSTITUTE

Since economists are in the dark about a range of issues, it behooves us all to have fora such as this one where we can come together and debate and exchange views about what is happening in the world and how to tackle economic problems. My own remarks are going to be focused on the financial crisis, and I will try to tie these comments to the economic choices that we face in Canada.

The Asian crisis of 1997-1998 is the third of the 1990s, the first having been in Europe in 1992-1993, and the second centred in Latin America in 1994-1995. I think it is safe to say that more financial turmoil is on the way. It is simply much less certain where and when it is going to take place. But I think it is also fair to say that the current crisis is deeper than the previous two and has elicited the now famous comments by Alan Greenspan, the U.S. Federal Reserve Board Chairman, that deflation may, in fact, be on the horizon.

Now, in my view, one of the root problems underlying the financial crises that we have been confronting is the rather aggressive program of financial liberalization that has been pursued, particularly by the G-7 countries, and through them the IMF and the World Bank, and its corollary, the integration of financial markets.

The reason I think this has been a root cause of financial instability is that it gives foreign financial investors the ability to buy and sell financial assets in other countries with less and less hindrance or regulation. This has allowed speculators and investors who are interested only in maximizing short-term returns to exploit interest-rate differentials or yield differentials and to shift large amounts of money when these differentials change or are expected to change. In my view, without financial liberalization, some of the so-called contagion effects, whereby a financial crisis spreads from one country to another, would be far more contained.

The whole process is driven by the institutionalization of savings in the OECD countries. Pension funds, insurance and mutual funds, even in 1994, held something like $20 trillion, and much of this money is looking for outlets with high returns. The problem is that public policy at the international level is accommodating these pressures wrongly. But because of the increasing openness in financial markets, according to the IMF, hedge funds, proprietary traders and speculative-type mutual funds have grown to well above $100 billion, and these funds often leverage money through the banking system to enable them to mobilize capital in the order of five to 10 times as much as the funds that they have.

In other words, speculative funds could be in the order of magnitude of about a trillion dollars in the world economy. So it is not surprising that this magnitude of speculative funding causes asset bubbles and speculation in stock and real-estate prices in various places around the world. Don't forget that this process started in the 1980s when a real-estate speculative boom in the United States led to large-scale insolvency in the savings & loan sub-sector of the U.S. financial sector.

Now, in contrast with speculative funds of $1 trillion, I should point out that the total reserve assets of all central banks of emerging markets (emerging markets being defined as developing or in-transition countries) amounted to only $822 billion. This is a very interesting juxtaposition of relative orders of strength. Furthermore, if you look at what resources the IMF has at its disposal, which will amount to only $290 billion after the current quota increase (if it in fact goes into effect and is approved by countries such as the U.S.), this amount again is considerably less.

There are some ironies to all of this. For example, there was a net capital inflow into emerging markets, in the order of $1.2 trillion, in the six years 1990 to 1996. But almost half of this net capital inflow flowed out again—$575 billion, to be precise. It is accumulated as foreign-exchange reserves, which typically means purchases of U.S. bonds and Treasury bills. For example, net foreign purchases of U.S. bonds increased five-fold from 1993 to 1996 to $294 billion, of which Hong Kong and China collectively accounted for $32 billion.

Now, this was an attempt by the emerging-market countries to build up their reserve assets to try and protect themselves against speculative attack and financial instability. But you can see that, for many of these countries, it has been in vain. Moreover, when you borrow dear and lend cheap—which is what emerging-market countries are doing—you are paying dearly to foreign investors for financial inflows and then reinvesting in relatively low-yielding U.S. securities. This ends up imposing a fairly high fiscal cost on the emerging markets, which the IMF estimates to be in the order of $10 billion a year.

Another irony, of course, is that the current balancing of OECD budgets and the levelling-off of debt obligations actually might be making the financial system more risky. The reason for that is that, because government bonds are becoming more scarce, investors in the institutional market (pension funds, mutual funds, etc.) are having to invest more and more of their portfolios in relatively riskier assets—i.e., in corporate bonds and more risky equities. And this imparts a riskiness to the financial sector which we have not seen for a long time, certainly not since the days when government bonds were more plentiful.

The problem with all of this is the role of the IMF and the G-7 countries, whose response to crises has been to step in and bail out private creditors in countries like Korea and Indonesia and Thailand. The result has inevitably been that ordinary people in these economies are the ones who pay the price, because of the stringent economic-policy reforms which the adjusting countries are forced by the IMF to undertake, and which lead to falling incomes, falling employment, and the loss of social security for workers and lower-income people.

So how do we fix this state of affairs? George Soros, the famous (or perhaps infamous) American financier, has been saying some very interesting things lately about the way the international financial system operates. He should surely be in a position to know because he has been working the system quite assiduously, and profitably, for some time now. In a recent issue of *Atlantic magazine*, he writes that: "Financial markets are inherently unstable, and international financial markets especially so. The instability of financial markets can cause serious economic and social dislocation.

"Markets," he adds, "cannot be left to correct their own mistakes because they are likely to overreact and behave in an indiscriminate fashion."

The IMF has also come under increasing criticism from some mainstream economists. Geoffrey Sachs of Harvard and, more surprisingly, Joe Stiglitz, the chief economist of the World Bank, a former president of the Council of Economic Advisors in the U.S., have both taken issue with the IMF's policies in Asia. They argue that in these countries economic fundamentals have in fact been sound, whether you measure those fundamentals in terms of GDP growth, savings-to-GDP ratio, or the fiscal-surplus-to- GDP ratio.

Ratios of these indicators in the East Asian countries have in the past, and up to very recent times, been far above ratios in the OECD countries. Therefore, the stock policy response by the IMF of disinflation, of compression of income, of fiscal compression and monetary compression, leading to short-term interest rate hikes (for example, in South Korea, they have shot up to 30%) is simply wrong. The criticism from Stiglitz is basically that what we want to do in the Asian crisis countries is not make matters worse, but make matters better. If they are worsened, the possibility arises, of course, that there will be a recessionary contagion that will spread around the globe. I think that is the concern that is facing decision-makers in this country.

In general, I have a great deal of difficulty with prescriptions of further financial liberalization, which have also been urged for the countries in crisis—Indonesia and Korea, in particular. I would argue that these prescriptions are exactly in the wrong direction, if in fact what we want is more financial stability and certainty. It is worth noting that financial sectors or countries that have relatively closed financial sectors, such as China and Malaysia, have done very well. There has not been speculation against the Chinese currency. While there has been against Malaysia's, it has been much more contained.

It seems that we are simply relearning the lessons of the Great Depression when the financial sector was a transmission mechanism for depression between countries and simply made bad things worse everywhere. All we need now is a trade war to complete the scenario that we saw in the 1930s. It remains to be seen whether in fact the Asian countries, with their rather drastically devalued currencies, will trigger such a trade war.

So, where do we go from here? What are the alternatives? One response is that of George Soros himself. He suggested that an international regulatory authority, which he calls the International Credit Insurance Corporation, be set up. This authority would guarantee loans to investors for a fee. The authority would set limits to the total amounts borrowed under insurance. So they would look at each country and decide the limits of its credit-worthiness and issue insurance up to a ceiling, and after that you are out of luck. If you are an investor, you will not have the benefit from insurance, at least from this particular agency, and you are on your own.

I find this proposal interesting. We do not have anything like that right now. But the problem that I have with Soros's particular proposal is: Would it tackle the root problem or would it simply address the symptoms? More to the point, might it simply shorten investor-horizons even more, and would it benefit speculators rather than those who are more interested in long-term investment?

As I said before, it is no accident that China has been an oasis of stability in Asia. China has received an enormous inflow of foreign capital, as everyone knows. But 80% of that capital inflow—in 1996, for example, $42 billion out of the $51 billion capital inflow—took the form of foreign direct investment, rather than financial investment in bonds and stocks. Compare that 80% in FDI in China with 22% in Thailand and 34% in Indonesia, and 39% higher in Malaysia.

Compare that with 50% in Chile. Chile has also been rather discouraging of short-term speculative inflows through a border withholding tax of 30% on all foreign borrowings of maturities of less than a year. I think that particular policy has served Chile very well in the financial turbulence, or the "tequila effect" that followed the peso crisis in 1994/1995.

In conclusion, I would argue that slowing down or impeding financial mobility may, in fact, improve the efficiency of the financial markets, if it in fact brings down the rate of returns to financial assets to equality with the rate of returns on real assets. The problem that we have now is with financial mobility. Speculators are free to switch their assets from country to country, going to where the returns are highest, and of course the returns are going to vary because of fiscal and monetary policies. But this may have no bearing whatsoever on real returns to capital in any real economies.

There are two ways of tackling this problem. One is at the national level, through the kinds of policies that Chile has adopted. At an international level, as much as this might seem out of fashion, I think that it is still germane to talk about mechanisms like the Tobin tax—taxes on currency transactions which would be very burdensome on frequent short-term financial trades, but negligible on longer-term stability-enhancing financial flows. We have done some work at the Institute lately which indicates that, if the tax were levied in the right way, it would actually be technically feasible.

The work that we have done suggests that, if you levy it at the netting stage of currency transactions, rather than at the deal-making stage or the final-settlement stage, you can in fact impose such a tax. But I think that, to be politically feasible, such a tax would have to be imposed at least by all the G-7 countries, if not most of the OECD countries.

Finally, maybe there is room for a Soros-type regulatory institution, as long as it impacts on or penalizes the behaviour of creditors as well as borrowers. It is worth noting that, in a recent conference at the IMF, several prominent economists, including Paul Krugman, Carmen Reinhardt, John Williamson and Robert Mandel, all agreed that recent currency crises have not been based on overly expansionary policies or poor credibility, or deterioration of economic fundamentals, and as such have been very hard to predict. I think that reality is going to stay with us for some time.

Canada's own Robert Mandel said that currency crises will continue to occur until the international monetary system can find a way to support all countries' exchange rates—in other words, to go back to a much more, if not rigidly fixed, then relatively more fixed exchange-rate regime than we have now.

PRESENTATION BY ALEXA MCDONOUGH, LEADER, NEW DEMOCRATIC PARTY

Faced with a government that balanced the books by unbalancing society, the CCPA and CHO!CES have provided a voice for the last three years for a more balanced approach, one that puts people and human needs ahead of corporate bottom lines. It is the same fight NDP caucus members have been bringing to the House of Commons, the same fight we brought to the federal election in 1997. I know there are voices here today for the many different aspects of that balanced approach.

But I would like to focus this morning on the two areas that I believe are the most critical for Canada's future. They are two areas where the government's approach is doing the most damage, the two areas where I believe our voice is needed most urgently. It is critical that the upcoming federal budget address, first, the erosion of opportunities facing young Canadians and, secondly, the increasingly stark division in our society between the most privileged and wealthiest segment of society, and the rest of Canadians.

When it comes to young people, how quickly we have accepted that they will face bleaker prospects than their parents did. Many young people have told me that graduating from high school is terrifying, not because there are so many choices they have to make, but because there are so few choices available to them. The doors to the future have been slamming in the faces of Canada's youth. And Ottawa has been doing a lot of the slamming.

Take education. Since 1980, the federal government has cut support for education in half. Most provincial governments have recouped those cuts, mainly at the expense of students. In the last 10 years, tuition fees have increased 240 per cent. The result of those increases is the disturbing fact that the average student debt load this year will be $25,000. Increasingly, that shuts out students from all but the wealthiest families from post-secondary education, the single biggest factor that determines future income and success in the new economy.

It is not much better in the workforce. Since 1980, we have seen the proportion of young families living in poverty double, from 20 per cent to 42 per cent. Think about that. Two out of every five young families starting their lives together in poverty. That figure is horrifying, but I cannot say it is surprising. There are 400,000 young Canadians out of work right now. Our newest workers are also those least likely to find a job.

Despite the government's endless proclaiming of the economy's performance, the reality is that overall unemployment exceeded 9 per cent for 86 consecutive months, finally dipping below that figure only last month. The reality is that the only real job growth in this *decade* has been in *self- employment.* In the NDP's dissenting opinion on the Finance Committee's pre-budget report, Nelson Riis reminded us that 87 per cent of the *new* jobs created since August 1989 actually came from *self-* employment.

If those are the jobs of the future, we have a problem. Forty-five per cent of them pay less than $20,000 per year. Moreover, the gap between the self-employed and paid workers widened constantly through the 1990's.

It is time to open doors again for young people. Surely an economy that cannot do that is failing, no matter what other measures you use. The next budget must include serious action to open up educational opportunities again. One big step would be to make accessibility a national standard in education, in the same way the Canada Health Act sets national standards for medicare. Of course, the moral authority to do that only comes if Ottawa is living up to its own responsibilities. So the second crucial step is to reinstate this year's $550-million cut to transfers—in other words, to reinvest in education.

Third, there has to be a national effort to tackle student debt. This would include a *needs- based* national grant system for students. The announced Millennium can serve as the initial base of that system.

Ensuring educational opportunities is part of the answer. Ensuring *employment* opportunities is just as important. Here, is anything, federal neglect has been even more noticeable. When the Finance Minister means business, he sets targets and timetables for achieving them. That is what he did with the deficit. It is what he does for inflation. It is what heays he will do with the debt. But it is not what he is willing to do with jobs. And that has to change.

The top economic priority in Mr. Martin's 1998 budget ought to be to set targets to reduce unemployment by at least one per cent per year. There need to be specific strategies to achieve those targets—with jobs for young people at the centre. And these have to be *genuine* strategies. We have seen more than enough "boutique" programs for youth—intended only to fill the shop window, and conceal the fact that the store is empty.

There are many avenues open to the government. One of the most promising is a community investment requirement for the banks—having them reinvest a portion of their profits in the communities that produced them. Another is to end the Bank of Canada's obsession with fighting inflation ahead of all other social ills. By some estimates, that exclusive focus is preventing Canada from creating half a million more jobs over the next five years.

A jobs-focused budget would mean a world of difference for young Canadians. It would go a long way toward addressing the second critical area I want to discuss: the growing gap between the most privileged parts of Canadian society and the rest of us. Increasingly, Canada is moving toward a winner-take-all society. A few people do really well; everyone else has problems. Call it the Titanic economy. On that ill-fated ship, roughly two-thirds of the passengers in first class survived, while the same percentage of passengers in steerage perished.

Since 1980, the average family has seen its before-transfer income drop by 3.9 per cent, while the richest families actually saw their incomes rise. Canada now has the second-worst record on income inequality in the industrialized world. Incredibly, for a country as prosperous as ours, we have seen child poverty increase by 45 per cent from 1989 to 1995. The poverty families are facing is severe. The average poor family would have to make another $9,000 per year just to make it *up* to the poverty line.

There is a cascade effect when families have their financial backs to the wall. They cannot make ends meet. They cannot afford education for their children. The family just slips further and further behind.

A decent job can break that cycle. That is why a jobs-centered budget is so important. But we should also be aiming to find ways to give working families a break, such as removing the GST from essentials like children's clothing, school supplies and home heating fuel. Canada should also be setting clear targets for the elimination of child poverty.

The announcement early in 1997 of a new national child benefit is a first tentative step in the right direction. Let me say how proud I am of Premier Roy Romanow, who pushed hard for the national benefit, and Premier Glen Clark, whose government in B.C. has shown the kind of difference such a benefit can make.

It is tragically easy to convince ourselves that nothing can be done, that opportunities for our young have vanished forever, that greater equality for our citizens is only a pipe dream. But that is nonsense. The fact is that there is tremendous new prosperity in Canada. Just look at bank profits and corporate bottom lines—they are improving by leaps and bounds.

The question is: how do we ensure that every Canadian gets to share in that new prosperity? I pose that question, that challenge, not only to the federal government, but to all of you here today. Let us work together, think together, and fight together for the solutions Canada needs—for our young people, for every Canadian.

PRESENTATION BY BILL ROBSON,
SENIOR POLICY ANALYST, C.D. HOWE INSTITUTE

This is a valuable exercise. I think it is a very good thing to do to get together and try and design a budget. My own impression is that it has less impact on the policy debate than you might wish, and what I want to do is talk about some pitfalls I see in the Alternative Budget process, make some suggestions about avoiding them, and perhaps ending up with a document that has more impact than its predecessors.

Since I was invited here to make at least one criticism, I will make it. It is that the substance of the Alternative Federal Budget seems to reveal a reluctance to acknowledge limits. Now, we have gotten familiar with certain battle lines over limits when it comes to budgeting on macro-budget issues, like whether government borrowing matters, or whether we should worry about high taxes. Less familiar, though, as yet, are limits that we are gradually discovering in our ability to translate good intentions with the resources that we do have into good results. And the era of balanced budgets is going to be one where borrowing and taxes will be a bit less salient as political issues, so I want to spend a bit of time on that second issue of the programs as well.

But first I am going to go back to some very familiar territory, and I apologize for bringing monetary policy up, but I am taking a cue from Jim's technical paper (posted on the CCPA web-site), which maintains that we could have had the original federal deficit-reduction timetable met or bettered without any spending cuts, on the strength of lower interest rates and faster economic growth. In the paper, Jim acknowledges that maybe the spending cuts could be argued to have helped bring about some of the interest rate declines, but then argues that the Bank of Canada could have brought them about in any event, and got us out of the hole.

In the wake of Tony Blair in the U.K. having decided to give the Bank of England autonomy in setting interest rates, I am going to go out on a limb and identify this line of argument as Pitfall No. 1. Now, I want to try and contain the area of disagreement here a little bit. I am uneasy about the way the Bank of Canada conducts policy on the basis of movements in the dollar. I do not think that it makes sense, if the dollar is falling because of a deterioration in the economic outlook, to raise short-term interest rates. That does not seem to make sense to me. But that is a question about means rather than ends. I have my own preferences for what I would like to see the Bank of Canada steer by. But at the end of the day, I think it is appropriate for it to try and get the economy growing at a rate that is healthy, but not enough to bring about higher inflation.

Now, if you are going to enlist the Bank of Canada as a support for fiscal policy, and ask it to print more money on that basis, you have to argue one of two things. You have to argue either that higher inflation is okay, or that you are going to somehow short-circuit the process by which faster money growth is going to lead to higher inflation. Choosing No. 1, that higher inflation is okay, seems to me to acknowledge that there is a pitfall, and step into it at least up to your knees. I do not think necessarily past your knees, because you can certainly have a reasonable debate about whether a bit more inflation would be okay. Pierre Fortin, I know, gets a good hearing when he argues that higher inflation is useful, essentially because it fools workers into accepting wage-cuts without noticing it. And that has been a popular argument, I think, around this table, although not phrased exactly in those terms. But that is the substance of his argument.

The harder thing to be up front about, though, is the question of what you would do if you did that—if you notched up inflation a bit—and discovered that the world was still unpleasantly familiar once inflation was higher. Would you do the same thing again? Well, if there is no point at which that search for a happier life through higher inflation stops, then you are on a familiar slippery slope that we have been on before and not found tremendously rewarding.

If you choose Option No. 2 and say we are going to short-circuit the process, then you are in a pitfall that is right over your head. Last year's Alternative Federal Budget had a recommendation that the Bank of Canada should start buying federal debt at a rate that, in rough and ready terms, I think, would have about tripled the amount that it held over five years, tripled the monetary base in Canada, and by my way of thinking, probably roughly tripled prices as well. There were suggestions about how you might avoid that. You could reimpose reserve requirements on the banks, ration credit in various ways, and basically prevent the banks from extending new money and credit on the basis of this faster-running printing press right at the centre of the Bank of Canada.

I can say a lot of things about reserve requirements and other sorts of new taxes on the financial sector. But at the end of the day, I guess my question would be: How is this easier monetary policy going to kick-start the faster economic growth you are talking about if this chain that leads from faster money printing at the centre to faster credit, faster lending, more money growth, more employment, and so on, at the end of the chain, if it's broken part way? I will not say much more about that, but I really do not see any sensible answer to that question. You want to get the central bank to help out, but then at some point you break the chain and it is a real problem. I do think the Bank could steer a steadier course, and give us low and stable inflation with fewer painful twists and turns than we do get. But I think, if you argue much beyond that—that a significant portion of our social programs can be financed by the printing press—you get us into a hole. The size of that hole depends on how you want to treat the inflation question and where you might stop.

I will draw a curtain over that for the time being and move on to a second place where I think that there are problems that various budget critics get into. And this is true of various political stripes. That is with the impact of taxes and spending on the economy. I think it is true on the demand side as well as the supply side.

On the demand side, I want to key off Jim's technical paper again, because one of the reasons that he argues that Paul Martin could have hit his deficit targets without the spending cuts is because he says that federal spending has a multiplier of 1.5. So for every dollar that the federal government spends, whether financed through new taxing or borrowing, there is an additional 50 cents in activity generated in the economy.

Well, it is a bit like the monetary policy argument to me. If only it were true, then if we were to raise the size of our public sector to, say, Swedish levels, all slack in the economy could disappear and new financing for all kinds of programs would roll in effortlessly because of all the extra activity that would spin off tax revenues, just as it has in Sweden. The same sort of argument gets made on the tax side, though, all the time. You have heard this, too. Tax cuts stimulate demand so much that they pay for themselves. Either way you take that, there is a big pitfall there. There is just no empirical basis for arguing that these demand-management policies through government budgets work. Part of the reason is straightforward. New spending or tax cuts tend to see a lot of the purchasing power that they release just leak across the border through imports. That is just as true if you give your civil servants a pay hike as it is if you cut taxes. Part of the reason is more speculative. Economic models that have high multipliers tend to assume that people are blinkered, backward-looking duffers, who do not form expectations about the future, and do not recognize when situations change. People in the real world, however, react to changes in fiscal policy in all kinds of ways. They can change their spending and saving patterns. They can change the rates that they ask on any loans that they make.

I will be the first to admit that we do not know all the ways that people react, but certainly people who build models of these things have tended over time to make their multipliers get smaller and smaller and smaller. They are typically now less than one. But beyond that, the whole idea of multipliers—this idea that there is a summary measure that you can use to say how much a given change in a government budget is going to change the economy—is in trouble, for the reason that Arthur Donner was talking about earlier. Different taxes and different types of spending have very different effects. And that brings me to the supply side.

If I focus on taxes first, it is very hard to think of a tax that does not change people's incentives in one way or another. Some taxes may encourage work, more than probably discourage it. And all of them certainly will create rewards for changing your activity in ways that make you harder to tax. Now, there is a line of literature that looks at income taxes, particularly, and concludes that the cost of the economy, over and above the dollar that is taken out of someone's pockets, might be in the order of 30-50 cents on the dollar.

It is easy to neglect these costs and it is easy to fall into what I see is a second major pitfall, if you do. I remember Neil Brooks, not exactly a Reaganite, upbraiding his fellow members of the Ontario Fair Tax Commission, in a minority report, for neglecting all these things. He did not necessarily think they were that important, but he did see their omission in that report as a major problem.

Over and above the economic decisions taken at the margins, I want to raise something else that Pierre Fortin often emphasizes, that might not get such a good hearing, if I did not say it for him here. It is this: Taxes tax people's honesty. I think of high taxes being like the marijuana laws. They turn a lot of people, who would otherwise be law-abiding, into criminals. And whatever your political orientation, I do not think you should be casual about that.

Now, moving into the third area I want to touch on, there is more than one supply side. If it was really true that every dollar in tax did an extra 50 cents' worth of damage to the economy, the economy would have imploded long ago. But, in fact, although it grows more slowly than it used to, it still does grow. The reason for that clearly is that lots of government spending provides benefits that are over and above the dollar that ends up in a person's pocket. But this brings me to this third major issue, which is the need to choose carefully which programs to support and which to let go.

Looking at last year's Alternative Federal Budget, it occurred to me that the nature of the coalition that comes together to produce this budget presents an acute challenge when it comes to setting priorities. To someone from outside that coalition, I do not know that it was very well met last time. As you will probably recall, the 1997 Alternative Federal Budget started off with a long list of very commendable objectives, all the way from full employment to a more just, sustainable and peaceful world order. When it got more specific, looking at the spending side of the federal budget, it recommended increases in 24 of the 26 areas that it identified. Only Defence and Veterans Affairs did not make the cut. Agriculture and business subsidies did make the cut. They showed very substantial increases.

In the framework outlining job impacts, the single biggest category of benefit was the hiring of more federal civil servants. Now, when it comes to presenting Canadians with an alternative to current federal practices that might be worth serious consideration, I think that this inability to prioritize and make some trade-offs is a third major pitfall. Now, it is easier to talk about avoiding this pitfall than it is to do it. But it seems to me that the crafters of the Alternative Budget have to be empowered to make a few choices, asking which areas of spending we can be most confident about, and that they yield benefits that outweigh the costs of taking the resources away from somewhere else.

I think that, when you work your way down the list of federal programs, there are a large number about which it is hard to be that confident. Andrew Jackson has a list in his paper: investment in physical infrastructure; investment in federal research and development; investment in training and in post-secondary education. I do not think that in any of those areas anybody is doing any serious analysis of whether the benefits are reasonable in comparison with the costs. My own suspicion is that, in the case of the first two, they are; in the second two, they probably are not.

I do not deny that the money is welcomed by the people who receive it. I do not deny that administering the programs creates nice jobs. But of course that is true of any government program. Some federal money does not do much additional good beyond those things, and I am afraid that some of it does harm. Certainly, some of it could be done better by provinces or local governments.

So I will simply conclude that, to an outside observer, last year's Alternative Budget did not show much evidence of attention to these considerations. But I do not think you can advocate more money for everything, because real budget-making involves choices.

PRESENTATION BY ANDREW JACKSON,
CHIEF ECONOMIST, CANADIAN LABOUR CONGRESS

Living standards in Canada have not increased during the 1990's. In fact, real average family income fell by 3.9 per cent between 1989 and 1996. This dismal performance contrasts with the experience of the United States and most of Western Europe, where real per capita income has grown by between 6 per cent and 13 per cent since 1989. Canadian living standards are thus falling in both absolute and relative terms.

Strikingly, the view of the Department of Finance is that long-term economic growth will continue to be very slow—just 1.9 per cent in the first decade of the next century, and still lower thereafter (See Table 1). For the purposes of planning the Canada Pension Plan, it assumes a long-term growth rate of just 1.5 per cent.

Long-term economic growth—and thus the prospect for rising living standards—is a function of the growth of the labour force, capital investment and productivity. There is general agreement that productivity is the most essential long-term determinant. Certainly it is desirable that growth should come from increased efficiency, rather than from a long-term trend to increased hours of work.

Trend-annual total-factor productivity (TFP) growth in Canada was 1.5 per cent per year from 1965 to 1975. It has been 0.2 per cent ever since, with a very modest recovery in the 1990s. The Department of Finance forecasts trend-future TFP growth of just 0.4 per cent. This dismal projection implies very little future relief from stagnant living standards.

The "orthodox" view is that macro-economic policy has little or nothing to do with the long-term growth rate. All that macro-economic policy can do is to ensure that the economy reaches its potential growth rate, which is determined by trend productivity growth (exogenously determined by the rate of technical progress) and by the growth of the labour force. On this view, there is no scope for stimulating growth by way of macro-economic policy, once the economy is operating at full capacity. The latter, in turn, is defined by the level of the so-called non-accelerating inflation rate of unemployment or NAIRU. Once a short-term cyclical output gap has been closed, any attempt to boost growth through macro-economic expansion is held to result in higher inflation.

The Alternative Federal Budget (AFB) has argued that this view is wrong and destructive, and that restrictive macro-economic policy based on a very low inflation objective can keep growth well below potential. The high real interest rates imposed to secure low inflation dampen capital investment, restrictive fiscal policy lowers public investment, and continuing high levels of unemployment lead to an erosion of "human capital." Restrictive macro-economic policy has not resulted in a one-time adjustment cost—as argued by the Department of Finance, the Bank of Canada, the Organization for Economic Co-operation and Development (OECD) and others—but in on-going costs due to "hysteresis" effects.

Some evidence at least can be found for this view in the United States, where the economy has grown faster than orthodox economists believed possible. As Pierre Fortin and others have argued, the economy can grow faster, if macro-economic policy is somewhat more tolerant of inflation. The lesson from the United States is also that the costs and risks of pushing down the unemployment rate have been greatly exaggerated.

This having been said, trend productivity growth remains the most important determinant of long-term growth, and the determinants of productivity growth are much broader than the macro-economic environment. Labour productivity has risen significantly faster in much of Western Europe than in the United States, despite restrictive macro-economic policies.

There is no consensus among economists regarding the structural determinants of productivity growth. Neo-classical economists stress the importance of low taxes and "free markets." Other economists stress the importance of public investment in education, human capital, infrastructure, and research and development, as well as intervention in the investment decisions of the private sector (as in active industrial and managed trade policies).

The dominant view by far in Canadian policy circles has been that deregulation, privatization, free trade and a smaller public sector will lead to more rapid productivity growth. This view was strongly expressed in the 1984 "Agenda for Economic Renewal" paper of the Department of Finance, in successive OECD reports on Canada, and—in more nuanced form—in the Department of Finance's *Jobs and Growth* papers. Most recent "structural reform" policies have been promoted on the basis that they would boost potential growth. The Department of Finance estimated that the Canada-U.S. Free Trade Agreement would result in a 2.5 per cent gain in real GDP because of faster productivity growth, and that the GST would result in a 1 per cent gain in real GDP.

In point of fact, there is little or no evidence of a pick-up in productivity growth from the "free- market" oriented "structural reforms" of the past decade and more. In the 1990's, Canadian labour (and TFP) productivity performance has been poor, even compared to the United States, which has not performed strongly itself (except in manufacturing). As shown in Table II, we have lagged significantly behind the US, particularly in manufacturing, and the gap appears to have been growing rather than narrowing. The gap is no doubt partly explained by weaker output growth in Canada (an average of 1.4 per cent vs 2.0 per cent in the 1990's), but productivity performance, particularly in manufacturing, should have converged because of the Free Trade Agreement and North American Free Trade Agreement (after all, more manufacturing output is now sold in the United States than in Canada).

Neo-classical economists are very puzzled that the projected boost to potential growth from "structural reform" has not come about. For example, the OECD noted in its 1996 country report on Canada that "structural reforms should contribute to creating an environment for sustained growth. The numerous initiatives in this area since the mid 1980's have been slow in producing the expected gains in economic efficiency and growth potential."

Again in 1997, the OECD reported that "over the past decade or so, structural policy initiatives have opened up both domestic and international markets for Canadian producers and, at the same time, considerably reduced government involvement in economic affairs. Recent actions have maintained this course, tackling continued structural impediments. Despite the reforms' focus on improving economic efficiency, the expected positive effects on productivity and potential output have yet to materialize."

The noted philosopher of science Sir Karl Popper argued that theories which are contradicted by the evidence should be reformulated and retested, while historians of science note that theoretical paradigms are in fact defended by all kinds of ad hoc arguments. The official line today is that structural reform will ultimately pay off, once we have passed through a period of "painful adjustment." At least the OECD is honest enough to admit that there is no evidence that growth is picking up due to the free market "reforms" implemented over the past decade or so.

What alternative conclusions might be drawn from Canada's dismal economic performance? And what are the implications for macro-economic fiscal policy?

First, it is reasonable to suspect that macro-economic policy has made a difference. Part of the Canada-US productivity gap is almost certainly due to the slower rate of output growth in Canada. Certainly, productivity gains are likely to be meagre in an economy operating well below capacity, such as the Canadian economy in the 1990's.

Secondly, fiscal policy should be directed towards promoting future productivity growth. A very important aspect of the Alternative Federal Budget is increased public investment in areas which could reasonably be expected to have a long-term payoff—investment in physical infrastructure, federal R&D and training programs, and investment in post secondary education. Both R&D and training programs address and help remedy the long-standing tendency of the Canadian business sector to invest inadequately in innovation and in skills. There is extensive economic research showing that public investment in these areas yields considerable returns.

The AFB also proposes greater support for investment in private industry, by way of the sector development funds financed in part from surplus profits of the financial sector. The AFB recognizes the need for some regulation of the private investment process to overcome long-standing structural problems of the Canadian economy—notably the underdevelopment of sophisticated industries such as machinery and equipment, and continuing over-reliance on the resource sector. Recent productivity performance in manufacturing suggests that deregulation and free trade have not produced the expected benefits, and that the case for more interventionist policies must be revisited.

Canada has achieved a fiscal surplus at a very substantial cost in foregone growth and future growth potential (in addition to the large costs inflicted on the disadvantaged via cuts to social programs and public services). The dismal productivity record of the 1990's—and the almost equally dismal future projections of the Department of Finance—should kindle a major public debate over what kinds of fiscal policies can increase our potential to grow. The AFB can make an important contribution by developing a long term growth strategy, and by documenting the key importance of public investment and regulation of private investment in such a strategy.

TABLE 1
LONG TERM ECONOMIC PROJECTIONS
(DEPARTMENT OF FINANCE)

Year Growth	Potential Output Growth	Productivity (TFP)
1997 - 99	2.3	0.4
2000 - 09	1.9	0.4
2010 - 2015	1.3	0.4

TABLE 2
CANADIAN AND U.S. LABOUR PRODUCTIVITY TRENDS IN 1990S

	Canada	U.S.
Business Sector		
1990	-1.6	0.8
1991	1.1	0.6
1992	1.6	3.4
1993	1.0	0.2
1994	1.8	0.5
1995	0.5	0.1
1996	0.3	1.0
average	0.7	0.9
Manufacturing		
1990	1.7	1.8
1991	0.4	2.5
1992	3.9	3.6
1993	1.7	2.1
1994	4.4	3.1
1995	1.2	3.4
1996	1.1	3.8
average	2.1	2.9

Source: Statistics Canada, The Daily, June 5, 1997.

PRESENTATION BY MANFRED BIENEFELD, SCHOOL OF PUBLIC ADMINISTRATION, CARLETON UNIVERSITY

We need urgently to think about the confines, context, and constraints within which governments put together their budgets. In 1995, Paul Krugman wrote that the Mexican peso crisis was, in his view, the beginning of the end of the Washington consensus. (Krugman also discusses how it was that the Washington consensus ever came into being, given the fact there was so little empirical or historical evidence to support it.) If Krugman was right, then surely the Asian crisis means that the game is up. The bankruptcy of this approach to economic policy simply has to be evident at this point. To place the future of the economy and of our citizens in the hands of an increasingly volatile global financial market is irresponsible, considering that its regulation is constantly talked about, but in private is recognised as being virtually impossible. If it is true that these markets and institutions are the only proper ones to make those judgements about risk and about resource allocation, then who is to second guess them? If we say they should have the job and we say there should be a regulator to oversee the risk, then what we are saying is that the regulator knows the risk better than they do. And if that is true, then the prevailing way of thinking has to change.

The truth is that these policies have been an abdication of responsibility; they have been a mechanism for redistributing income massively, worldwide and nationally. The evidence is clear. The impact on growth and welfare has been highly ambiguous and in most cases negative. In the United States, real wages are now lower than they were in 1973. And it seems to me that we have a way of understanding this.

The 1920's and 1930's were uppermost in the minds of the architects of the Bretton Woods system. They constructed a liberal trading system, but were mesmerized by the absolute necessity of ensuring that this system would have safeguards preventing it from collapsing into the turmoil and instability of the 1920's and 1930's. So they built two absolutely central safeguards into the system: capital controls and fixed exchange rates. Keynes wrote beautifully and extensively on how capital controls had to be a permanent feature of such a system. Even Morgentaler, the Secretary of the Treasury in the United States, stressed that the system must never again fall into the hands of the financial speculators.

In a world where capital flows were managed, we would have to insist on relatively fixed exchange rates. Not because we do not understand those first-year textbook arguments about the exchange rate being a price, but because we understand that in a world of instabilities, flexible exchange rates may themselves become a source of instability.

Of course, when the world was induced to shift to the more flexible exchange rates, there were theorists or ideologues who assured us that this would produce greater stability. They claimed that the real exchange rate was what mattered and that the nominal exchange was really just an epiphenomenon. And indeed, if the market worked perfectly, then flexible exchange rates would bring stability. In theory anything is possible. But the evidence is in. That argument about flexible exchange rates is not true. It was not true in the 1920's or 1930's and it is not true now. That is why Bretton Woods was created in the first place. Dornbush and Frankel did a huge empirical study which concluded that the proportion of the huge increase in fluctuations in real exchange rates that could be explained with reference to the economic fundamentals was "close to zero."

I am glad to say that the news has reached certain parts of the financial press. George Soros tells us in no uncertain terms that private banks are entirely inappropriate instruments for allocating international finance. They do not actually care about the long-term structural adjustment of economies and they say so when you speak to them.

An editorial in the *Financial Times* recently had this to say: "Is banking part of the private sector? As the crisis in East Asia unfolds, the answer turns out once again to be both yes and no. Profits go to private owners, but losses, if big enough, to taxpayers. As a result, supposedly safe institutions assume vast risks, the result being endemic financial instability." This is not a minor issue. The prevailing argument says that the real economy should constantly be adjusted to price signals. But if the price signals and exchange rates are so volatile and so irrational, then the argument makes no sense.

We had an inkling of this through the 1970's and 1980's. But there was always Asia. Asia was the beacon on the hill. Asia was the model. Asia was the place where the sound policies were actually implemented. Because, whenever you said, "O.K., I understand the theory. I do not find it very plausible. Where is your evidence?" the answer was that they did not have much evidence, but they had Asia. The financial markets agreed and poured money into Asia. They were voting with their cheque books.

Then Asia collapsed. Now the story is being rewritten. Shameless people talk about Asia as though it were some kind of corrupt hell hole of corruption, and as though it were obvious that this would happen. There was an article that said: "You know, in Asia, bankers take decision on the golf course instead it doing it from balance sheets." Can you imagine the tone of these discussions?

The greatest irony is that I have a clipping from the *Far Eastern Economic Review* from the late 1980's, which has extensive interviews with people they call "financial gunslingers" who were just leaving Tokyo because, while they had made billions (the numbers are quoted in the article, they are absolutely enormous), the bubble had burst. They were saying: "There is nothing more to be done in Japan now. We are off to Asia to do the same thing."

Well they did. And they made enormous amounts of money. Now Asia is being restructured in a world where the Mexican finance minister is sent to Thailand to give advice on how to run the economy. Monty Python's Flying Circus could not do better. Mexico, which is disintegrating, where the society is on the skids (I am going there in two weeks and I cannot believe what the people at the embassy are telling me)! Crime rates are exploding and the middle class has been destroyed. Yet the economics literature labels it a success story because the financiers got repaid.

When South Korea joined the OECD, the *Financial Times* declared that it would have to stop mollycoddling labour and get rid of employment security etc. The Koreans were reluctant, but they have come on side. And the mechanism has been the same as ever. It is the same recipe that has been used to destroy our welfare state. The speculative bubble of the 1980's and the property markets distorted prices beyond belief, inflating public deficits, and these deficits were used to bludgeon the welfare state.

There are five lessons to be learned here:

1) banking is a public trust which cannot be run as a profit-maximizing activity. Indeed, if you went back to read the financial texts of the 1950's, they generally tell you exactly that. Because generally competition in banking will simply lead to unsupportable risks.
2) International capital movements need to be managed and controlled. The benefits of these movements are much smaller than is generally alleged. Even the financial institutions themselves constantly agree and admit that development in every society has and ought to be fundamentally driven by domestic savings.
3) Once capital movements have been moderated, exchange rates must be relatively fixed and policy must be organized around maintaining those relatively fixed levels. They have to be adjustable in the end, but that has to be a policy objective.
4) The efficiency of markets ultimately depends on monetary and exchange-rate stability
5) Human welfare is much more dependent on the existence of stable and cohesive communities and societies than it is on marginal efficiency at any level, particularly because that marginal efficiency can alter so dramatically in very short spaces of time. And this ultimately requires a degree of sovereignty, which again Keynes wrote about extensively, that allows societies to make trade-offs. Trade-offs that can never and will never be made by the market as such—trade-offs between efficiency and social stability; trade-offs between efficiency and sustainable development; trade-offs between short- and long-term horizons. And those choices, those value-judgements have to be made by societies through a political process. But we have to create a world in which that is possible. And that requires interest rates and profit rates that vary from society to society, because that is an implication of making those choices, and Keynes rightly said that if we create a world in which there is one profit rate (which is a world where capital movements are completely deregulated), those choices will no longer be open to people. That is the central issue which would create space for alternative budgets even more beautiful than the one we see here.

Presentation by Andrew Sharpe, Executive Director, Centre for Study of Living Standards

I shall present a framework for understand the relationship between living standards, economic well-being and fiscal policy. The Centre for the Study of Living Standards is doing a project on the state of living standards and quality of life in Canada, and I shall borrow from it in my presentation.

The basic definition of living standards I am using is personal income on a per capita basis in dollar terms. Personal income is composed of a number of components. Labour income is by far the most important, accounting for about two thirds of it. But in addition to labour income, transfer payments represent an important component, about 14 per cent of personal income, as do investment income and unincorporated business income.

A second definition of living standards is disposable personal income per capita in real terms, which is basically personal income minus taxes. That is also an indication of transient living standards, although it is probably not as good as the first one, personal income per capita, because if taxes go up, then disposable income goes down. But you are not necessarily worse off because you receive benefits in the form of government services. However, if the increased taxes are used to pay down debt, for example, then you are not receiving any benefits directly and you may feel you are worse off if taxes go up.

What do I mean by economic well being? That is a much broader concept than living standards. Using some work by Lars Osberg on definitions of economic well-being, the Centre for the Study of Living Standards has developed an index of economic well-being. That index includes four basic components. 1/ What we call consumption flows. 2/ Measures of stocks of wealth. 3/ Indicators of inequality. 4/ Indicators of insecurity in society. We have developed weights for those four basic components, and they are obviously very subjective. Other people may prefer other weights. But we have weighted consumption with .4, wealth and stocks with .1, and insecurity and inequality with .25 each, in the construction of an aggregate index of economic well-being. This index is still in its developmental stages, but we have some preliminary results I can share with you today.

The key component of well-being is the flow of consumption. We draw our measure of consumption from the national accounts, although we adjust it for a number of factors, such as the cost of commuting, the cost of crime, the cost of accidents, and the cost of pollution. We also include government spending on goods and services and unpaid work. In the future we hope to include an adjustment for the increased life expectancy of the population. For our indication of the stock of wealth in society, we look at the capital stock, the stock of R&D, stocks of natural resources, and stocks of foreign debt, which really are negative stock, in the sense that we are worse off if they go up. We also are developing a stock of human capital, because one could argue that we will be a lot worse off in the long run if we run down our human capital.

In terms of the component of inequality, we use the GINI coefficient for total income and also rates of poverty. Finally, for insecurity, we use the unemployment rate and the rate of the duration of unemployment. We realize that is inadequate and we are developing a measure of the probability of job loss, which is the key determinant of insecurity as well as an indication of the overall social safety net.

That is a very quick overview of what is in this index. Now, what has happened to trends in living standards and economic well-being in the 1990's? Turning first to living standards, I think the key term I would use there would be "disastrous". Basically the 1990's have been a dismal decade for living standards in Canada. Between 1947 and 1981, personal income per capita grew at an annual rate of over 3.2 per cent in real terms. In the 1980's, the growth rate was about 1.5 per cent a year. In the 1990's, between 1989 and 1996, we were falling at .8 per cent per year. We do not have data yet for 1997. That will show some improvement, so it will be slightly less if you go from 1989 to 1997.

In 1996, per capita personal income in real terms was about 5 per cent less than it was in 1989. In terms of disposable income, it was even worse. We were 9 per cent below 1989 level in 1996, because of increased taxes in the 1990's. In fact, if we want to get back to 1989 levels by the year 2000, we will need 1.3 per cent growth in personal income per capita from 1996 to the year 2000 and 2.3 per cent growth in personal disposable income per capita. I should note that it took 11 years for personal income to recover to 1929 levels after the Depression. There is a possibility that we will not have regained the 1989 peak by the year 2000, 11 years later. The 1990's would show a worse performance in terms of growth for personal income than the 1930's. I hope that does not happen.

In terms of transient and economic well-being, the situation is even worse than for living standards. In terms of per capita income, our overall index was down 12 per cent between 1989 and 1996. In terms of the overall components, in terms of consumption, there was actually not much of a change. One reason was that unpaid work increased. That offset some of the declines in government spending on goods and services and on personal consumption. In terms of wealth, the index was down about 5 per cent and that was linked to increased foreign debt and also some decline in our stocks in natural resources.

In terms of inequality, the index was down 15 per cent and that was largely due to increases in poverty. Actually, income distribution has not become more unequal, at least until recently. Data from 1996 data show a large increase in income inequality. But there was not a major increase in inequality in terms of total income, as opposed to wage income, in the 1980's and 1990's. In terms of economic welfare, we are even worse off in terms of our measures of real income.

What is the relationship to fiscal policy in all this? First off, fiscal policy has a number of effects on living standards. Obviously, transfer payments directly affect income and consumption, and government services also directly affect a broad measure of consumption in society. Of course, taxes can reduce disposable income, although that might be offset through increased transfer payments or increased expenditure by government on goods and service taxes.

In terms of well-being, there are similar links. Transfer payments affect consumption. Government infrastructure expenditures affect stocks of wealth. The stock of R&D is affected by government spending and government policy. Government transfer payments greatly affect inequality; in fact, they have been the major factor in preventing an increase in inequality up until recently. Finally, the social safety net is very closely linked to government programs, such as UI. So there are very direct links between fiscal policy and both living standards and economic well-being.

What impact has fiscal policy had on living standards and economic well-being in the 1990's? First off, it is very important to make the point that the key factor affecting living standards is not fiscal policy. It is really the overall state of economic growth in the economy and in particular employment growth. Employment growth since 1989 is about .6 per cent a year compared to 1.6 per cent in the 1980's. There has been a major fall in the employment/population ratio. In addition, we have had much lower productivity growth. That is one of the reasons we have had less growth in real wages.

Those are the key factors driving living standards and, of course, those standards reflect monetary policy. I concur with Andrew Jackson's overall assessment of macro-economic policy, and monetary policy in particular. It explains a much inferior economic performance in the 1990's compared to, say, the United States or earlier periods in our economic history. So fiscal policy is not the key, but it is conditioned a lot by the overall economy and it also has a number of effects on these indicators of well-being that I have mentioned.

Transfer payments held up quite well in the early 1990's. They were cut in recent years. But up until around 1994, they were growing at quite a rate. In fact, the share of personal income that came from transfer payments increased by over 2 percentage points between 1989 and 1994. So transfer payments were doing fairly well, though they were cut in 1995/1996. Government services have also been cut and that has led to some fall in the indicators of economic well-being. Recent cuts in transfer payments have led to a cut in consumption and have had a negative effect on well-being. The cuts in government expenditure on infrastructure have reduced the stock of capital and had a negative effect on well-being. Cuts in education expenditures are going to have a very negative long-term effect on capital formation. Overall, fiscal policy has recently had a very negative effect on both measures of living standards and on measures of economic welfare.

What about the future? I think there is a great potential for fiscal policy to contribute to bringing back the upward trend in living standards and economic well-being that we saw up to the 1990's. Thanks to economic growth we shall have the fiscal dividend and a large part of that can be used to improve living standards and economic well-being.

I would identify 4 key priorities for improving living standards and economic well-being.

1. A tax cut for low-income individuals. That would result in faster growth in disposable income overall, and particularly for these individuals. The best way to accomplish this would be full indexation of benefits and brackets, and reduced marginal tax-rates for low-income individuals. I think that would go a long way towards improving overall consumption, particularly among lower-income individuals. It would also, of course, reduce inequality, which is part of the overall index of economic well-being.
2. Human capital has to be a key determinant of long-run growth, yet we have cut a lot at the post-secondary level in recent years. Increased expenditure on education would have an effect on the stock of human capital.
3. Increased child tax benefits would have a major effect on inequality by reducing the rate of child poverty and contributing to increased economic well-being.
4. Lower unemployment would improve economic security, but reversing some of the cuts in UI would too, by increasing the percentage of people covered by Unemployment Insurance in the future.

PRESENTATION BY MIKE MCCRACKEN,
CHAIRMAN, INFORMETRICA

Unemployment seems to be stuck around 9 per cent. Real per capita incomes are stagnant or declining. Income distribution appears to be worsening. Certain groups are falling further behind. Fiscal limitations seem to be prevent us from doing anything about unemployment and other concerns. There is an instability in the current account balance and there is some concern about our international competitiveness, even at our low exchange rate.

Real wages have not been keeping up with productivity. A large gap has opened up between real wages and productivity. The promise that real wages would in some sense be influenced by growth and productivity has not been kept. Indeed, productivity was almost 16 per cent higher in 1996 than in 1981, whereas real wages were only about 6 per cent higher. A 10 per cent gap has opened up between real wages and real labour productivity. That is fundamentally why we have had weak real disposable income and reduced real consumption over this period.

We anticipate 3.5 per cent growth this year, the best year since 1994. Under current policies, 1998-1999 will bring somewhat less rapid growth. The good news is that growth will be slightly more rapid in Canada than in the United States over this period. But keep in mind that they are operating at the moment with a substantially lower unemployment rate, even though it may be an overestimate of the tightness of their labour market. The key message is that the robustness of the growth in the economic recovery in the 1980's, where we averaged over 4 per cent growth (1983-1989) is not being repeated in this recovery. Nor is there any sense that we will be moving back vigorously. As a result, the unemployment rate remains fairly high, 9.2 per cent on average in 1997. It will stay around 8 per cent in 1998 and 1999.

Earlier today, Alexa McDonough commented on the high rate of youth unemployment. We are currently running about 16 per cent. That might come down to as low as 14 per cent with these improvements but it will still be very high, and substantially above the United States, something which prior to 1981 was not a characteristic of the Canadian economy.

The participation rate and employment ratio are behind this. We have seen participation rates decline. But the percentage of people 15 and over working as a share of the population—the employment ratio—has declined from 62 per cent in 1989 to about 58 per cent. This is what Pierre Fortin has referred to in his presidential address to the Canadian Economics Association as the "Great Canadian Slump." It is a peculiarity of Canada. This kind of slump and sustained lowering is not evident in the US numbers. We are wasting $80-100 billion in foregone output. This level of waste is much more unforgivable than the transaction cost of unemployment insurance, which some people consider a bit high.

Between 1989 and 1997, there was a drop of about 13 basis points in the employment ratio for females aged 15-19, and a similar drop in the 20-24 year-old group. We think this reflects people staying in school longer and increasing their post-secondary education. That should have some positive longer-term effects. When you look at the male unemployment levels, however, the drop is across all age groups, or all but those 65 and over.

There is a debate in a slack economy as to whether education helps the individual quite substantially. But whether it does anything overall for the economy is not as clear. We have had rising employment ratios or enrolment ratios for some time now and no strong evidence that they are showing up yet in our productivity, although a major effect may only discernable there after many years.

The gap between productivity and real wages will continue to narrow through 2006, but by no means back even to the levels that we had in the mid-1980's. Finally, real income is down, real disposable income per household, with 1981 equal to 100, is today at about 94, down from a peak of about 105. That is the decline that has occurred. By the year 2006, we may able to get back to the level of real disposable income per household that we had in 1981. We will have had no improvement in real income per household for 25 years and for a good part of that period, we will have operated substantially below it. That is a pretty dismal performance.

Even though they are currently lower, real interest rates (this is the industrial bond rate, long term and relative to the GDP deflator) are still running in the 5 per cent range. And that still greatly in excess of the real growth that we are looking at. The real issue for government finance is the way in which real interest rates unfold. We would argue that much could be gained if we focussed first on substantially low real interest rates, below the real growth or long-term potential growth of the economy. This is the desirable and necessary policy if any kind of sensible stability is to be returned to the economy.

We are not going in that direction. There is pressure growing for experience-rated UI and a soon as that occurs the employers will pressure the government to cut the benefits even more. Limited indexing continues and there are more user fees. Deficit phobia has been reflected here today in the idea that we must run a balanced budget or a mild surplus, even though we are running huge primary surpluses at the moment. This kind of an atmosphere is likely to lead to further cuts in expenditures including transfers to the provinces. At the same time, if we continue with high unemployment and immigration in the 250,000 range, I expect that we will increasingly see a backlash on the immigration front, something that we could have avoided. That is the good news.

The bad news is things could get a lot worse. Certainly a major recession could hit the US and the world economy. The betting is that it is unlikely the US will continue to go along without someone touching the policy levers and screwing things up. The world economy is subject to increasing uncertainty at the moment, as unemployment rates go double digit now in most of the European countries and the Asian debt difficulties begin to show up in cutbacks in spending and cutbacks in employment, in particular layoffs in factories and mines supplying Asia as we have seen recently in B.C.

But we can also create our own nightmares. Inflation rates can pick up substantially and the Bank of Canada can raise interest rates substantially from current levels in order to deflate the economy. That is the mechanism, it is no magic. We could have some additional panics, more and more financial institutions closing their doors, whether that be restricted only to Canada, or more likely internationally. And if that is not enough, we have people working hard on trying to create another referendum in Quebec to add to the uncertainty.

What not to do in this whole world is easier to say than what to do, so let us start with what we would not do. Do not raise interest rates permanently. Do not get immersed in the debate about whether potential growth is 2 or 2.5 per cent. We are sitting here with a very large output gap in Canada. We ought to be arguing about how quickly we reduce that gap, not whether the potential underlying growth rate is 2.3 or 2.8 as the current debate in the US is being framed. Do not cut taxes for the rich, in spite of pessimism there may be about the size and magnitudes of some multipliers. The one thing there is general agreement on is that tax cuts on those who would save them are likely to ensure that there is no multiplier effect in the economy. Do not focus on running surpluses and reducing the debt. Stop increasing economic security through these cuts to social programs and removing protections in labour markets, whether that be minimum wages or not enforcing current legislation.

Some sensible policies: Adopt a full-employment target. The pace of change in the unemployment rate should be at least one percentage point. I would like Mr. Martin to thump on things and say: "Come hell or high water we will deliver that!"—meaning that he would try to go for two or three, just to make sure that he reaches that objective with the same vigour that we have seen in his deficit reduction effort. How far do you go on that? My own target is 4 per cent at the present time, but if we get there and feel we should go further, I am prepared to debate it at that time.

We need the move to stimulus on both the fiscal and monetary side. It does us no good to go in opposite directions. Operation Twist, if you will, is not what we need in this economy. It is, I think, important to begin talking about and developing incomes policies as alternatives to high unemployment as a way to control inflation. Whether we need them or not, as we move towards full employment at some point in the future, it would be appropriate to have at least some better incomes policies than the current ones. We do have an incomes policy at the moment. We basically say we will keep inflation between 1 per cent and 3 per cent and, by God, if it gets out of that range, we are going to create massive unemployment! That is the current incomes policy. I cannot imagine that a group of people could not devise a somewhat more sensible one than that, that does less damage to the economy.

We could certainly start looking at a guaranteed annual income or social wage, or whatever you want to call it, for high unemployment areas. We could start it in areas where unemployment stands at 30 per cent or 40 per cent. There is no sense in worrying much about the incentive effects of a guaranteed annual income in that particular environment. I doubt that the level would be so high as to trigger a great mobility of people into rural areas, the far North or other areas in which unemployment rates are particularly high. We should keep looking seriously at changes in working time. You could also think of paid educational leave as a thing to foster. The net consequence of that, if it is significant in time and duration, is that it does require increased employment to replace some of those people who would otherwise be covered. The federal government could show some leadership in that area.

Since the government no longer allows individuals to receive UI benefits if they quit their jobs, there is no rationale for making individuals pay UI premiums anymore. Cutting employee UI premiums would give you a $4 to 6 billion tax-cut bang. And it would go to the lower-income working people. If employers paid the UI and CCP premium without an upper limit, that would also take away the incentive to overtime.

One possibility is to raise minimum wages, but do it for adults with a high school education or the equivalent. This would give people an incentive to stay in school and earn that degree or certificate. You might even go further and prevent employers from hiring people who are not so certified, but that is perhaps too draconian.

We should not overdo debt reduction. A balanced budget and stable debt should be achieved through growth in the economy, not by focussing only on the debt per se. Should we balance the budget in a recession or move to increase restraint? I think that one of the key roles of government is to stabilize the economy and perform a counter-cyclical policy. In an open economy, I do not think we are going to get much of a payoff from debt reduction. If anyone can convince me that a declining debt/GDP ratio will give you lower real interest rates, I am prepared to listen. I know that it works the other way: lower rates will bring down the debt/GDP ratio.

How large is the gap and how far do we have to go? I think something in the order of 8 per cent to 10 per cent growth in GDP would be a good start. Assuming that 2 to 2.5 percentage points of growth translate into one percentage point of unemployment, then that gives you a good starting point for assessing how much do you have to do. Unfortunately, with current policies, and even average good luck, we may only make little progress in the next decade.

PRESENTATION BY MICHAEL MENDELSON, SENIOR FELLOW, CALEDON INSTITUTE

My aim is to provide a ballpark quantitative analysis of the alternative fiscal strategies on the debt. A lot of the discussion about the debt has a theological veneer around it. Debt reduction is regarded as intrinsically virtuous. Somebody in a blue suit and white shirt can stand up and say that we ought to be reducing the debt more rapidly, and have an air of credibility about them. I would argue instead that this is a financial and economic question. Like any other financial and economic question, it must start with a discussion of what the numbers are. Anyone who claims that the debt ought to be reduced more quickly, without providing the numbers to substantiate that argument, is not to be taken seriously.

I developed a fiscal model of the federal debt. It is a fiscal model, not an economic one. For those who are economists, that means that the economic assumptions are exogenous not endogenous. It projects the debt to 2008/2009. It allows you to look at various scenarios very easily to see what the debt level would be under different assumptions.

I began by developing a base case, which I characterize as a maximum reasonable debt reduction case. This is the scenario that would prevail with no change in policy. In it, the government meets its present commitments and provides a little bit for real per capita increases in costs, but nothing else. There are no more cuts. Then I compare other scenarios to that base case. The main measure that I look at here is debt burden. By that I simply mean the ratio of federal government debt to the gross domestic product (GDP).

Certain assumptions are built into the base case and the other scenarios, such as GDP growth and inflation. The main policy variables are spending and tax decisions and I have put in two types of them. One is the annual increase in transfers to people, to provinces and of course direct federal spending. Those are tied to the inflation rate, and so on, in the model. The second one is the possibility of one-time shocks, one-time policy decisions affecting the economy.

The main assumptions on the base case are that we see real GDP growth at levels of 3 per cent, 2.8 per cent and then 2.5 per cent, an inflation rate of 2 per cent, interest averaged on the government debt of 7.25 per cent. Currently it is about 7.8 per cent. The current commitments I put down as a billion dollars each in tax cuts, personal transfers and program spending. That is probably a little bit of an overstatement. But I have tried in the base case to err on the side of small 'c' conservatism, to ensure that I am not overstating or understating the case. The annual change in spending that I provide in order to be cautious is fairly generous. I have transfers to persons growing at the same rate as GDP. I have transfers to governments growing at the rate of inflation plus 1.5 per cent (as the approximate population growth figure), which would have real transfers to provincial governments per capita remaining constant over the period. And I also have direct programs growing at the rate of the Gross Domestic Product.

The result of all of this is a very rapid reduction in the federal debt as a percentage of GDP, from its current level of approximately 70 per cent to just about 20 per cent—20.05 per cent to be exact—in the year 2008/2009.

I then look at a number of scenarios. In Scenario 1, I said : "Let us leave everything the same and increase spending substantially." In the model, all the spending was just pumped in 1998/1999. Of course, that is just a simplifying assumption. You would not necessarily want to do things that way in real life—you might, but perhaps not. But that is a simplifying assumption. So I looked at an additional $ 9 billion of spending and what the impact would be. The consequence is that we continue to have a very rapid decrease in debt burdens.

I looked at a number of other scenarios in the paper, but tried to keep well within my target range, so as to satisfy the central bank. I will only put two up here. In scenario 2, I ask what happens if the economic assumptions are just a little bit better? What does that mean for spending? There will be some interplay between the economic assumptions and fiscal policy. These economic assumptions are more optimistic obviously, but they are also more mainstream. The Royal Bank, Scotia McLeod, and CBIC have just put out revised forecasts. I might not have them in the right order, but for next year they were 3 per cent, 3.3 per cent and 4 per cent. Some might argue that 2.7 per cent is high for the ongoing period. But then, if we did get 1 per cent productivity and 1.5 per cent population growth, it is not outlandish to imagine the potential of closing our gap in economic potential over that period. So I assume a little higher inflation rate, 2.2 per cent as well.

But then I put in $12 billion. What happens, not entirely by coincidence, is that you end up with exactly the same debt burden and the same accelerated debt repayment in scenario 2 as you would in scenario 1.

Now, I did do sensitivity analysis on all of these with what happens if you have a 1 per cent decrease in interest rate or 1 per cent increase, or whatever, and I can say that in almost every instance, in every instance, in fact, you end up still with a continuing decrease in debt burdens. The reason for that is well understood, I think, around this table. That is because we have achieved a very significant primary balance in our budget that is our revenue over our spending, not counting public debt interest. Now the public has, unfortunately, no comprehension of that reality. I hope that is one of the realities that the Alternative Budget could help to bring to light.

I tried to do some international comparisons. For a variety of reasons, it is not that easy to do, namely because the figures that I was giving you were all on a public accounts basis. International comparisons have to go on a national accounts basis. I did some recalculations on some fairly rough assumptions about the relationship between public accounts and national accounts and provincial debts—rough assumptions, but I think probably erring on the side of overstatement. In all three scenarios I have evoked, we end up with the second lowest debt burden among the Group of Seven nations.

The first conclusion I would draw from all this is that under almost any sensible scenario, we are going to have accelerating and rapid reduction in our debt burdens. Of course there are things that we could do that would reverse that. But they are not really on anyone's table, as far as I can see. The main difference between alternative fiscal strategies in regard to reduction in debt burden is not *where* you end up, but *when* you end up there. If your target is 20 per cent or 25 per cent, the difference is one of time. The difference between getting to a debt/GDP ratio of 20 per cent under the base case, where we do not increase spending, and getting there when we increase spending by $10 billion is about 2 years.

The real choice is between reaching a debt/GDP ratio of 20 per cent in ten years, or taking the opportunity to reinvest in our social and economic infrastructure and in other possibilities for real improvement in the lot of Canadians—particularly low-income Canadians who have bourn the brunt of the cuts over the last few years—and reaching the 20 per cent ratio in 12 years. I am not making a judgement about which is the correct choice. I have simply offered you a quantitative analysis of what the real choice is, so that a reasonable judgement can be made.

PRESENTATION BY BOB DALE,
CHIEF ECONOMIST, NATIONAL UNION OF PUBLIC AND GENERAL EMPLOYEES

The "conventional" or "received " wisdom says that the range of public policy options is limited. It says that public policy is limited to those options consistent with the "neo-conservative" economic agenda. Those options are also held to be consistent with "sound " economics.

Neo-conservatives claim that:

- A main reason for our economic problems is that "government is too large," "too intrusive," and a "burden" on the more "efficient" private sector.
- Social programs and other entitlements must be trimmed, to jolt us from our lethargy and make us more productive. Workers have to be more "flexible".
- Companies have no choice but to downsize and restructure. If they don't, global competition will leave them far behind.
- It's not government's role to create jobs. Putting the right economic framework in place, and giving the private sector more freedom to operate, will ensure that jobs are created.

These ideas exert a major influence on public policy decisions around the world. They are today's "conventional wisdom ". The problem is that this agenda is ultimately based on an economic model built on idealized, theoretical, "never-never land" assumptions.

Economists typically feed data into complex mathematical models. Because they use a scientific approach in their analyses, and because they use those complex models with mysterious mathematical formulae, many people—even a lot of economists—seem to think that economics is a science.

It isn't. In the sciences, theories can be tested under controlled laboratory conditions, to come up with results that are predictable under a wide range of circumstances. That just isn't possible when we deal with human behaviour.

Economics describes so-called "rational " behaviour under a set of assumptions which are quite theoretical, idealized, and highly unrealistic. As sociologists and psychologists know, in the "real world" human behaviour can be volatile and influenced by a limitless variety of "non-scientific" factors—especially ones that have nothing to do with "rational" behaviour in market settings and can't get quantified in fancy mathematical models.

The economic theory underlying most of today's public policy decisions—the "price-auction" model—is based on the ideal of a "perfectly competitive" economy. As economists, we know full well that it's an ideal that doesn't exist, never did exist, and never will exist. A pity it's so influential in our public policy decisions.

Well, so what? They have their theory, we can have ours. Politicians can weigh the merits of both.

Unfortunately, it isn't just a matter of theory. About 25 years ago, the world economy began to suffer from the effects of inflation and oil price hikes. Unemployment soared. Economic growth stopped. Despite evidence that tight monetary and fiscal policies were behind these problems, people looked for a scapegoat, and found it in Keynesian economics—the theory that said that government had to be an active player in the economy, to create jobs and re-distribute wealth and income more fairly.

Based on the theories of Professor Milton Friedman, neo-conservative politicians and their big business supporters began to argue that there was "too much government." They said that "free markets," based on the model of perfect competition, would turn the economy around. They said that the main job of government was to help markets work well, through removing barriers to economic efficiency. They said that because re-distributing income and wealth interfered with "efficiency" in markets, this should only occur in some "targeted" way, or through private charities.

In short, what these politicians and corporate spokespersons saw in Milton Friedman's economic theories was a way of justifying some preconceived ideas: namely, that government should get off people's backs; and let higher income individuals and corporations lead us down the road to prosperity.

Thus, when dealing with unemployment, a current policy approach has been to amend labour laws, in some very regressive ways. The theoretical basis for this is that it will create employment, through making workers and wages more "flexible." This means that wages can be pushed down more easily, and make workers more eager to take on jobs at these lower wages. This is based on the law of supply and demand: when the price of a "factor of production" like labour goes down, it's supposed to stimulate demand for that "factor."

This doesn't necessarily happen in the "real world." In the "real world," we have laws about minimum wages and the fair treatment of workers. We also know that we need a liveable wage, to attain and maintain a decent standard of living. Sometimes we have to remind people about all this, and to fight for our rights.

Because of "real world" conditions, wages aren't quite as "flexible" as economic theory says they should be. As a result, more "flexible" labour markets rarely, if ever, bring about greater levels of employment.

The reaction of policy makers has often been to propose more regressive changes to those labour laws in the interest of bringing about the flexibility that right-wing economists say must be there. Wouldn't it be far more sensible to just admit that the policy doesn't work in the "real" world, and focus on something more productive, like public investment to create jobs?

By the way, there is also a basis in the same economic theory for job creation through increasing demand—say through public investment—instead of trying to manipulate the conditions under which labour is supplied. That part of the theory isn't mentioned all that often today

Government spokespersons trot out economic theory and jargon to show us that "there is no alternative" to their policy prescriptions. Corporate lobby groups echo these sentiments. These views have captivated the media, "independent" research organizations, and even some provincial governments who should know better.

A corollary is the view that more "people-centred" policies, like those contained in the Alternative Federal Budget, aren't really "do-able". Those who put forward such "alternative" perspectives are portrayed as representatives of "special interests", dreamers, or just plain stupid. In fact, the supposedly "sound economics" our governments rely on are the real problem.

I get frustrated when I talk to people about the Alternative Federal Budget, and they tell me that while the sentiments are right, it just can't be done. Why? Well, because some politician, financial analyst, or economist on TV has said so. Isn't it time ordinary citizens had a better understanding of what economics is, its uses, its limitations—and its misuse in public policy? And isn't it time we , as economists on the progressive left, took responsibility for making a contribution to that process? Specifically, shouldn't we be de-mystifying economics, and coming clean about its weaknesses?

This is the fourth year we have been working on the Alternative Federal Budget. We've made a lot of progress, putting together an intelligent, readable document, with a workable set of economic options. We've even gotten some good press. Why is it we aren't viewed as being as credible as an economist who works for a bank, or a research organization funded by multinational corporations, when it's obvious that economist has a vested and direct financial interest in the provisions that will emerge in the federal budget? To be taken seriously, economists can't come up with something that goes too far against the prevailing wisdom. They also know that their prescriptions have to satisfy whomever is paying their salaries.

Policy-makers and politicians today use or rely on a highly theoretical, idealized economic model; and they use it in some very selective ways, to "justify" a pre-determined political agenda. Ordinary citizens, the victims of that agenda, know from bitter experience that it is wrong. But they often feel powerless in challenging it, because of the apparently "sound" economic reasoning that gives its policies credibility.

It's time to put a stop to this. It's not enough for us to know that our solutions are better, if we can't convince ordinary citizens. I therefore call on my fellow economists to focus their attention on educating ordinary citizens about economics—what it is, its uses, its limitations, and its abuses. In simple, everyday language, not in the jargon many of us like to use.

We must show ordinary people that economics is not some "natural," scientific, indisputable truth. It should—it must—be challenged, even when it is spouted by finance ministers and so-called economic "experts." Especially those who work for organizations with vested financial interests.

We have to help ordinary people gain the confidence they need to oppose public policies that hurt them, that weaken the framework of society—even when those public policies seem perfectly consistent with the prevailing economic wisdom.

If we do this, we'll go a long way in helping ordinary people recognize that the "people-centred " public policy proposals in the Alternative Federal Budget are far more logical—and far better for them—than those based on the "sound " economic reasoning of neo-conservative governments and their spokespersons.

Background Papers

Dismantling a Nation: The Provincial-Territorial Blueprint for National Social Programs

by Cindy Wiggins

Over the past 15 years, Canada's social union has undergone massive change. Virtually every national social program—UI, post-secondary education, health care, social assistance, Old Age Security—experienced severe fiscal restraint, as did important public services and institutions. The federal government identified the deficit as the reason for steep cutbacks, even though a major study by Statistics Canada showed that spending on social programs contributed only minimally to the increase in the deficit (6%). Further, federal public services and assets were privatized, and a significant decentralization took place of the federal responsibility for national programs such as housing and the labour market.

The role of the federal government in the provision of programs and public services was radically minimized under the rubric of 'diminished expectations.' The public was led to believe that governments could no longer afford the programs and services which had brought greater equality and security within Canadian society. The notion of organizing ourselves on the principle of collective responsibility increasingly was replaced with the principle of individual responsibility. This fundamental shift in public policy—and thus in the values which underpin it—was evident in the federal government's failed attempt to reform social programs during the Social Security Review process in 1995.

After the failure of the Social Security Review, social policy came completely under the control of the Department of Finance. Federal budgets became the instruments for making social policy. The 1995 federal budget outlined the government's intent not only to cut social spending further, but also to profoundly restructure national social programs. As a result of this budget, program spending was decreased to the level of 1951 as a share of the economy.

Federal funding cuts have not been made without consequence.

A complete restructuring of the Unemployment Insurance system lowered benefits, imposed extra penalties on workers in seasonal and insecure jobs, and ensured that fewer unemployed workers would be eligible to receive benefits. Now only about 40% of people who become unemployed will qualify for UI. In times of sustained high unemployment, as we have experienced for the last 10 years, the unemployed will be forced to apply for social assistance.

Perversely, the implementation of the Canada Health and Social Transfer (CHST) in 1996 marked a massive restructuring of national social programs for health, education, and social assistance. Seven billion dollars was cut from these programs.[1] At the very time when more unemployed people needed to turn to social assistance because of the UI changes and continued high unemployment, the federal cash transfer for social assistance was cut, and the provinces/territories were released from their obligation to provide income assistance to people in need, regardless of the reason for the need.

The CHST eliminated all national conditions for federal funds for social assistance, with the exception of the residency condition. This allowed provinces to impose workfare requirements as a condition for the receipt of social assistance. This is contrary to key United Nations' covenants which Canada has signed prohibiting forced work.

The CHST threatens access to higher education as universities and colleges raise tuition fees to offset the loss of federal funds and turn to the private sector for an infusion of dollars into the system. The consequences are predictable: fewer and fewer low- and middle-income people will have access to higher education. If they do, they will emerge with staggering debt loads. Secondly, greater private sector involvement in funding education threatens the integrity of academic freedom and the level of basic research undertaken, as private funders use their influence to focus curriculum and research in ways which meet their interests.

Public health care is at risk under the CHST. Although the effects will be gradual, they will nevertheless be devastating. The cap on federal cash funding at $12.5 billion under the CHST (health share about $6 billion) means that, as the federal cash contribution diminishes over time as a share of total public health spending ($52 billion), the provinces and territories are likely to conclude that continuing to meet national standards for health care in the *Canada Health Act* is no longer worthwhile in return for the inadequate share of federal funding. The decline in transfers to the provinces for health care already has led to diminished coverage of insured medical services, making conditions ripe for privatization.

Although decent, affordable housing ought to be a national priority, successive federal budgets have devolved responsibility for social housing to the provinces and territories, as well as cutting federal funding for housing.

In addition to concern about the impact of reduced social protection and a smaller role for government in the provision of social programs, the loss of public sector jobs as a result of this process is a key concern. Public sector jobs have been an important source of better-paying jobs for women in particular, and also for disadvantaged minority groups. The loss of public sector jobs has negative consequences for these Canadians and also to the economy as a whole.

These changes have profound implications for the nature of national social programs and for the social and economic security of Canadians overall. Moreover, it has serious implications for the historic role of the federal government in ensuring the very existence of a national social fabric and the values such a system represents.

In an important way, these changes have begun to alter our concept of Canada as a social union, and, in doing so, our understanding of what national unity has meant in practice. We are witnessing unprecedented change in the nature of fiscal-federalism, the system which determines how the federal and provincial and territorial governments relate to one another, work together, and the areas for which each level of government has responsibility.

The social union has been changed largely without real public debate about the implications of those changes, both now and in the future. A diminished social union in which the federal government plays a limited role in both the financing and the nature of national social programs has the consequence of turning the economic and social security of Canadians over to the marketplace, thus threatening traditional Canadian values of equity, caring, and sharing.

While Canadians were told that these changes were essential to achieve deficit reduction targets, they were about far more than that. The federal government chose to restructure the economy and the social union in the interests of capital accumulation, which requires vast reductions in social programs and a disciplined labour force, i.e., a labour force which is weakened by high unemployment, lower wages, and less effective trade unions.

Within this time frame, the issue of national unity has remained a difficult, unresolved question. The failure of the Meech Lake and Charlottetown Accords and the sovereignty referendum in Quebec in 1996 are important parallels to consider when analyzing the downsizing of national social programs and the devolution of federal responsibility to the provinces and territories.

This is the context within which the provincial and territorial governments began making plans to take on a much larger role in the development and provision of such programs specifically, and in the management of the social union in general.

In the 1995 federal budget, the federal government proceeded down what it called an "irrevocable path" (a plan to divest itself from the funding of and responsibility for the social safety net). Provincial-territorial governments consolidated their collective opinion, first articulated in 1994, that federal off-loading made it imperative for them to have a stronger say in the devolution of national social policy. Governments identified the need to balance both financial arrangements and the roles and responsibilities for all social programs. Provincial-territorial governments have two critical goals: to dilute the effective enforcement of national standards, and to ensure that social programs are 'flexible.'

What follows is an analysis of the provincial blueprint for Canadian social policy and of the resulting re-design of the social union as documented in the papers prepared by provincial- territorial governments since 1995 and the *Final Communiques* issued by the Annual Premiers' Conferences:

- *Ministerial Council On Social Policy Reform: Report To The Premiers*, December 1995.
- *Issues Paper On Social Policy Reform and Renewal: Next Steps* Prepared for the 1996 Annual Premiers Conference, prepared by the APC Provincial-Territorial Working Group on Social Policy Reform and Renewal.
- *New Approaches to Canada's Social Union: An Options Paper* prepared by the Provincial-Territorial Council on Social Policy Renewal (PTC). April, 1997.
- *Progress Report To Premiers*, July 1996. Prepared by the PTC.
- *Final Communiques* of the Annual Premiers' Conferences, 1994-1997.
- *The Calgary Declaration*, 1997.

* * *

Background—The Provincial-Territorial Process

The 1994 Annual Premiers' Conference issued a *Final Conference Communique* noting that it was time for provincial-territorial governments to assume a "*more cooperative leadership and coordination role*" with respect to programs under their jurisdiction, primarily as a result of federal cuts to national social programs. A Ministerial Council on Social Policy was struck, mandating the minsters of social services, education, and health to develop a provincial and territorial vision for national social policy.

By the 1995 Annual Premiers' Conference, this position had solidified. The *Final Communique* noted that provinces must work cooperatively and "... *take on a leadership role with respect to national matters that affect areas of provincial jurisdiction and speak with a common voice on the essential elements in the national debate on social policy reform.*"

The Ministerial Council put before the premiers and territorial leaders for their consideration a position paper, *Ministerial Council on Social Policy Reform and Renewal.* The need for provinces/territories to take on a greater leadership and coordination role in social policy was reiterated [p.1]. Fifteen principles were set out for social program reform, including the setting of "... *guiding principles and underlying values for social policy reform*" [p.4].

By March 1996, this blueprint had been endorsed by all provincial-territorial governments, with the exception of the Government of Quebec which did not participate in the process.

The 1996 Annual Premiers' Conference marked the release of a further paper, *Issues Paper on Social Policy Reform and Renewal: Next Steps.* It built on the December '95 document and called for the creation of a Federal-Provincial- Territorial Council on Social Policy Renewal which would form the basis for upcoming federal-provincial-territorial negotiations. This was agreed to by the Prime Minister's office on the basis of the need "*...to work with the provinces and territories on the recommendations of the Ministerial Council Report*" [p.2 August '96].

A Provincial-Territorial Council on Social Policy Renewal (PTC) was established to move the renewal agenda forward as outlined in the August '96 *Next Steps* report.

The PT Council produced a paper in April 1997 entitled *New Approaches to Canada's Social Union: An Options Paper* which reaffirmed the provincial-territorial determination to clarify the role of both orders of government in national social programs. The rationale for this remained the unacceptability of federal unilateral actions and cuts in funding. Stronger language emerged in this Report with the statement that "*federal unilateralism must end*" [p.3].

The *Options Paper* identified a strong desire to develop new approaches for intergovernmental cooperation and partnership and for the management of the federation in the future. It outlined a series of possible frameworks under which a restructured social union could operate.

In July 1997, the Council issued a *Progress Report To Premiers* outlining progress to date in key areas: a National Child Benefit; a National Children's Agenda; Benefits and Services for Persons with Disabilities; Health; Financial Arrangements; Labour Market Matters; Aboriginal Peoples; Education; Housing; Public Input, and Gender Equity Issues.

The *Final Communique* of the 1997 Annual Premiers' Conference reaffirmed once again the intention to take a leading role in issues of national social policy and in re-designing the federation. The Ministerial Council on Social Policy Reform was mandated to develop the "*set of guiding principles and underlying values for social policy reform and renewal*" [p.3] which had been identified as a priority in 1995.

The Premiers issued a statement of principles for national unity called *The Calgary Declaration* and promised to consult their respective residents on this document.

THE PROVINCIAL-TERRITORIAL RATIONALE FOR SOCIAL PROGRAM REFORM

Key factors driving the desire of the provinces and territories to devolve and disentangle social programs were identified in the December '95 Ministerial Council Report to the Premiers.

- Cuts in federal transfers to the provinces/territories have reduced federal support for provincially-delivered national social programs, resulting in increased provincial-territorial costs for health, higher education, and social services.
- At the same time, the federal government continues to set conditions and standards for the receipt of federal funding for these programs. Most irksome to the provinces and territories is that the federal government "*... unilaterally interprets the conditions of the Canada Health Act and imposes fiscal penalties on Provinces ...*" [p.2 December '95].
- Economic restructuring and associated labour market impacts have resulted in high structural unemployment, a loss of high- wage, resource sector jobs, an increased polarization of jobs, (high-wage, high-skill vs. low-wage, non-standard jobs), and a demand for 'passive' income support. The report notes that "*both kinds of jobs (high- and low-wage) reflect the dignity and value of work.*" [p.2 December '95].
- Changes in the structure of the family and demographics of the population have implications for both the mix of programs and associated costs.
- All governments must reduce deficits and spending levels. The *Final Communique* of the Annual Premiers' Conference reiterated that costs needed to be reduced [p.2 December '95].
- Core Canadian values were redefined to include fiscal responsibility [p.4 December '95].

The provincial-territorial rationale for demanding a stronger and larger role for provinces/territories in social programs is threefold.

1. If federal financial support is insufficient to support national cost-shared social programs, then the federal government ought not to have the authority to enforce national standards which result in increased costs to provincial and territorial governments. "He who pays the piper calls the tune." Clearly, the provinces/territories want to minimize the effectiveness of national standards for social programs so that they can be made more 'flexible,' a code word for downsizing and reduced access.
2. The provinces/territories view the changes in the labour market as unalterable, if not permanent, features of the labour market. In other words, unemployment will remain high and the march towards a lower-wage economy is inevitable. That being the case, a corresponding increase in the demand for income support will be unsustainable, in their view. The reference in the December '95 *Report* to an increased demand for income support implied that this is an inappropriate response from people who are victims of a low-wage, high-unemployment economy. Hence, the provinces and territories feel a strong need to take greater control over the national social programs they deliver, primarily to ensure they control access, and thus the costs. To some degree, national standards and conditions prevent such control.
3. It is clear all through the December '95 *Report* that the fundamental goal of the provinces/territories is to reduce social spending overall. While the rhetoric implies that the proposed reforms would have positive results, in fact just the opposite is true.

It is quite striking that there is not a single statement in the December '95 *Report* identifying job creation and economic growth as the most powerful measures for reducing social expenditures, alleviating financial pressures on existing programs, and bolstering government treasuries. The provincial-territorial rationale is pessimistic, regressive, and narrowly focused on fiscal concerns rather than on the public interest.

By 1997, a new rationale had emerged to justify the redesign of the social union which was clearly intended to convince the public that the motivation behind this initiative was well-reasoned and good-intentioned. The 1997 *Options Paper* spoke for the need to "*assure Canadians of the continuing priority that provinces/territories attach to maintaining viable and effective social programs that meet the needs of all Canadians*" [p.2]. Other key elements included increasing public confidence in the sustainability of social programs, improving accountability and transparency in the decision-making process, and clarifying and coordinating the roles and responsibilities of each level of government.

THE BROAD PERSPECTIVE OF THE PROVINCIAL-TERRITORIAL VISION FOR SOCIAL POLICY

In examining the various papers and communiques, several broad but key themes emerge which form the foundation of the provincial-territorial blueprint for restructuring the social union and the management of the Canadian federation. These themes are underpinned by two important prerequisites: the federal government must maintain its responsibility for equalization payments; there must be a recognition that provinces/territories have differing abilities to provide programs because of differing revenue-generating abilities, and that variations exist in the demand for and cost of social programs.

PRINCIPLES FOR SOCIAL POLICY REFORM

The December '95 *Report* sets out principles for social policy reform based on the mandate to "*develop a set of guiding principles and underlying values for social policy*" which are "*general rules or codes of conduct to guide all governments in the design and delivery of social policies.*" [p.4].

The principles fall under four broad categories. The first category speaks to accessibility and meeting only the basic needs of Canadians. Phrases like 'reasonable access,' 'Canadians most in need,' and 'enhanced self-sufficiency' reflect a narrow vision of social policy, rather than one based on traditional Canadian values of creating equality in society through an equitable distribution of income and wealth, and on the notion that collectively we can minimize the risks inherent in work and throughout life [p.5].

The second category identifies our individual and collective responsibility for health, education, and social security, and affirms the dignity and independence of the individual, the latter of which can be decoded to mean that individuals rather than the state have the greatest responsibility for economic and social security. This category of principles identifies the need for both levels of government to participate in "*the establishment, maintenance and interpretation of national principles for social programs*" [p.6].

The third category speaks primarily to the affordability, effectiveness, and accountability of social programs. The statements here are so fuzzy that it is difficult to determine the underlying message, except for one which is blatantly transparent: the provinces/territories want the federal government to resume their constitutional financial responsibilities for Aboriginal Peoples, both on and off reserve [p.6].

The final category identifies the need for social programs which are "*flexible, responsive and reasonably comparable across Canada*" [p.7]. While some of the statements here could give a warm fuzzy feeling, the code word 'flexibility' is key. What is clear is that, when provinces and territories note the need to be "*responsive to changing social and economic conditions, regional priorities and individual circumstances,*" it can be safely assumed that they are not talking about improved living standards and greater equality. Rather, the intent is to minimize, if not eliminate, the national nature of these programs by giving greater control of them to the provinces and territories [p.7].

UNILATERAL FEDERAL ACTION

Provinces and territories have long been dissatisfied with unilateral federal actions in the field of social programs which they view as their sole jurisdiction. The dissatisfaction is on several levels. The Ministerial Council *Report* in 1995 noted, "*Initiatives to eliminate government deficits and managed debt should not result in a unilateral shift of costs from one government to another*" [p.17]. The 1997 *Options Paper* notes that, while the federal government once cost-shared national social programs, severe funding cuts have driven the provincial-territorial share of social spending up to 80% of the total. The intention to prevent unilateral federal action is clear: "*Federal unilateralism must end.*" [p.3].

This is a legitimate complaint on the part of the provinces and territories. It makes it difficult to make long- term plans, and unilateral cuts to funding put significant and unexpected pressures on provincial-territorial finances. People still expect the same level of services and hold the provinces/territories responsible for those services, so they bear the political fallout. This is not to say that some provincial governments would not be making cuts anyway, but, nevertheless, federal unilateralism with respect to funding is a legitimate complaint.

The provinces/territories take the view that the federal government also acts unilaterally in the setting of conditions which dictate the design of social programs. The Ministerial Council *Report* states that the federal government "*unilaterally interprets the conditions of the Canada Health Act and the Canada Assistance Plan, and imposes financial penalties on Provinces.*" [p.2]. Both the 1996 *Issues Paper* and the 1997 *Options Paper* point out that the federal government unilaterally imposes conditions on social programs. Clearly, the provinces and territories resent such conditions. This resentment is a key factor driving the provincial- territorial bid to take a greater leadership role in national social programs now that they are responsible for the lion's share of social spending. For this reason, the provinces/territories intend to see that the federal spending power is limited, and that the roles and responsibilities of each level of government are clarified and/or redefined.

NATIONAL STANDARDS

Provincial-territorial governments are not fond of federal national standards for social programs because they stand in the way of full provincial control over the programs they deliver, including accessibility and eligibility, adequacy and costs. It is not surprising, then, that the December '95 *Ministerial Report* [p.7], the August '96 *Issues Paper* [p.2], the April '97 *New Approaches To Canada's Social Union* [p.3], and the *Final Communique* of the August 1997 Annual Premiers' Conference [p.2] refer to the need for social programs to have "adequate flexibility" to respond to local needs. These are code words for weaker national standards.

When looking at the section in the December '95 *Report* entitled *Principles to Guide Social Policy Reform and Renewal*, the vagueness of these principles indicates that the intent is to dilute national standards beyond the point of enforcement. They also reflect an extremely limited view of the social welfare state as indicated by phrases such as 'reasonable access,' 'protecting Canadians most in need,' 'promoting self-sufficiency,' 'ensuring the dignity and independence of the individual,' 'partnerships,' 'flexibility,' etc. The weakness of the principles to guide the reform of social policy is demonstrated by the following general principles [p. 5-7]:

- social programs must be affordable, effective, and accountable;
- social programs must be flexible, responsive, and provide reasonably comparable levels of service across Canada;
- social programs must be accessible and serve the basic needs of all Canadians; and
- social programs must reflect our individual and collective responsibility.

They sound nice, but are a far cry from national standards. They are too vague to ever be enforceable. Further, it is difficult to imagine provinces actually coming to an agreement as to what standards would be appropriate for each program. It is easy to imagine that the standards provinces might agree on would be motivated more by an attempt to control costs rather than to ensure adequate services.

The federal government has the power under the Constitution to use its spending power to intervene in areas which are primarily provincial jurisdiction. Medicare and the Canada Assistance Plan are two areas where the spending power has been utilized to create social programs which were national in scope. In both cases, national standards or conditions were attached to the federal dollars, thereby influencing the way provincial-territorial programs were designed and delivered.

For example, the *Canada Health Act* requires that provincial health insurance plans be universal, accessible, portable, comprehensive, and publicly administered. A key condition under CAP required that programs not require forced work as a condition for receipt of social assistance, so workfare was prohibited. The federal government had the right to impose financial penalties on the provinces if the conditions were not met.

These conditions irk the provinces/territories to no end because they are not free to do whatever they like. The desire to have a greater say in the setting and enforcement, if any, of national standards or conditions is really at the heart of the provincial/territorial blueprint for new rules for the social union.

The 1995 Ministerial Council *Report* calls for the development of "*a set of guiding principles and underlying values for social policy*" which are "*general rules or codes of conduct to guide all governments in the design and delivery of social policies.*" [p.4]. The report states that "*there is a continuing and important role, to be defined, for both orders of government in the establishment, maintenance and interpretation of national principles for social programs.*" [p.6]. At the end of the report the language is stronger: "*The use of the federal spending power should not allow the federal government to unilaterally dictate or prescribe how social programs should be designed or managed.*" [p.18].

The 1996 *Issues Paper* reaffirmed this position by calling for the development of "*intergovernmental mechanisms and processes to develop and promote adherence to national principles or standards in the area of social policy.*" [p.13].

The 1997 *Options Paper* again cited as a key objective "*the joint creation of national social policy principles, standards or outcomes measured through cooperative intergovernmental processes.*" [p.3]. Further clarification later in the paper indicated that principles or standards should be developed, reviewed, and interpreted through a cooperative process. Such a process could take the form of a formal advisory mechanism, public discussion or consultation, but would require a joint mechanism for the imposition of sanctions. The 1997 Annual Premiers' Conference *Final Communique* mandated the Ministerial Council on Social Policy Reform and Renewal to "*draft a set of guiding principles and underlying values for social policy reform and renewal.*" [p.3]. The list of areas for which guiding principles are to be developed is so long and varied that it is clear that the issue of enforceable standards or conditions is to be cast off the table.

The *1995 Final Communique* of the Annual Premiers' Conference specifies that the national standard of comprehensive medical services in the *Canada Health Act* must be changed to include a commonly accepted definition of medically necessary services. The provincial-territorial plans for the national standards under the CHA were made much clearer in the Conference of Provincial-Territorial Ministers of Health Report, released in 1997, *A Renewed Vision For Canada's Health System*. The provinces and territories want to develop a 'new administrative mechanism' for the *Canada Health Act* which would involve the creation of an "*expert advisory panel consisting of knowledgeable persons chosen for their expertise in the Canada Health Act and the realities of provincial and territorial health systems*" and "*would make recommendations to both levels of government on the interpretation of the principles of the CHA*" and "*on provincial-territorial adherence to the principles.*" [p.9].

Without a doubt, the provinces/territories' blueprint involves a massive stripping of federal power in the provision of key social programs. National standards form the backbone of truly national programs in which equity via accessibility and affordability are fundamental values.

Even if provinces could agree on some level of standards, and then agree that a standard had been broken without the federal government having the authority to impose a fiscal penalty, the standards would be completely unenforceable. Moral suasion on the part of some provinces towards others is simply no substitute for enforceable, truly national standards. A panel of experts to interpret and enforce the *Canada Health Act* would result in a cumbersome and difficult process, the rationale for which is clearly to eliminate the federal authority from the enforcement of the *Act*.

Further, it must be noted that federal-provincial- territorial decision-making is inherently an undemocratic process which takes place behind closed doors, without scrutiny from either opposition parties or the public. In short, the process lacks accountability. The same criticism would apply to inter-provincial decision-making. The setting and enforcement of national standards must have a high level of accountability in order to maintain the integrity of the programs.

THE FEDERAL SPENDING POWER—THE KEY TO NATIONAL STANDARDS

The intent to limit the federal role in social programs is expressed most clearly in the proposal for extreme limits on the federal spending power, which has been instrumental in the creation and development of national social programs. The December '95 Report states that "*federal activity in the areas of sole provincial responsibility should occur only after federal-provincial-territorial consultation, and provincial agree-*

ment on how federal spending can be effectively applied." [p.10]. The 1996 *Issues Paper on Social Policy* calls for "*new approaches to the use of the federal spending power to ensure that the federal government cannot continue to unilaterally use it to impose conditions on social programs.*" [p.5], and "*the federal government must go further and commit itself to seeking provincial agreement on all federal spending in areas of provincial jurisdiction.*" [p.10].

The April '97 *New Approaches To Canada's Social Union: An Options Paper* expands the new approach to the federal spending power by calling for the development of guidelines which would include opt-out compensation, consent alternatives, program scope, and financial arrangements [pp.9-11].

The *Options Paper* identifies possible ways to impose limitations on the federal spending power which was first identified as a major goal in the restructuring of the social union in December 1995. The consent options include a simple majority of provinces, a majority of provinces representing a threshold percentage of the population, provinces representing the majority of the population, and unanimity of provinces. Each of these options is repeated to include the territories [pp. 8-10].

The scope of new limits on the federal spending power include new and existing cost-shared programs and all other federally funded programs.

Such an approach differs dramatically from the current use of the federal spending power which does not require unanimous consent of the provinces. The provincial- territorial blueprint implies that full consent of all provinces would be required for future—perhaps even for continued—use of the federal spending power in the setting of standards and conditions. Such constraint would make it next to impossible to create new national social programs such as child care.

The August '96 *Issues Paper* is very clear on this. In listing the ground rules for future negotiations, the Report states that "*Each government comes to the negotiations as an equal partner,*" leaving the federal government without the authority it has traditionally had in national programs [p.3]. The provincial-territorial approach is a full limitation on the federal spending power and would effectively prevent the federal government from acting in the national interest in the future (should any government even wish to do so again), as far as social programs are concerned.

The effect of such curtailment on the federal spending power would be enormous. Rather than allowing the federal government to take a leadership role in national social programs and policy by using its spending power, the federal government would be reduced to one of 13 partners around the federal-provincial-territorial negotiating table, all with an equal voice on matters of national importance, at least in the sphere of social programs.

The federal government capitulated to this view in the 1996 *Speech to the Throne* by committing itself to placing strict limits on the federal spending power. In future, the government "*will not use its spending power to create new cost-shared programs in areas of exclusive provincial jurisdiction without the consent of the majority of the provinces. Any new program will be designed so that non-participating provinces will be compensated, provided they establish equivalent or comparable initiatives.*" [Speech From The Throne, 1996].

Clarifying the Roles and Responsibilities of Each Level of Government

A key feature of the provincial-territorial blueprint is the intent to clarify and re-balance the roles and responsibilities of both levels of government in the field of social policy. The rationale for this is two-fold: the first has to do with the provincial-territorial stance that, as the federal government offloads its financial responsibilities onto the provinces, there should be a commensurate transfer of authority and resources for the devolved area. The second rationale has to do with prohibiting the federal government from interfering in areas of provincial-territorial jurisdiction.

In the early stages of developing this social policy blueprint, the idea of disentanglement was referred to—-the notion that only one or the other level of government ought to have responsibility for a particular program or jurisdiction. Where both levels of government need to be operative, it must be on the basis of cooperation and full agreement.

The December '95 *Report* does indeed argue for the separation of federal and provincial-territorial roles with respect to social programs, and this view is reaffirmed in the August '96 *Issues Paper* by calling for the need to clarify federal and provincial-territorial roles "*in all areas of social policy.*" [p.2 August '96]. The responsibility for individual programs would be based on which order of government can best deliver the service and would ensure that the level of government with the responsibility would have the "*authority and resources to do the job.*" [p.10 December '95]. This is repeated in the August '96 *Report.* [p.3, p.10]. The *New Approaches to the Social Union* paper notes that a key element in any new approach to the social union "*will be the delineation of clear roles and responsibilities for each order of government,*" and, as these areas are realigned, "*commensurate resources must also be transferred so that the order of government charged with the responsibility of delivering services has the authority and resources to do the job.*" [p.2].

The 1997 *Options* paper outlines several new mechanisms to clarify and realign the roles of each level of government which would then be used as the basis for the future management of the social union. The paper suggests any new mechanism agreed upon could be formalized through inter-governmental agreements, legislation or constitutional amendment, but recommends the inter-governmental approach as the best option, likely for two reasons: firstly, in the past, this approach has taken place in an undemocratic fashion behind closed doors; and secondly, both legislation and constitutional amendments remain extraordinarily difficult options in light of the unresolved national unity question.

The five options presented in the paper are as follows:

1. a federal-provincial-territorial approach which would include the development of a framework agreement on broad overarching issues to guide social policy renewal with sub-agreements in specific areas of national concern or developing such a framework limited to one area of concern at a time such as the federal spending power;
2. the provinces/territories could develop a framework agreement on overarching issues to guide social policy renewal in areas of provincial jurisdiction or develop a step-by-step approach in specific areas which would eventually form part of a larger framework agreement;
3. build a federal-provincial-territorial framework agreement in combination with the provincial-territorial agreement on key priority issues;
4. build small federal-provincial-territorial agreements in combination with provincial-territorial agreements on a step-by-step basis which would eventually form part of a larger agreement; and
5. develop mechanisms to strengthen inter-governmental dialogue on social policy and increase opportunities for dialogue.

A news release during the 1997 Annual Premiers' Conference seemed to favour the negotiation of a broad framework agreement on the social union to address such issues as common principles, the use of the federal spending power, and new ways to manage and resolve disagreements. Health and education were identified as priority areas for discussion.

Another news release indicated that there is interest on the part of provinces/territories in re-balancing roles and responsibilities of each level of government in areas beyond social policy, such as the environment.

Putting this vision into practice requires a fundamental redesign of the Canadian federation or the social union, involving devolution, disentanglement, and a greatly reduced role for the federal government which, in some cases, amounts to *de facto* constitutional change, as was the case in the federal government's commitment to limit the use of its spending power.

At this point, it is difficult to tell just how much devolution of federal responsibility the provinces and territories envision, and exactly what level of disentanglement is being called for. At a minimum, it is clear the provinces/territories are keen to develop a new mechanism for managing the social union which would limit the federal authority in the areas of national social programs, in particular in the enforcement of the *Canada Health Act*.

It is also clear that there is serious concern about the federal offloading of financial responsibility for Aboriginal peoples. In earlier papers, the provinces/territories called for the federal government to resume full responsibility for the funding of programs for Aboriginal peoples.

The December '95 *Report* recommended that the federal government *"accept full responsibility for all programming for Aboriginal people, both on and off reserve, with a gradual transfer of authority to aboriginal communities."* [p.2]. In the August '96 *Issues Paper,* the federal government was rightly accused of abandoning its constitutional responsibility for Aboriginal peoples living off reserves. This has resulted in increased costs for the provinces at a time when federal funding is diminishing for other national social programs which are delivered at the provincial level, and at a time when it is expected that, in some provinces, Aboriginal people will form a significant portion of the labour force in the not-too-distant future. It was correctly noted that resolving this issue is *"vitally important to the future of our country,"* and that input on this resolve must include input from Aboriginal communities [p.12].

However, the 1997 Annual Premiers' Conference called for a comprehensive approach, noting that provinces/territories have differing revenue-generating capacities which affect their ability to raise funds for such programs. It may be that the current thinking is to take on responsibility in the area of Aboriginal peoples in return for federal dollars or perhaps a transfer of taxing authority.

The provinces/territories have identified other specific program areas in which the roles and responsibilities of each level of government need to be clarified. These are outlined below, but again, the lack of sufficient detail makes it difficult to tell what level of decentralization and disentanglement the provinces/territories are seeking.

The question of services and support for people with disability is one example where the direction remains unclear. The December '95 *Report* calls for *"possible consolidation of government income support for individuals with long-term and significant disabilities into a single national program"* which would streamline administration, disentangle federal- provincial-territorial jurisdiction. While the December '95 *Report* spoke of a jointly-managed but federally delivered program, the

August *Issues* paper refers only to reviewing existing programs, identifying gaps and overlap, and preparing a progress report.

While this may be a sign that provinces-territories want right out of providing disability programs, it is clear that they want input into all federal decisions regarding the development of such a plan. It is worrisome that the August paper notes the wide array of disability assistance, including social assistance programs, housing, Workers' Compensation, the Canada Pension Plan, and private sector, long-term, disability plans. The proposal has all the makings of a universal disability plan, which could have some merits, but, again, the devil is in the details, and the prospects for progressive thinking and action are dim. In support of this view, the proposal calls for any new national plan to be constructed within current expenditures, which will not rescue people with disabilities from poverty.

The provinces-territories are happy with the decision to transfer labour market programs and services funded through the federal government's new Employment Insurance program, but are unhappy with the fact that not enough funds are being transferred and that the amounts designated are not open for discussion. This is contrary to the provincial view that the transfer of responsibilities ought to be accompanied by 'commensurate resources,' and that the federal government ought not to have the authority to act unilaterally. It is annoying to the provinces-territories that the federal government is not willing to be reduced to an 'equal partner.' That being said, it is not completely unreasonable for provinces-territories to expect that their views should be taken into account for programs they are expected to deliver, but it should not be on the basis of equal partners.

The December '95 *Report* called for the *"possible harmonization or integration of income support for other working age adults (currently provided through UI and social assistance)"* [p.14]. This was dropped from the August '96 *Issues Paper*. This may or may not still be on the agenda, but it is not up front at this point. In any case, this earlier proposal has serious implications for maintaining the social insurance component of the social security system. Still on the agenda, however, is a proposal to integrate employment and training services delivered through EI so that provinces can include people currently outside the labour market, such as youth, people with disabilities, and Aboriginal peoples. This, too, has implications for maintaining EI as a social insurance program.

There has been a constant call for renewed financial arrangements in light of federal government cuts to social programs and in light of the *"unilateral nature of federal decisions regarding the use of the federal spending power in areas of provincial jurisdiction."* [p.9 August '96].

A 1997 Annual Premiers' Conference news release called for negotiations on renewing existing financial arrangements. The premiers remain firm in their demand for the transfer of commensurate resources which are both adequate and predictable when federal responsibilities are transferred to the provinces and territories. Key issues include the imbalance in the respective share of program financing between each level of government; the continuing federal claim that taxing authority granted to the provinces in the late 1970s constitutes a part of the federal transfers for programs, and the differences in the ability of provinces and territories to raise tax revenues to meet the constitutional requirement for relatively comparable access to social programs and public services across the country.

The more important point in a discussion about financial arrangements is the inadequacy of funding for social programs by all levels of government as things currently stand. While all the provincial papers try to cast the provincial- territorial vision for renewed and reformed social programs in a progressive light, the fact of the matter is that the real goal of the reform has never been to reduce poverty and lessen income disparity. The need for a significant increase in funding for social programs has never been recognized. Concern over deficits, balanced budgets, and limiting the authority of the federal government are the true motivating factors behind the call for reform and renewal. Taken from this perspective, overall, the proposals can only be termed as regressive.

IMPLICATIONS FOR THE CANADIAN FEDERATION

Minimizing the role of the federal government in national social policy and its capability to act in the national interest would prove detrimental to most Canadians. The federal government has a constitutional responsibility for ensuring that all Canadians have comparable access to public services which include, among others, health care, public pensions, post-secondary education, income support, and a healthy environment. This is a fundamental principle of the federation and it has served us well. Indeed, it underlies a long-held value of Canadians that achieving greater equality of social and economic circumstances for all people is of key importance to building the kind of country we want for ourselves and future generations.

Complete separation of the federal and provincial responsibilities for social programs, and an effective end to the federal spending power, could limit the ability of the federal government to act in the national interest in the way it has in the past. It could mean the end of national social programs for health, education, and social assistance which have made a significant contribution to higher living standards for Canadians than otherwise would have been the case. The likelihood of introducing new national social programs would be remote. While it is true that the CHST has initiated the direction outlined by the provinces and territories to some extent, the federal government still plays an important role in these programs, and thus in promoting the social and economic well-being of Canadians. However, as noted earlier, the CHST is badly flawed.

It is worthwhile remembering here that the Rowell-Sirois Report on how the federation would best be managed noted that the very nature of a loosely-knit federation such as Canada necessarily requires a degree of jurisdictional overlap in order to ensure a national influence in matters of national importance, such as the social and economic well-being of the Canadian people. Cooperative federalism has been important to the functioning of the federation, even though improvements must be made to the democratic functioning of inter-governmental processes. In addition, limitations on the federal government with respect to unilateral changes in funding arrangements would be a welcome change.

For this reason, the Alternative Federal Budget recognizes and affirms the important role of the federal government in the provision of national social programs. The federal government has the responsibility to distribute the benefits of the economic union, and it is only the federal government which has the levers at its disposal to act in the national interest in this way. It can influence employment levels and thus the revenues with which to cost-share social programs within the areas of provincial jurisdiction. It can mitigate the impacts of economic downturns and recessions through the use of its spending powers. It has sought to redistribute income in an equitable way to all Canadians through national programs such as the Canada Assistance Plan and the OAS, although there is still a long way to go in terms of achieving a truly egalitarian society.

Not all provinces have the same capacity to raise revenues for programs. The federal spending power has ensured that the poorer provinces can afford to implement important programs. In this sense, the federal spending power has been a key instrument in alleviating the variance in economic conditions within the federation and in the ability of individual provinces/territories to raise taxes from region to region. It can exert pressure on reluctant provincial governments to come on board with needed national programs, such as Medicare. It is doubtful that we would ever have had a national system of public health care with universal access, regardless of the ability to pay, were it not for the flexibility of our constitutional arrangements, especially with respect to the federal spending power.

Equally important is the role the federal government has played in setting national standards and conditions for the programs it funds. While this is a long-standing thorn in the sides of provincial-territorial governments, the federal authority to set standards is of great benefit to Canadians. National standards are key to ensuring that national objectives for the effectiveness of social protection are met, and that the goal of equity remains a crucial priority in public policy. To lose sight of this, as does the provincial vision for public social policy, would clearly not be in the public interest.

Quite simply, without national standards, there would be no such thing as a national social security system. Rather, there would be the proverbial patchwork quilt of programs across the country. Adequacy would depend on where one happened to reside. In the current environment, where fiscal restraint and minimal government are the overriding objectives, the absence of national standards would certainly spark a race to the bottom with respect to social programs as provinces compete to cut spending in order to lower taxes in order to attract business investment. Certainly, the current eagerness of some provinces to gut labour standards as a means of attracting investment is a clear parallel to what would happen on the social front.

Having made these comments, the fact remains that the federal government bears a great deal of responsibility for the direction in which the provinces and territories are headed. Massive federal funding cuts have set the stage. What is crucial here is to re-establish a serious federal presence in the field of progressive public policy, both social and economic. Only by doing so can we assure ourselves as a nation that the race-to-the-bottom scenario will not occur. The Alternative Federal Budget makes this commitment.

CONCLUSION

It is widely understood by Canadians that national social programs are defining features of the country. For many, they represent the values of caring and sharing and are seen as rights of citizenship. Medicare is recognized by Canadians to be of critical importance to their well-being and as a source of great security. People intrinsically understand the value of national social problems regardless of their (government- media-manufactured) concern about the deficit. Thus, it is important that Canadians understand what the provincial- territorial vision for social programs could mean to their social and economic security.

The provincial-territorial vision for the reform of social policy is taking place in the context of massive changes to social programs initiated by the federal government. While the ideology of some provincial governments certainly favours reducing social spending in any event, it is true that cuts in federal transfers for health, education, and social assistance, as well as cuts to UI, have placed a heavy burden on provincial government treasuries. As the deliverer of social programs, provincial and territorial governments have to deal with the expectations of the public about the level and quality of services provided. Trying to meet public expectations for services in light of a declining revenue base has no doubt been difficult. It is not surprising that provincial governments have concluded that greater control is needed over the programs and their costs.

However, the direction envisioned by the First Ministers would fundamentally change the nature and workings of the Canadian federation in a way which does not serve the interests of the majority of the Canadian people. The extreme limits on the federal spending power, the weakening of enforceable national standards, and a strict division of roles and responsibilities for programs would severely diminish the federal role in national social programs. Doing so would threaten the continued existence of a truly national system of social security which, to a large degree, has ensured equitable levels of public services across the country, and has promoted greater equality of social and economic conditions among the people of Canada.

The decentralizing thrust of the proposals with respect to the setting and enforcing of national standards would give the provinces and territories much greater control over health care, post-secondary education, and social assistance in terms of access to these programs, as well as their comprehensiveness. The absence of strong national standards would undoubtedly lead to inequitable access to programs and services from one province to the next. The potential for a race-to-the-bottom with respect to social program protection would be a very real prospect, and with that, an inexorable move towards putting in place the social and economic parameters for the realization of a lower-waged economy.

While the specific proposals for an Integrated Child Benefit and a Disability Income Support Plan have some merit, this would only be the case if there were a commitment to increased funding for these programs so that they would act to decrease our disgraceful poverty levels. Clearly, the intent in these areas is not to put forth recommendations for progressive social policy, but rather to separate federal and provincial responsibilities.

Overall, the provincial-territorial proposals would not contribute to the rebuilding of the social security system, but would more likely lead to its further deterioration.

---

1 During the 1997 federal election, the Liberals announced that only $6 billion would be cut under the CHST in a misleading attempt to convince Canadians that the Liberal Party was firmly committed to the preservation of a public system of health care. Due to the lack of knowledge regarding the nature of the CHST, it was not noted that the federal government had no authority to ensure that the extra $1 billion going to the CHST would be used by the provinces for health care since no strings are attached to federal cash transfers for the health, education, and social assistance programmes governed by the CHST legislation.

Towards Engendering Budgets,

by Isabella Bakker, York University and

Diane Elson, University of Manchester

Foreword

Access to and transparency of the budget process have been one of the fundamental objectives of the Alternative Federal Budget (AFB). This technical paper offers another dimension of the democratization of fiscal politics. We argue that not only must budgets be written with people in mind but that budgets must also reflect the often different circumstances of women and men in both paid and unpaid activities.

Budgets should also recognize that, although men and women may live together in households, this does not necessarily mean that all incomes are pooled and shared on an equal basis. Budgets do have different impacts on women and men; we need to know what these are and what the short- and long-term macroeconomic effects of all fiscal policy decisions will be for women and men. This is important for gender equality objectives—and also for other objectives, such as the well-being of those who need the care of others (children, sick and disabled people) which includes boys and girls, as well as men and women.

Introduction

The budget, on the face of it, appears to be a gender-neutral policy instrument. It is set out in terms of financial aggregates—totals and subtotals of expenditure and revenue, and the resulting budget surplus or deficit. As usually presented, there is no particular mention of women, but no particular mention of men, either.

However, this appearance of gender-neutrality is more accurately described as gender-blindness. The way in which the federal government's budget is usually formulated ignores the different, socially determined roles, responsibilities and capabilities of men and women. These differences are generally structured in such a way as to leave women in an unequal position in relation to the men in their community, with less economic, social and political power, but greater responsibilities for caring for those who need the care of others.

The presence of gender differences and inequalities means that a gender-blind budget in practice tends to have different impacts on men and women, boys and girls; and in turn they tend to have different responses to the budget. Depending on how the budget, and the public services which it finances, are structured, the outcomes for men and women can be unequal. For instance, the cuts in social spending initiated by previous budgets and solidified by the 1995 budget, have not been gender-neutral but have instead contributed to reinforcing rather than ameliorating gender inequality in Canada, and worsening the position of those who need the care of others.

SOCIAL SPENDING AND GENDER

EXAMPLE 1:

Women continue to be disproportionately dependent on social assistance because of their position in the labour market, the lack of more comprehensive welfare and child care programs, and the increase in single-parent, female-headed households. Women constitute approximately 90% of lone parents in Canada, and 69% of lone parents receive some income from welfare programs (Woolley 1995: 1). Social assistance is decidedly and increasingly gendered in terms of its recipients, as well as the reasons they cite for applying for social assistance. One study conducted in 1992 in Ontario, for example, found that women more often accept social assistance because of parenting responsibilities while, in contrast, men cite joblessness as their reason (Woolley 1995: 7).

EXAMPLE 2:

The reduction of federal transfers, combined with a greater decentralization of service provision, has special implications for women both as paid and unpaid care providers. In 1993, 62% of the total income of women aged 65 and over came from transfer payments, compared with 47% of men (Statistics Canada, 1995: Table 7.13). While senior women's share of income from transfer payments is greater than that of men, their average dollar amount of the total transfer payments is lower: $9,100 was the average in transfer payments for senior women, $10,900 for senior men. 37% of all income to lone-parent families versus 19% to male-headed lone-parent families and 9% of two-parent families came from transfer payments (Statistics Canada, 1995: 90).

The shift from CAP to the CHST, and the implications for social programs and services, will have a powerful impact on assisting women to contend with social and economic inequality. Often presented as strictly budgetary changes, these decisions in reality are decisions about women's equality and women's rights.

A major concern for gender equity advocates is related to the status of welfare-related spending compared to other spending in the transition to block funds under the CHST. Keeping welfare and social services a separate transfer, rather than combining them with health and post-secondary education transfers, will ensure that the weakest political actors in the federal transfer mix can maintain a safety net.

The reduction of federal transfers, combined with a greater decentralization of service provision, also has special implications for women, both as paid and unpaid care providers. Women employed in delivering social services could experience job losses or salary cuts with a reduced CHST transfer to the provinces. Women as volunteers in non-profit community agencies and as care-givers in the home will become the 'shock absorbers' of fiscal offloading. This not only has costs in terms of women's coping strategies in difficult times, but it also leads to gender-based distortions in the market.

If women are required to pay a "tax" in terms of their unpaid caring work before they can engage in income generating activities in the market, they are not able to compete on an equal footing; they do not enter with the same flexibility and mobility as their male counterparts. This is particularly relevant when we consider that women's poverty is strongly linked to care-giving responsibilities (Woolley, 1995: 8). Statistics show that 23% of women of childbearing age (25-44) work part-time because of personal and family responsibilities (Table 6.8, Statistics Canada, Women in Canada, 1995).

A gender-blind budget, then, not only contravenes goals of gender equality, but also makes it more difficult for that budget to have positive impacts on economic growth and human development. A gender-sensitive budget makes good economic sense, because it enhances the contribution the budget can make to economic growth, human development, and to the empowerment of women and men.

In addition, a gender-aware budget framework supports the AFB's vision of a Canadian society grounded in the values and goals of full employment; reduction of inequality; eradication of poverty; economic equality between women and men; protection of all rights; strong social programs and public services; environmental sustainability and sustainable development for all peoples (AFB Papers 1997).

The existing conceptual frameworks and statistics used to create budget scenarios are gender-blind. They fail to recognize that:

- women's contribution to the macroeconomy is underestimated because of missing and biased markets and incomplete statistics;
- there is an unpaid economy (which has been variously labeled 'domestic', 'social reproduction', 'reproductive' or the 'care' economy) in which women do most of the work of maintaining the labour force and keeping the social framework in good order—both vital services for the paid economy;
- the parameters of aggregate production, savings, investment imports and exports in the paid economy may be sensitive to different patterns of gender relations and gender distribution of resources.

Research is under way to develop gender-sensitive conceptual frameworks and national economic statistics which can reveal linkages and feedbacks between gender relations and macroeconomic outcomes.[1]

Here we draw upon that research to clarify a conceptual framework within which the issue of a gender-sensitive budget may be approached, with emphasis on:

- measuring women's contribution to the economy;
- engendering macroeconomic models; and
- gender and budget strategy.

1. Measuring Women's Contribution to the Macroeconomy

More of women's work than of men's work is not counted by national economic statistics because, although women's formal market contribution is high in Canada, a great deal of women's work continues to take place in:

- informal sector employment,
- domestic or reproductive work, and
- voluntary community work.

Informal sector employment is market-oriented employment in small workshops, family businesses, subcontracted work undertaken in the home ('homeworking') and work as domestic servants. It includes three types of occupational status: employee, self-employed (both of which are paid), and unpaid family worker in which the worker does not herself receive money) but the family member (often the male household head) directing the business does receive payment. In principle, informal sector employment should be included in the gross national product (GDP), but is often omitted because of the shortcomings of statistical surveys.

Domestic work or 'reproductive work' is the work of managing a household, cooking, cleaning, keeping home, clothing and domestic equipment in good repair, and caring for family members and friends and neighbours. In principle, it is excluded from the GDP; it is defined in the United Nations System of National Accounts as lying outside the production boundary. But the work of the care economy is vital for keeping the social framework in good repair, and for maintaining and reproducing the labour force.

Voluntary community work includes unpaid activity in all kinds of civic associations, both secular and church- based. It includes everything from self-help groups of mothers getting together to run a children's play group or secure improvements in neighborhood safety, to support work for large international charities. Again, these activities are in principle excluded from the GNP—and often are regarded as leisure activities. But for many poor people, especially poor women, such activities are vital to get access to needed resources and provide some security. Voluntary work makes a vital contribution to sustaining the social framework, particularly the sense of civic responsibility.

Reproductive work and voluntary community work could in principle be done by men or women, but these kinds of work have been socially constituted as more the responsibility of women than men in most countries, including Canada.

ACCOUNTING FOR THE UNPAID ECONOMY

• Global estimates suggest that women's unpaid work produces an output of $11 trillion, compared to a global GDP of about $23 trillion (UNDP, 1995:97).

• Economic Gender Equality Indicators of the Federal-Provincial/Territorial Ministers Responsible for the Status of Women (1997) serve to underscore the continuing gap between women's contribution to paid and unpaid work and their resources (income, assets, institutional decision- making). The gender equality indicators are all expressed as indexes using ratios of women to men, where 1.0 represents equality, in the sense that there would be no gap between women and men. Ratios above or below 1.0 indicate inequality or imbalance for that particular indicator. The indicators compare adult individuals and show averages for women and men and trends over time.

The total income index (average of the total income received by women and the average of the total income received by men) in 1995 was at 0.56, meaning that overall, women in Canada received 56% of income compared to men. The gender gap remaining between 0.56 and 1.0 was 0.44. This is a rise compared to the gender equality index for total income in 1986, which was 0.49.

CHART 1:
GENDER EQUALITY INDEX FOR TOTAL INCOME, 1986, 1991 AND 1995

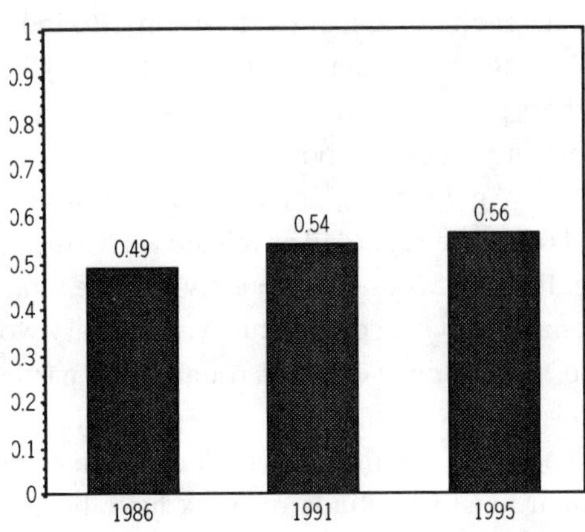

Gender Equality Indexes use ratios of women to men. A ratio of 1.0 is the point where women and men are equal in relation to that index. Below 1.0, women's income and earnings are less than men's; above 1.0, they would be greater.

Source: Statistics Canada, Survey of Consumer Finances.

The total workload indicator examines the extent of gender equality in overall workload when different types of economic activity are combined. It is based on hours spent doing both paid market work and unpaid work of economic value such as child-oriented work; performing household work and volunteer work. When total workload is divided into paid and unpaid work, the female/male ratio for paid work is 0.6 and for unpaid work 1.73 (for 1992). This unpaid work is a significant part of women's resources, work distribution patterns (within paid work and between paid and unpaid work) and leisure time.

CHART 2:
GENDER EQUALITY INDEX FOR PAID WORK AND UNPAID WORK, 1986 AND 1992

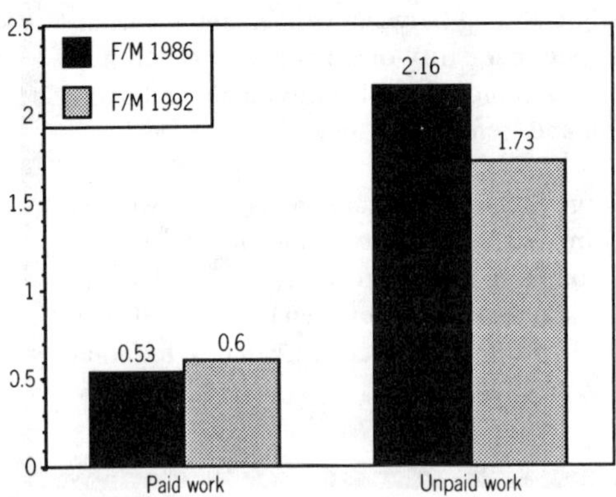

Gender Equality Indexes use ratios of women to men. A ratio of 1.0 is the point where women and men are equal in relation to that index. Below 1.0, women's workload is less than men's; above 1.0, it is greater.

Source: Statistics Canada, General Social Survey

A good deal of progress has been made in Canada in measuring women's domestic or reproductive work and voluntary work compared to other countries. However, little attempt has been made to introduce such results into fiscal policy making. Part 2 will provide some suggestions for how this might be done.

WOMEN IN THE PRIVATE SECTOR COMMODITY ECONOMY

Women have continued their entry into the paid work force. This trend has been a pronounced one since the early 1960s when approximately one-third of women over the age of 15 were active in the labour market, rising to current female labour force participation rates of 57% (in 1997).

In Canada in 1994, 1.6 million women, 26% of all those with jobs, worked part-time, compared to just 9% of men. In fact, 69% of all part-time workers in Canada were female, a relatively stable figure over the last two decades (Statistics Canada, 1995: 65). Almost half of all women working part-time (34% indicated that they wanted full-time employment but could only find part-time work.

Part-time workers generally earn lower hourly rates than full-time workers and receive less fringe benefits and employment protection. The ILO (1993) notes that an increasing amount of part-time and temporary work is involuntary and that there is a growing incidence of underemployment and less job security and earnings capacity for women workers. Analysts have suggested that this raises concerns about labour market restructuring and flexibility in employment.

As long as flexible employment is associated with marginalization of the workforce, then there is a higher probability that workers in these positions (mostly women and ethnic minorities) are bearing an unequal burden of the costs of structural change. For example, involuntary part-time employment for women is primarily due to their inability to secure a full-time job; for their male counterparts, working part-time involuntarily is mainly for economic reasons.

In 1994, 34% of all female part-time workers in Canada indicated that they wanted full-time employment (Statistics Canada, 1995: 66). Relatedly, as long as social investment in the caring for children and other dependents is not recognized or granted sufficient priority, women will likely continue to bear a disproportionate share of these tasks, as is partly reflected in their over-representation in involuntary part-time work and among discouraged workers. In this sense, women may be providing the flexibility that allows men's working patterns to remain less flexible. Women's lack of bargaining power, within and outside of the household, limits their labour market power and tends to bias their participation towards low-skill, part-time work.

A reflection of women's limited bargaining power is the persistence of gender pay differentials. On the one hand, women's share of earnings has also increased due to their increased presence in the labour market and declining gaps in average earnings. In 1981, women workers received 29% of all earnings, and by 1995, this share had increased to 68%.

FIGURE 1:
AVERAGE EARNINGS OF ALL WORKERS AND FULL-TIME FULL-YEAR WORKERS BY GENDER, 1981 AND 1995

Source: CCSD, 1997. Are Women Catching up in the Earnings Race?, p.7.

However, significant distributional disparities remain in earnings between women and men. In 1984, 60% of all workers (full-year, full-time) earned $28,000 or less, but 77.4% of female workers fell into this earning range. Ten years later, 57.4% of all workers and 70.9% of female workers earned $28,000 or less, indicating that women continue to be over-represented at the bottom of the earnings distribution (CCSD, 1997: 11). Women did make gains in the middle and top earnings deciles over this period. For instance, in the top three deciles (of $42,000- plus earnings) women accounted for 21.2% of earners, up from 14.4% in 1984.

Wage data in Canada seem to confirm one of the characteristics of restructuring: that women's gains are at least as much a result of the deterioration of men's jobs as they are the result of improvements in women's position (Armstrong, 1996: 40). As Armstrong notes: "When the 1991 wage data were released in 1993, a great deal of attention was paid to the significant decline in the wage gap. Between 1990 and 1991, the female-to-male earnings ratio increased to 70% from 68% for full-time, full-year workers.(49). She notes that it is the drop in male average income that explains a good deal of the decline in the wage gap. This observation is confirmed by Statistics Canada for 1993, as well (Statistics Canada, 1995: 86).

Persistent vertical and occupational segregation continues to lie at the source of pay differences. Skill valuation and the influence of bonus systems also play a significant role in certain aspects of pay differentials (EC, 1992). According to the Organization for Economic Cooperation and Development (OECD, 1993), rising wage inequality in the public sector also contributes to the overall trend of steady or rising inequality in women's earnings.

Explanations vary from continuing occupational segregation to the contracting-out of consulting and support services. Some authors have argued that shifts in employment away from manufacturing toward services are contributing to income polarization. As a result, wages and earnings are no longer clustered around the middle of the wage distribution, but are moving towards an hourglass configuration where wages tend to be clustered at the top or the bottom. Emerging jobs are polarized according to earnings and skills which favors the feminization of employment (Standing, 1989). This may be a gain for women in terms of overall economic participation, but results in the incidence of more precarious and low-income forms of economic activity.

In terms of occupational restructuring, several key trends can be discerned. First, men's and women's jobs are becoming more similar because many of the traditional jobs held by men are not as good as they used to be. Restructuring of good managerial jobs that men held and women are making inroads into often creates jobs that are becoming more similar to traditional women's work. In this process, men's and women's work has become more similar and more men are taking on jobs in areas traditionally dominated by women (Armstrong, 1996: 46).

Another implication of earnings, skill and job polarization is that, as women continue to be drawn to either pole of employment, the disparity among them will increase. In 1994, 70% of all employed women were working in teaching, nursing and health-related occupations, clerical positions, or sales and service occupations (Statistics Canada, 1995: 67). This does reflect a decline from a decade earlier when 77% of women were employed in these areas.

At the other pole, some gains in several professional fields such as management and administrative occupations (43% in 1994 versus 29% in 1982) and in diagnostic and related positions in medicine and health care (32% of doctors in 1994 versus 18% in 1982) have contributed to a somewhat better occupational distribution between women and men. This has economic as well as political implications. Pay equity (equal pay for work of equal value) and equal employment opportunity legislation, for example, assume a commonality of interests among women, but economic restructuring appears to be creating both material differences and skill divisions within female ranks The increasing polarization or segmentation among women signals, for some authors, a class-based divergence of interests among women in the labour force (Bakker, 1990).

What all of these trends suggest are both new opportunities for women to be economically active and new structures of inequality exacerbated by the process of restructuring. The policy implications of this are far-reaching and will require a rethinking of standard employment equality legislation to address not only differences between women and men, but also to target women who are at the lower end of the workforce in terms of job stability and remuneration.

For example, if polarization leads to more men in "bad" jobs or overall employment conditions are lowered, then parity of male and female wages (pay equity) could be realized. However, such equality could be taking place at lower average wage levels. Given women's concentration in the service sector and the continued importance of this area of economic activity in the future, the public sector can play an important role in shaping the mix of services and the structure of employment.

Analysts of women's employment patterns are increasingly expanding their focus to encompass broader economic policies. For example, macroeconomic strategies that target deficit reduction via public expenditure cuts should also incorporate a gender-based analysis of the costs and benefits of such policy decisions (See Appendix 1 for an example of how this has been done in South Africa and Australia). Shifting caring activity from the paid to the unpaid economy may result in increased pressures on women's 'choices' in the labour market, influencing their participation in more precarious forms of employment.

WOMEN IN THE PUBLIC SERVICE ECONOMY

The public sector has been declining as a source of employment in Canada, with the private sector and self-employment growing. While the public sector provided 20% of all jobs in 1976, it supplied 15% in 1996. This sector continues, however, to be a more important source of employment for women than for men. In 1996, 18% of all employed women worked in the public sector, compared to 13% of all employed men (CCSD, 1997b).

The quality of jobs remains better than either in the private sector or self-employment with better wages, working conditions and benefits.

More than two-thirds of women in the public sector earn at least $15 an hour, compared to less than one-third in the private sector. These relatively better wages also contribute to greater wage parity between men and women in this sector (CCSD, 199b:19).

Public sector downsizing, then, has particular implications for women workers, threatening the economic gains they have made over the last several decades. In addition, families and households experience a number of social and economic costs associated with job loss in this sector. Women as volunteers in non-profit community agencies and as care-givers in the home will become the 'shock absorbers' of fiscal offloading. These issues are taken up in the next section.

Women in the Household and Community Care Economy

Overall, Canadians spend more time in unpaid work (work of economic value producing a set of goods and services that are marketable) than in paid work (Status of Women Canada, 1997: 20). Unpaid work includes child-oriented work, providing help to relatives and friends, performing household work such as meal preparation, laundry and maintenance, and volunteer work.

This definition of work of economic value was developed by Statistics Canada in the 1970s and is found in the Total Work Accounts System. An individual's total workload, according to this definition, is the number of hours per day, averaged over a seven-day week, doing paid or unpaid work. From this, female/male ratios for the total workload index have been derived.

Chart 3 shows the pattern of imbalance in the dual-earner household, and patterns of paid and unpaid work distribution in other types of households.

Another way to capture unpaid work activities is to look at time use. Chart 4 from the General Social Survey of 1992 reveals that women spend more time on unpaid work at virtually all stages of the life cycle as compared to men (about 1.0 hours per day). This number actually increases for women over the life cycle and doubles when full-time employed women become mothers, even though they remain employed full-time. For men, unpaid work also increased over the life cycle peaking with retirement.

Women's and men's time allocation can be influenced by a number of factors, including conditions in the labour market, financial and taxation policies, the availability and affordability of child care, family and community support, number of children, and presence of elderly relatives. With unpaid work there is also an additional factor: it can be transferred to and from the market:

CHART 3: PAID AND UNPAID WORK PATTERNS FOR WOMEN AND MEN EMPLOYED FULL-TIME IN THREE HOUSEHOLD TYPES, 1992

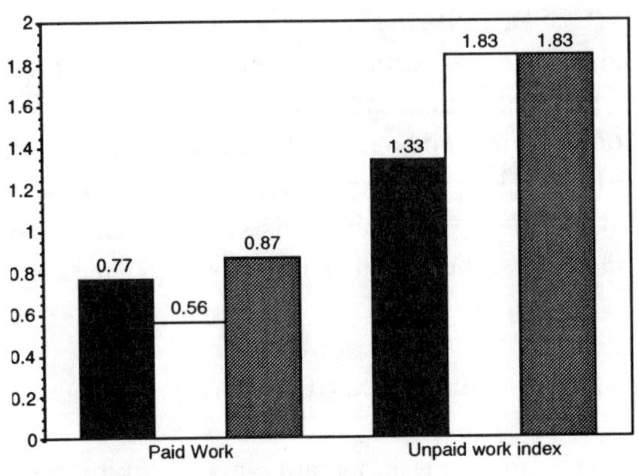

Dual-earner with young child: women and men, 20 to 44, with a child under 6, where both spouses are employed full-time

Primary-earner with young child: women and men, 20 to 44, employed full-time, with a child under 6, and a husband or wife who is not employed full-time (although the spouse may have some paid work).

No young children: women and men, 20 to 44, employed full-time, who have no young children at home (they may be single or married and they may be childless or have children 6 or over - includes lone parents with older children).

Even when women are employed full-time, they assume a smaller share of paid work and a larger share of unpaid work than men in comparable household situations.

Source: Status of Women Canada, 1997. Economic Equality Indicators.

CHART 4: AVERAGE TIME SPENT ON UNPAID WORK ACTIVITIES BY SELECTED POPULATION COHORTS AGED 15 AND OVER

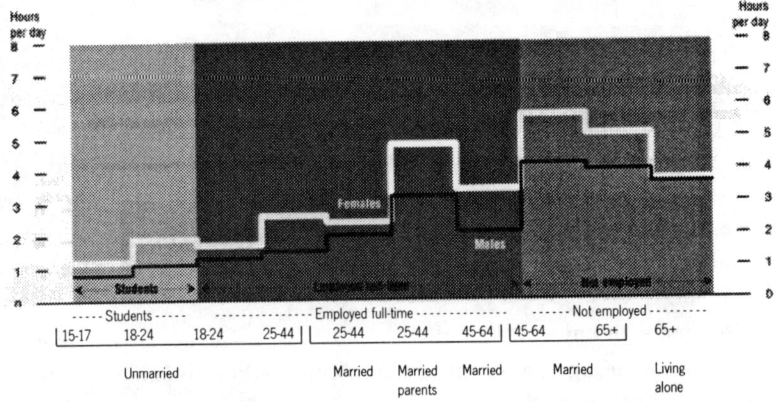

Comprises households chores, family care, shopping and volunteer work.
Source: Statistics Canada, General Social Survey, 1992

Source: Statistics Canada. 1995. As Time Goes By..., Chart 5.8.

Market goods and services, either publicly provided or privately delivered, can replace unpaid work, if there is enough income to meet the cost. Alternatively, when income falls or services are not available, unpaid work may increase to compensate. Detailed analysis to better understand the relationship between income and total work patterns will likely become more essential to policy-makers in the future (Status of Women, 1997: 25).

There are a number of tracking projects currently under way in Canada which will no doubt help to establish the links between economic cycles and unpaid work. One is the Elliot Lake Tracking Study (ELTS), supported by HRDC, which includes a Social and Institutional Costs Sub-Project that examines the impact of mass layoffs on workers, families and communities.

One of the main goals of this study is to assess the capacity of local social services to handle the total effects of mass layoffs in a resource-based community. In other words, one component of this study is to get at the hidden costs of adjustment by defining well-being to include four essential elements—productivity, equity, empowerment and sustainability—not just for the individual, but for families and communities.

ELTS has also found evidence to support the buffer effect—that unpaid work in households expands to make up for shortfalls in income.

ELLIOT LAKE TRACKING STUDY—
EVIDENCE OF HOUSEHOLD BUFFER EFFECT

In the 1996 survey, the women were asked whether they had made any of the following changes: cutting back on the amount and quality of food eaten, engaging in bulk or group shopping, making meals from scratch, vegetable gardening, canning or preserving, hunting or fishing, eating fewer snacks and junk foods, eating less often in restaurants, and using food banks. The analysis of these data indicated that more than three-quarters of the women had used at least one of these methods of coping with reduced income after the layoffs and 10 percent had used four or more (up to 11 of the 12 of these strategies.

(Mawhiney, Social and Institutional Costs Sub-Project, ELTS, October 1997:9)

Neither national accounts, nor satellite accounts, in themselves, can indicate what policies are appropriate. A conceptual framework or model is required in which to use them. But statistics are important for making inputs and outputs visible; without this visibility, it is difficult to get them included in models and seen as significant by policy-makers. So the goal of the AFB in this capacity is to make visible what women and men actually do, to establish an accurate picture and indicators that link economic relationships with other forms of data concerning different groups in the economy. What follows is a conceptual model that brings to light these interconnections.

2. ENGENDERING MACROECONOMIC MODELS: BRINGING THE CARE ECONOMY INTO NATIONAL INCOME FLOWS

We can incorporate the care economy into macroeconomic thinking by focusing on the circular flow of national output—seeing national output as a product of the interaction of three economic domains: the private sector commodity economy, the public service economy, and the household and community care economy.

The creation of wealth in a country depends on the output of all three domains. Sometimes there is a tendency to assume that the wealth-creating sector is the private commodity economy, while the public service economy and the household and community care economy spend what the private commodity economy has produced. This mistaken view results from considering the circular flow of national income in isolation from the circular flow of national output (See Diagram 1).

The three domains of the economy are <u>interdependent</u>. The private commodity economy would be unable to create wealth for use by the government, and by families and communities, if the government and families and communities did not in turn create wealth for use by the private sector. The wealth of a country consists not only of the commodities produced by the private sector, but also the public services produced by the government (law and order, communications networks, health and education) and by the care economy (human capacities, social cohesion).[2] This interdependence is shown in Diagram 1.

DIAGRAM 1: THE CIRCULAR FLOW OF NATIONAL OUTPUT: A GENDER AWARE MODEL

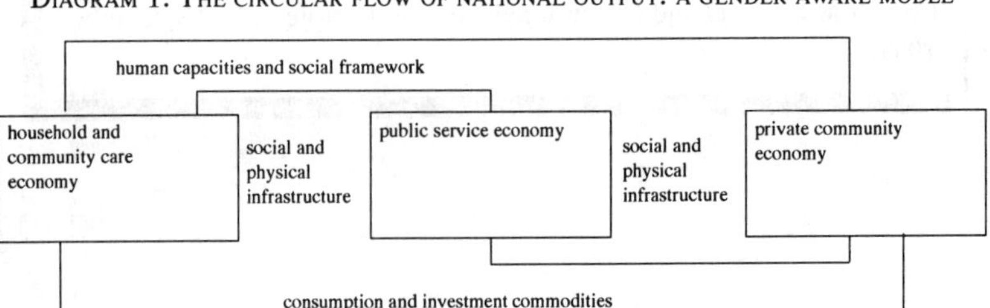

The private sector commodity economy produces market-oriented goods and services primarily in response to the profit motive. It includes the private formal sector and the informal sector. In principle, these sectors should be fully covered in the national accounts. In practice, there is under-counting of informal sector activities. Men and women both work in the commodity economy. Overall, the formal part of it is relatively male-intensive, though less so than formerly, and the informal part relatively female-intensive.

The public service economy produces a social and physical infrastructure which is used for consumption and investment in the commodity economy and the care economy. These services correspond to public sector output in the national accounts. The public service economy is market- oriented to the extent that its employees are paid wages, and it is financed through taxation, user fees and borrowing (and, sometimes, by increases in the money supply). But it is less market-oriented than the commodity economy because it delivers many services free at the point of consumption. Ideally, it should be citizen-oriented, but unfortunately it is often bureaucrat-oriented. Men and women both work for wages in this sector. Overall, it is less male-intensive than the formal commodity economy, though probably more male-intensive than the informal commodity economy.

The care economy produces family and community-oriented goods and services as part of the process of caring for people. Work in the care economy is not paid, though it may be supported by transfer payments from the government (such as pensions and child benefits). It is regulated by social norms rather than by commercial or bureaucratic criteria. The economy is excluded, as a matter of principle, from the UN System of National Accounts.

Both men an women work in the care economy, but overall it is relatively intensive in the use of female labour. The care economy contributes to the welfare of the individuals receiving care, but it also contributes to the activities of the commodity economy and the public service economy by supplying human resources and by maintaining the social framework (supplying what some economists call human capital and social capital to the commodity economy and the public service economy). The relative size of the three sectors can vary depending on the level of development and economic strategy pursued.

Like all pictures which draw boundaries, this picture is something of an oversimplification, since the commodity economy is not totally guided by commercial principles; and the public service economy does not always service the public; nor is the care economy totally guided by selfless altruism. Nevertheless, there is an important difference between being paid to look after children as a private sector nanny or child minder, or as a public sector nursery school assistant, and looking after one's own children. This is not only a personal difference. The costs of child care in the commodity economy and the public service economy show up in the national accounts, and are taken into consideration in policy decisions. But the costs of child care in the care economy do not show up in the national accounts and are therefore not taken into account in policy decisions.

As we have pointed out, conventional macroeconomic models ignore the care economy as a producer of human capabilities and upholder of the social framework. They do include a household sector in the framework but only as a source of personal consumption and personal savings. The only constraint which the household sector can impose on such models is the constraint of insufficient demand to buy the output of the marker-oriented economy.

In effect, by ignoring the care economy, macroeconomists treat it as if it is able to supply whatever quantities of human capacities and social support are required by the commodity economy and the public service economy, regardless of the level of investment in the care economy. If it can do this, then it is safe to ignore it from the point of view of macroeconomic policy, and macroeconomists are right to do so. The assumption is equivalent to an assumption that women's time is available in unlimited quantities, (in more technical terms, that the supply of women's labour is perfectly elastic) (Elson, 1995a).

Economists would point out that making welfare comparisons is not the main use to which national income estimates are put. They are instead used as macro indicators of the situation of a country—if the economy is expanding or contracting, the tightness of labour markets and balance of payments problems, for instance. However, it has been recognized that this sort of macroeconomic analysis needs to be done beyond aggregate estimates of total national income and supplemented by a great deal of detail on the structure of GDP by sector, by type of product, by type of expenditure, and so on.

Detailed supporting tables which show the inputs and outputs of different industries and other activities have been developed, along with social accounting matrices which link economic relationships with other data on the social characteristics of different groups in the economy (Beckerman, 1991: 488). We suggest seeing the inclusion of the care economy as a part of these broader efforts.

There will always be and should always be an important role for the care economy. The question is rather whether there will be sufficient resources in the care economy to enable it to respond to the demands made on it. If the care economy is overburdened, there will be negative feedbacks to the commodity and public service economies which will reduce their productivity and increase their costs, because of inadequate maintenance of human resources and of the social framework.

The tangible signs of this will be work-days lost and lower productivity through ill-health and stress; rising public and private expenditure on insurance, policing, social workers, repairs to make good damage to public and private property and health services to make good damage to human capacities. These negative feedbacks will affect the level and growth of output of the public and private sectors.

Beyond a point, investment in the care economy will be necessary to increase its capacity; it cannot be treated as a bottomless well from which water can always be drawn. This investment can come both through the provision of public sector services and through the provision of decent jobs in the private commodity economy.

Much of the investment required by the care economy is best supplied through public services free at the point of delivery, since it consists of social and physical infrastructure (health and education services, water, sanitation, lighting, roads, electricity, etc.) which need to be accessed by women who do not have much purchasing power.

Historically, the improvement of productivity in the care economy has gone hand in hand with provision of such public services (Folbre, 1994). But the public service economy is financed by taxes on the formal sector economy which overall is male-intensive; whereas public services most important to the functioning of the care economy tend to be more used by women. This creates the conditions for a potential mismatch between the level of public investment required to improve the productivity of the care economy, and the level of tax revenue forthcoming to finance this. It creates the conditions which may generate budgetary strategies which rely on expenditure cuts which simply transfer costs from the public sector service economy, where they do show up in the national accounts, to the care economy where they do not show up in the national accounts but are visible to those who think to look, in a deterioration in the health and capacities of families and communities.

Ultimately, these policies will be self-defeating if they are pushed too far. The social framework will give way, or other categories of public expenditure (on police and prisons, for instance) will rise, undermining the budget strategy.

An alarming new trend in Canada has been the passage of balanced budget amendments which will likely exacerbate social and economic disparities and prevent equality-seeking public initiatives to support the care economy. Balanced budget amendments now exist in five provinces (Alberta, British Columbia, Manitoba, Saskatchewan and Quebec) and the Territories. These statutes and laws have important political, economic and legal impacts through their enshrinement of fiscal conservatism

(Philipps, 1996). For one, they constrain governments in their fiscal policy decisions by establishing caps on spending and taxation. In particular, establishing tax limits (Manitoba, Alberta, BC) restricts the ability to generate new revenues through taxes and narrows the range of fiscal choices open to government. Such laws increase the likelihood of user fees which will be easier to implement than taxes, but often have negative distributional consequences. These laws and statutes also discourage government from pro-active policies to promote equality because provincial balanced budget legislation in particular is likely to generate increased pressure for regressive spending cuts whenever revenues decline. The political costs of spending money to eradicate poverty or to address the impacts of restructuring on people will indeed be perceived as high.

Finally, balanced budget laws undermine the crucial role that government spending plays in stabilizing the economy during private sector recessions. Without the ability to engage in counter-cyclical spending, governments will have to meet a fall in demand levels through spending cuts which may well postpone recovery. The AFB rejects fiscal limitation laws as the answer to our budgetary problems, as these laws blame governments for exercising power irresponsibly when it is markets and the private accumulation of economic power that need to be regulated in the interests of citizens.

3. GENDER AND BUDGETS

A gender-analysis needs introducing into the design of policy so as to ensure that:

(i) efficiency in the use of resources is properly defined. All too often, efficiency is defined only in relation to the use of paid labour in the private and public sectors of the economy. Caring labour in families and communities is left out because it does not have a market price. Measures which seem to increase efficiency in the use of paid labour can in fact simply be transferring costs to the unpaid care economy. The overall effect can be a reduction in efficiency, resulting from human resource depletion and deterioration of the social framework;

(ii) mobilization of new resources takes account of the fact that women's labour is not an under-utilized resource, but an over-utilized resource, in limited supply; and that households are internally differentiated and tend not to pool all their resources. This means that the impact of different taxes will vary by gender: income tax will have more immediate impact on men, while VAT on basic household consumer goods will have a more immediate impact on women. The ultimate incidence will depend on intra-household relations;

(iii) reorganization of the pattern of expenditures takes account of the fact that some externalities are gender-specific. Given the existing division of labour, women's work in the care economy produces services with benefits far beyond families, raising productivity in the private commodity economy and the public service economy. There is a particular need to enable women to increase their productivity in the care economy, but there are no market prices signalling the returns to such investment;

(iv) the issue of sustainability is understood very broadly, going beyond financial sustainability to encompass the sustainability of the social framework, and of the economy of care that is so important to maintaining it.

A key issue of aggregate budgetary policy is the extent to which a budget deficit is sustainable. This is conventionally judged in terms of whether it will tend to lead to financial problems, such as accelerating inflation; balance of payments crises; or an increasing and unsustainable debt burden. Inflation and balance of payments problems are likely if the public and private sectors are already fully utilizing their capacity; if labour is fully employed and the government keeps increasing the money supply to finance a growing deficit.

If the deficit is instead financed by borrowing, this will be less inflationary, but may tend to drive up interest rates, especially if financial markets have been deregulated. This in turn means that more and more future tax revenue will be pre-empeted to service the debt. It may also deter private investment, "crowding out" private investors because they cannot afford the high interest rates.

The sustainability of a budget surplus is not conventionally judged to be a problem because a surplus does not tend to lead to financial problems. But it may lead to unemployment, low levels of capacity utilization, and an overburdening of the care economy, with consequent social and economic problems, and a breakdown in social cohesion.

The likely sustainability of a budget deficit can be tested by using a computable macroeconomic model to stimulate the likely outcomes with a range of different values for variables. But the answers will depend on the assumptions built into the model on such issues as the extent to which increases in money supply lead to inflation; or increases in borrowing drive up interest rates; or increases in interest rates deter private sector investment. Negative feedbacks from overburdening the care economy are not built into such models.

The sustainability of a budget deficit in practice is also influenced by more intangible factors, such as the climate of opinion and the institutional structures of a country—what Taylor (1988) calls the Social Matrix and Khan (1993) calls the interface between institutional organization and policy regime. That is, the sustainability depends on the configuration of power and values as well as on the size of the deficit itself.

The extent to which any deficit leads to financial problems is influenced by factors such as the organization of financial markets and "market sentiment" and the organization of wage negotiations and the degree of importance attached to the "social wage" provided by public sector services. It is influenced by whether there are cooperative or competitive responses to budgetary policy, and the kind of "social bargaining" that takes place about policy. There are important feedback effects from the expectations and actions of major players in the economy.

One of the factors that is usually assumed to be constant is the social framework of norms, rules and values (what some economists call the 'social capital'). For instance, for an economy to work well, there needs to be a fund of good-will, trust, and acceptance of and obedience to the law; plus some institutions that provide social stability and security, even though the economy is changing; institutions that can cushion individuals against shocks and see them through times of transition and restructuring.

Family and community institutions in the care economy are important pillars of the social framework, generating and maintaining it. However, the social framework may not be invariant to the macroeconomic policy: high and rising deficits that generate hyperinflation may tent to lead the social framework to crumble; but so also will severely deflationary policies in which the deficit is cut rapidly and extensively, creating widespread unemployment and idle capacity.

Some economists are now starting to pay attention to the interrelation between macroeconomic policies and the social framework, and to ask whether in some circumstances too rapid an attack on inflation runs down to dangerous levels the fund of good-will and acceptance of social norms that is needed for economies to function well. They do not, however, connect the maintenance of the social framework to women's unpaid work in the care economy, as we have done here.

Nevertheless, economist who are worried about depreciation of social capital do see the need to consider the sustainability of the budget deficit/surplus in a wider framework, not just emphasizing its implications for financial variables such as the rate of inflation and the balance of payments, but also for growth and human development. There is an urgent need to develop operational macroeconomic models that take account of these feedbacks.

Several policy areas illustrate these connections:

1. TAX CUTS

The clamor for tax cuts is part of an ideology of privatization which sees a diminished role for governments. Several assumptions underpin tax cuts. A great deal of faith, for example, is placed in market forces and their ability to generate and distribute wealth in an adequate manner through the consumption and investment decisions of individual persons and firms. It signals, as Lisa Philipps suggests (1996b), a downgrading of the traditional post-war emphasis on distributive equity within tax policy.

Given fiscal pressures such as deficit reduction, it also undermines the state's ability to provide minimum levels of social security for those faring badly in the market or those who work in the care economy. It remains at best unclear, given remaining gender-based economic disadvantages, to what extent women will benefit from the increased consumption power supposedly generated by tax cuts.

2. DE-UNIVERSALIZATION OF BENEFITS

Since the late 1980s, successive governments have undermined the principle of universal entitlement to social welfare benefits. Both Family Allowance and the Old Age Security (OAS) program were shifted to being targeted programs. OAS has been a universal program paying a monthly flat-rate, inflation-indexed benefit to all Canadians at age 65. The 1995 federal budget announced that the government would abolish OAS and the Guaranteed Income Supplement (GIS) by 2001, replacing them with a new income-tested Seniors' Benefit.

As Monica Townson has pointed out (1997), the OAS benefit has been especially important for women because it did not depend on their being in the paid work force. Women who had never worked outside their own homes could get an OAS benefit in their own names at age 65. The new Senior's Benefit, however, will be income-tested based on family income. This means that a married woman's right to benefits is going to depend on the income of her spouse, since men generally have higher incomes both before and after retirement.[3]

The switch to a benefit based on family income undermines women's economic autonomy and assumes that married couples split income evenly; the change also converts the system away from an income replacement plan to a social assistance program targeted on those with the lowest incomes. Clearly, there is an assumption that people can provide for their retirement through private pension plans and RRSPs.

By the year 2005, someone earning $86,000 per year (three-and-one-half times the average earnings of a female worker) will be able to contribute $15,500 to an RRSP, resulting in a tax refund of $7,750, almost double the annual OAS benefit now paid to seniors (NAC, 1997). Data on the distributive impact of tax incentives for private retirements savings clearly show a gender and class bias. Similarly, the Family Allowance was abolished and replaced with a Child Tax Benefit paid only to certain households.

There are two ways in which these policy shifts represent a form of privatization with particular implications for women. First, the trend to de-universalize benefits suggests that poverty or low incomes are an exceptional circumstance in a person's life rather than a systemic problem that society has a stake in resolving. Women's lower incomes and wealth are factors suggesting they will be particularly vulnerable to the shrinking social safety net and the narrowing of support for social programs through targeting (Philipps, 1996b). Second, measuring need according to joint spousal income overlooks a good deal of economic and sociological literature which demonstrates that income within households is not necessarily shared on an equal basis.

FROM TOOLS TO ACTION: IDENTIFYING OPTIONS FOR INTEGRATING GENDER INTO PUBLIC EXPENDITURE POLICIES

Establishing the importance of gender-aware budget frameworks is a necessary but not sufficient goal. A key goal of the AFB is to create structural change in both the prevailing budget orthodoxy and in how decisions are made about different economic and social priorities. A number of tools are available for integrating gender into public expenditure policies. These can be carried out discreetly or in conjunction with each other, depending on the resources, scope and commitment of those involved in the production of the next AFB.

1. Review the AFB process and the contents of the AFB. The goal here is to review the practice of the Steering Committee and to begin to identify points where the analysis and recommendations could be modified to take account of gender differences and inequalities. This would involve disaggregating along gender lines the various public expenditure areas discussed in the AFB, such as unemployment insurance, training and health care, for example, and making recommendations that are gender-sensitive.
2. Monitor the next federal budget and determine its impact on unpaid work and time use. This is to make visible the implications of the national budget for household time budgets and to reveal the importance of unpaid work in social reproduction (unpaid caring work). Time use data can be used to reveal the interconnections between the government budget and household time budgets. Canada does have regular estimates of monetary value of unpaid work since 1978 and time-use surveys were initiated in 1986. In addition, tracking studies such as the Elliot Lake one could be broadened.

3. Develop a satellite process of gender-aware policy evaluation along the lines of the South African model. In the South African case, this case was a joint initiative taken by a group of NGOs and the Parliamentary Joint Standing Committee on Finance to examine the likely gender impact of key areas of public expenditure and taxation (see Appendix 1 for a detailed discussion).

Gender differences and inequalities can restrict the ability of budgets to achieve national economic goals because men and women play different economic roles and have different economic responsibilities. Both on equity and efficiency grounds, gender-sensitive models mean changes in budget priorities. To bring about changes in priorities, development of new tools to appraise budgets and the building of broadly-based coalitions to support the use of these tools to bring about change, are required.

Yet the first stage in changing priorities is to change understandings. Here we have looked at national budgets through women's eyes, disclosing interconnections which are missing from gender-blind visions. Including women's empowerment and the economy of care within macroeconomic policy frameworks can contribute to sustainability and growth in ways that in the long run benefit us all.

APPENDIX

South African women's groups and NGOs have conducted an alternative women's budget project over the last two years, drawing partly on Australian government practice in the 1980s. The aim is to evaluate whether policies that underlie budget appropriations are likely to reduce, increase, or leave unchanged the degree and pattern of gender inequality.

SOUTH AFRICA EXAMPLE

Starting point: Budgets affect women in their multiple roles.

There are three different gender roles which differ from society to society.

REPRODUCTIVE ROLE	PRODUCTIVE ROLE	COMMUNITY ROLE
• service receiver • transfer recipient (child benefit, UIF) • user of household infrastructure • consumer • indirect tax payer • user of technology • sexual being	• breadwinner and economic citizen • wage-earner • person requiring access to capital • direct tax payer • public service employee • worker on public works programme • user of technology • receiver of direct and indirect incentives and rebates • beneficiary of affirmative access, restitution • farm workers	• political citizen • service receiver • victim/survivor of violence • occupant of (unequal) spaces (farm dwellers, rural dwellers) • member of different groups (race, age, location) • exercising control over resources generated by government expenditure

The goals of the Women's Budget are:

1. to assess the impact on women of all government programs;
2. to influence three types of spending decisions:
   i) specifically targeted programs,
   ii) programs aimed at change in departments, and
   iii) mainstream programs.

Specifically identified gender-based expenditures of government departments and authorities.		**Equal employment opportunity expenditure by government departments and authorities on their employees.**		**General or mainstream budget expenditure by government departments and authorities assessed for its gender impact.**
Women's health programmes; special education initiatives for girls; employment policy initiatives for women; and so on.	+	***Training for clerical officers or women managers; rewriting job descriptions to reflect equal employment opportunity principles; provision of creche facilities; parental leave provisions; and so on.***	+	***Does the education budget, minus the above two types of expenditure, reflect gender equity objectives? Who are the users of hospital services? Who receives agricultural support services? and so on.***

= Total Budget

With these goals in mind, the researchers focused on four sectors for the 1996-97 Budget:

i) welfare
ii) education
iii) housing
iv) work

and integrated two cross-cutting themes: taxes and public sector employment.

Each chapter of the Women's Budget starts from:

1. a problematic statement outlining the major gender issues in that particular sector;
2. a description of state involvement in the sector; and
3. possible reprioritization and alternatives—wherever possible, costs are estimated.

This model serves as an annual monitoring exercise that allows for an analysis of change over time.

Source: Debbie Budlender (ed.) The Women's Budget (South Africa), Institute for Democracy in South Africa, Cape Town, 1996.

PUBLIC EXPENDITURE AND TAX INCIDENCE ANALYSIS

Another model of incorporating gender-sensitive analysis into budget frameworks is to conduct an incidence analysis.

Goal: to assess how gender-inclusive the expenditure or tax is by comparing the distribution of spending between men and women, boys and girls.

Need to: establish the annual cost of any service minus user fees, then try to determine who used these services (by income groups, by gender); taxes are the same—with good household budget data, can see to what extent women and men manage different income streams and have different expenditure possibilities.

Until recently, most benefit incidence studies did not report gender-based disaggregations. However, a recent study for Ghana illustrates the possiblities of gender-disaggregated analysis: Lionel Demery, Shiyan Chao, Rene Bernier and Kalpana Mehra. "The Incidence of Social Spending in Ghana." PSP Discussion Paper Series No.82, Poverty and Social Policy Department, World Bank, 1995.

REFERENCES

Armstrong, Pat. 1996."The Feminization of the Labour Force: Harmonizing Down in a Global Economy." in Bakker, Rethinking Restructuring: Gender and Change in Canada. Toronto: University of Toronto Press.

Bakker, Isabella. 1996. "Deconstructing Macroeconomics Through a Feminist Lens." in Janine Brodie, ed. Women and Canadian Public Policy. Toronto: Harcourt Brace.

———. 1990. "Pay Equity and Economic Restructuring: The Polarization of Policy?" in Judy Fudge and Patricia McDermott, eds. Just Wages: A Feminist Assessment of Pay Equity. Toronto: University of Toronto Press.

Beckerman, Wilfred. 1991. "National Income." in J. Eatwell, M.Milgate and P.Newman (eds.) The New Palgrave World of Economics. New York and London: Norton.

Canadian Council for Social Development. 1997. Are Women Catching up in the Earnings Race? Katherine Scott and Clarence Lochhead. Ottawa: CCSD, Paper No.3.

Canadian Council for Social Development. 1997b. Public Sector Downsizing: The Impact on Job Quality in Canada. Christopher Clark,. Ottawa: CCSD, Research Report.

Elson, Diane. 1997. Integrating Gender Issues Into Public Expenditures: Sic Tools. University of Manchester, graduate School of Social Sciences, GENECON Series, April.

———. 1995a. Gender Neutral, gender-Blind or Gender Sensitive Budgets?: Changing the Conceptual Framework to Include Women's Empowerment and the economy of Care. University of Manchester, graduate School of Social Sciences, GENECON Series,.

European Community/ Commission of the European Communities. 1992. The Position of Women on the Labour Market. Brussels: Women of Europe Supplements, No.36.

Folbre, Nancy. 1994. Who Pays for the Kids? Gender and the Structures of Constraint. London and New York: Routledge.

Mawhiney, Mawhiney, Anne-Marie. 1997. Social and Institutional Costs Sub-Project Analytic Paper. Elliot Lake Tracking Study. Mimeo. October.

NAC. 1997. Review of the Situation of Women in Canada Report, 1993-1996. Mimeo.

OECD. 1993. Organization for Economic Cooperation and Development. 1993. Women and Structural Change in the 1990s. Paris: OECD. Report by Gunther Schmid.

Philipps, Lisa. 1996. "Tax Policy and the Gendered Distribution of Wealth." in Bakker, Rethinking Restructuring: Gender and Change in Canada. Toronto: University of Toronto Press.

Philipps, Lisa. 1996b. "The Rise of Balanced Budget Laws in Canada: Fiscal (Ir)Responsibility. Osgoode Hall Law Journal. vol.34, no.4, winter.

Statistics Canada. 1995. As Time Goes By...Time Use of Canadians, General Social Survey. Ottawa: Statistics Canada, cat.#89-544E.

————————. Women in Canada. Third Edition. Ottawa: Statistics Canada, cat.#89-503E.

Status of Women Canada. 1997. Economic Gender Equality Indicators. Ottawa: Status of Women Canada.

Townson, Monica. 1997. Protecting Public Pensions. Ottawa: Canadian Centre for Policy Alternatives.

Woolley, Frances. 1995. Women and the Canada Assistance Plan. Ottawa: Status of Women Canada.

Footnotes

[1] See Cagatay, Elson and Grown, eds.1995, Special Issue of Feminist Economics, November, 1996; Bakker, 1996 Philipps, 1996).

[2] GNP is not a good indicator of economic welfare nor welfare in a wider sense. As Wilfred Beckerman notes: "Apart from the conceptual problems ... there are many other limitations on the GNP as a measure of economic welfare, such as the failure to allow for externalities (e.g., the failure to include pollution, congestion and so on, as negative items); the difficulties involved in evaluating home-based produced output or subsistence output which may be very important in poorer countries; the common failure to value the output of most public service in a welfare-oriented manner instead of in a cost-of input manner; the failure to include the output of many public facilities and the failure to allow for many other non-market activities - of which housewives' services are on of the best-known examples; the failure to allow for differences in leisure or working conditions; and, above all, the failure to reflect the degree of equality in the distribution of income ("National Income," The World of Economics, 1991: 487). See also David Cosby, "A Genuine Progress Indicator for Canada," Alternative Federal Budget Papers 1997, Ottawa: CCPA/Choices.

[3] Statistics Canada reported that in 1995 the median income of married women aged 65+ was $9,661 while for married men it was $20,848 (cited in Townson, 1997: 9).

Over the Rainbow: The Balanced Budget, How We Got It, And How to Hang Onto It, by Jim Stanford

Introduction

Dorothy: *"Toto, I have a feeling we're not in Kansas any more. We must be over the rainbow."*

The federal government will, for all intents and purposes, balance its budget during the current 1997-98 fiscal year. The government's net financing requirements turned negative during the summer of 1997, meaning that it is already beginning to pay down its "market" debt (that portion of the federal debt that is due to financial lendors, rather than owed to the government itself). In national accounts terms, the budget was already essentially balanced during the second quarter (April-June) of 1997, when the total deficit of the federal government equaled barely $1 billion (or just 0.1 percent of Canada's GDP). Even in stricter public accounts terms (which includes delayed obligations arising from public sector pension programs and other accounting debts), the federal government is now running consecutive monthly surpluses. For the fiscal year as a whole, counting year-end adjustments to be made next spring, the government may still show a small accounting deficit—and Finance Minister Paul Martin is doing his best to inflate this deficit through a variety of accounting tricks (including the front-loading of future expenses, and his continued $3 billion "contingency" reserve). But in concrete economic terms, the federal government is now in a balanced fiscal position for the first time in over twenty years, and approximately two years ahead of Martin's own deficit-reduction timetable.

It seems like only months ago that Canadians were being warned of impending fiscal catastrophe: we were approaching the "debt wall," we were saddling our offspring with a painful legacy that would take generations to pay off, the Canadian dollar was allegedly viewed in the same light as the Mexican peso. Now, just 30 months after Martin's famous 1995 budget speech, it seems that the problem has been solved far faster than anyone anticipated. The social and economic pain resulting from historic government cutbacks has paid off. We now can eagerly anticipate the fiscal dividend to come, a natural reward for the tough medicine we have swallowed.

The fact that a crisis of such multi-generational proportions could be resolved in 30 months suggests firstly that the crisis was perhaps not so immense as was portrayed. Nevertheless, all sides in the fiscal debate concurred that the federal deficit had to be reduced. And while disagreement continues over the means that were followed—Martin's painful and one-sided focus on sharply reducing program spending—the fact that the deficit is now history is nevertheless a good thing for all concerned. It sets the stage for a gradual reduction in debt servicing costs (which totaled 30% of all federal revenues in 1996), and allows the reallocation of these funds to more constructive purposes (new program spending, tax cuts, or debt reduction).

There are still lessons to be learned, however, from Canada's fiscal "near-death" experience. First, it is worth examining more carefully how the great turnaround was achieved. It turns out that the cuts in program spending—despite their painful consequences—were not actually the critical ingredient in the deficit-reduction recipe. More important was the decline in interest rates and the consequent acceleration in economic growth in Canada over the past two years. Ironically, this is exactly the strategy that *critics* of the "slash-and-burn" school of deficit reduction have proposed as the foundation for an alternative, more humane path to a balanced budget: reduce interest rates, boost and sustain economic growth, and cut the deficit while preserving public programs. In fact, Martin's program spending cuts could have been *avoided altogether*, yet Martin's original deficit-reduction timetable still have been met, on the strength of lower interest rates and economic growth.

Secondly, in light of the continued restrictive direction of macroeconomic policy in Canada—namely, a single-minded commitment to maintaining very low inflation rates, regardless of the consequences for other economic variables—it is not at all clear that the combination of low interest rates and accelerating economic growth that has been so successful for the federal government will be allowed to continue for much longer. At time of this writing, the Bank of Canada had increased its trend-setting interest rate twice in three months, and Governor Gordon Thiessen had warned explicitly about more increases (and a higher dollar) to come. Officially, the federal government supports the Bank's get-tough approach with inflation—despite still-stagnant prices, an official unemployment rate of 9%, and *true* unemployment (counting discouraged and involuntary part-time workers) of 13 or 14%. The financial community, with a few notable exceptions, has also strongly endorsed the Bank's approach.

If current strong economic growth and job-creation is deliberately slowed down, however, the consequences for the federal government's fiscal balance will be severe. It has been argued, in previous *Alternative Federal Budgets* and elsewhere, that it was high interest rates and chronic unemployment (dating back to the post-1981 shift in macroeconomic policy) that caused the fiscal crisis of Canada's governments, not "out-of-control" spending. Furthermore, we show here that it has been *low* interest rates and more rapid growth that have mostly fueled the dramatic improvement in federal finances over the past two years, not Martin's painful spending cuts. But unless this lesson is learned quickly by our macroeconomic policy-makers, we are bound to cut short current beneficial fiscal trends, shortchanging Canadians of billions of dollars in potential fiscal savings.

Under an ideal Bank of Canada "soft-landing" scenario, according to which the Bank raises interest rates and slows real GDP growth to a more "sustainable" 2.5% per year, the coming fiscal "dividend" for the federal government is fully $70 billion smaller over the next five years than if the Bank allows current rates of growth to continue. This will be the direct cost to Canadian taxpayers of our status-quo low-inflation economic policy: over $70 billion in foregone program spending (or tax cuts) over just 5 years. If the Bank of Canada goes too far in its effort to restrain inflation, causing stagnation or even recession (as occurred early in 1995), then the much-vaunted fiscal dividend virtually disappears. On top of the damage that will be done to labour markets and economic growth by the pre-emptive hikes in interest rates that are presently planned by the Bank of Canada, therefore, another important consequence will be the arresting and possible reversal of the recent improvement in federal government finances.

II. What Happened?

> Glinda: *"She brings you good news, or haven't you heard.*
> *When she fell out of Kansas, a miracle occurred."*

> Dorothy: *"It really was no miracle, what happened was just this."*

According to national accounts data, the federal government deficit declined from over $31 billion in the second quarter of 1995 (immediately following Paul Martin's historic budget, and prior to the implementation of his announced cutbacks) to almost zero just two years later, during the second quarter of 1997.[1] A number of factors contributed to the rapid erosion of the deficit, including the program spending cutbacks, some announced tax increases (and the unannounced tax increases that result from "bracket creep"—the failure to index the tax system to inflation), higher tax revenues that automatically accompany economic growth, and the post-1995 decline in interest rates.

The overall improvement in the deficit can initially be decomposed into three broad components:

i) the reduction in program spending;
ii) increases in tax revenues; and
iii) savings on interest payments.

These latter two components can be further decomposed. Some of the growth in taxes results automatically from economic growth—which generates more income against which existing taxes are levied. But some of the growth results from tax increases: either explicit tax increases (which have been very rare in the Liberals' deficit-reduction scheme), or the implicit tax increases that result from the less-than-full indexing of the tax system to inflation and other factors (often referred to as "bracket creep"). Similarly, the net reduction in the government's interest payments can be decomposed into two portions: the savings resulting from the decline in interest rates, less the *increase* in interest payments resulting from the continued growth of the federal debt. In summary, then, we can identify five mutually exclusive fiscal changes that together produced the sum change in the total federal deficit over the two-year period being considered:[2]

i) the reduction in program spending;
ii) "bracket creep" and other tax increases;
iii) increased tax revenues resulting automatically from GDP growth;
iv) savings resulting from lower interest rates; and
v) higher debt service charges resulting from continued growth in the debt burden.

The first four components all contributed toward the reduction of the deficit; the last term offset some of this improvement.

A federal fiscal "dividend" is estimated on the assumption that "core" nominal program spending by the federal government increases from its budgeted 1998 levels ($103.5 billion) at a rate equal to the sum of inflation plus population growth. This, in essence, freezes "core" federal program spending at its 1998 level, in real per capita terms.[3] With tax revenues rising automatically with economic growth, a budgetary surplus arises in 1998 and thereafter. This, in theory, is the "dividend" that will become available for some combination of new program spending, tax deductions, and actual paydown of the federal debt.[4] In the more optimistic status- quo scenario—the "soft landing"—the projected surplus grows to over $20 billion by the year 2001.[5] If continued economic growth is stalled by the Bank of Canada's tightening, however, then the estimated surplus almost disappears until fiscal 2000, and is much smaller than in the "soft landing" projection in following years. With a macroeconomic commitment to sustained expansion, however, then the funds available to the federal government swell dramatically, creating an estimated surplus of $50 billion by fiscal 2002 (see Figure 1 and Table 1).

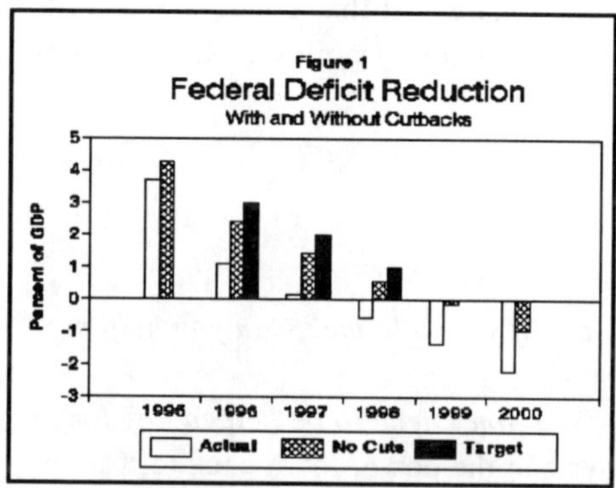

In other words, there will be a huge fiscal cost imposed on Canadians and their governments as a result of the pre-emptive tightening this year of monetary policy. If the Bank of Canada allowed current growth rates to continue for just another four years, still leaving the economy a considerable distance from full-employment, the federal government would have an *additional* $70 billion to spend on new programs, tax cuts, or debt repayment, compared to an optimistic "soft landing" scenario, over the next five fiscal years. The coming "dividend," then, will be almost cut in half by the continued top priority placed in macroeconomic policy on maintaining Canada's ultra-low inflation rate. If real growth is stalled by the Bank's tightening, then the "dividend" may virtually disappears altogether.

TABLE 1
ESTIMATED FEDERAL FISCAL "DIVIDEND"
CONTRASTING ECONOMIC SCENARIOS ($ BILLIONS)

	Status-Quo Policy Stalled Growth	Soft Landing	Alternative Policy Sustained Expansion
1998	3.2	7.1	11.7
1999	2.4	11.4	20.7
2000	5.7	16.3	29.4
2001	9.4	21.7	39.4
2002	13.6	27.3	50.8
5-year Total	34.3	82.4	152.0

Canadians are demonstrating that they are already skeptical of the Bank of Canada's quick action to slow down our long-delayed economic recovery. Imagine, however, their reaction if the Bank were to present the federal government with a bill for $70 billion, as the ultimate fiscal cost of its emphasis on continued low inflation.[6] In the wake of the unprecedented belt-tightening and sacrifice that Canadians have (needlessly) endured for the sake of putting our fiscal house in better order, the notion of the federal government "spending" $70 billion over five years in support of this dubious goal of low inflation would spark an outright taxpayer's revolt. Yet that is exactly the ultimate cost that Canadians will bear if the current restrictive direction of monetary policy in Canada is endorsed and continued.

CONCLUSION

Dorothy: *"Oh, will you help me? Can you help me?"*

Glinda: *"You don't need to be helped any longer.* You've always had the power to go back to Kansas."

Canada's business and political leaders are presently filled with pride at the apparent success of efforts to reduce the federal deficit through program spending cutbacks. The rapid improvement in federal finances since Finance Minister Paul Martin's historic 1995 budget is proof, the argument goes, of the wisdom of the spending cutbacks. An upcoming fiscal dividend will be our reward for the difficult but wise measures Martin imposed.

Looking back on the sources of the rapid improvement in federal finances, however, suggests a very different story. The tough spending cuts were actually only a secondary factor in the federal government's fiscal turnaround. More important was a favourable macroeconomic environment, marked by much lower interest rates and a consequent acceleration of economic growth. In this macroeconomic context, Martin's original deficit-reduction targets could have been met even *without* the spending cuts.

What's done is done, of course, and Canada's difficult experience over the past two years cannot be rewritten. It is crucial, however, that our macroeconomic policy-makers examine more carefully the factors that created the present fiscal balance. The much-vaunted fiscal dividend will be dramatically and needlessly reduced if the Bank of Canada continues with its policy of cutting short our recent strong economic growth. And if this tightening should accidentally stall Canada's recovery altogether (as occurred in 1995), then there won't be a fiscal dividend. The present top priority placed on maintaining ultra-low rates of inflation needs to be reconsidered; the goal of low inflation needs to be balanced against other goals (including job-creation and the continued fiscal repair of our public sector). Otherwise, taxpayers and unemployed workers alike are going to pay a very high price indeed in the coming years for the preservation of Canada as the low-inflation promised land.

APPENDIX

The overall improvement in the federal deficit can be decomposed into three components:

The total change in the deficit (D) equals the decline in program spending (P) plus the increase in tax revenues (T) plus the decline in debt servicing charges (DS). These latter two components can be further decomposed as follows:

The growth in taxes equals the tax-to-GDP ratio in 1997 (t_{97}) times GDP in 1997 (GDP_{97}), less the corresponding sum for 1995. Similarly, the reduction in debt service charges equals the government's average effective interest rate in 1995 (i_{97}) times the outstanding stock of federal debt at that time (B_{95}), less the corresponding sum for 1997. The average effective interest rate is defined simply as the ratio of federal debt service charges during the period to the stock of debt outstanding at that time. Disaggregating and rearranging terms, we obtain:

The five terms on the right-hand side of the equation can be interpreted consecutively as follows:

i) reduction in program spending;
ii) "bracket creep" and other tax increases—which have increased the share of federal tax revenues in overall GDP;
iii) increased tax revenues resulting from GDP growth;
iv) savings resulting from lower interest rates; and
v) higher debt service charges resulting from continued growth in the debt burden.

The first four terms all contributed toward the reduction of the deficit; the last term offset some of this improvement.

A similar set of calculations to those presented in Table 1 can be performed using the federal government's official Public Accounts data (instead of the National Accounts data utilized above). This approach yields somewhat different results, due to definitional differences, and the greater seasonality of the Public Accounts data series. The analysis presented in Table 1 is repeated below, using Public Accounts data for the same time period (from the second quarter of 1995, immediately following Martin's historic budget speech, to the second quarter of 1997). The same general conclusion is generated: a more favourable macroeconomic climate has been considerably more important to the overall deficit-reduction effort than has the reduction in program spending (which accounted for just 30% of total deficit reduction in the Public Accounts analysis). New revenues resulting from "bracket creep" appear to be more important in the Public Accounts analysis, accounting for over one-third of total deficit reduction (versus just 10% in the National Accounts analysis). This result, in particular, must be interpreted cautiously because of strong seasonal patterns in the revenue streams reported in the Public Accounts data.

TABLE 2
DECOMPOSITION OF FEDERAL DEFICIT REDUCTION
2ND QUARTER 1995 TO 2ND QUARTER 1997

	2Q 1995	*2Q 1997*
Nominal GDP ($billion)	$773.8	$828.0
Total Federal Revenue ($billion)	$147.0	$160.3
"Tax Ratio" (% of GDP)	19.0%	19.4%
Program Spending ($billion)	$130.3	$116.8
Debt Service Payments ($billion)	$47.9	$44.7
Deficit ($billion)	$31.1	$1.2
Opening Debt ($billion)[1]	$545.7	$593.3
Effective average interest rate (%)	8.77%	7.53%
Sources of Deficit Savings:		
	Billion Dollars	*Percent of Total*
Improved Macroeconomic Environment		
GDP Growth	$10.3	34.4%
Lower Interest Rates	$7.3	24.5%
TOTAL	$17.7	58.9%
Reduced Program Spending	$13.5	45.0%
Tax Increases	$3.0	10.0%
Increased Debt Burden	-$4.2	-13.9%
TOTAL	$29.9	100.0%

Source: Canadian Economic Observer, Statistics Canada Catalogue 11-010, Tables 1 and 3.
[1] Closing debt at March 31 each year, reported in federal Budget Plan and Economic and Fiscal Update.

Finally, it should be noted that the total benefits of improved macroeconomic conditions for the federal budget probably *exceed* the value of the third and fourth components listed above (GDP growth and lower interest rates, respectively). Since federal program spending still varies counter-cyclically with the state of the macroeconomy (through mechanisms such as unemployment insurance payouts), the improved state of Canada's economy over the past two years may have contributed to the achieved reduction in program spending. In contrast, the preceding analysis has assumed conservatively that *all* of the program spending savings resulted from the pro-active fiscal restraint of the government. The fact that actual 1996-97 federal program spending was more than $4 billion less than Martin's original budget may reflect this additional positive fiscal consequence of stronger economic conditions. Thus the program cutbacks probably account for *less* than the 45% share of budget savings that was reported in Table 1, while improved macroeconomic conditions account for *more* than the 59% estimated share reported in Table 1.

FOOTNOTES

1 Similar calculations to those reported here can also be conducted using Public Accounts data, instead of National Accounts data. See Appendix for discussion.

2 See Appendix for a complete algebraic description of this disaggregation.

3 Of course a freeze in nominal spending, in the context of continuing inflation and population growth, still translates into a real cutback in the services that government delivers. Nevertheless, the social and economic consequences of a freeze would have been far less severe than those that have actually prevailed.

4 This is conservatively within the range of estimated multiplier effects that have been commonly used in estimates of the fiscal drag impact on overall GDP and employment of government cutbacks; other studies imply significantly stronger multiplier effects. See, for example, "Government cutbacks: a checklist," Mike McCracken, Informetrica, May 1994; or "When will the fiscal brake be released?", Jeff Rubin and John Lester, CIBC Wood Gundy, Occasional Report #15, August 1996.

5 The counterfactual exercise assumes the same interest rates that have prevailed in practice; see below for discussion of this assumption.

6 See Jim Stanford, "Is there a risk premium in Canadian interest rates?", *Canadian Business Economics*, Fall 1997, for a full critique of this view.

7 It is certainly the view of the Bank of Canada itself. For example, Governor Thiessen recently explained the post-1995 fall in interest rates by stating that Canada's economy "needed a substantial amount of monetary stimulus to respond to the degree of fiscal restraint and problems associated with a major restructuring of the economy." See "Dollar set to climb, Thiessen says," *Globe and Mail*, p. B1, October 8, 1997.

[8] The rise in the government's effective average rate is not as large as the rise in short- term rates due to the fact that interest rates on longer-run bonds (which make up a significant portion of total federal debt) are not expected to increase as much as short-term rates.

[9] Some other estimates of the coming fiscal "dividend" assume a continued nominal freeze on program spending at the budgeted 1998 levels. However, this would translate in practice into a need for ongoing *continued* real program cutbacks (since that frozen spending will be insufficient to keep up with inflation and population growth). Thus the size of the estimated "dividend" in these studies cannot be equated with the volume of spending available for *new* programs (since some of that so-called "dividend" would be needed just to maintain the real delivery of existing programs).

[10] This methodology is somewhat misleading, in that if some or all of the dividend is "spent" on new programs or tax cuts, then the size of the dividend itself will be somewhat smaller in future years—since the net federal debt will be no longer falling in absolute terms (as would be the case if the dividend was allocated to debt repayment).

[11] This is quite consistent with the base-case projections of the Royal Bank, CIBC Wood Gundy, and other forecasters, updated to reflect the lower-than-expected 1996-97 deficit announced recently by Paul Martin; see "Canada's new fiscal order," *Globe and Mail*, p. D1, October 11, 1997.

[12] This is to say nothing of the huge social and economic costs resulting from the continued high levels of unemployment that are a necessary feature of the status-quo approach.

Tax Relief for Those Who Really Need It, by Hugh Mackenzie

From its inception in 1995-96, the Alternative Federal Budget (AFB) has focused on macroeconomic and taxation policies needed to rebuild the capacity of the federal government to pay for the public programs we need. We have argued that the main driving forces behind the growth of the deficit in the first place were macroeconomic—high interest rates and high unemploymen—and that reversing these policies is the key to an alternative economic future.

Canada's experience since the Liberal government's obsession with the deficit began in 1994-95 demonstrates this point. Of the $43 billion turnaround in the fiscal position of the federal government since then (from a deficit of $37 billion in 1994-95 to a projected surplus of $6 billion in 1998-99), more than $31 billion is the direct result of reductions in interest rates and economic growth.

This change has important implications for the AFB's tax policies as well. Reduced interest rates and higher economic growth have already done much of the job of rebuilding Canada's fiscal capacity. Over the next two years, even the relatively modest growth projections of the federal government will add roughly $7 billion a year to revenue. The growing revenue base will be sufficient to fund over 70% of the AFB spending program in 1998-99, and over 90% of the program by the end of a two-year planning period.

The AFB program of public service renewal and job creation can be funded—with a balanced budget, and with a declining ratio of debt to GDP—with the general tax increase limited to a one-time-only levy on bank profits for 1998-99. This dramatic reduction in the amount of new revenue needed to fund the AFB makes it possible to shift the focus of AFB tax policy towards providing tax relief for Canadians who really need it.

WHO HAS BORNE THE BURDEN?

The income of the average family in Canada is lower today than it was 20 years ago. On top of that, average families now pay a larger share of tax in Canada, thanks to the "tax reforms" of the Mulroney Government that increased taxes on average families at the same time as they reduced taxes for the wealthy. And in the 1990s, average families have been the infantry in the Liberals' war on the deficit as funding has been cut for programs vital to the security of middle- and lower-income Canadians, programs such as Medicare, post-secondary education, unemployment insurance, and social services.

The story for the wealthy has been dramatically different. Although the incomes of average families have not been growing, the economy has grown. Wealthy Canadians are getting wealthier. Executive incomes keep going up at a rate far higher than the incomes of people whose work pays their salaries. The average CEO in a large corporation in Canada now gets more than 40 times the pay of the average employee. The banks chalk up one record profit year after another.

Canada has been going through wrenching adjustments in the past 20 years in the face of free trade and counterproductive national economic policies. The cost of those adjustments has not been shared fairly.

THE POLITICS AND ECONOMICS OF TAX RELIEF

Reflecting what must be the height of political hypocrisy, the right wing—the authors and most enthusiastic supporters of the policies that have heightened inequality in Canada—have become advocates of tax relief. But arguments from the right are self-serving in the extreme. They claim that the only way to provide tax relief is to cut back even further on the public services on which Canadians depend. And the tax relief they offer is tax relief for the rich and powerful. Their idea of tax relief is to eliminate the tax on the unearned income—capital gains— of the rich and privileged. Their idea of tax relief is to reduce income tax rates across-the-board—a move that gives most of the benefit to those with the highest incomes.

Middle- and lower-income Canadians, who are struggling through a "recovery" that is taking a long time to trickle down, are being told that the only way to increase their after-tax incomes is to sacrifice vital public services.

At the same time, the apologists for the privileged have been out in force. In its 1997-98 budget, the federal government took the unusual step of issuing a background paper explaining why it was NOT increasing the level of taxation on the rich.[1]

In that paper, the government attempted to address three of the highest-profile criticisms of the fairness of Canada's tax system:

- the fact that some Canadians with high incomes either pay no taxes at all, or pay taxes at a very low effective rate;
- the use of "family trusts" by wealthy families to avoid paying capital gains taxes on family assets; and
- the fact that Canada, unlike most other countries in the OECD, does not impose either an annual net wealth tax or a wealth transfer tax.

The paper claims that the phenomenon of high-income Canadians paying tax at very low effective rates is transitory, and that "non-taxability typically results from an unusual mix of circumstances." That claim is not supported by the evidence. A study conducted by Statistics Canada for the Ontario Fair Tax Commission found that people with high incomes who paid tax at low effective rates in any given year tended to be in that position on a consistent basis, from year to year.[2]

The paper suggests that the problem of "family trusts" was solved in amendments made in 1995 to the Income Tax Act. In fact, the amendments addressed only a portion of the problem created by the use by taxpayers of trusts and other devices to avoid the payment of capital gains taxes. These "estate freezes" continue to cost Ottawa millions of dollars every year.

Finally, the paper recycles an old claim that local property taxes and corporate capital taxes in Canada are really wealth taxes, and that, when you count these taxes in the total, Canada actually taxes wealth more heavily than other OECD countries. This argument is ridiculous. The property tax is not a wealth tax. It does not take into account mortgage debt—it applies to the gross value of property. It is paid by tenants, who have no ownership interest in the taxed property. And it is a tax on only a portion of wealth holding—a portion that drops dramatically as wealth increases.

Corporate capital taxes are used by both provincial governments and the federal government as substitutes for corporate income tax—especially in the financial services sector. The "Tax Fairness" paper itself combines corporate income and capital taxes in its tables and charts dealing with corporate taxation in Canada.

It is not true that the only way to provide tax relief for middle-income families and individuals is to cut back further on public services. The revenue potential is available to support genuine tax relief.

Now that the problem of the deficit is behind us, and now that the economy has begun to grow again and federal revenue is increasing, we are in a position to reform the tax system—to use the revenue raised by filling gaps, closing loopholes, and ending wasteful subsidies delivered through the tax system to fund real tax relief for lower- and middle-income families and individuals.

THE AFB TAXATION PROGRAM

In summary, the AFB tax program for 1998-99 consists of:

1. Significantly increased tax credits for families with children, offset by reallocating tax expenditures from corporations and high-income individuals;
2. Tax relief for low- and moderate-income individuals and families, offset by a combination of a tax on wealth transfers in excess of $1 million and the introduction of two new tax brackets targeted to the highest-income individuals in Canada;
3. The creation of an Atmospheric Fund of $1 billion supported by revenue from a modest carbon tax and the savings from cancelling tax preferences for the oil and gas industry;
4. Increased general revenue for the fiscal year 1998-99 only, derived primarily from a temporary surcharge on bank profits, and a one-time increase in revenue from tougher enforcement of existing tax laws.

Our program meets our fairness and environmental objectives with no increase in the overall level of taxation in Canada as a share of GDP.

Our fairness objectives are met through a combination of enhanced personal income tax credits, financed through reform of the tax expenditure system, and income tax rate reform, financed through a combination of the elimination of preferential rates of taxation on income from capital—both capital gains and dividends; reform of the system of taxation of incorporated small business; and the introduction of a tax on transfers of wealth in excess of $1 million on death.

Tax relief is funded by addressing directly serious problems with the fairness of our tax system.

TAXATION OF INCOME FROM CAPITAL

The core of AFB's taxation strategy for 1997-98 will be a series of measures designed to restore balance to the tax system by increasing taxes on capital and income from capital. It will do so carefully and strategically. In this increasingly integrated world economy, no country can make tax policy without reference to its impact on capital mobility.

Although there is considerable debate over the impact of tax systems on the location of real economic activity, there is little doubt that mobility of tax bases enhanced by global economic integration imposes real limits on taxation of income from capital. The weakness of current national corporate and personal income tax systems in dealing with the pressures of mobility is widely recognized, as are the difficult implications of this weakness for individual national fiscal systems. As Michael Daly, who served as secretary to the EC committee on company taxation from 1990 to 1992 points out:

> *The increased mobility of capital in a single market and the greater scope that it provides for aggressive tax planning and tax evasion will increase the extent to which taxes are borne instead by other, less mobile, factors, such as labour (except, possibly, highly skilled and therefore more geographically mobile individuals), land, or consumers. That may undermine taxpayers' confidence in the fairness of member states' income tax laws and thus their acceptability.*[3]

Individual nations will continue to face downward pressures on their systems of taxation of income from capital. These pressures can be resisted effectively only through international agreement on a common set of rules and standards for the taxation of income from capital. In the absence of such an agreement, significantly increased reliance on taxes based on ability to pay is unrealistic.

This problem demands a strong response from the government of Canada, not just in words in its budget, but in strong and concerted action with other countries concerned about this phenomenon. We need new international financial institutions and agreements to secure the principles of fair taxation on which the social consensus of democratic societies is based. Canada, as one of the countries most negatively affected by the flight of tax bases to the lowest common denominator, should be at the cutting edge of these efforts. Canada, for example, should be a champion of "Tobin" taxes on international currency transactions.

These constraints are faced by all countries, not just Canada. And it is clear from international comparisons that other countries have been much more successful in maintaining their fiscal capacity in the face of these pressures than Canada has been. One of the goals of the 1998-99 Alternative Federal Budget is to reverse that trend.

ELIMINATING TAX PREFERENCES FOR INCOME FROM CAPITAL.

Nearly 30 years after the Carter Commission made the phrase "a buck is a buck" famous in its recommendations for a tax system that treated all sources of income the same way, regardless of their source, a buck in Canada is not a buck.

The dividend tax credit and the capital gains exclusion

The current personal income tax provides a tax credit for dividends from Canadian corporations and exempts 25% of all capital gains income from taxation. There are two arguments typically advanced for the current dividend tax credit system. First, it is argued that the dividend tax credit provides an incentive for Canadians to own shares in Canadian corporations and therefore benefits the Canadian economy by acting as a magnet for investment. Second, it is argued that the dividend tax credit is needed to "integrate" the personal and corporate income tax systems.

With regard to the first argument, it is worth noting that the dividend tax credit does not apply to the most significant holders in Canada of shares of Canadian corporations—pension plans, RRSPs and mutual funds—and because it does not apply to foreign investors, it is irrelevant in the perpetual debate about the need to attract offshore investment capital to this country. As a mechanism for encouraging investment in Canada, it is very expensive and of questionable value.

As for the second argument, the only respect in which the dividend tax credit actually functions as a mechanism for integrating the personal and corporate tax systems is for small business personal corporations. For dividends from publicly held corporations, it does not play that role. It does not apply to all dividends paid to the benefit of Canadians; and it is paid irrespective of whether the corporation paying the dividend actually paid any corporate tax. As noted above, it would be much less costly and much more effective to design a mechanism for integration specifically for small business personal corporations, as is done in the United States, and to abolish the general dividend tax credit.

At a rough estimate, an integration mechanism would take up $200 million of the $840 million tax expenditure value estimated for the dividend tax credit for 1998.[4]

This restructuring of the integration system also eliminates the main general argument for the exclusion of 25% of capital gains from taxation. We see no case based on fairness to give preferential tax treatment to unearned income. The general 25% exclusion should be eliminated. Any replacement measures should be considered only in the context of the targeted integration mechanism for small business personal corporations. Elimination of the preference for capital gains from the personal income tax would generate an additional $445 million.

Although the elimination of the $100,000 lifetime capital gains exemption has removed the most outrageous of the capital gains tax exemptions introduced by the Mulroney government in the mid-1980s, there are two much more generous exemptions that must be addressed: the $500,000 exemptions for capital gains on sales of farming and small business assets.

While the arguments advanced for retaining these exemptions take full advantage of popular sympathy with and support for farmers and small business people, they tend generally to obscure the facts. These very costly exemptions are not measures designed to preserve family farms and small businesses. They are in fact available only when these assets are sold. And, while the image conjured up of the beneficiaries of these exemptions is of the struggling "Mom and Pop" business or small family farm, the maximum of $500,000 in capital gain clearly puts the beneficiaries in another league.

We believe that the provision that existed for farming assets prior to the introduction of the capital gains exemption was more than adequate, and should be re-introduced. That provision permitted a rollover of the capital gains base when farming assets were transferred within a family. The gains would be taxable once the assets were sold to a third party.

We do not believe that a similar provision for small business assets generally is necessary or desirable.

One argument that should be addressed, however, is the assertion that, for farmers and small business people, the capital gain on their farming and small business assets represents their savings for retirement. We believe, however, that this concern should be addressed directly, through the design of the RRSP system. Specifically, we would propose that farmers and small business people be allowed increased contribution room in the RRSP system, with the additional allowed contributions established on a basis that is consistent with and bears a fair relationship to the RRSP provisions applicable to taxpayers generally.

In the same category is the 25% exclusion from tax of the proceeds of employee stock options. This is a clear give-away to the most highly paid executives in Canada, and as such cannot be justified under any circumstances.

WEALTH TAXATION

Canada is virtually alone in the OECD countries in not having a wealth tax of any kind. Only Australia and New Zealand share with Canada the dubious distinction of not taxing wealth in any form. In effect, this country is a tax haven when it comes to wealth taxation.

Most countries with wealth taxes raise between 0.3% of GDP and 0.75% of GDP from these taxes. The United States, for example, raises about 0.3% of GDP from this source. In Canada, estimates for the Ontario Fair Tax Commission suggest that a tax on wealth transfers at death which exempted the first $1 million in wealth from taxation would raise between $2 and $5 billion.

Such a tax would exempt transfers between spouses, and would apply both to bequests and to substantial gifts prior to death.

To reduce the potential for tax avoidance, such a tax would take effect on Budget Day, with implementing legislation and detailed design developed over the succeeding taxation year. The substantial body of work on the design of wealth taxes done by and for the Ontario Fair Tax Commission could serve as a useful starting point in the design of a national wealth transfer tax.

Given the experience with wealth taxation in the 1970s, when competition among provinces led to the elimination of wealth transfer taxation in Canada, wealth transfer taxation would be strictly national, with no provision for additional wealth taxes by agreement with provincial governments.

There are two principal arguments advanced against the imposition of a wealth transfer tax in Canada. One argument holds that property taxes in Canada are actually a form of annual wealth tax, and that the absence of such a tax in Canada is not a gap in the system. The other is that, because Canada taxes capital gains on death, the imposition of estate and inheritance taxes would amount to double taxation and would itself therefore be unfair. Neither of these counter-arguments is valid.

There are a number of problems with the property tax argument. First, the property tax as it is levied in Canada is a tax on the value of the housing occupied by the resident and taxpayer. It applies whether the occupant is a tenant or the owner. Second, it is not a tax on net wealth. It is based on the gross value of the property, taking no account of mortgage debt. Thus a $100,000 house which is mortgage-free draws the same tax as a $100,000 house with a $75,000 mortgage, despite the fact that the wealth represented by the first house is four times the wealth represented by the second house. Third, and most important, property taxes apply only to real property, the principal form in which lower- and middle-income families hold their wealth. They do not apply to the financial assets that make up the principal assets of the wealthy. Thus, as a wealth tax, the property tax is regressive in the extreme.

It is also worth noting that the United States relies on residential property taxes to approximately the same extent as Canada, and also levies a wealth transfer tax.

The double-taxation argument is equally suspect. While it is true that capital gains are deemed to have been realized and are subject to tax on death, and that therefore a wealth transfer tax would be levied at the same time as the capital gains tax, that coincidence in timing does not make the case for double taxation. To see why, it is necessary to consider why capital gains are taxed on death in the first place.

Capital gains are taxed because they represent income to the taxpayer. Technically, gains should be taxed as they accrue. Because the valuation of capital gains is difficult until the asset is actually sold, and because taxation of gains that have not yet been realized could cause liquidity problems for taxpayers, capital gains taxes are generally deferred until the gain is actually realized when the asset is sold. When gains are taxed on death in Canada, the tax is actually being imposed on income that should, in principle, have been taxed as it accrued during the lifetime of the taxpayer.

It is no more double taxation to tax both estates and capital gains on death than it would be to collect both an estate tax and income taxes owing from wages and salaries earned during the taxpayer's lifetime. Capital gains taxes and estate taxes are different taxes levied on different bases for different purposes. The estate tax is a tax on transfers of large amounts of wealth between generations. The capital gains tax is a tax on income earned during a taxpayer's lifetime that has been deferred until death.

The only legitimate problem with taxing both gains and estates on death is one of cash flow. In the United States, which has both a gains tax and an estates tax, this relatively minor problem is addressed by allowing capital gains to be rolled over so that it becomes an obligation of the person inheriting the property.

At a minimum, we would expect that Canada could generate at least the same percentage of GDP from wealth transfer taxation as the United States. With a more aggressive approach to tax design and administration, perhaps modelled on the German system,[5] and at the level relative to GDP of the United States, we would anticipate raising approximately $3 billion annually from a wealth transfer tax in Canada.

CORPORATE INCOME TAXATION

Although there has been a great deal of discussion of the issue of tax expenditures in Canada in recent years, these measures continue to be used by governments to deliver hidden subsidies to corporate taxpayers and as instruments of social policy in the personal income tax system.

The extent of the tax expenditures provided for in the Canadian income tax system is such that it has caught the attention of as conservative an institution as the International Monetary Fund. In a June 1995 report, the IMF singled out for attention the small business tax credit, which has the effect of reducing tax on the first $200,000 of earnings of Canadian- controlled private corporations, the tax incentives for manufacturing and processing, research and development, exploration and development and regional tax incentives.

The IMF report concludes: (p.106)

These preferences are relatively generous and their effectiveness in promoting investment does not appear to have been large. For example, the threshold for the small business tax rate is considered to be high by international standards (a preferential rate is provided on corporate income up to $US75,000 in the United States). Similarly, Canada's system of tax incentives for R&D has been described as one of the most favourable among industrialized countries.

With public spending at all levels under much tighter scrutiny and fiscal capacity in Canada under such strain, both political and economic, it is time for a major assault on tax- delivered subsidies to the business sector. Such tax expenditures must be shown to be of clear benefit to the Canadian economy and be justified annually alongside alternative measures, just as spending programs must now be justified in the estimates process.

In the past, many of these subsidies have been justified on the basis that they offset higher corporate tax rates in Canada compared with those in other countries. Whatever merit those arguments may have had in the past, they do not hold up today. Corporate tax rates in Canada compare favourably with those in other countries.

SMALL BUSINESS TAXATION

Canada's preferential rate of taxation for earnings of Canadian-controlled private corporations is extremely generous by international standards, and far too generous under the current economic and fiscal circumstances. Although one of the most obvious problems was addressed in 1994 when the small business benefit was restricted for very large Canadian-controlled private corporations, two other serious and costly problems remain.

One of the rationales for the small business tax rate is based on the theory that the tax system should be neutral as between different forms of corporate organization. In other words, the amount of tax that an individual pays should be the same whether he or she carries on business as an individual or in a partnership or through a small business corporation. While the theoretical system which was the original rationale for the 12% rate achieved this balance, changes in the personal income tax system at both the federal and provincial levels now mean that there is a significant tax advantage to operating as an incorporated small business rather than as an individual.

Calculations by the Ontario Fair Tax Commission suggested that in Ontario the small business rate would have to be a full six percentage points higher to restore neutrality to the system.

The second problem concerns the small business threshold highlighted by the IMF report.

Even with the changes adopted by the federal government in 1994, the total value of the small business credit is estimated to exceed $2.7 billion for 1998. We estimate, conservatively, that reform of the system to reduce the threshold to the Canadian dollar equivalent to the US$75,000 threshold and integrating the personal and corporate tax systems below that threshold would generate an additional $346 million.

We believe that the economic benefits associated with small business development can be realized with a tax-based incentive much closer to international norms.

CORPORATE TAX CREDITS AND DEDUCTIONS

The use of the tax system to stimulate economic development and to influence investment patterns in Canada is well developed and has a long history. Consistent with our belief that public industrial policies have an important role to play in shaping Canada's future economic destiny, we support the use of tax incentives as one of a number of industrial policy instruments available to governments.

At the same time, however, we believe these tax-system delivered subsidies should be treated as tax expenditures, not just for the purposes of the now-annual reporting on tax expenditures published each December by the Department of Finance, but also for all purposes connected with the management of public money. At a minimum, this requires disclosure, accountability, annual approval, regular review and value-for-money audit—the same standard that applies to all other areas of public spending.

The current system of tax preferences is a gold mine for tax accountants and lawyers, and an open invitation to corporate taxpayers to stretch a very weak system of checks and balances to the limit.

One of the characteristics of tax-delivered subsidies is that they tend to be open-ended, with eligibility determined in the first instance by the taxpayer, subject to verification by officials of Revenue Canada. This type of system places the official, and therefore the general public, at a disadvantage, because it requires judgments about matters related to the expenditure area (regional development, or exploration and development, or research and development) to be made by officials whose expertise is in taxation. The most infamous example of the problems that can be encountered with this kind of system is the scientific research tax credit, which cost Canadian taxpayers billions before the government was able to get the program under control.

The basic criterion for continuing with a tax expenditure can be summed up in the following straightforward question: would the provision be considered acceptable and justifiable if it were provided through an otherwise identically designed direct grant program?

After the reduced tax rates for small business and manufacturing and processing, the most significant tax expenditures in the corporate tax system are the provision for deduction of depreciation for tax purposes at rates in excess of economic depreciation; the fast write-off for Canadian exploration and development expenses; and the scientific research and experimental development tax credit.

ACCELERATED DEPRECIATION

The corporate income tax provides for rates of depreciation for tax purposes at rates in excess of those normally reported under generally accepted accounting principles for a wide variety of different types of assets. Most were originally justified on the argument that incentives for increased capital spending had an important role to play in improving productivity in Canada's resource and manufacturing sectors.

Canada's economic structure is radically different than it was when most of these provisions were brought in. Corporate finance has also changed a great deal, as alternative forms of finance such as leasing have become much more prominent. One of the signs of these two types of changes is that the finance and services sectors accounted for more than 90% of the net tax expenditure cost of accelerated depreciation in 1992, the most recent year for which figures are available.

With economic development concerns still focused on the resource and manufacturing industries, it would appear to be difficult to justify this type of tax expenditure on incentive grounds to do with economic development. Even to the extent that the tax benefit claimed by the finance and services sectors actually represent depreciation on leased property used in other sectors, it can hardly be said that these are incentives to those sectors.

Furthermore, major changes have already been made in tightening up depreciation rules, with no apparent negative effects on the economy.

Part of the 1998-99 AFB plan would be a review of depreciation rates in the corporate income tax to bring them into conformity with economic depreciation as reflected in generally accepted accounting rules. The objective would be not to eliminate all tax preferences, but to require that they continue to be justified on economic policy grounds in comparison with alternative direct spending programs.

One area in particular demands immediate action, however. With world-wide concern growing over the impact of "greenhouse gases" on climate, the continued granting of substantial tax preferences for oil and gas exploration and development is difficult to justify. The 1998-99 AFB addresses that issue as follows, and directs the revenue savings into an Atmospheric Fund established to support greenhouse gas reduction strategies across Canada.

The fast write-off permitted for investments in exploration and development is one of the largest tax expenditures in the income tax system. Although the write-off is available in both the oil and gas and mining sectors, 75% of the benefit goes to the oil and gas sector. In addition to costing the federal treasury substantial sums of money, these special provisions have the effect of creating a preference in favour of non-renewable resource extraction and renewable resource production and recycling. While it is often argued that these preferences should be equalized by providing a corresponding benefit in the renewable energy and recycling sectors, we believe that the appropriate response is to eliminate the preference for non-renewable resource industries. Based on the most recent estimates available from the Department of Finance, for 1992, we estimate that this measure would generate $568 million in additional revenue.

Other provisions of the corporate income tax work against environmental objectives for the resource sector by limiting the deductions for site reclamation and rehabilitation to expenses actually incurred. While this may make sense for most activities, it works against the environmental goal of having funds set aside while profits are being generated to provide for rehabilitation when the profit stream has ended.

We would allow resource companies to deduct contributions to tax-free adjustment and rehabilitation funds, provided that the funds are held in trust for future expenditures on site reclamation and rehabilitation and community and employee economic adjustment.

THE SCIENTIFIC RESEARCH AND EXPERIMENTAL DEVELOPMENT TAX CREDIT

The tax credit for research and development has, justifiably, come under intense public scrutiny with the revelation that corporations such as banks have been able to take advantage of the credit against expenditures that are undertaken in the normal course of business and would not meet any reasonable definition of research and development activity. We believe that support for research and development should be maintained as an element of Canada's economic strategy. But rules should be tightened up to ensure that only legitimate research and development activity qualifies, and to guard against the emergence of another Scientific Research Tax Credit fiasco. The AFB for 1998 would restructure and tighten the SR&ED credit to reduce its cost by 50%. We estimate that this would its cost by $508 million.

THE DEDUCTION FOR MEALS AND ENTERTAINMENT

Even with the changes introduced in the 1990s, Department of Finance estimates for 1998 show that the deduction for meals and entertainment still costs $210 million in the corporate tax system and a further $95 million in the personal income tax system. These deductions should be totally disallowed.

In addition, rules analogous to those used for employer-provided automobiles should be introduced to limit similar types of deductions where the potential for abuse is great. Abuse of travel allowances could be restricted by limiting deductions to an accepted standard—the amounts paid to public employees on business, for example.

LOBBYING EXPENSES

It is estimated that the Ottawa-based lobbying industry is valued at $100 million a year. Assuming (conservatively) that provincial and municipal lobbying expenditures add another two-thirds to that total, we estimate that the deduction of lobbying expenses by corporations in Canada costs the Federal treasury $50 million a year. While we have no objection in principle to lobbying as an activity, provided it is subject to full disclosure and is conducted in an above-board manner, it is unacceptable that taxpayers would provide a subsidy for what is clearly self-serving and self-interested activity. This is not activity in the public interest; it is activity in a private interest and should not benefit from an implicit subsidy by taxpayers.

Disallowing corporate tax deductions for excessive executive salaries

The huge and widening gap between average wages and salaries in Canada and the salaries and bonuses paid to corporate executives at the top end of the scale is of real concern to many Canadians. They frankly have trouble understanding how any executive could be "worth" the high six- and seven-figure salaries that are becoming commonplace in Canadian big business. They understandably look with some skepticism at the self-sustaining process by which corporate directors who themselves receive salaries determine the salaries and bonuses of others. And they listen to the protestations of corporate leaders about competition with other jurisdictions for talent, and wonder how countries like Japan manage to survive with ratios of top salaries to average wages and salaries much smaller than those found in Canada.

Society cannot prevent corporations from paying these salaries. But it can make its disapproval clear by denying corporations a tax deduction for salaries in excess of what is considered a reasonable relationship between executive salaries and what average working people earn. We propose that earnings in excess of 10 times the average wage be disallowed as a deduction for corporate income tax purposes. This would not prevent corporations from paying high salaries to employees who, in the opinion of the shareholders of the corporation, deserve such remuneration. But it would require that such salaries be paid out of the after-tax profits of the corporation.

Corporate minimum tax

The ability of many profitable corporations to structure their affairs so as to pay no corporate income tax has been a major issue of fairness in the federal tax system for more than 20 years. Every year, literally billions of dollars in profits are received by corporations that pay little or no corporate income tax. It is important to stress that these untaxed profits arise because corporations are able to take advantage of legitimate provisions of the corporate income tax and not because anyone is doing anything illegal or illegitimate.

Given this perspective, there are two approaches that could be taken. One would be to focus on the provisions themselves, and eliminate those which are felt not to be worthy of support. This first approach would imply the elimination of most tax preferences. The other would be to take the position that, while the individual provisions may be worthy of support, the result— profitable corporations paying no tax—was not intended; that corporations should not be able to stack favourable tax provisions so as to eliminate their tax liability. This approach would suggest the application of a minimum corporate tax that would override special tax preferences.

We favour a mixture of these approaches. We believe that many of the tax expenditure provisions of the income tax are excessively generous or unwarranted. At the same time, we support the use of appropriate tax-based incentives in Canada's economic policy framework. Some corporate tax expenditures should be retained. But we believe that the phenomenon of profitable corporations paying no tax must be seen as an unintended result of the application of these incentives—an unintended result which is not acceptable. Further, we believe that the tax system must respond effectively to the need to ensure that institutions that derive significant economic benefit from participation in the Canadian economy should make a contribution to the support of the public services that help to sustain that economy.

The crucial decision in designing a minimum corporate tax is the definition of the tax base. Untaxed profits arise from a number of provisions of the corporate income tax. Not all of these provisions should be added back into the corporate tax base for minimum tax purposes. The most detailed and careful analysis of corporate tax provisions to date was conducted by the Corporate Minimum Tax Working Group of the Ontario Fair Tax Commission, whose report was published in 1992.

The Working Group concluded that such deductions as prior years' losses, the dividend income received from other corporations, and equity income of subsidiaries should apply to the base for a corporate minimum tax as well. The Group found that, of $18.5 billion earned by profitable, non-taxpaying corporations, $2 billion was non-taxable because of prior years' losses, $9 billion was non-taxable because inter-corporate dividends are not taxed; $850 million represented equity income taxable at the subsidiary level; and $700 million was non-taxable because of provisions unique to Ontario.

Of the $6 billion remaining, $3.3 billion was attributable to Ontario. Translated to the national level, this would imply the existence of about $8.25 billion in untaxed corporate profit in Canada. This remaining amount is a reasonable estimate of the base for a corporate minimum tax. If the rate of corporate minimum tax were set at half the nominal federal corporate income tax rate, the average rate of tax would be approximately 12%, yielding a revenue estimate of $1 billion.

Making an allowance of half to account for higher-than- normal profits in the base year of 1989 and erosion of the base attributable to changes in behaviour, we estimate revenue of $500 million from such a tax. Taking into account differences in rates and the size of the base, this is roughly equivalent to the estimate of $100 million for Ontario's corporate minimum tax.

WITHHOLDING TAXES ON CANADIAN EARNINGS OF FOREIGN CORPORATIONS

To ensure that investors and other non-residents active in the Canadian economy are placed in a tax position comparable to that of Canadians, Canada levies a withholding tax at a standard rate of 25% on income earned in Canada by non-residents. While this rate is generally applicable, reciprocal treaty arrangements with other countries reduce that rate to lower percentages. Under these arrangements, Canadians working in the other nation pay the same reduced withholding tax. These treaty rates can vary depending on the source of the income.

Canada, however, has gone one step further and acted unilaterally to reduce or eliminate withholding taxes on a number of categories of income, including copyright royalties, royalties for the right to use other property; interest on deposits; interest on long-term government debt; dividends; and management fees. Since this income is taxable in the home jurisdiction of the non-resident and taxes paid by that non-resident in Canada are generally creditable against domestic taxes, this change in tax treatment doesn't even accrue to the benefit of the taxpayer. It amounts to a transfer to the home government of the non-resident income recipient. We would restore withholding taxes to their previous levels, and examine all such taxes to ensure that such earnings are subject to tax at a level equivalent to the taxes paid by Canadians on such investment earnings, or to the taxes paid by Canadians on earnings in other jurisdictions.

A SURTAX ON BANK PROFITS

Most Canadians have been shocked by the fact that Canada's chartered banks managed to earn steadily increasing profits throughout the most difficult recession to hit this country since the 1930s. The recently announced massive merger of the Royal Bank and the Bank of Montreal merely reinforces the public sense that these corporations are consumed by greed and oblivious to the public interest.

What the banks seem to have forgotten is that they owe their privileged position in our economy to public regulation, which protects their status as one of a very limited number of institutions permitted to take deposits from the public. When the banks claim that their profits derive from their efficiency and managerial genius, they conveniently forget that, without public regulation, they would not exist.

Each year, the major banks seem to achieve new heights of profit excess, regardless of the state of the Canadian economy. In 1997, the six largest chartered banks reported profits in excess of $7 billion.

For the year 1998 only, the AFB would establish an excess profits tax, applicable to financial institutions. Excess profits would be defined as that portion of an institutions rate of return on shareholder equity that is in excess of the approximate average rate of return for all corporations in the non-financial sector—10%.

A MORE PROGRESSIVE PERSONAL INCOME TAX SYSTEM

Tax rate reform

When the income tax system was last changed, by the Mulroney government in the 1980s, the rate structure was flattened. Rates of tax on the highest-income individuals were reduced substantially. At the same time, the rate structure for low- and middle-income Canadians was flattened. The personal income tax system was made less progressive. And middle-income Canadians' after-tax incomes were squeezed.

The squeeze got tighter, later in the 1980s, when an across-the-board 3% surtax was introduced.

The 1998 AFB addresses this problem. Effective April 1, 1998:

- the across-the-board 3% surtax will be eliminated;
- the lowest rate in the personal income tax will be reduced from 17% to 16%;
- the current top rate of personal income tax will be increased from 29% to 30%;
- income between $100,000 and $150,000 will be taxed at a new rate of 33%; and
- income over $150,000 will be taxed at a new rate of 35%.

The combined effect of these changes will be to reduce the low rate to 16% from an effective rate of 17.51% (including the 3% surtax). The current middle rate will drop to 26% from an effective rate of 26.78%. The current top rate remains approximately the same, increasing from an effective 29.87% to 30%.

In proposing new rates for high income earners, we have taken into account the issues of international comparison raised by others in opposition to measures that improve the fairness of the tax system. While we accept in general the argument that Canada's top marginal tax rates have to be monitored carefully in relation to those in other countries, we believe that there is room in the current system for an increase in marginal tax rates applicable to very high income individuals.

The addition of two federal tax brackets to the current system—a rate of 33% on taxable income in excess of $100,000 and a rate of 35% on taxable income in excess of $150,000—would still leave regular top marginal tax rates below 60% and would generate a substantial amount of additional revenue.

Personal income tax credits

Canada's system of refundable tax credits and tax-based child benefits provides a useful vehicle through which to deliver targeted tax relief. In the 1998-99 AFB, these benefits are targeted to families with children.

Despite a lot of self-righteous posturing about addressing Canada's growing and unconscionable problem of child poverty, child poverty continues to increase. The principal culprits have been:

- the high unemployment created by a decade of anti-job Federal macroeconomic policies;
- cutbacks in social assistance benefits and funding under the Canada Assistance Plan by provincial governments and the federal government; and
- cutbacks in unemployment insurance that have reduced eligibility to 43% of the unemployed.

The much ballyhooed new federal-provincial initiative, so far, is little more than a cynical exercise in mutual back-slapping by federal and provincial governments. So for, the program itself has actually reduced benefits flowing to many families with children, and has provided only token increases for others.

The AFB makes a major assault on child poverty. It increases the child tax benefit by a total of $870 per child over a two-year period. It also increases the adult portion of the GST credit by $60.

RE-THINKING TAX ASSISTANCE FOR RETIREMENT SAVING

The special tax treatment accorded to retirement savings is by far the most significant tax expenditure in the personal income tax system, with a cost in foregone revenue of nearly $22 billion in 1993—$16 billion after taking into account tax paid on withdrawals.

The Mulroney-era reforms of the system of tax assistance for retirement saving increased contribution limits significantly and tied those limits more closely to income. Increasing the maximum RRSP contribution has been of great benefit to people with higher incomes, who can save 18% of their income, but has offered little to working people.

The skewed distribution of the tax subsidy for retirement income delivered through the RRSP system is well documented. For example, in 1993, over 46% of RRSP contributions were made by the top 12.5% of tax-filers. Because the deduction for contributions is worth more, the higher your income, the distribution of the tax subsidies is even more heavily weighted towards the top end.

The benefits from the tax-subsidized retirement system— both RRSPs and pension plans—are heavily skewed in favour of people with high incomes. For taxpayers with incomes over $100,000, average tax-subsidized retirement saving (RRSP contributions plus pension adjustments) in 1994 was $12,662, and 80% of taxpayers in that income group either belonged to a pension plan or contributed to an RRSP, or both. People in that income range made up only 7.7% of taxpayers.

In the $40,000-to-$50,000 income range, 80% of taxpayers participated, but the average contribution was $5,191. Only 18% of taxpayers had incomes above $50,000. In the $20,000-to-$30,000 range, the average contribution was only $2,335 and only 25% of taxpayers participated.

Data made available in 1996 for the first time have cast further doubt on the role of RRSPs in providing for retirement income. According to Statistics Canada, between 1990 and 1994 Canadians under age 65 withdrew $16.6 billion from RRSPs and used a further $4.4 billion in the Home Buyer's Plan. Those withdrawals were disproportionately from middle- and lower-income tax-filers, raising serious questions about the role of the RRSPs in the retirement income system.

Tax assistance for retirement saving is paid for though general taxation. We are all paying for the generous improvements Brian Mulroney made in the tax position of high-income savers.

There are a number of problems with the current system. The maximum pension—and therefore the maximum RRSP equivalent— eligible for tax subsidy is far higher than the maximum pensionable earnings under the Canada Pension Plan. Assistance is delivered in the form of a deduction, rather than in the form of a credit. The result is that higher income taxpayers get a larger tax subsidy for the same amount of retirement savings than lower-income taxpayers. And the conservative assumptions used in determining the RRSP equivalent to a pension plan mean that RRSPs are treated more favourably than pensions.

Given the skewed distribution of the benefits from the current RRSP system, it would be possible to reduce the maximum contribution and restrict the amount of tax subsidy with no negative impact whatsoever on the vast majority of contributors to RRSPs. Changes could be designed to redistribute some of the subsidy provided for retirement saving from high-income savers to provide a real incentive for retirement saving for lower-income taxpayers.

The 1998 AFB proposes a reform of the system of tax-assisted retirement saving that would redistribute the tax subsidy, while leaving the total amount of tax expenditure unchanged.

CONSUMPTION TAXES

The GST

The introduction of the GST has been one of the most controversial tax changes in Canadian history. It was introduced just as Canada was headed into its worst recession since the 1930s. No attempt was made to offset in any way the substantial shift in tax from corporations to individuals that was buried in the change from the Manufacturers' Sales Tax to the GST.

Sales tax payments tend to decrease as a proportion of income as income goes up—-the classic definition of a regressive tax. At the same time, the GST raises a substantial amount of revenue that is badly needed to pay for public programs which themselves have a very strongly progressive impact.

With the improved fiscal situation, the AFB considered carefully the most effective way to deliver tax relief to low- and moderate-income families and individuals. We concluded, after an analysis of the impact of various types of tax changes by income group, that enhancing tax credits would be the most effective way to deliver relief to low- and moderate-income individuals and families, and that tax rate reform in the personal income tax system would be the most effective way to provide relief for middle-income taxpayers.

The 1998 AFB therefore does not propose a reduction in the general rate of the GST. Instead, tax relief for low- and middle-income families and individuals will be delivered through income tax rate and credit reform.

We do, however, make proposals for change in the GST in two areas: reading material and financial services.

Reading material

The application of the GST to Canadian magazines and books has turned this country into one of the world's highest-taxed jurisdictions for reading material. The 1998-99 AFB completely removes the GST from books and magazines.

Financial services

One of the significant gaps in our taxation system is its treatment of financial transactions. While we have concluded that a broadly-based tax on financial transactions themselves is not practical as a domestic tax, we believe that a tax on the financial services would be appropriate. We have a great deal of difficulty understanding why you have to pay the GST when you buy a shirt, get a haircut, or hire a lawyer, but not when you use the services of an investment advisor or stock broker. The fact that these services are used disproportionately by the highest-income individuals makes this exemption extremely regressive.

In the 1998-99 AFB, therefore, we propose that brokerage fees and other financial transactions fees be added to the base of the GST.

Longer-term GST reform

In the longer term, there are a number of possible options for reform of the GST. The GST could be replaced by a European- style value added tax. Such a tax could build in higher rates of tax on luxury items and lower rates on necessities so as to make the impact of the tax less regressive. The rate structure could also be adjusted to reflect environmental objectives by, for example, taxing (re)used products or products made from recycled materials at a lower rate or by taxing toxic substances at a higher rate. The general rate of tax could also be reduced as finances improve and social programs are renewed.

GST reform could also be addressed in the broader context of the division of taxing responsibilities between the federal government and the provinces and territories. One option would be for the federal government to vacate the sales tax field entirely, in exchange for an expanded role in the taxation of capital and income from capital. Such an exchange would give provinces exclusive jurisdiction over a tax base which it is relatively easy for provincial governments to defend in exchange for a tax base which is much more easily defended by the federal government than by provincial governments.

Cigarette and Tobacco Taxes

In addition to its impact on both the substance and the image of the campaign to reduce smoking in Canada, the federal decision to reduce taxes on cigarettes and tobacco in certain provinces has cost the federal government hundreds of millions of dollars in lost revenue.

It is apparent from the data that are now coming to light that the strategy announced last year was ill-conceived and ineffective. It was based on an assumption about the scale of smuggling far in excess of what is apparent from the new data. Extrapolations from the data suggest that smuggling accounted for a far smaller share of the Canadian cigarette and tobacco market than was suggested by the tobacco industry and pro-industry lobbyists. It also suggests that the option of much tougher enforcement—never seriously considered by the federal government — would have been effective at a fraction of the eventual cost in lost revenue.

In addition, the mechanism introduced to persuade provincial governments to follow Ottawa's lead by tying additional federal tax cuts to provincial tax cuts placed Ottawa in the ridiculous position of providing an incentive for increased lowest-common- denominator competition among provincial governments. In our view, this is an unacceptable position for a federal government to adopt.

The federal government has already moved part way towards reversing its policy with the recent increases in tobacco taxes. Completing the reversal of this policy would be an important further step in putting Canada's anti-smoking policy back on track.

Environmental taxation

Interest has been growing in the use of the tax system to achieve environmental quality goals. Increases in consumption taxes such as the excise tax on motor vehicle fuels raise additional revenue to help compensate Canadians for the environmental impact of gasoline consumption and act as a modest disincentive for motor vehicle fuel consumption. One of the effects of tackling the issue of subsidies to the oil and gas industry in the income tax system would be to level the playing field between renewable and non-renewable energy production.

The 1997-98 AFB introduces two tax measures with explicit environmental objectives: significant restrictions on the tax preferences provided for non-renewable resource exploration, development and extraction (see above, under tax expenditures); and a modest carbon tax as an atmospheric user charge. We estimate that a nominal tax of $4.00 per tonne of carbon contained in energy consumed in Canada would raise an estimated $500 million.

The revenue from these two measures provides the funding for the creation of an Atmospheric Fund, with an annual cash flow in excess of $1 billion, to be directed towards the reduction of greenhouse gases.

Enforcement of existing tax laws

The Mulroney government clearly undermined public confidence in the tax system when it took the side of tax evaders and restricted the scope and scale of tax enforcement by federal government tax authorities. Although it goes without saying that the most unfair tax is one which some taxpayers can choose not to pay, by reducing the likelihood of audit and restricting the activities of auditors, the Mulroney government's attack on tax administrators made it easier for unscrupulous taxpayers to cheat the system, and therefore make chumps out of every Canadian who supports the system by paying what he or she owes.

We believe that significant increased revenue could be raised by turning up the heat significantly on tax cheats. Such a move would raise additional revenue directly. The Auditor General has found that an investment in tax enforcement generates many times the amount in additional tax recovered.

The attitudes given comfort by that policy continue to be reflected today in Mike Harris's "boys will be boys" attitude towards tax evasion and outright theft of sales tax revenue by small business operators, as highlighted in the Ontario Provincial Auditor's report.

The 1994 Report of the Auditor General revealed that arrears of taxes then stood at more than $6.6 billion. The Auditor General also noted that GST audits in particular were completely inadequate. While we would accept that recovery of all of this foregone revenue is not possible, we believe that recovery of half of this revenue over a five-year period is a reasonable objective. This would generate one-time revenues of approximately $600 million each year for five years.

While the improved enforcement activity contemplated by this proposal would provide an ongoing boost to revenues at the same time as it addressed the unpaid tax backlog, for the purposes of our budget projections we are treating these gains as a one-time revenue improvements.

The taxation of income from self-employment is becoming a major problem for the tax system. Every wage earner in Canada knows someone who enjoys a comparable lifestyle and who boasts of paying little or no income tax as a consequence of being able to "write off" expenses that others cannot. It is clearly impossible to expect that the system will be able to deal with these issues on an issue-by-issue basis. There are simply too many self-employed taxpayers to be able to defend the tax base through the audit process. We believe, however, that it is time for a crackdown on tax evasion through self-employment administered through the establishment of tax deduction rules similar to those applied to employer-provided automobiles. For example, general rules could limit the of the deduction available for a home office or a home-based compu

Maintaining tax bases internationally

As we noted above, individual nations face limitations on their ability to tax income from capital imposed by the mobility of capital and the consequent ability of high-income individuals and corporations to shift their taxable income among jurisdictions to find the most favourable jurisdiction from a tax perspective.

The international trend towards reduction of taxes on income from capital relative to taxes on income from employment can only be reversed in the longer term through international agreements that establish common definitions and approaches, provide for the sharing of information among jurisdictions, and require minimum levels of taxation. As a country with a relatively small, open economy, Canada should be at the forefront of efforts to create such agreements.

FOOTNOTES

1 "Tax Fairness", Budget 1997, Department of Finance, Canada, 1997

2 Brian Murphy, Michael C. Wolfson, and Ross Finnie (Statistics Canada Analytical Studies Branch). "A profile of High- Income Ontarians", in *Taxation and the Distribution of Income,* Research Studies, Ontario Fair Tax Commission, 1994

3 Daly, Michael. 1992 "Harmonization of Corporate Taxes in a Single European Market: Recent Developments and Prospects." Canadian Tax Journal, 40(5) p. 1054

4 Tax expenditure data are based on projections of the Department of Finance published by the Government of Canada in "Tax Expenditures", 1997

5 In the German system, all estate transfers are captured in the system, including transfers to residents of the jurisdiction from estates outside the [illegible] transfers from residents of the jurisdiction to beneficiaries out[illegible]iction, and transfers of property located in the jurisdiction to [illegible] outside the jurisdiction to beneficiaries outside the jurisdic-

Toward a Green Alternative Budget,

by the Environment Working Group

Principles of Environmental Policy

The following ten principles of environmental policy covering all the aspects of environmental protection should be adopted.

1. Primacy of prevention

   Traditionally, there are three modes of environmental protection: 1) the *prevention* of environmental degradation by refraining from activities and the use of materials that *create* degradation, pollution and waste; 2) the *control* of emissions and products to *mitigate* the effects of detriments, once they have been created; and 3) the *remediation* or *clean-up* of contaminated sites and areas. The *primacy of prevention* says that we should focus on, and give a priority to, preventive measures as the most effective, and often the least costly, environmental protection strategy.

2. The Precautionary Principle

   The most useful expressions of this principle include the notion that full scientific certainty should not be required for a prudent and effective environmental strategy to be pursued; that risk assessments are not usually necessary as a scientific precondition of environmental strategy; that the onus of proof of safety rests with those responsible for a process or material; that limited resources should be conserved, not depleted; and that any discharge or emission should be regarded as a detriment unless proved to be harmless. When in doubt, adopt the environmental strategy which is the least likely to be harmful.

3. Just Transition

   The concept of *just transition* encompasses a series of measures designed to protect the livelihood of workers adversely affected by environmental programs and legislation. When a major initiative is taken, such as the sun-setting or banning of a major industrial chemical, or climate change measures aimed at severely eroding or sun-setting a whole industrial sector, workers should not be required to bear the full brunt of the environmental measures. Among the options for transition programs are: 1) an equitable program of industrial restructuring and retraining to recruit laid-off workers from the affected industries to the new alternative industries or ventures; 2) a program of retraining and re-employment in the affected industries; and 3) a placement service inside and outside the affected industries, which may include severance pay, counselling, retraining, adjustment programs.

4. Weight of Evidence

   Instead of a single scientific test such as a risk assessment or epidemiological study, detriments are assessed on the weight of all the evidence, for and against.

5 The Critical Load Principle

   This requires that the amount or the concentration of pollution that the natural environment can withstand without permanent damage (or critical load) shall not be exceeded. Where no critical load or threshold has been established, pollution and waste are to be *minimized*.

6. Cradle to Grave and Life Cycle Analysis

   In assessing environmental detriment, we have to consider the extraction, processing, production, transport, use or consumption, and disposal of materials. The factor most commonly left out of life cycle analysis is workers' health, safety and well-being in the production, processing and transport phases of the life cycle of materials/products.

7. Best Available Technology

   This principle requires that poor technical solutions, especially at the processing stage, not be an excuse for poor practice if better technology is available.

8. Sustainable Use

   This principle requires that renewable resources shall be used sustainably and that non-renewable resources shall be conserved while renewable substitutes are developed.

9. Full Cost Accounting

   In addition to "what to do and how to do it," there are two monetary principles to be observed, of which the first is full cost accounting. Environmental impacts, which are "externalities" with respect to conventional pricing mechanisms, are to be included or internalized in the price of goods and services.

10. THE POLLUTER PAYS PRINCIPLE

The second monetary principle is that the generator of pollutants and wastes must pay the cost of avoidance or remediation. As it is, many contaminated sites are "orphaned", with great difficulty in tracing the polluter, even if it were established public policy to have the polluter pay.

These ten principles amount to what has been called a green screen to assess policies and programs. It needs to be emphasized that the adoption of these principles, collectively, would amount to a radical new basis for environmental policy-making. For instance, prevention of environmental degradation, far from being the prime concern, is currently relegated to a distant third, behind the control and remediation of environmental detriments. Business has made quantitative risk assessment (QRA) into a central and exclusive rationale for environmental policy, so that it serves not merely to mediate the move from the recognition of detriments to their removal, but to prevent any public moves towards elimination or control. In the name of "good science," risk assessment is the antithesis of the precautionary principle.

Just transition entails a recognition that environmentalism must incorporate social as well as ecological values if it is to become a practical alternative to current practice. Just transition comprises a central element in our proposals on climate change and pollution prevention.

In *full cost accounting*, environmental impacts are "externalities" to be included or internalized in the price of goods and services. Producers of goods and services, through the externalization of environmental costs, pass on costs to consumers. Citizens pay these costs either in taxes to pay for remediation of damage, or through bad health, pollution, loss of wilderness, recreation, etc. Much of these costs are passed on to future generations and to non-humans.

Lutz Wicke estimated that the external costs arising from environmental degradation in West Germany represented over 5% of GDP in 1985. He included only domestic effects on air, water, soil contamination and noise. Adding external costs arising from injuries and environmentally caused illness, soil erosion, climate change, biodiversity losses and for damage exported or imposed on future generations, externalities represent at least 10% of German GDP. [In the U.S. Ralph Estes estimated the cost of workplace cancer in 1994 as US$275 billion. The global external effects from burning fossil fuels alone were estimated at about 14% of global GDP in 1988.]

Transplanting the German figures of 5-10% of GDP to Canada, we can get a ballpark figure of the amounts involved. In 1996/7, Canada's GDP was $797 billion, and therefore 10% and 5% of GDP represent approximately $79.7 billion and $39.8 billion, respectively. In 1996/7, federal government total budgetary revenues were $135.5 billion or 17% of GDP. For 1996/7, federal program spending was $109 billion or 13.7% of GDP. In 1996/7, total provincial/ territorial program spending was about $134.7 billion or 16.9% of GDP. Therefore, total federal/provincial/territorial program spending for 1996/7 was $243.7 billion or 30.6% of GDP. If the value of environmental externalities is 10% of GDP, they are equivalent to nearly one third of all federal/provincial/ territorial program spending in Canada. Ecological tax reform is one way of internalizing the externalities.

AREAS OF ENVIRONMENTAL POLICY

A comprehensive policy of sustainability and environmental protection should cover five main areas:

Natural Resources: including mining, forestry, agriculture, and fisheries. It includes both the extraction and harvesting of resources and the quantities and modes of their industrial use ("natural resource inputs").

Energy: This includes the selection of energy sources with a preference for renewable energy sources and an assessment of the relative detriments of non-renewable energy sources. It also includes energy utilization, the efficiency and intensiveness of the use to which energy is put. Energy-intensiveness is not necessarily bad, if the social/environmental benefit of an activity is correspondingly high. Inefficiency, however, is always bad, and a needless environmental detriment.

Pollution and Waste: These are always to be minimized. The more toxic, persistent and bio-accumulative the waste, the more it is necessary to minimize discharges and emissions (non-product outputs).

Natural Conservation: The conservation of nature is not the same as the conservation of resources, though the latter can be a contributing factor in the conservation of the former. The aim of natural conservation is the retention or preservation of biodiversity, wilderness, wildlife, ecosystems and bioregions. In natural conservation, human beings are often seen, not as a part of the "social ecology" of the planet, but as a life form potentially and actually at odds with Nature. While the budgetary implications of natural conservation are not as strong as those of environmental protection, we will, in future reports, be more balanced in terms of the relationship between conservation and environmental protection, though these concepts overlap.

Consumer Issues: These include the reduction of (needless) consumption and the production of goods and services that are durable and reusable or recyclable.

Instruments of Environmental Policy Regulation: Regulation remains the single most effective safeguard of environmental protection. In the federal jurisdiction, the effluent control regulations under the Fisheries Act, governing emissions from pulp mills, mines and refineries, are among the most important, as are the ozone depletion regulations under the Canadian Environmental Protection Act. Generally, regulations are about control measures; the regulations proposed in connection with pollution prevention are rather different from traditional control measures. The proper enforcement of regulations requires an expansion in the budgets of the relevant government departments. Otherwise, regulation has far less budgetary impact than *economic instruments.*

Economic Instruments: Economic instruments provide an *incentive* to meet a standard. Economic instruments are a form of regulation in that they usually require legislation to implement or realize them, though they are usually regarded as less effective in meeting a policy aim than *hard regulation*. This is, admittedly, true of the pollution prevention proposals which follow. Among economic instruments are:

- *Subsidies* to encourage environmentally-friendly behaviour.
- *Green Taxes* including: *pollution taxes* on emissions or waste; *consumer taxes* on environmentally unfriendly products such as gasoline and domestic pesticides. These are not usually favoured, as they are regressive, however environmentally useful; *taxes on industrial materials* or taxes "at the front end" of the industrial process, such as a carbon tax related to climate change measures, and taxes on chemical inputs.
- *Tradeable Emission Permits*: in which the government usually sets a quota of allowable emissions or detriments, then issues licenses or similar up to that level, which must always of course be lower than current practice. The licenses can then be bought and sold, sometimes on a stock exchange. Such a system is in operation in the U.S. for acid rain emissions (sulphur dioxide), though nitrogen oxide emissions are excepted. It is also on the cards for carbon dioxide and climate change. In this case, tradeable emission permits are particularly inflexible, since one cannot in most cases change a production process in order to cut down on CO_2 emissions, but only shut down emitting industries to the detriment of all the workers in them. Environmentalists dislike emission permits because, like pollution taxes, they are a limited license to pollute, and also because businesses remain untouched by direct public regulation. As to the effectiveness of emission permits in meeting their declared aims, the jury is still out. We must also bear in mind that traditional regulations are only as good as the enforcement policy. A well-run economic policy instrument could well be better than regulations that are not properly enforced.

- *Depletion Quotas*: The government puts limits on the amount of selected resources allowed to be used, then arranges an auction, so that for x amount of a resource, its true market value is established. This is a novel idea, with a compelling logic, emanating from the ecological economics of Herman Daly. As an incentive to promote resource conservation and avoid waste, it is faultless.

Tax-based instruments attach a specific price to environmental degradation and, in effect, create an explicit market. In a regulatory environment, the market is implicit. The Ontario Fair Tax Commission, for example, developed a number of principles for environmental taxation: 1) there should be a mix of tax/price and regulatory approaches ; 2) Tax/price options work best where there are a large number of decision-makers and decisions to be influenced on the "receiving end"of the tax/price mechanism, where it is desirable to give those decision-makers a range of choices as to how to comply, including contracting out of the obligation, e.g., not buying a product; 3) regulatory options work best where there are small numbers of decision makers and are thus easier to regulate; 4) tax/price instruments work best when they are levied on the behaviour or decisions which we wish to influence; 5) regulatory options work best on *system* problems (e.g., a whole activity has to be shut down) as opposed to individual decision maker problems (e.g., an activity has to have its direction modified through the behaviour of a large number of decision-makers such as consumers); and 6) environmental behaviour is influenced by the tax system, even without specific environmental taxes—via the tax expenditure system.

VOLUNTARY MEASURES

Voluntary measures are of two sorts: those that build on, or exceed, the aims of regulation, and those that replace regulations to a greater or lesser degree. Voluntary measures comprise the third type of environmental policy instrument. The federal government is backing off the enforcement of regulations and devolving responsibility for them to the provinces under the guise of "harmonization". In contrast to Europe, and even the U.S., its policy of economic instruments is empty. This leaves it with what it asserts to be its third policy option, *voluntary measures*—projects and programs of which the most well-known is the Accelerated Reduction and Elimination of Toxics (ARET). The reporting arrangements for ARET are so vague that it is impossible to assess how successful the program has been. It has certainly been successful from the point of view of the chemical producing industry, which has avoided pollution prevention regulations while laughing all the way to the bank.

We recommend that:

- regulation, within a mix of instruments, is always the preferred policy option;
- where "green taxes" are to be adopted, we prefer taxation at the "front end" of the production process;
- green taxes should be "loop taxes" or dedicated revenue— dedicated to resolving the issues, especially the employment issues, which are the occasion for levying the tax in the first place;
- that green taxes should reflect the principles of ecological tax reform and should, at least in part, be offset by reductions in other taxes.

RESOURCE ISSUES

In the 1997 Alternative Federal Budget, the Taxation Group identified three important problems with the imposition of resource extraction taxes at the national level. First, while resource taxation is clearly an area of federal/territorial jurisdiction, taxes on the volume or value of resources extracted would almost certainly be interpreted as an invasion of provincial constitutional authority. Federal tax policies with respect to resource industries have been exercised through the corporate income tax, which remains the most appropriate focus of federal tax policy related to resources.

Second, a volume-based resource tax would generally bear no relationship to the economics of the particular resource operation or industry, and would therefore likely maximize the resulting economic disruption and the migration of operations abroad. This would not reduce virgin resource use and is not related to any identifiable environmental policy objective.

Third, a volume-based tax would likely interfere with provincial taxes designed to tax the economic rent (the underlying economic value of the resource itself) associated with resource extraction industries. In the end, the Taxation Group supported neither tax privileges for environmentally friendly industries nor the retention of the provisions of the Income Tax Act that provide incentives for non-renewable natural resource extraction. The Group did recommend the establishment of tax-free dedicated funds for natural resource extraction site rehabilitation.

In light of difficulties with the taxation of natural resources and our proposals for ecological tax reform, a new approach will be needed to resource conservation and utilization. There are, broadly, two new federal policy approaches. The first is an Advance Disposal Tax or National Product Design Fee. The fee would vary according to resource category, and with the degree of diversion from waste disposal in the resource category. Resource categories would include waste that is hazardous and difficult to manage such as household hazardous waste, batteries, oil and tires; residential short-life products such as newspapers and packaging; durable products and various categories of waste such as food/yard, inorganic chemical waste, organic chemical waste; and construction and demolition waste. Fee levels would be based on the cost of diverting the waste from landfill at the end of the product's useful life. Fees would be charged to the producer, in the case of domestic producers, or the importer, in the case of imported products. The fee would be earmarked for waste diversion.

Provinces would be able to opt out of the system, provided they had an equivalent provincial program in place. Though the scheme is aimed at waste reduction, it would have the effect of conserving resources in that the most wasteful uses of resources are the ones subject to the highest fees.

The second approach is that of resource depletion quotas, as advocated by Daly. The government puts a limit on the amount of selected resources allowed to be used, then arranges an auction, so that for any given amount of a resource, the true market value is established. In the system of resource depletion quotas, the policy objective of resource conservation is the prime concern, with waste reduction as a policy consequence.

Neither scheme is a conventional taxation measure. Both policies would need major shifts in ecological priorities and ecological tax reform before they would stand a chance of finding a place in economic policy and thus in any budget.

We thus recommend future policy work on resource taxation, and as a concrete measure we propose the removal of resource subsidies.

ENERGY ISSUES: CLIMATE CHANGE MEASURES

Our climate is changing. The average annual surface temperature of the planet has increased by somewhere between 0.3 and 0.6 degrees celsius since the late 19th century, and global sea levels have been rising. There is now a broad scientific consensus, represented by the more than 2,000 scientists involved in the Intergovernmental Panel on Climate Change (IPCC) that "...the balance of evidence suggests that there is a discernible human influence on global climate". This human-induced climate change, produced primarily by greenhouse gas emissions released through the combustion of coal, oil and natural gas to produce energy, is perhaps the most significant environmental threat facing Canada as we enter the 21st century.

If no action is taken to reduce global emissions of greenhouse gases, the IPCC projects that average global temperatures will increase by another one to 3.5 degrees celsius by the year 2100. This is expected to result in significantly higher sea levels; more extreme rainfall events; major disruption to one-third of the world's forests; the loss of one-third to one-half of mountain glacier mass; fundamental shifts in global agricultural production; and increased incidence of infectious diseases. Within Canada, climate change threatens our Arctic ecosystem as well as natural resources like forests, fisheries and agriculture, and the economic activity that depends on them.

Canada made a commitment to stabilize its greenhouse gas emissions at 1990 levels by the year 2000, and is now involved in international negotiations that are likely to result in strengthened, legally-binding commitments to control greenhouse gas emissions in the post-2000 period. To meet its commitment, Canada has relied largely on voluntary action by corporations. This approach has failed. Between 1990 and 1996, carbon dioxide emissions in Canada increased by more than 10%. The federal government now expects Canada's greenhouse gas emissions to be 19% above 1990 levels by the year 2010.

A number of models have attempted to examine the economic impact on Canada of taking action to reduce greenhouse gas emissions, and a wide range of results have been produced–ranging from significantly negative to slightly positive, in GDP terms. All of these modelling exercises tend, however, to overestimate the costs of taking action to address climate change. Virtually no models consider the costs of inaction (the costs of mitigating or adapting to future climate change), or the multiple benefits of action to reduce greenhouse gas emissions (reductions in emissions that contribute to acid rain and urban smog). In addition, most of these models significantly underestimate our capacity for technological innovation.

Taking action to reduce greenhouse gas emissions will produce economic benefits. One of the pillars of a successful climate change response strategy is to improve the efficiency with which we use energy. By using energy more efficiently, we reduce energy bills, producing savings for energy consumers. We also create jobs because actions to improve energy efficiency (e.g., building retrofits) are more labour-intensive than actions to produce new energy supply (e.g., new coal developments).

In addition, the investment of energy bill savings back into the economy generates further economic activity and job creation. As a result, investments in energy efficiency tend to create about four times as many jobs as equivalent investments in new energy supply. (Comparative Analysis of Employment from Air Emission Reduction Measures–Pembina Institute, January 1997). These positive impacts are on top of the multiple environmental benefits generated by avoiding the need to exploit new energy resources.

Another pillar in a successful climate change strategy is to produce more energy from renewable energy sources like solar energy, wind energy, small hydro, and biomass. Once again, the environmental benefits are clear. In addition, studies completed to date indicate that investments in these technologies tend to produce approximately 50% more jobs than investments in conventional large-scale energy development from mega-hydro, oil, coal, and nuclear. Moreover, there is a rapidly growing market for renewable energy technologies overseas, particularly in developing countries.

Canada's current climate change response strategy fails to capture the potential job creation opportunities, or the economic and environmental benefits, associated with actions to improve energy efficiency and increase the use of renewable energy sources. Doing so will require Canada to move beyond voluntary actions to address climate change to the adoption of a mix of regulatory, fiscal, and voluntary measures to reduce greenhouse gas emissions.

A Carbon Tax

To be effective, the package of measures that make up a greenhouse gas emission reduction strategy must include fiscal instruments that adjust market signals to make greenhouse gas emissions reduction more attractive and greenhouse gas emissions production less attractive. Such measures can be targeted at specific activities or sectors, or can be broad-based and have an impact across the entire economy.

A carbon tax is the most straightforward broad-based fiscal instrument to address climate change. Similar taxes have already been implemented in a number of European countries (Finland, the Netherlands, Norway, Sweden) many of which have instituted such a tax as part of a broader ecological tax reform which has resulted in the reduction of other taxes at the same time. By taxing energy sources according to their carbon content (i.e., coal is taxed more than oil, which is taxed more than natural gas), a carbon tax would send a market signal that would increase the attractiveness of all of the key policy responses to climate change (energy efficiency improvements, greater use of renewable energy, and switching from high-carbon to low-carbon fossil fuels).

We propose a carbon tax of $25 per tonne of carbon that would be applied to fossil fuels, on the basis of their carbon content, at the point of combustion. For example, the tax would be imposed on:

- fossil fuel producers who use fossil fuels to provide the energy needed to recover and process coal, oil, and natural gas;
- electric utilities that burn fossil fuels to produce electricity;
- industries that burn fossil fuels on site to meet their energy needs; and
- consumers who use fossil fuels to power their vehicles (e.g., gasoline) or to provide energy services in their home (e.g., natural gas).

At $25 per tonne of carbon, this tax represents a moderate level of taxation that is well within the range of carbon taxes already in existence in European countries. It certainly does not come close to fully reflecting the environmental costs associated with the production, distribution and use of fossil fuels. For consumers of energy, this carbon tax would result in the following price increases:

- Gasoline–$ 0.0161/litre (2.7% increase on 60 cents a litre).
- Home Natural Gas Heating– $ 0.0128/cubic metre (17.6% increase on 7.26 cents per cubic metre).
- Coal for Electricity Generation–$ 11.86/tonne of coal (approximately a doubling of price for Alberta utilities, and approximately a 20% increase in price for Ontario Hydro).

By applying the tax at the point of combustion, it would send a clear signal to fossil fuel users and provide an incentive to reduce carbon dioxide emissions. The tax should be clearly identified and visible to the energy user. If Canada produced the same level of carbon dioxide emissions in 1999 as it did in 1995, this carbon tax would raise revenues of $ 3.14 billion.

ECOLOGICAL TAX REFORM

Most economic analysis indicates that the impact of a carbon tax on economic activity and employment levels is critically dependent on what happens to the revenues generated by the tax. Generally, economic models indicate that ploughing the tax revenue into general revenues or using it to reduce government debt produces a less positive result than taking steps to ensure the tax is "revenue-neutral" (i.e., other taxes are reduced by an amount equivalent to the new revenue generated by the greenhouse gas tax). According to the models, the effects are often most positive when the taxes reduced are taxes on the use of labour (e.g., payroll taxes).

A carbon tax should represent the first step toward a broader ecological tax reform. In essence, this new tax on something we do not want (carbon dioxide emissions) should be offset by tax reductions in things we want to encourage (employment, investment, and other forms of economic activity). While there are several taxes that could be reduced to meet this objective, we suggest that the federal GST, as a highly visible and politically unpopular tax (and because it is relatively easy to model), be reduced. We recommend that more work be done to examine what specific tax reductions in an ecological tax reform initiative would provide the greatest overall benefit to Canadians as part of the preparatory work for next year's Alternative Federal Budget.

PROGRAM SPENDING

A climate change strategy that relies only on a carbon tax is unlikely to be the most effective strategy. Government programs, as well as additional fiscal, regulatory and voluntary initiatives will be required. This is particularly true with a carbon tax as modest as the one proposed here, which will in some cases provide only a small incentive to reduce some sources of greenhouse gas emissions (e.g., the impact on gasoline prices is relatively small because gasoline is already taxed far more than any other energy source).

As a result, we have not proposed reducing other taxes by an amount equivalent to the revenues generated by the carbon tax. This is to ensure that new resources are available for investments in programs that will reduce greenhouse gas emissions. Nor are we proposing that any of the carbon tax revenues be directly tied to specific greenhouse gas emission reduction programs.

The Rational Energy Program developed by the Canadian Climate Action Network proposed 44 measures (including a carbon tax) to reduce greenhouse gas emissions in Canada. These measures include:

- fuel economy standards for automobiles;
- energy efficiency standards for new buildings and building retrofits;
- revenue-neutral feebate on new vehicles;
- national vehicle inspection and maintenance program;
- expanded government energy efficiency programs;
- tax incentives for cncrgy efficiency investments in industry;
- gas and electric utility least cost planning;
- decrease and eventual elimination of subsidies to the fossil fuel industry; and
- increased research, development and commercialization support for energy-efficient and renewable energy technologies.

The cost of this package of measures to the federal government was estimated to be at least $628 million per year, upwards of 20% of the revenues generated by the carbon tax. Modelling by Natural Resources Canada indicated that these measures would reduce carbon dioxide emissions to at least 8% below 1990 levels by the year 2010. In addition, this package of measures was found to reduce Canada's sulphur dioxide emissions by 24%, emissions of volatile organic compounds by 13%, and nitrogen oxide emissions by 16%.

Informetrica, which analyzed the Rational Energy Program from a macroeconomic perspective, projected that it would produce a net increase of 1.5 million jobs in Canada over 15 years. In addition, the modelling work concluded that the Rational Energy Program would have a positive impact on GDP in early years and noted that any negative impacts on GDP that might develop in the longer term would be proportionately small.

While the Rational Energy Program demonstrates that a well-designed climate change mitigation strategy can produce net benefits for the economy, some sectors of the economy will suffer losses. For example, although the Rational Energy Program produces a net increase in jobs in Canada, some sectors (e.g., resource-based goods, energy, food/beverage/tobacco, electrical/electronic, and government and social services) experience job losses.

Accordingly, there is a need for funds to support the transition for workers from sunset industries to sectors experiencing growth. This revenue, or at least a portion of it, could be directed to workers displaced by climate change measures, particularly in the hard energy fuel cycle—from mining through processing, distribution, sales and service. Ideally, such a transition program would help these workers enter the energy efficiency and renewable energy industries.

While the carbon tax seems to be unfair to workers in the hard energy fuel cycle, it should be remembered that the alternatives are far worse. In particular, the favoured alternative to the carbon tax is a system of tradeable emission permits. This system, unless backed by a package of other measures similar to those of the Rational Energy Program, would be unfair, limited and inflexible. Such a system would (assuming it worked) provide limited incentives for efficiency in coal-fired power plants, leaving other sources of greenhouse gases untouched. Older plants would close, leaving workers without jobs and without any expectation of compensation, retraining or placement in other industries.

There is also a case for just transition for consumers as well as workers. For example, in the area of home heating, differential pricing could be instituted to ensure that the price of energy to heat an average home was low and affordable, with any excess energy use charged at a much higher rate. This could serve to encourage energy conservation and retrofitting, without unduly penalizing the less-well-off in society. It is critical that any climate change mitigation strategy include measures that ensure that the cost does not fall unduly on lower-income citizens and consumers.

The implementation of a carbon tax is only the first step in a process designed to ensure that increasingly strong market signals are provided to reduce greenhouse gas emissions. Accordingly, we recommend the following:

- a schedule of gradual but steady increases in the carbon tax in future years. For example, a commitment to increase the carbon tax by $5.00/ tonne of carbon every three years for the next 15 years.
- As the tax revenue increases from the carbon tax over time, it will have a larger impact on overall economic activity and provide a stronger signal for greenhouse gas emissions reduction. Accordingly, there should be a commitment to increase the percentage of carbon tax revenue offset by reductions in other taxes over time, to more fully reflect the principles of ecological tax reform.
- a commitment to expand, over time, the carbon tax to cover emissions of other sources of greenhouse gases where there is international agreement that emissions can be measured or estimated with a high degree of confidence. The Kyoto Protocol (signed in December 1997) brought five other greenhouse gases, in addition to carbon dioxide, under the terms of the agreement to reduce emissions by 5.2% by 2012.
- While it is often difficult to measure emissions of greenhouse gases other than carbon dioxide, it is often possible to measure reductions in emissions of other gases. For example, it is hard to estimate methane emissions from a landfill, but methane that is captured from a landfill and used to produce energy can be easily quantified. There should be a commitment to provide such reductions with a tax credit, equivalent to the amount of CO^2 emissions they offset. These "credits" could be applied against a company's own tax, or they could be sold to other carbon dioxide emitters, providing them with enhanced flexibility at no environmental cost.

The AFB Steering Committee accepted in principle our recommendations on climate change measures. The Steering Committee agreed to a significant first step in the development of a Canadian Action Plan to reduce greenhouse gas emissions. The 1998 AFB calls for a $1 billion National Atmospheric Fund, half of which is to be financed by a modest carbon tax of $4 per tonne [and the rest by savings from the elimiination of tax subsidies to the oil and gas sector.] This Fund will provide loans to municipal governments that support the development and implementation of actions to reduce greenhouse gas emissions at the municipal level. Municipal governments will be expected to repay these loans from the savings generated as a result of investments made with the Fund. It is hoped that these monies will also help leverage additional amounts from provincial and municipal governments, and the private sector. The interest earned from the Fund can be used to provide grants to cover project development costs and small community initiatives to fight climate change.

While the full $1 billion will initially be available to municipalities, $430 million is ultimately earmarked to support *just transition* for workers displaced by actions to protect the climate.

POLLUTION AND WASTE

In accordance with the *primacy of prevention* principle, we emphasize the prevention of pollution and waste, as opposed to mere control or remediation. The definition of pollution prevention put forward by the federal government in 1995 and subsequently accepted by the provinces and territories is: *the use of processes, practices, materials, products or energy, that avoid or minimize the creation of pollutants and waste and reduce the overall risk to the environment or human health.*

The definition implies that pollution prevention rests on the key concept of toxic substances use reduction, which has become a technical discipline known as Toxics Use Reduction (TUR). This generates pollution prevention action at the workplace level. Bans, phase-outs, use-restrictions, elimination or sun-setting of toxic chemicals at the national or provincial levels are also a part of the drive towards pollution prevention, though as yet very little Canadian legislation requires pollution prevention measures and planning.

The advantage of pollution prevention in minimizing the creation of waste is that it benefits the work environment, community health, and the physical environment alike. It is clearly superior to emission control measures once a pollutant is created, since these have a limited effect on protecting the environment and human health, and do nothing at all to protect the health of workers inside the chemical-using facility. Another advantage of pollution prevention methodology is that it obviates the need for the technique of risk assessment. Instead of using risk assessment as a technique for intervening as little as possible in environmental protection, pollution prevention can be instituted to minimize the creation of pollutants whenever the opportunity exists. It rests squarely on the precautionary principle.

Over the past five years, the Canadian Labour Congress has developed a National Pollution Prevention Strategy. The main elements are as follows:

The first step is for the federal government to set down a standard of pollution prevention, including *pollution prevention planning,* as a universal national goal in federal undertakings or federally-regulated workplaces. For constitutional reasons, the federal government cannot legislate pollution prevention in workplaces not subject to federal regulation. The federal government can only lay down national pollution emission control regulations at "the end of the waste pipe," which are not the same thing. So the federal standard is a flagship for a national standard.

Since the federal government cannot legislate pollution prevention for the whole country, it has to rely on economic instruments in order to aim for a national standard. The CLC proposes a tax on chemicals, preferably the 178 chemicals that are on the National Pollutants Release Inventory (NPRI). The revenue from this tax is then transferred on a prorated basis to those provinces and territories that: a) meet the federal standard; and b) have a compliance policy not weaker than the federal one.

The traditional Canadian environmental program called on the federal government to eliminate or phase out a short list of specific chemicals or classes of chemical. The CLC supports this but links it with a transition program for displaced workers as a sine qua non (no transition, no sun-setting). The revenue for transition would be raised by extending the existing chemical taxation scheme, building on its taxation infrastructure.

A tax on chemical inputs–import, manufacture, processing and use–would aim to raise tens of millions of dollars to finance a national standard of pollution prevention. An example of this is a scheme in operation in Massachusetts. A large number of chemicals are on a list of those liable to taxation. In practice, 251 are taxed, rather more than those currently on the Canadian NPRI. There is a minimum base rate of $1,100 U.S. per designated chemical, plus a differential rate, based on whether the chemical is manufactured/processed, or only used. The highest cap (the maximum that a workplace–not a company–can pay per year) is $31,100.

Designated chemical use in Massachusetts is 1.3 billion pounds per year. An average of 600 workplaces a year are taxed, since the tax is on workplaces rather than companies or corporations. The number of workplaces taxed in 1996 fell to 524, partly due to the success of the TUR program in reducing the use of toxic substances and partly due to the delisting of such substances as metal alloys from the lists of chemicals liable to taxation. The system raises about $4.5 million per year from a population of about 6 million.

If a similar system were to operate in Canada, this would raise about $30 million Canadian annually, enough to finance a national standard. Preliminary work done on a Canadian version suggests that the rate of the tax should be higher than that for an U.S. state and the corresponding revenue would be much higher than $30 million.

A Canadian corporate tax on toxic chemicals would work somewhat differently, through the NPRI, which is a less ambitious version of the U.S. Toxics Release Inventory (TRI). The NPRI requires the reporting of emissions rather than patterns of chemical use; the TRI requires both.

There are proposals both to increase the numbers of chemicals on NPRI and to require the reporting of pollution prevention activities, i.e., the pattern of chemical use. Such data would be required to form the basis of the chemical taxation scheme proposed (unless the chemicals concerned were first identified through NPRI, then chemical use reporting required, then the levying of the tax, which Massachusetts calls a "dedicated fee" to run its TUR program).

Either way, the NPRI is a good basis on which to rest the taxation scheme. Substances on the NPRI list are selected because of their toxicity and their potential for environmental degradation. There is no case for saying that the tax is arbitrary or does not address the issue of pollutants in the Canadian environment. In 1996, 1,173 companies reported emissions under NPRI, in proportion a smaller number than Massachusetts with a population of 6 million and 500-600 companies reporting. The lesson is that, to yield an adequate tax, the taxation rate must be higher than Massachusetts and more chemicals have to be added to the NPRI list, at least for the purpose of tax liability.

We do not expect the 1998 Alternative Budget to adopt the chemical taxation system advocated by the CLC. Instead, we propose that the principle be established of sectoral taxation with dedicated revenue.

The Taxation of Selected Chemicals

The 1997 AFB Taxation Group recommended the taxation of a very limited number of chemicals, and mentioned mercury as one possibility. What follows is a discussion of selected chemicals.

Ozone Depletors

The Montreal Protocol contains a list of ozone depletors scheduled for phase-out. Some of these have short-term imminent deadlines and there is no point in trying to tax them. Hard regulation is enough. With others, however, the deadlines are more distant, e.g., the HCFCs with a final phase-out by 2030, and methyl bromide with a final phase-out in 2010. Here, taxation as an incentive to plan for each of the quantity reduction deadlines would be a useful move. It is self-fulfilling—the less you produce, the less you are taxed.

Mercury

Mercury and its compounds occur both through deliberate use and as an unwanted contaminant. Getting a tri-national agreement through NAFTA on mercury abatement has proved to be difficult, making a national tax, in principle, an attractive idea. The trouble is that the quantities of mercury involved are small and it would be administratively difficult to calculate the quantities in each of its applications and as a contaminant. In addition, the main sources as a contaminant include coal, oil and natural gas burning, all of which would be subject in any case to a carbon tax. In all, mercury is not a good candidate for chemical taxation.

DIOXINS AND FURANS

Similar arguments apply to dioxins and furans. These are highly toxic contaminants produced mainly by industrial burning, in very small amounts. A tax on dioxin outputs would be too complex to administer effectively and would lead to the suspicion that businesses would pay the price of dioxin pollution without changing their economic behaviour. Banning sources of dioxins such as medical waste incineration is a far better strategy.

PERCHLORETHYLENE (PERC)

The main use of PERC is as a solvent in dry cleaning. It is estimated that about 15,000 tonnes of PERC are used in Canada each year, of which about two-thirds are used as a solvent in the dry cleaning industry. Environmentalists agree that the use of PERC should be substantially reduced or eliminated. Perchlorethylene is on the federal government's initial list of Priority Substances and it was a subject of the Strategic Options Process (SOP).

In a minor breakthrough, the Consultative Group listed among its recommendations a levy (raw material tax) on PERC to pay for a training and certification program for dry cleaners. This of course is a loop tax. It could easily be adapted to finance an alternative work program so that workers can remain in the industry, doing non-PERC related jobs, e.g., wet cleaning.

However, the revenue would be small, showing that establishing a principle is far from establishing a full chemical taxation program. The price charged by the manufacturers/importers to the dry cleaning industry is about $1,116 per tonne. A tax or levy of 10% would yield about $1,116,000, which could be dedicated to transition measures but which is not enough to fully finance an alternative work program.

Appendix

ALTERNTAIVE FEDERAL BUDGET COORDINATORS:
Bruce Campbell, Robert Chernomas, Greg Selinger

CANADIAN CENTRE FOR POLICY ALTERNATIVES SECRETARIAT:
Bruce Campbell, Shannon Daub, Ed Finn, Kerri-Anne Finn, Agathe Gauthier, Seth Klein, Paul Leduc Browne, Arun Purkayastha, David Robinson, Diane Touchette

WINNIPEG WORKING GROUP:
Jean Altemeyer, Buffie Burrel, Joanne Bousher, Robert Chernomas, Neil Cohen, Victor Dobchuk, Donne Flanagan, George Floresco, Essylt Jones, Eugene Kostyra, Phil Lancaster, Shirley Lord, David Martin, Pauline Riley, Greg Selinger, Harold Shuster, Louise Simbandumwe, Murray Smith, Jerry Sopko, Don Sullivan, Phil Trottier

POLICY WORKING GROUP CO-ORDINATORS:
Macro-economic policy: Jim Stanford, Isabella Bakker
Taxation: Hugh Mackenzie, Eugene Kostyra
Unemployment Insurance: Neil Cohen, Kevin Hayes
Employment Creation and Industrial Policy: Andrew Jackson, Rianne Mahon
Training: Jerry Sopko, Jennifer Stephen
Agriculture: Bob Stirling
Fisheries: Mary Desroches
Forestry: Fred Wilson
Social Policy: Cindy Wiggins, Irene Haig
Health: Colleen Fuller
Education: Errol Black, Denise Doherty-Delorme
Income Support/Poverty: Kapil Khatter
Child Care: Wendy Atkin
Housing: Sharon Chisholm
Pensions: Monica Townson, Bob Baldwin
Foreign Policy: Brian Tomlinson, John Dillon, Muriel Smith
Environment: Robert Hornung, David Bennett
Aboriginal Issues: Phil Lancaster
Women's Issues: Lorraine Michael, Joan Grant-Cummings
Visible Minorities and Immigration: David Onyalo
People with Disabilities: David Martin
Social Economy/CED: Paul Leduc Browne, Todd Scarth
Urban Issues: Matt Sanger
Rural Issues: Moira Hanrahan
Justice: Graham Reddoch
Youth: Cristobal Young, Nadene Rehnby
Culture: David Robinson

POLITICAL ACTION AND COMMUNICATIONS COMMITTEE COORDINATORS:

Marcella Munro, Phil Trottier

AFB STEERING COMMITTEE:

Wendy Atkin	Child Care Advocacy Association of Canada
François Bélanger	Confédération des syndicats nationaux
Peter Bleyer	Council of Canadians
Deborah Bourque	Canadian Union of Postal Workers
Bruce Campbell	Canadian Centre for Policy Alternatives (Chair)
Jocelyn Charron	Canadian Federation of Students
Bob Chernomas	CHO!CES
Sharon Chisholm	Canadian Housing and Renewal Association/ Campaign 2000
Duff Conacher	Democracy Watch/Community Reinvestment Coalition
Kathleen Connors	National Federation of Nurses Unions
Bob Dale	National Union of Public and Employees
John Dillon	Ecumenical Coalition for Economic Justice
Denise Doherty Delorme	Canadian Federation of Students
Bernard Dufresne	Canadian Conference of Catholic Bishops
Michael Farrell	National Anti-Poverty Organization
Andrew Jackson	Canadian Labour Congress
Steve Jelly	Public Service Alliance of Canada
Larry Katz	Canadian Union of Public Employees
Paul Leduc Browne	Canadian Centre for Policy Alternatives
Serge Lord	Communications, Energy and Paperworkers Union
Hugh Mackenzie	United Steelworkers of America
Mike McBane	Canadian Health Coalition
Ross McLellan	Ontario Federation of Labour
Lorraine Michael	National Action Committee on the Status of Women
Shirley Mills	Canadian Association of University Teachers
Josephina Moruz	United Food and Commercial Workers
Marcella Munro	Canadian Labour Congress
Kathyrn Robertson	Ecumenical Coalition for Economic Justice
Marianne Roy	Solidarité populaire
Matt Sanger	Canadian Union of Public Employees
Pauline Sawh	Oxfam Canada
Greg Selinger	CHO!CES
Rick Smith	International Fund for Animal Welfare
Jim Stanford	Canadian Auto Workers/CCPA
John Staple	Canadian Teachers' Federation
Tim Stutt	Canadian Council on Social Development
Brian Tomlinson	Canadian Council for International Cooperation
Cindy Wiggins	Canadian Labour Congress

CANADIAN CENTRE FOR POLICY ALTERNATIVES

NATIONAL OFFICE:
804-251 Laurier Avenue West
Ottawa ON K1P 5J6
Tel: (613) 563-1341
Fax: (613) 233-1458
e-mail: ccpa@policyalternatives.ca
http://www.policyalternatives.ca

B.C. OFFICE:
815-207 West Hastings St.
Vancouver BC V6B 1H7
Tel: (604) 801-5121
Fax: (604) 801-5122
e-mail: ccpabc@intouch.bc.ca

MANITOBA OFFICE:
300-365 Hargrave Street
Winnipeg MB R3B 2K3
Tel: (204) 943-9962
Fax: (204) 943-9978
e-mail: ccpamb@policyalternatives.ca

CHO!CES: A COALITION FOR SOCIAL JUSTICE

409-275 Broadway
Winnipeg MB R3C 4M6
Tel: (204) 944-9408
Fax: (204) 957-1508